I0795085

Drawing a Hypothesis

Edition Angewandte
Book Series of the
University of Applied Arts Vienna
Edited by Gerald Bast, Rector

edition: 'ʌngewʌndtə

Drawing a Hypothesis

Figures of Thought

A Project by Nikolaus Gansterer

Second corrected edition

DE GRUYTER

Nikolaus Gansterer
Compiled in the years between 2005 and 2011,
while living and working in Maastricht, Nanjing, Rotterdam, Antwerp, Vienna, Mexico City, Los Angeles, Prairie City, Beijing, New York, Berlin and Ghent.

Library of Congress Cataloging-in-Publication data
A CIP catalog record for this book has been applied for at the Library of Congress.

Bibliographic information published by the German national library
The German national library lists this publication in the Deutsche nationalbibliografie; detailed bibliographic data are available on the Internet at http://dnb.dnb.de.

Book concept: Nikolaus Gansterer
Book design: Simona Koch
Cover design: Simona Koch and Nikolaus Gansterer
Cover illustration: Nikolaus Gansterer
Translation: Veronica Buckley, Aileen Derieg (text by Gerhard Dirmoser), David Ender
Proofreading: Dorrie Tattersall, Petra van der Jeught, Michael Karassowitsch
Image proofreading and technical assistance: Jo Frenken
Typesetting: Simona Koch

Models by Nikolaus Gansterer and Simona Koch
Photos by Nikolaus Gansterer, Tim Tom, Daniela Zeilinger

Typeface: Times New Roman
Printed on Munken Print Cream 90g, Hello Gloss 135g,
Levo Thin Print 60g, Munken Print Cream 300g (Cover)

Printed on acid-free and chlorine-free bleached paper TCF ∞

With 160 black figures, 4 tables, 42 coloured pages and 1 folding map.

1st Edition 2011: SpringerWienNewYork

ISSN 1866-248X
ISBN 978-3-11-054661-3

TABLE OF CONTENTS

APPENDIX

Index of Figures

INDEX OF FIGURES I

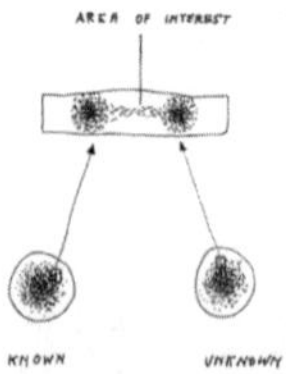

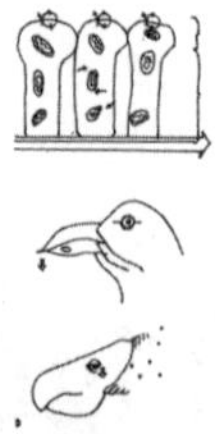

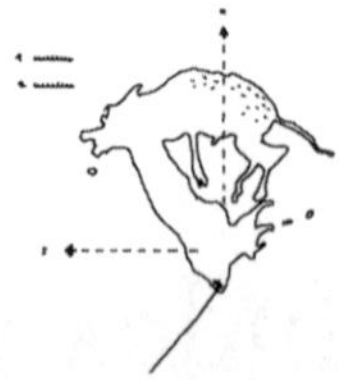

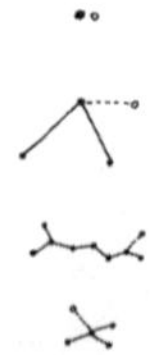

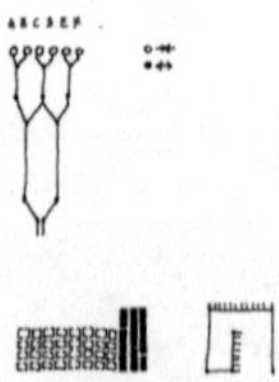

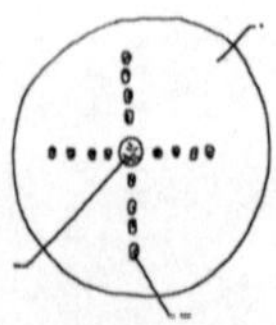

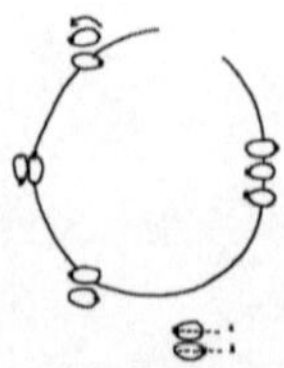

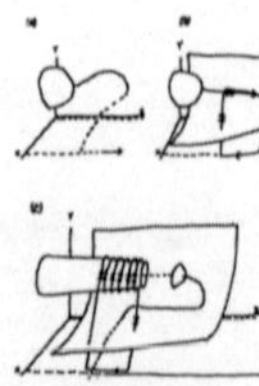

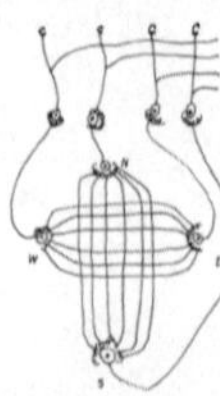

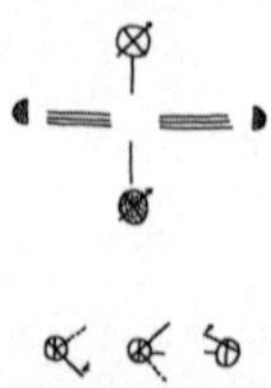

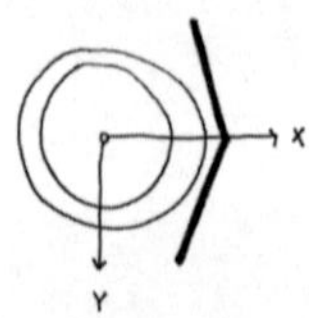

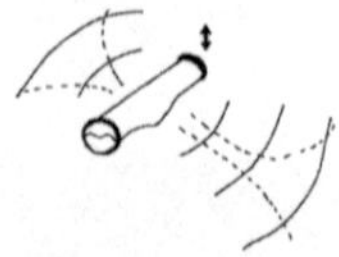

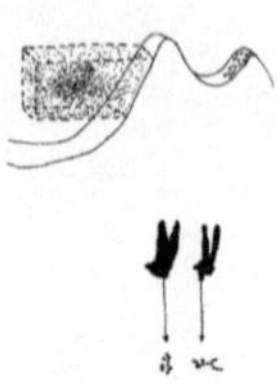

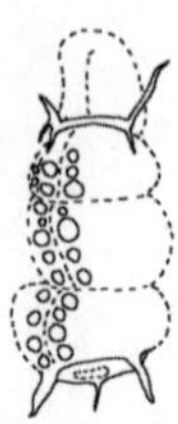

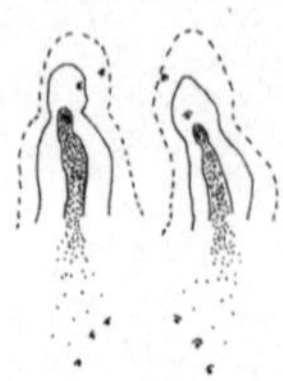

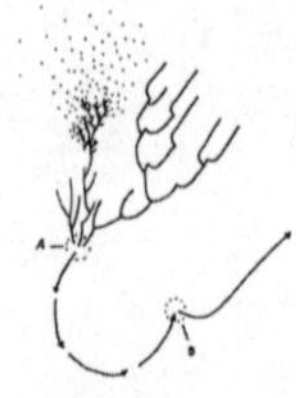

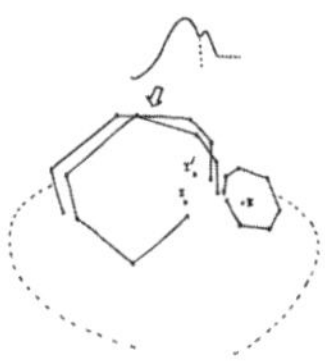

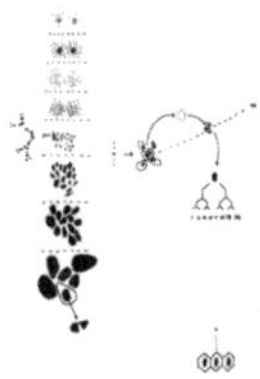

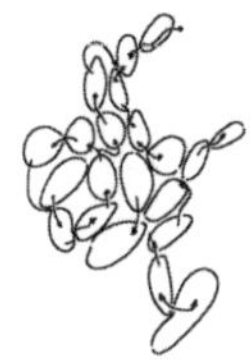

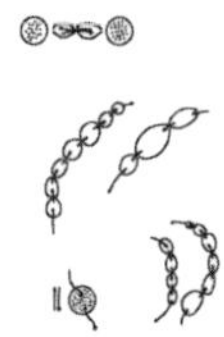

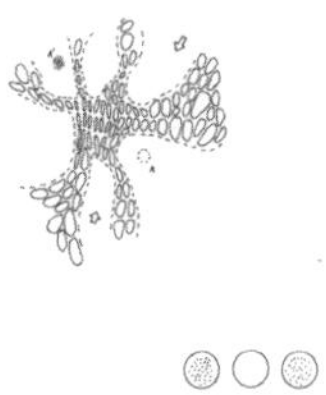

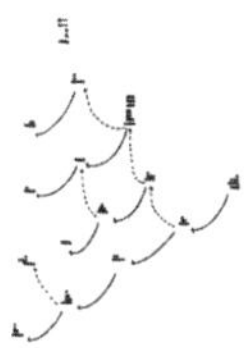

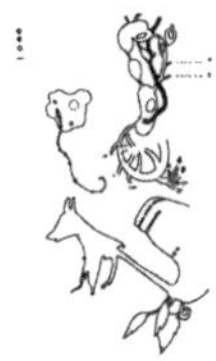

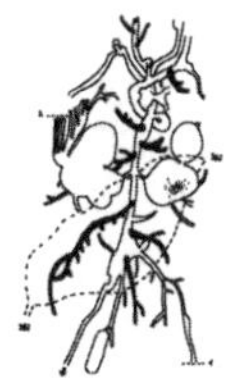

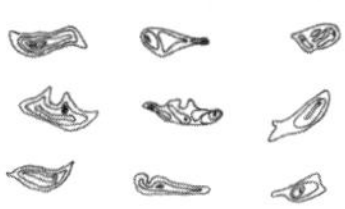

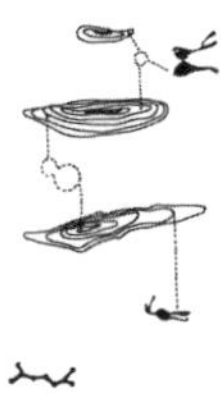

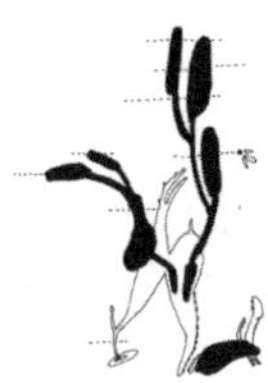

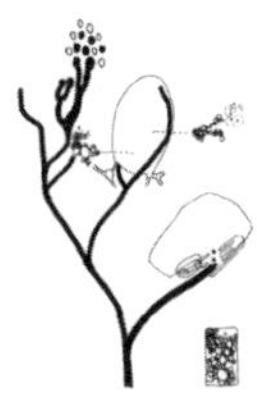

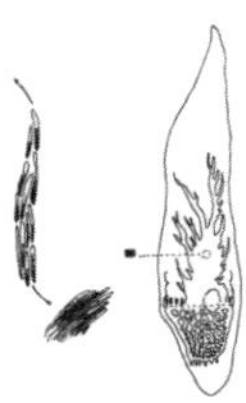

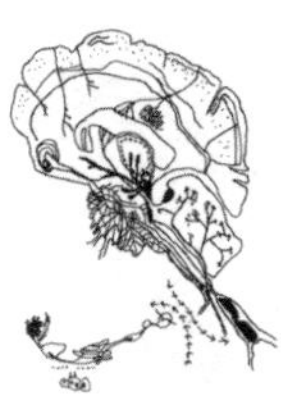

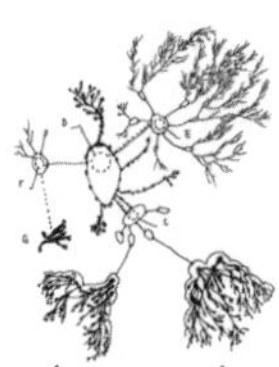

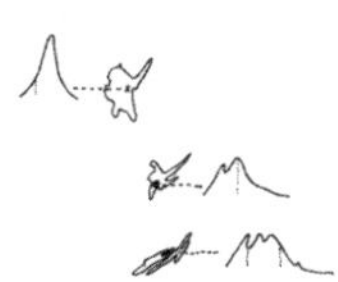

INDEX OF FIGURES II

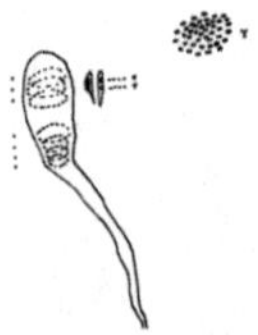

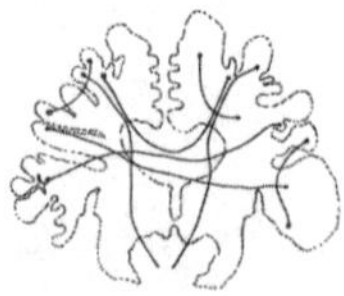

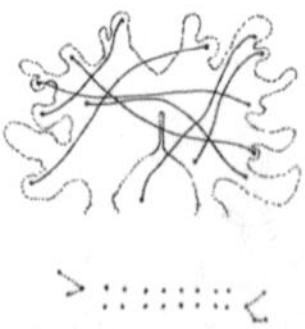

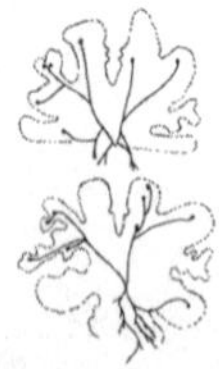

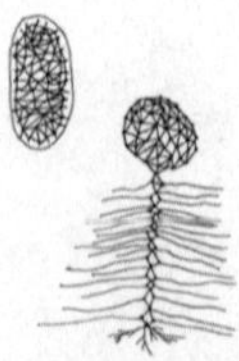

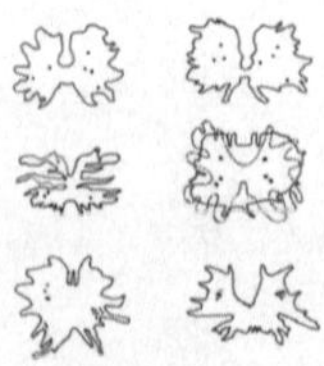

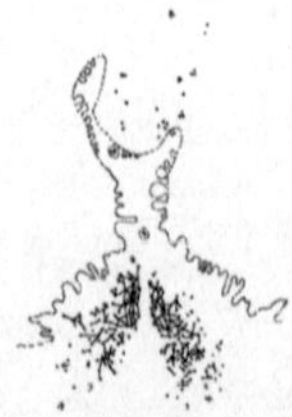

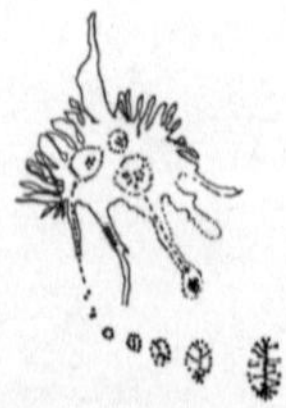

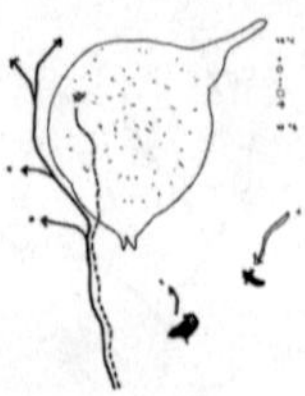

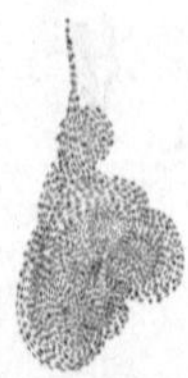

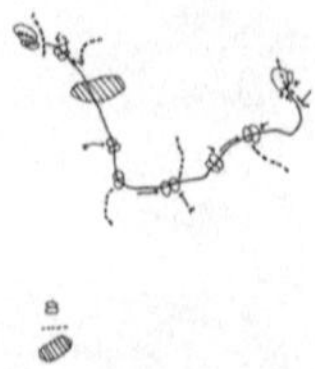

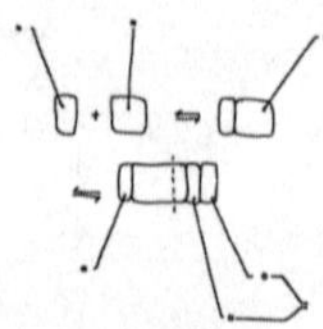

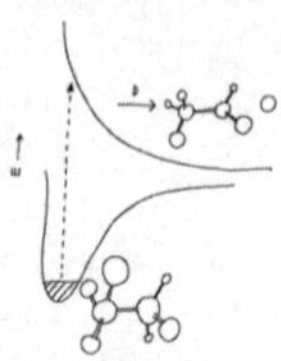

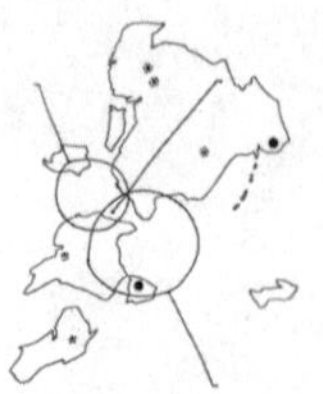

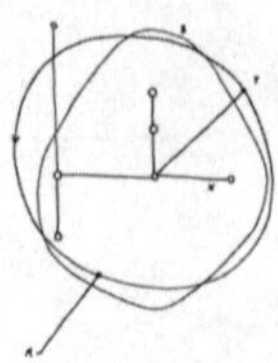

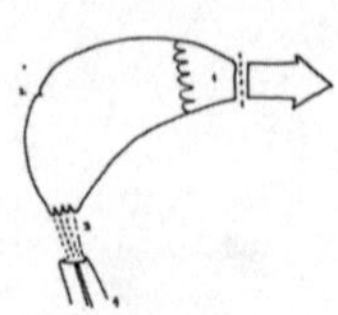

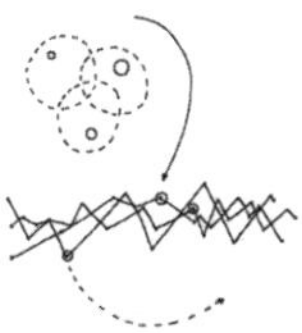

Fig. 03-11
→ p. 261, 273

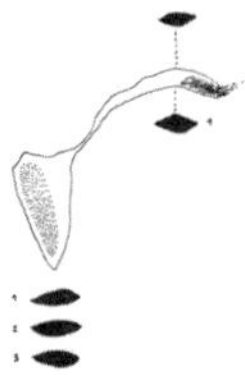

Fig. 03-12
→ p. 263, 274

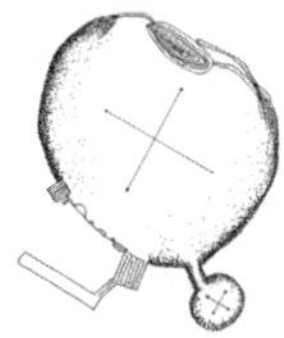

Fig. 03-14
→ p. 260, 272

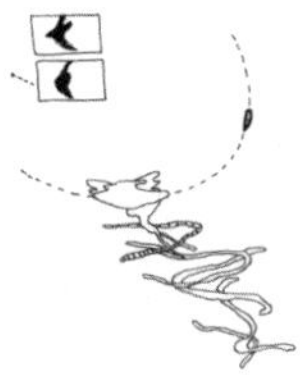

Fig. 03-16
→ p. 278

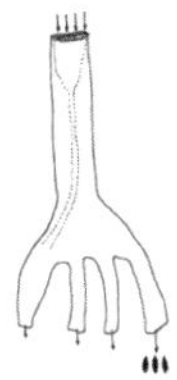

Fig. 03-17
→ p. 260, 262, 273

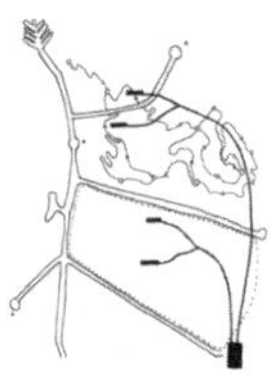

Fig. 03-19
→ p. 260, 272

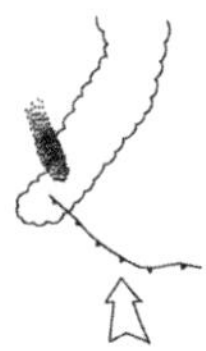

Fig. 03-24
→ p. 63

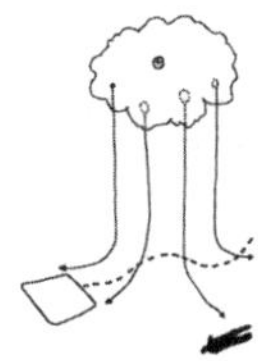

Fig. 03-25
→ p. 63

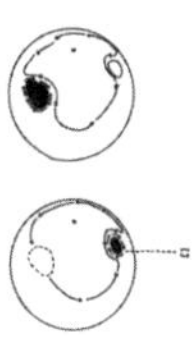

Fig. 03-27
→ p. 200, 327

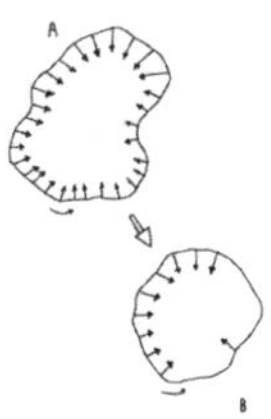

Fig. 03-28
→ p. 326

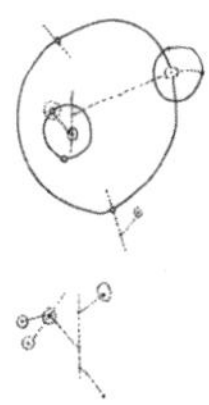

Fig. 04-08
→ p. 216, 327

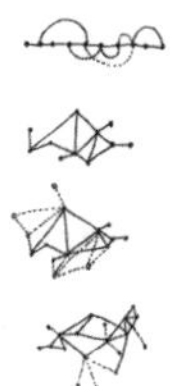

Fig. 04-09
→ p. 284, 309

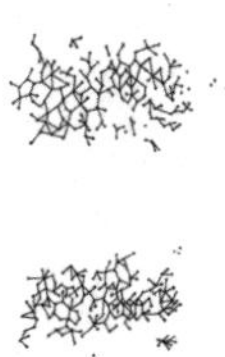

Fig. 04-10
→ p. 283

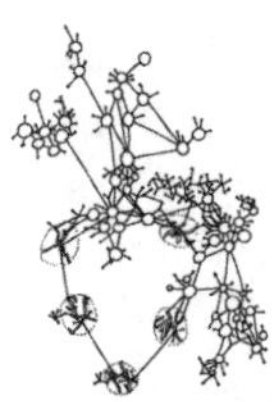

Fig. 04-11
→ p. 284

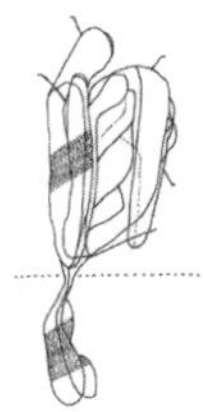

Fig. 04-12
→ p. 216, 267

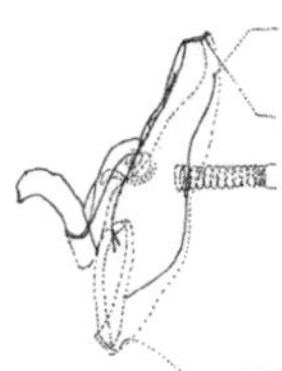

Fig. 04-15
→ p. 216

INDEX OF FIGURES III

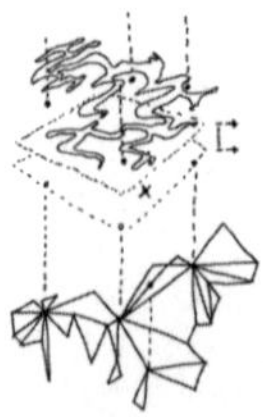

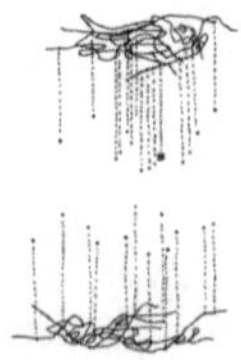

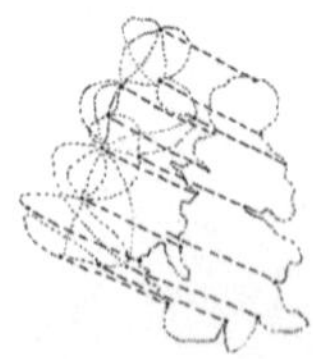

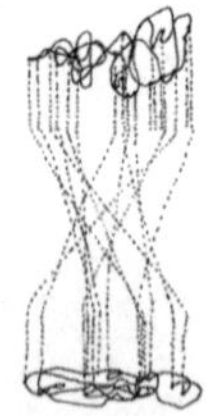

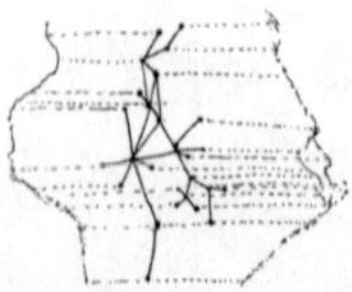

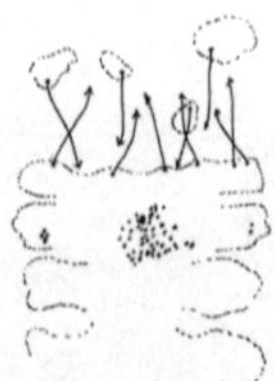

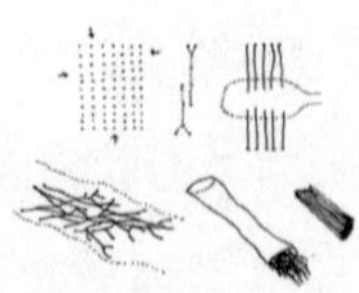

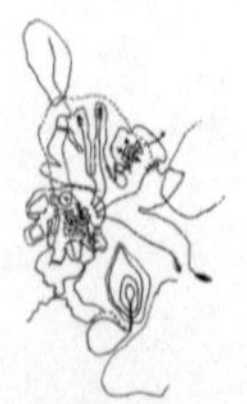

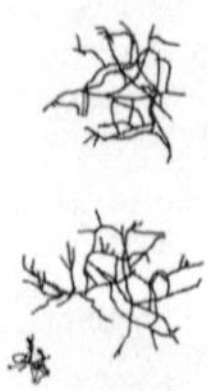

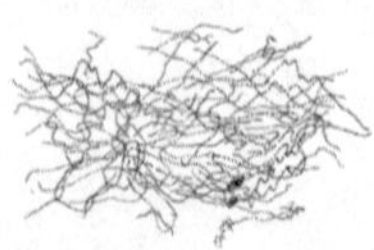

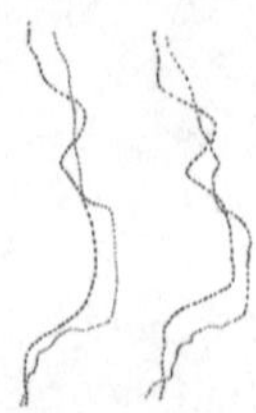

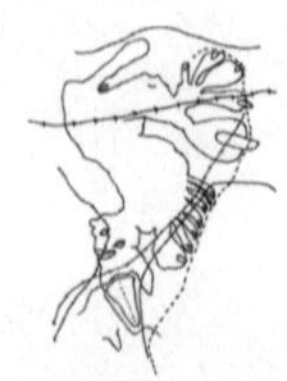

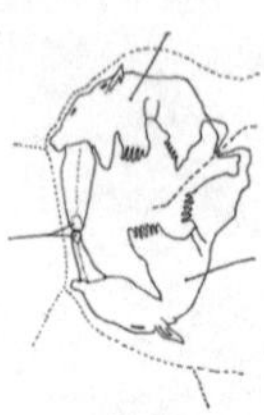

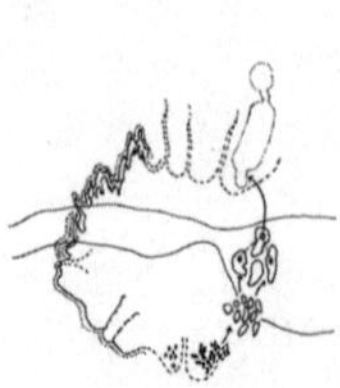

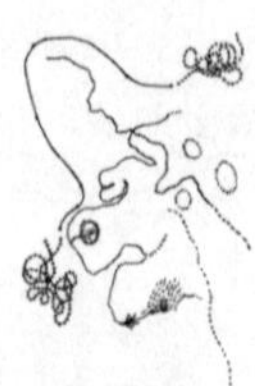

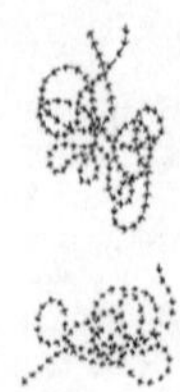

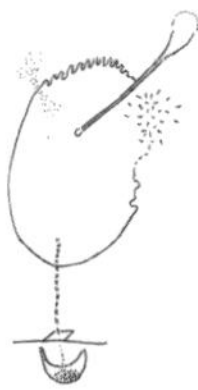

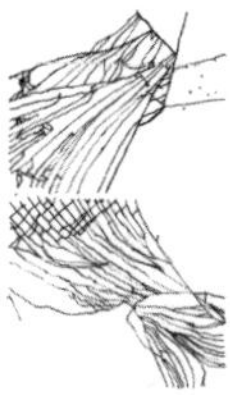

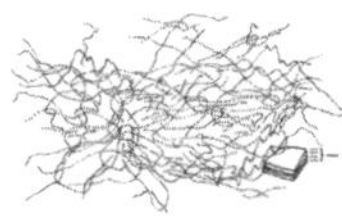

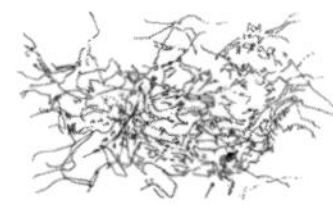

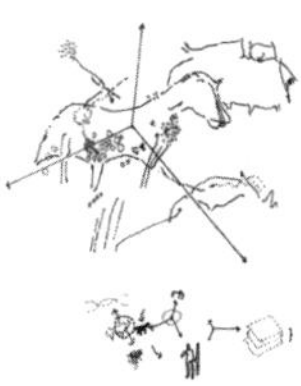

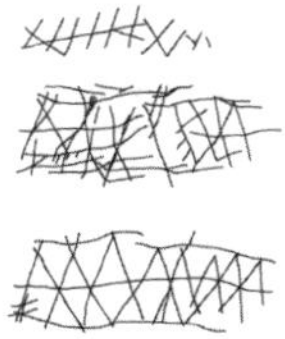

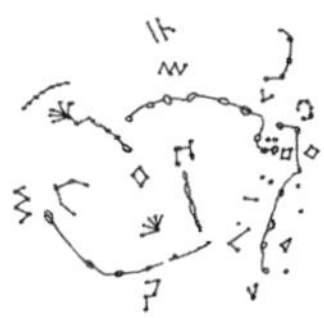

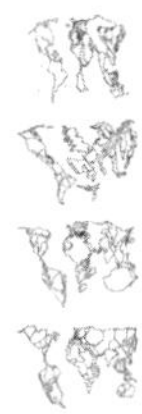

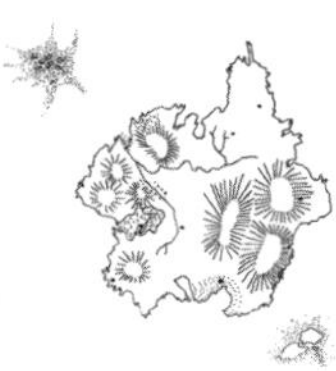

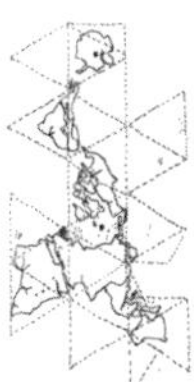

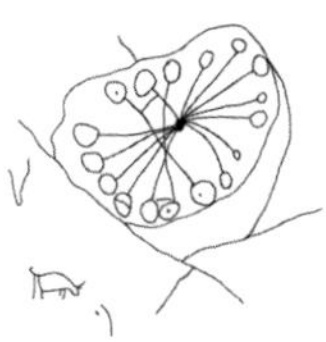

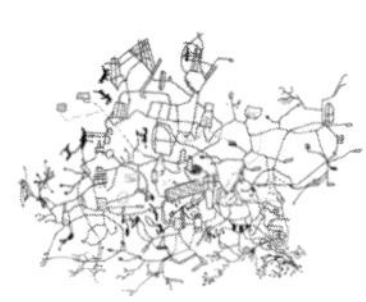

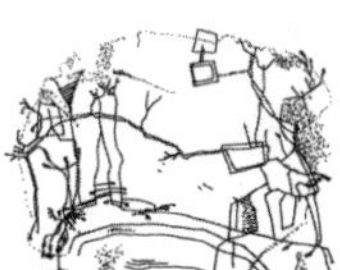

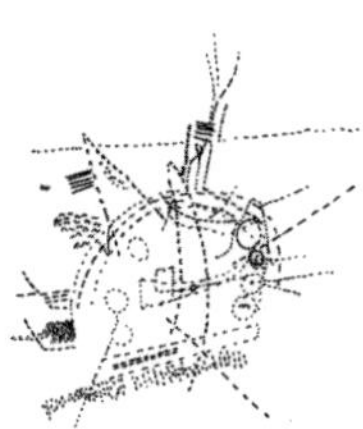

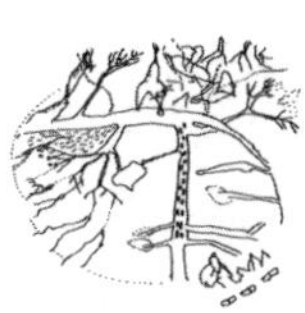

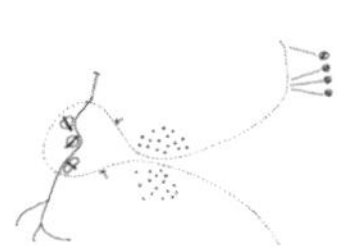

INDEX OF FIGURES IV

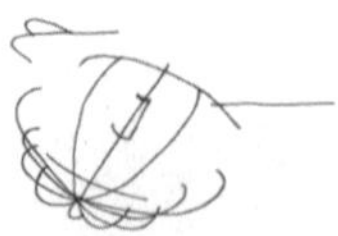

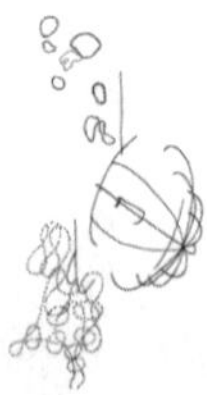

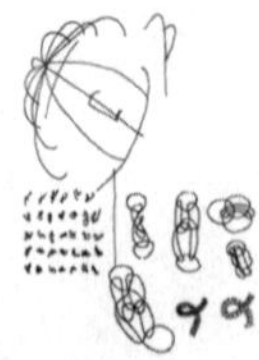

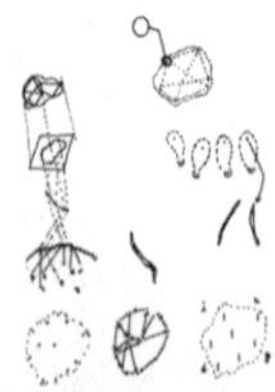

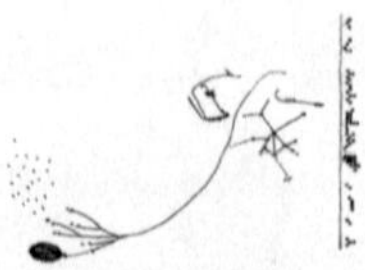

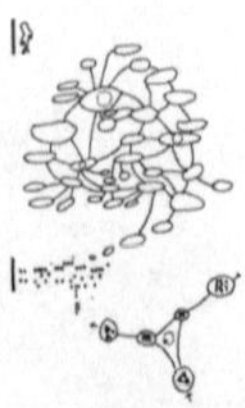

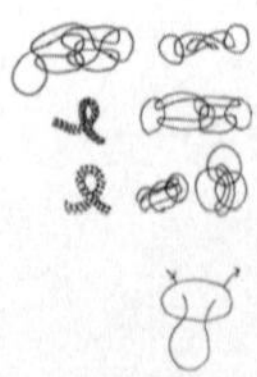

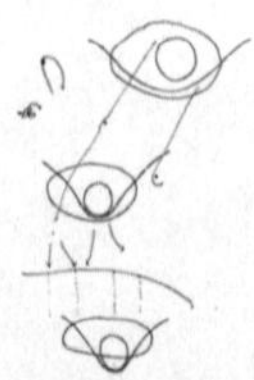

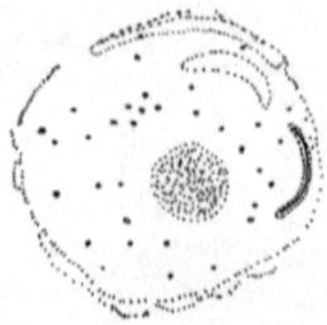

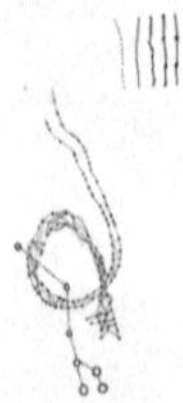

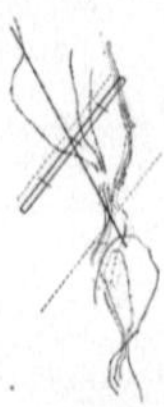

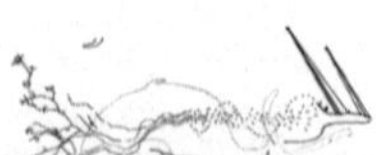

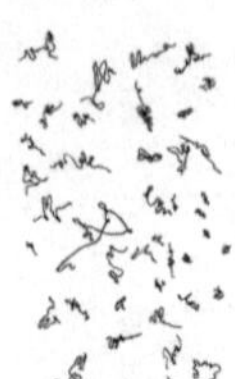

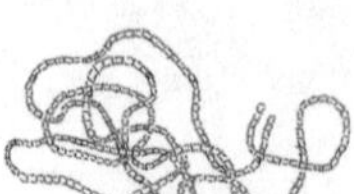

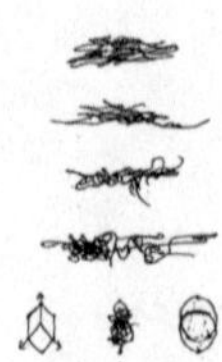

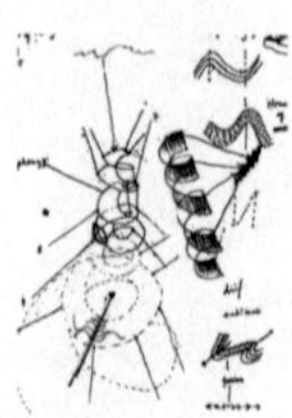

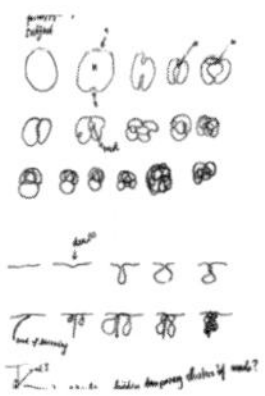

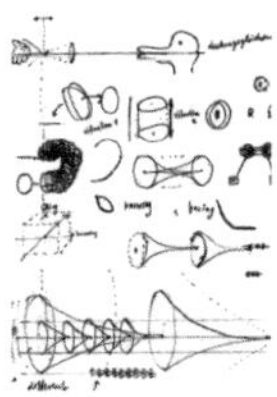

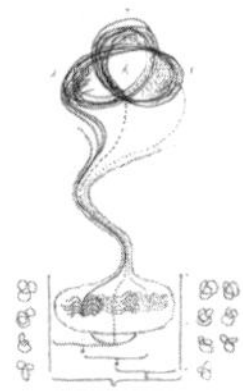

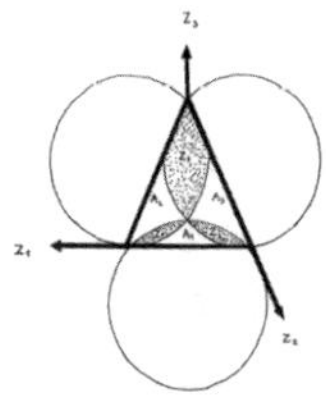

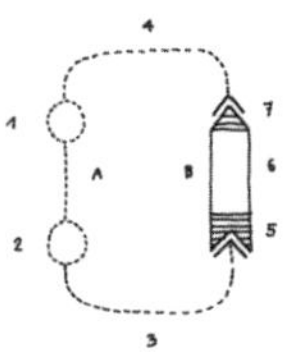

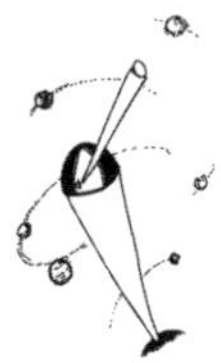

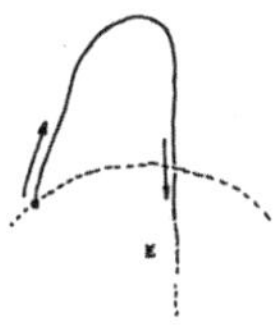

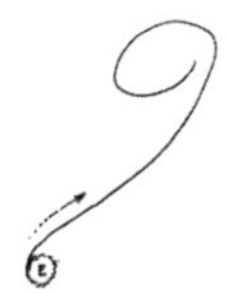

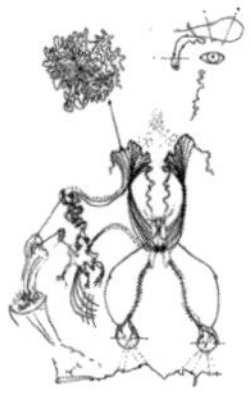

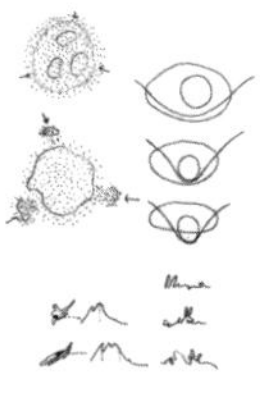

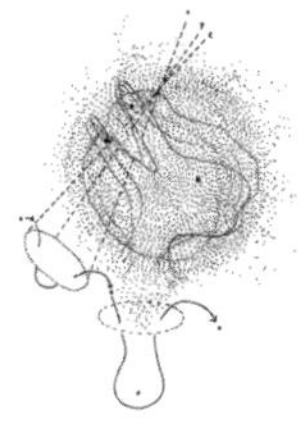

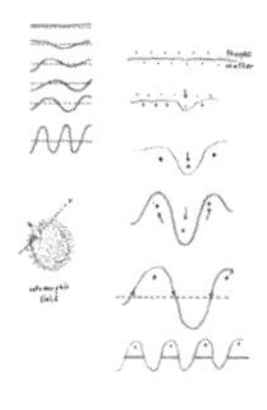

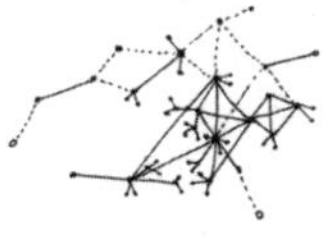

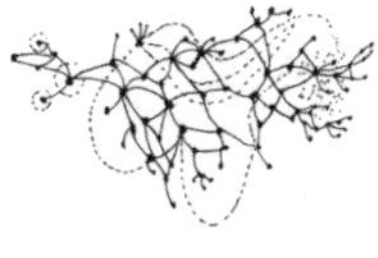

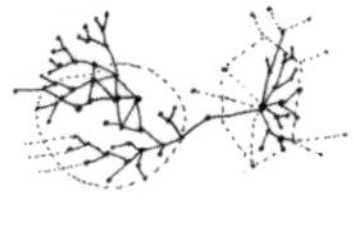

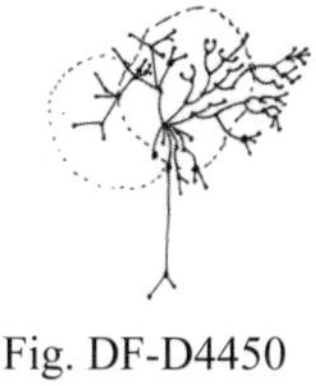

INDEX OF FIGURES V

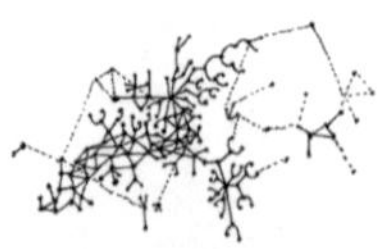

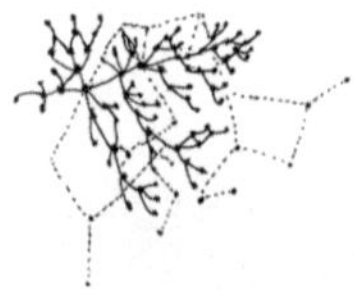

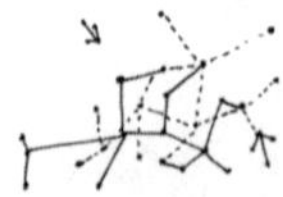

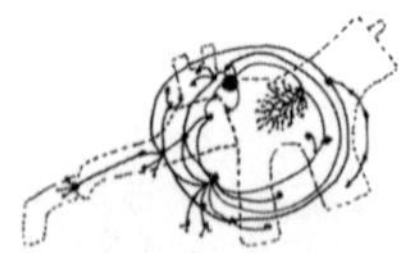

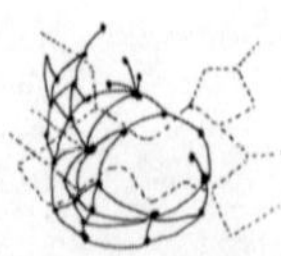

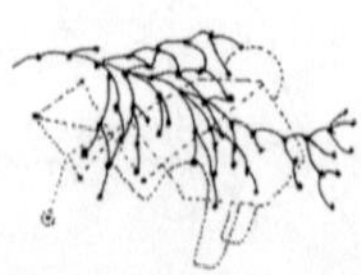

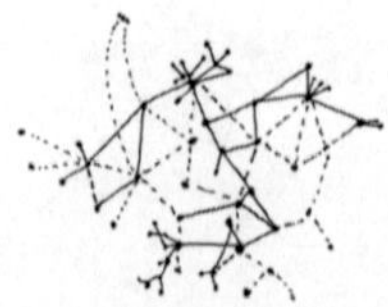

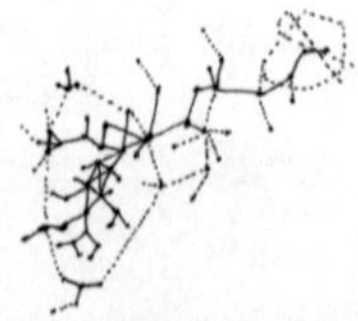

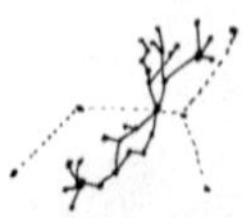

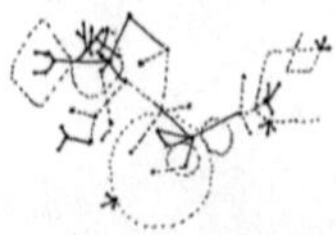

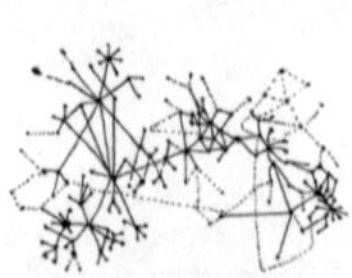

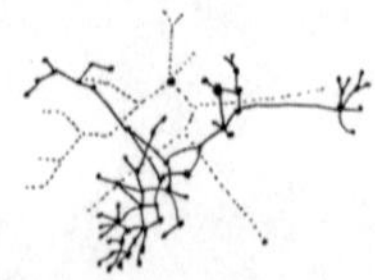

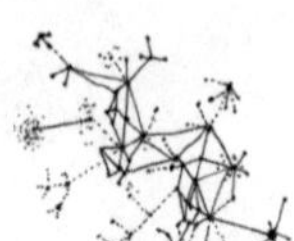

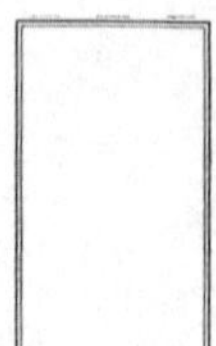

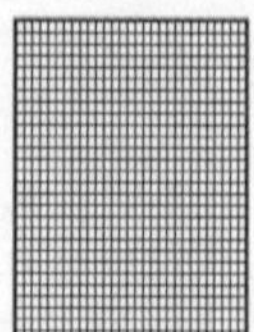

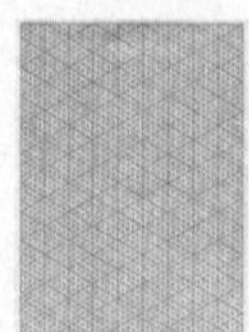

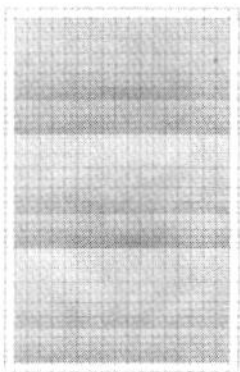

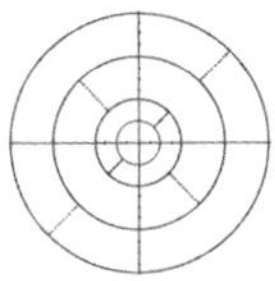

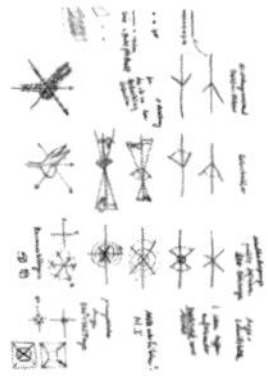

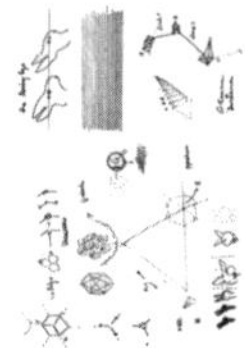

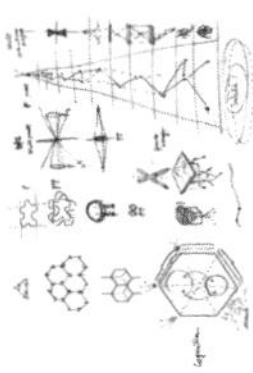

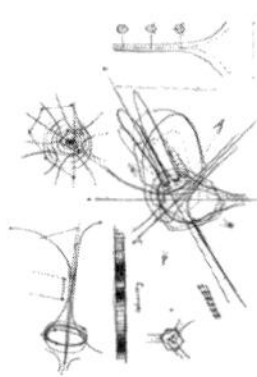

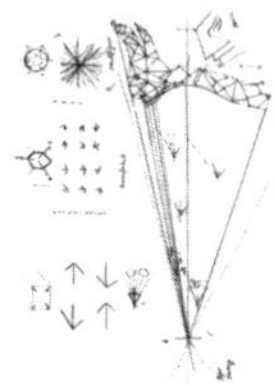

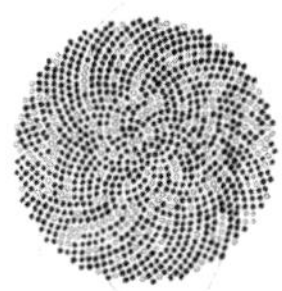

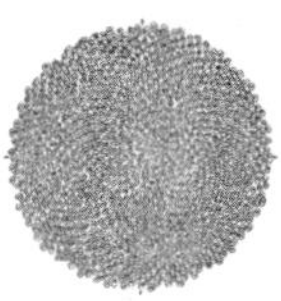

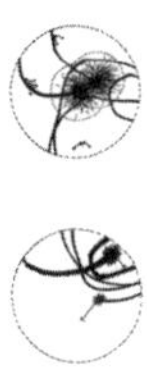

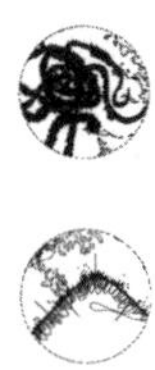

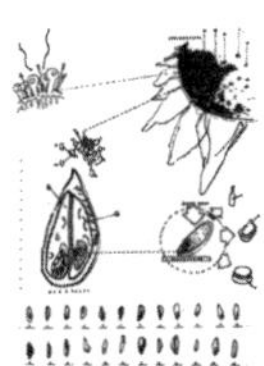

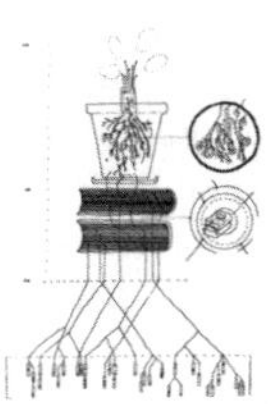

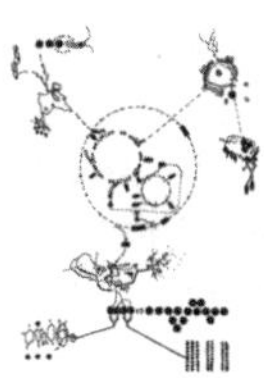

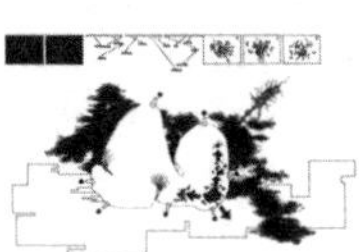

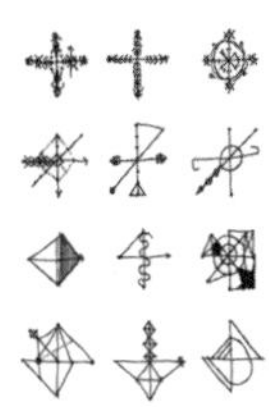

Preface

DRAWING A HYPOTHESIS

Nikolaus Gansterer

When the first edition of *Drawing a Hypothesis* was published in the year 2011, I was surprised and pleased that the work attracted wide interest. In the midst of the reverberations of a proclaimed diagrammatic turn, my question "how to do things with diagrams and in reverse what do they do with you?" found a strong echo among artists, researchers, scientists, theoreticians, and writers alike, and encouraged me to continue the research project, that has eventually also resulting in this second, corrected edition. The publication itself encompasses diverse voices, each of them approaching the complex and highly agile and flexible nature of the diagram, describing, denominating, invoking, and marking it, and thus developing highly individual notation forms of the diagrammatic.

The initial idea for this book originated during a two-year artistic research project (2005-2006) at the Jan van Eyck Academie in Maastricht, the Netherlands. My long-held fascination with diagrams, maps, networks and all graphical forms of visualising complex associations prompted me to approach the field from a genuine artistic point of view. This book has evolved from a five-year exchange with theoreticians, scientists and artists on the question of the hypothetical potential of diagrams. I began intuitively to collect, order, and study diagrams from books and the Internet. Endeavouring to understand how information is visually constructed within these representations, I internalised this language of images for myself by redrawing them. From this emerged a comprehensive archive of diagrams has emerged that is still growing and provides the basic resource for the research project. The longer I have been working with the material, the more I find myself asking how these figures were to be read, given their ambivalent nature between image, symbol and drawing. Moreover, how do they in turn configure our thought processes? What narrative forms can be found in these drawn figures of thought? And what happens when figures are removed from their original context? What poetic, performative and speculative action potential is then liberated?

Thinking Drawing – The pool of diagrammatic images, signs and symbols is a permanent part of our daily perception. The cognitive act of perceiving, translating and allocating occurs continuously when we compose thoughts and receive or process information. This process of sense-making always happens by establishing relations and through drawing connections: the structures of the semantic relationships embodied in the anatomical organisation of our brains allows us to interact with others by means of language and behaviour and is a diagrammatic operation per se. Since drawing mediates between perception and reflection, it plays a constitutive role in the emergence, production and communication of knowledge. From my perspective, the genesis of ideas is often directly connected with graphical thinking:[1] on the one hand, many theories genuinely did and do begin with a quick draft to capture an idea to delineate it for oneself or others; on the other hand, hardly any thesis rejects the forms of visual representation when communicating its contents. The drawing of figures thus reveals itself to be one of the oldest of mankind's cultural techniques, and to this day remains a fundamental instrument in any kind of artistic or scientific practice.

Reverse Engineering of a Theory – In my research process it soon became clear to me that I would have to open up my archive of figures to make them accessible to others in order to initiate a discursive analysis, thus clearing the path for research into the potential of drawings. The figures I had drawn myself served as a starting point for the hypotheses collected here. They quickly became associative catalysts of an animated exchange with a great variety of people from the most widely differing fields (artists, writers, scientists). I sent my drawings to several interpreters with a request for written interpretation a micrology[2] , so that in turn I could react to their texts with diagrammatic drawings. The associative process continued to work until the potential for action was exhausted.[3] Due to this discursive method, text and drawings constantly began to interweave, forming propositions and densifying to become reflective structural images. In mutual enquiry, the contingent relation between image and text with its suggestive efficacy that continuously constructs (apparent) evidence became tangible

1) For example, the largely unknown fact that Ludwig Wittgenstein originally developed the *Tractatus Logicus* in a parallel fashion, both graphically and in words, with hundreds of diagrammatical figures; the theories of Charles Sanders Pierce are also deeply interlinked with his graphical figures and *Existential Graphs* drawn by hand.

2) By the concept of *micrology* I mean a small model and theoretical structure, in itself coherent, that is informed by or stamped with the author's particular background of knowledge. Each of the invited authors chose an adequate figure of speech and self-consistent logic for their texts themselves. It was important to me not to predetermine any formal criteria for the text.

3) The "ping-pong experiment" didn't always work. Some of the authors I approached were not prepared to get involved in a process of this kind, or the *micrologies* got bogged down after a while. This book documents only a selection of these interpretations and communication processes.

by literally drawing a hypothesis[4]. This process of formation of individual hypotheses functioned as a poetic catalyst and inspired me beyond the figures already drawn to new models, objects, installations, and gestures, quasi to support, elaborate, and corroborate the fresh hypotheses in the course of their development. Due to this intensive process and exchange of thoughts, numerous ideas, hypotheses, theses and interrelations developed, eventually achieving the form of captions, (sci-fi) stories, and longer essays on the themes of figure, drawing, hypothesis, and diagram. The resulting contributions are of very different nature, reflecting their authors particular fields of knowledge in the fractious borderland between art, science, and fiction. This has generated a comprehensive compendium of figures of thought which straddles the border between scientific representability and artistic means. Without pretension to completeness, it reveals a rolling line that touches, penetrates, and goes beyond significant aspects of the diagrammatic enabling them as proliferators of a process of unfolding and maps of movement allowing destabilisation and discovery rather than being visualisers of information data and mere means of control and systematisation[5].

The figures it contains should always be understood in reference to Roland Barthes thoughts as something moving, changing, living, flexible and fluid in themselves[6]. Due to their ambivalent character, they reveal to us an enticing glance into the (rear-view) mirror of our consciousness, of the possible mental spaces between recognising and naming tracing diagrams as hyper-vital agents which are continuously re-, con-, and trans-figuring space between thinking – drawing – (un-)knowing.

Drawing on Drawing a Hypothesis – The publication in itself is devised entirely in a diagrammatic sense rather as a laboratory, workplace and a kind of interstation. After the first edition was published it therefore seemed only consequent to me to immediately to take the hypotheses collected in this volume as a point of departure, to employ and apply them; they are exemplary for the numerous different ways of reading and testing them, and translating them into various media and materials, thus continuing and developing them.

4) This precariously unstable and highly creative and poetic state of figures of thought during the immediate process of their formation is of course restricted by their current fixation in the shape of a book layout, and only tangible to a limited degree.

5) → Hypothesis #1, p. 29.

6) → Hypothesis #7, p. 110.

In the course of the book launches, in collaboration with the writer-artist Emma Cocker[7] I developed a series of performance lectures titled *Drawing on Drawing a Hypothesis.*[8] Using processes of cross-reading and live drawing, the performance lecture approached the publication as a reader might thumb through the book; where certain sections appear to be lingered over, while others are skimmed in search of key words and phrases, evocative fragments and extractions. The reading suggested that the book might not always need to be read in a linear or logical way, but rather be dipped into, allowing for detours and distractions within the event of diagrammatic reading itself. The lecture took the figures of thought at the heart of *Drawing a Hypothesis* as points of departure for exploring and performing the correlations between thinking and drawing. Addressing the shifting and ambivalent properties of image, symbol and drawing within the publication, it asks, "how can these visual artefacts be comprehended?"

Parallel to the performance lectures, I created a number of installation-based implementations of the hypotheses and extrapolations into spatiality in the framework of a series of exhibitions[9]. Through the juxtaposition and confrontation of special objects, murals, and video recordings of live drawings, as well as the implementation of spoken text passages, central aspects of the hypotheses were inter- and trans-medially enhanced to open spatial diagrams.[10]

Furthermore, in workshops and seminars with other researchers and students at universities and in various educational contexts, diagrams from the book were successfully implemented as teaching instruments, especially in order to activate and trigger the performative potential of individual research topics.

In all the mentioned extrapolations and translations of the hypotheses, especially the performative and poetic potential of the diagrams gained more and more importance in my own

7) → Hypothesis #6, p. 97

8) *The lecture Drawing on Drawing a Hypothesis* was presented a.o. at MUHKA, Antwerp; Kunsthalle, Vienna; PROGR, Bern; Kunsthall, Bergen; Pivo Gallery, Sao Paulo. At NGBK, Berlin and KNAW, Amsterdam together with Susanne Leeb presenting her research on diagrams, published in *Materialität der Diagramme. Kunst und Theorie,* Susanne Leeb (ed.), Berlin, 2012.

9) Installations were presented a.o. *Schaubilder/Diagrams,* 2012, Kunstverein Bielefeld; *A Study On Knowledge,* 2012, Forum Stadtpark Graz; *4th Athens Biennial,* 2013, Athens; *My Brain Is In My Inkstand,* Cranbrook Museum, Detroit; *When Thought Becomes Matter And Matter Turns Into Thought,* Kunstraum Niederösterreich, Vienna; *Thinking Matters, 2013,* Gallery Marie-Laure Fleisch, Rome; *Drawing Room,* 2013/14, Blickle Foundation, Kraichtal and Galerie im Taxispalais, Innsbruck; *Inventing Temperature,* 2014, *KCC,* London.

10) Cf. Nikolaus Gansterer, Christiane Krejs (eds.), *When Thought Becomes Matter And Matter Turns Into Thought,* Kunstraum Niederösterreich, (cat.),Vienna, 2013.

artistic work. I began to elaborate the performance lectures into *Translectures*[11] and to develop spatial, temporal, and medial connections. "Often a text, a drawing, or a material marks the starting point for different layers of interpretations and re-translations. Here, drawing – for me a medium of high immediacy – could turn the subject into a score, an ad-hoc diagram, a makeshift model, or an instruction for taking action, translating figures of thought into fragile forms of new materiality."[12] Within these performances the process of "drawing beyond drawing" increased, became central, and was extended along the categories of time and space, movement and speculation: a line of thought becomes a line on the paper, a line in space, a line verbalised, or even a line drawn with the whole body. My deep interest in new and innovative forms of diagrams – from *figures of thought* to *choreo-graphic figures* – as performative forms of aesthetic sense-making, as well as the development of embodied diagrammatics has led to the artistic research project *Choreographic Figures: Deviations from the Line*[13]. Both artistic research projects and their respective publications combine and interlace my observations and thoughts regarding diagrammatic figurations as epistemic agencies in theory and practice.

Index of Figures – In order to facilitate diagrammatic reading of the book on hand, let me make a few basic remarks concerning orientation. The figures themselves and all the various ways of reading them are the protagonists of this publication. The figures given in this book were drawn by hand by myself. Many of them were sent to more than one person for parallel interpretation allowing for knots, deviations, congruencies, undercurrents and unexpected overlaps. Consequently, these re-appear in several places in the book. To ensure easy tracking, the figures are numbered following the logic of their creation, and indicating their placing in my sketchbooks. The identifying number is given next to each particular figure as (Fig. XXX). An index and collection of all figures used in the publication can be found on the front pages, providing both a visual list of contents and an orientation guide. The reader is invited to navigate through the book, to leaf through and read into it with the help of the *Index of Figures*.

11) Cf. www.gansterer.org/translectures, for further contextualisation of Gansterer's concept of translectures.

12) Quote from an interview with the curator Nova Benway published in *Bottom Line Blog,* in the course of the exhibition project *Drafts,* 2013 at Drawing Center, New York.

13) Cf. The research project *Choreo-graphic Figures. Deviations from the Line* (2014-2017) was funded by the FWF – the Austrian Science Fund and resulted into the publication Nikolaus Gansterer, Emma Cocker and Mariella Greil (eds.), *Choreo-graphic Figures: Deviations from the Line,* Berlin/Boston, de Gruyter, Edition Angewandte, 2017.

The coloured image parts (→Plates I–III) are divided into three sections. Inspired by Aby Warburg's *Mnemosyne Atlas*, associative images were collected which emerged in the course of the project as a visual response to the contributions. They draw associative references between my own artistic work, the found and drawn figures, and the hypotheses developed out of these. The pink pages are a comprehensive collection of figures of thought, and are connected with the map at the end of the book. Inserted into the flap of the book cover, you will find a removable folding map (→*Questions of Order and Relational Characteristics of Figures of Thought*) which places key figures of thought within an ordered system. By means of drawing, I carried out a visual re-translation and contextualisation of the central manifestations of the diagrammatic which kept recurring in the course of the research project. The map broadly follows Gerhard Dirmoser's approach that positions basic diagrammatic forms along a Cartesian coordinate system.[14]

Acknowledgements – I wish to express my thanks to all the authors for their unique and fascinating interpretations and contributions, and for taking part in this experiment on probing and publishing new forms of diagrammatic sense-making. I would also like to express my gratitude to the involved institutions, namely the Jan van Eyck Academie, Maastricht; the University for Applied Arts, Vienna; and the Austrian Federal Ministry for Education, Arts and Culture, for the financial and active support which has made this research project possible. My special thanks also to Gerhard Dirmoser, without whose generous financial and moral support this second edition would never have come to pass.[15] Particular thanks are due to the artist and designer Simona Koch for investing so much love, inspiration and time in the project, for developing the exquisite design, and for bringing it to fruition with me, in the form in which you now hold it in your hands.[16]

Nikolaus Gansterer, Brussels, 2017

14) →Hypothesis #12, p. 153; →*Questions of Order and Relational Characteristics of Figures of Thought*, p. 26-27 and at the end of the book.

15) A detailed list of thanks and all supporters can be found here →*Acknowledgements*, p. 349.

16) The elaborate design won book prizes in the categories "The Most Beautiful Books of Austria" awarded in Vienna and "Best Book Design from all over the World", awarded at the Leipzig Book Fair, 2012.

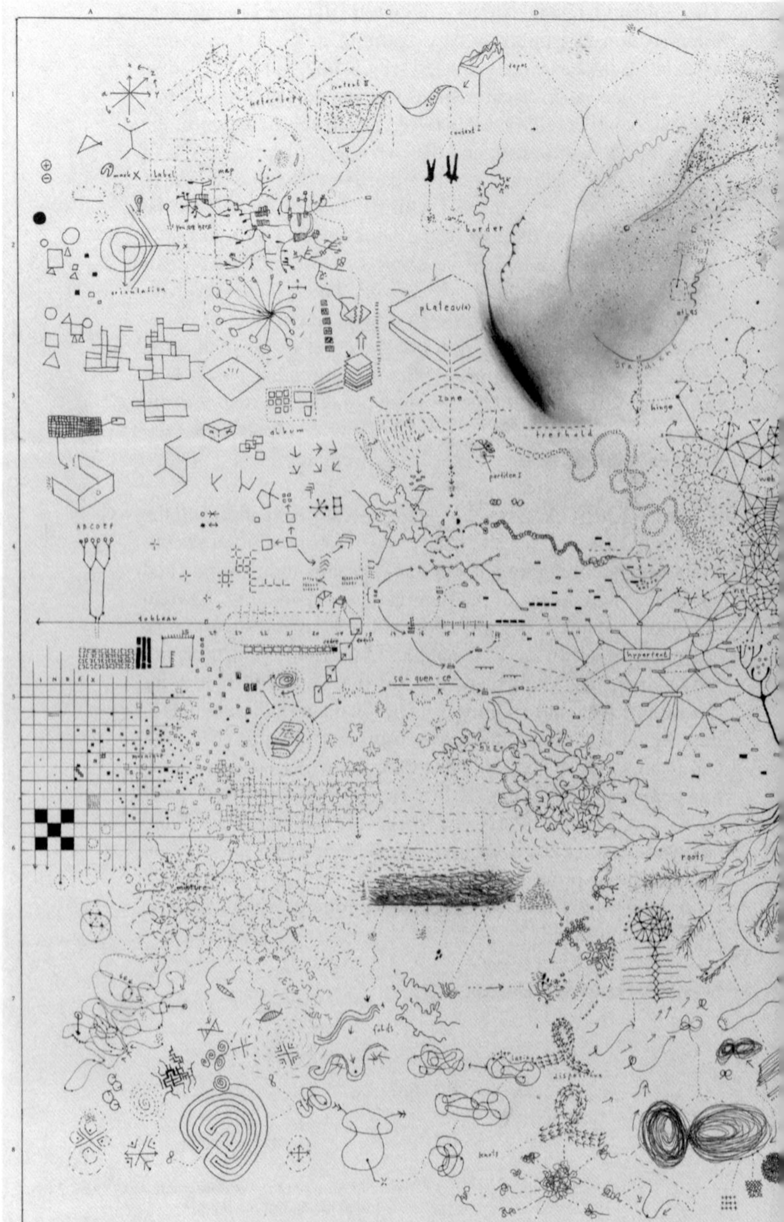

Map: Questions of Order and Relational Characteristics of Figures of Thought (→ removable folding map at the end of the book)

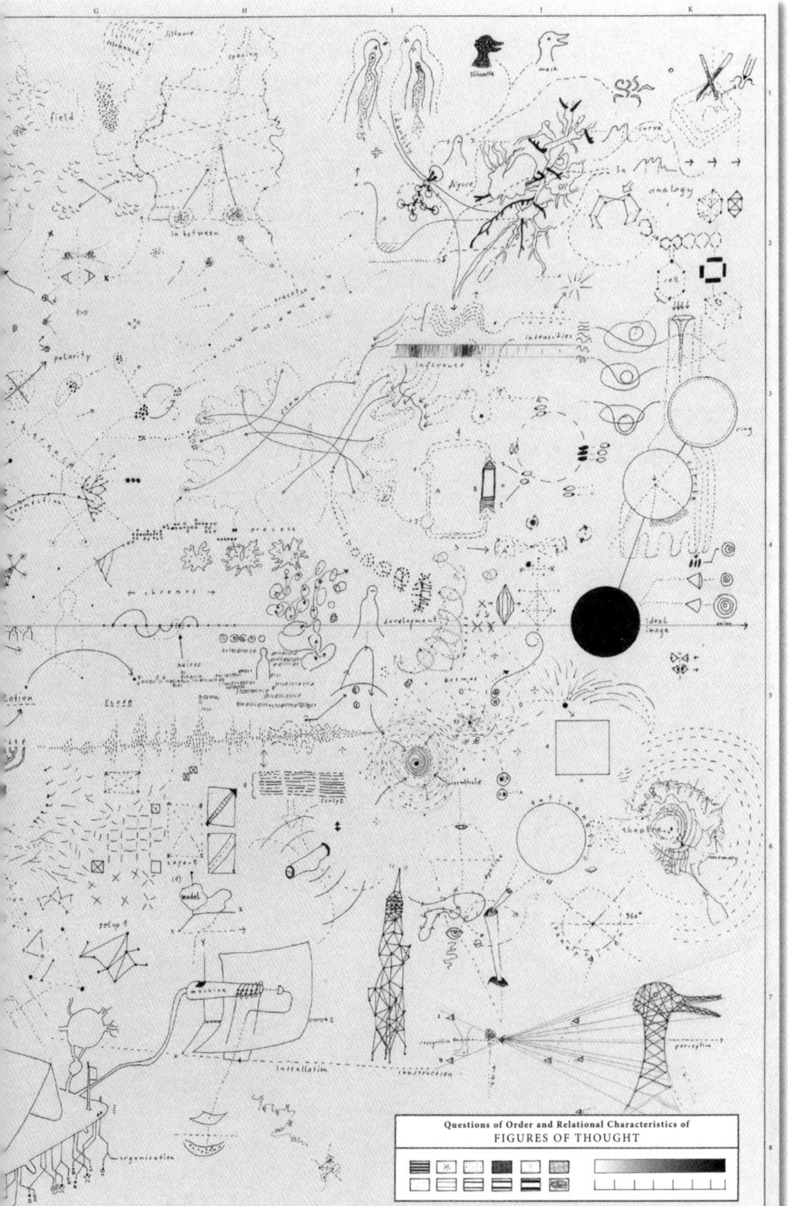
Questions of Order and Relational Characteristics of
FIGURES OF THOUGHT
©Nikolaus Gansterer 2011, after a diagram by Gerhard Dirmoser

HYPOTHESIS #1

"A Line with Variable Direction, which Traces No Contour, and Delimits No Form"*

Susanne Leeb

* Gilles Deleuze, Félix Guattari, *A Thousand Plateaus*, Minneapolis, University of Minnesota Press, 1987, p. 499.

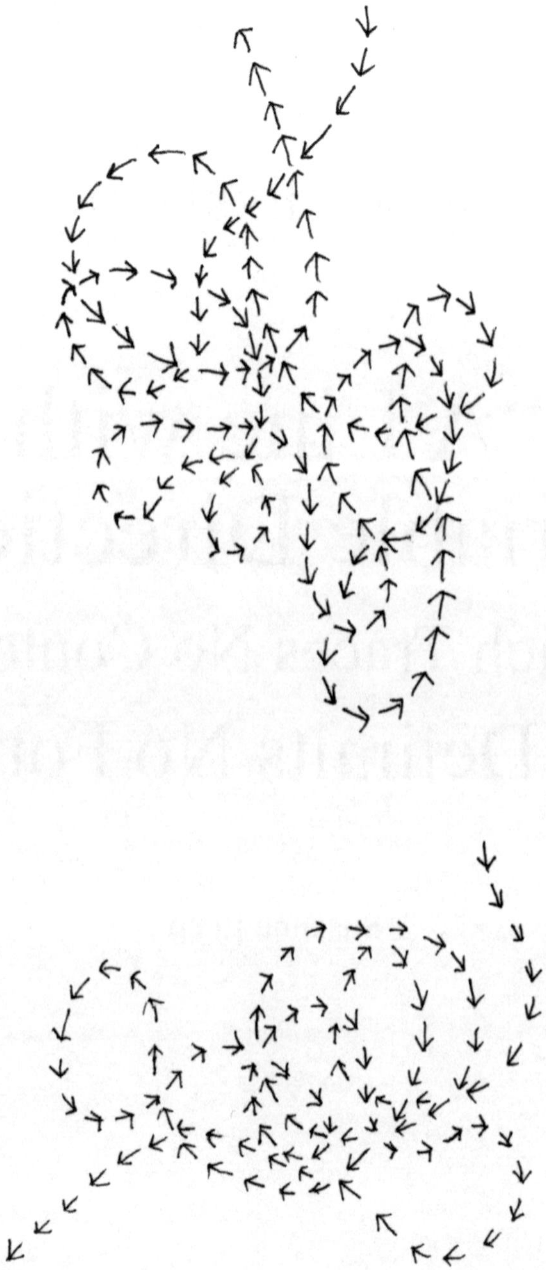

Fig. 06-12

There are currently at least two opposing ways of understanding the term 'diagram'. Some see diagrams above all as an aid to systematisation – "problem solvers, because they 'automatically support a large number of perceptual inferences, which are extremely easy for humans'"[1] –, while others see them as "proliferators of a process of unfolding" or "maps of movement"[2]. If in the former case the visual diagram is regarded in terms of the potential for order and visualisation, for example in mathematics, economics, statistics or pedagogy, in the latter case it is rather the structural possibility of putting relationships in the foreground, so conceiving of the diagrammatic as something which describes the alignment of words, shapes, objects and persons. If the first concept of the diagram is retrospective – by means of diagrams, a complex thought process or argument can be composed or a set of circumstances systematised – the second concept is projective, with vectors pointing in unknown directions. And while in recent years much attention has been paid to the first concept of the diagram in semiotics and image, but also in the science of cognition, the second concept of the diagrammatic has been marked by the power and subject theories of Michel Foucault as well as Gilles Deleuze and Félix Guattari. It is not a question, however, of two fundamentally different types of diagram; rather, this oscillation between systematising and openness is inherent in the diagram. Kenneth Knoespel calls to mind the Greek etymology of the word *diagramma*, whose roots suggest not only that "which is marked out by lines, a figure, form, or plan, but also carries a secondary connotation of marking or crossing out". Correspondingly, diagrams would not only take care of "order and stability" but would also be a means to "destabilisation and discovery"[3].

The same ambivalence also applies to those passages of text in which a more recent preoccupation with diagrams has its origin: for Foucault, the panopticon, with its specific structure of supervision, is a prototypical diagram which establishes a particular structure and sees to a smooth functioning of the

1) cf. John Mullarkey, *Post-Continental Philosophy. An outline*, New York, continuum 2006 in the chapter *Thinking in Diagrams*, here: p. 162.

2) Ben van Berkel and Caroline Bos, *Diagrams: Interactive Instruments in Operation*, in: *Any, Vol. 23*, 1998, pp. 19-23, here: p. 22.

3) Kenneth Knoespel, *Diagrams as plotting device in the work of Gilles Deleuze*, in: *Littérature, Théorie, Enseignement No. 19*, 2001, pp.145-165, here: p. 146.

mechanism – a network "which also pervades free milieus".[4] This means that the 'panopticon' supposes not only an architectonic form of construction, but also "a form of political technology"[5], which can be and is implemented in other places. Accordingly, Foucault defines the panopticon as a "type of implanting of bodies in space, of the dividing of individuals in
(→ PII/01) their relations to one another, of hierarchical organisation, of the arrangement of centres and channels of power, of the definition of instruments and intervention tactics of power".[6] The most important element of the diagram understood in this way is that it serves the description of the process whereby power relations are produced through relationships of strength. The diagram remains not external to the subject, but rather is essential for its formation. A diagram drawn would then be only a materialising of all those lines which connect the subject in its relationship to the social field. The fact that this makes an inner/outer distinction increasingly difficult notably resulted in the strong relationship of the diagrammatic to mental space. It abandons Euclidian
(→ PII/09) space in perspective form and conceives space topologically. Thus figures form, such as the twisting Möbius loop, in which the outer is also always the inner and vice versa.[7] Topology, in the words of the mathematician Benedict Listine, is the "science of the modal relationships of spatial entities [...] or of the laws of correlation, of the mutual position and the sequence of points, lines, surfaces, bodies, and their parts or aggregations in space, irrespective of ratios and proportions."[8] This implies,

4) Gilles Deleuze, *Foucault*, a. d. franz. von Hermann Kocyba (orig. *Foucault,* Paris, 1986), Frankfurt am Main, 1992, p. 65.

5) Michel Foucault, *Überwachen und Strafen. Die Geburt des Gefängnisses* (*Discipline and Punish: The Birth of the Prison*), translated from the French by W. Seitter (orig. *Surveiller et punir*, 1975), Frankfurt am Main 1994, p. 264. cf. also Petra Gehring, *Paradigma einer Methode. Der Begriff des Diagramms im Strukturdenken M. Foucaults und M. Serres*, in: *Diagrammatik und Philosophie*, ed. P. Gehring, et al., Amsterdam, Atlanta, GA:, pp. 89-120, p. 94: "A 'diagram' thus generates itself from the analyses of the highly effective machinery within the social body; the disciplining has the character of a diagram, as has delinquency, normalisation, the forms of sexual disparity, or even that panoptism which constitutes a particular kind of subject despairing about the incongruity of the view."

6) Foucault, transl. Ibid.

7) In topology cf. Stephan Günzel (ed.), *Topologie. Zur Raumbeschreibung in den Kultur- und Medienwissenschaften*, (*Topology. Towards the Description of Space in the Cultural and Media Sciences*) Bielefeld 2007; and: Wolfram Pichler, Ralph Ubl (eds.), *Falten, Knoten, Netze, Stülpungen in Kunst und Theorie* (*Folds, Knots, Nets, Reverse Drawing in Art and Theory*), Vienna, 2009.

8) Benedict Listing, *Vorstudien zur Topologie* (*Preliminary Studies in Topology*, 1847): here following Marie-Luise Heuser, *Topologie in der Mathematik* (*Topology in Mathematics*), in: Günzel, *Topologie*, pp. 183-200, here: pp. 190f.

however, that positional relationships – locations in space – are extremely important, whereby, as distinct from space perceived in the perspective view, "the authorial viewpoint is always immanent to the field of observation".[9] The point depends strictly on changes of location, which in their turn are decisive for the change of those divisions mentioned by Foucault, and also those of the respective (own) 'position', in the spatial as well as in the fullest metaphorical sense. Since just as the specific diagram of a power structure can be analyzed, so there is "no diagram which does not have among its points which connect it, relatively free or uncoupled points, points of creativity, of change, of resistance [...]."[10] If one follows Deleuze in this, every fixed point can become a pivotal point; or as Kenneth Knoespel puts it: "Rather than sequestering or policing the diagram in an axiomatic grid, Deleuze repeatedly emphasises the ways diagrams work to generate a kind of cognitive sweep that extends the possibilities of thought."[11] Every artistic work which attempts to produce spaces of thought and experience, and moreover, which are in confrontation with regulations and mechanisms of control, has shown that this cannot be understood voluntaristically.

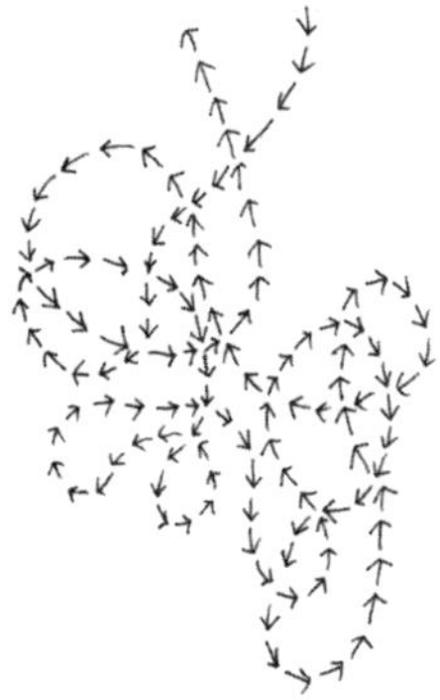

Fig. 06-12a

For this reason, diagrams are not only illustrations or systematisations of a set of circumstances, which – thanks to their spatial arrangement as writing – render two- or three-dimensional space productive as mental space, so that the intervals, distances, and locations also become meaning-giving and meaning-resolving elements.[12] As an operational drawing principle, they escape the insoluble dialectic of presence and absence which pervades the play of representation. In his famous essay *A City is not a Tree*, Christopher Alexander makes clear that particular diagrams are consequently restrictive, and opposes the hierarchizing and cross-connecting exclusive ramification of the tree diagram to the far more complex semiconductor diagram,

(→ PIII/05)

9) Eric de Bruyn, *Topological Pathways of Post-Minimalism*, in: *Grey Room 25* (Herbst (Autumn) 2006), pp. 32-63, here: p. 34.

10) Gilles Deleuze, *Foucault*, (orig. *Foucault*, Paris, 1986), translated from the French by Hermann Kocyba, Frankfurt/Main, 1995, p. 65.

11) Knoespel, p. 148.

12) cf. e.g. Michel Serres, who identifies a diagrammatic three-dimensionality in the paintings of Carpaccio. Michel Serres, *Carpaccio. Ästhetische Zugänge* (*Aesthetic Approaches*), Reinbek b. Hamburg, 1981.

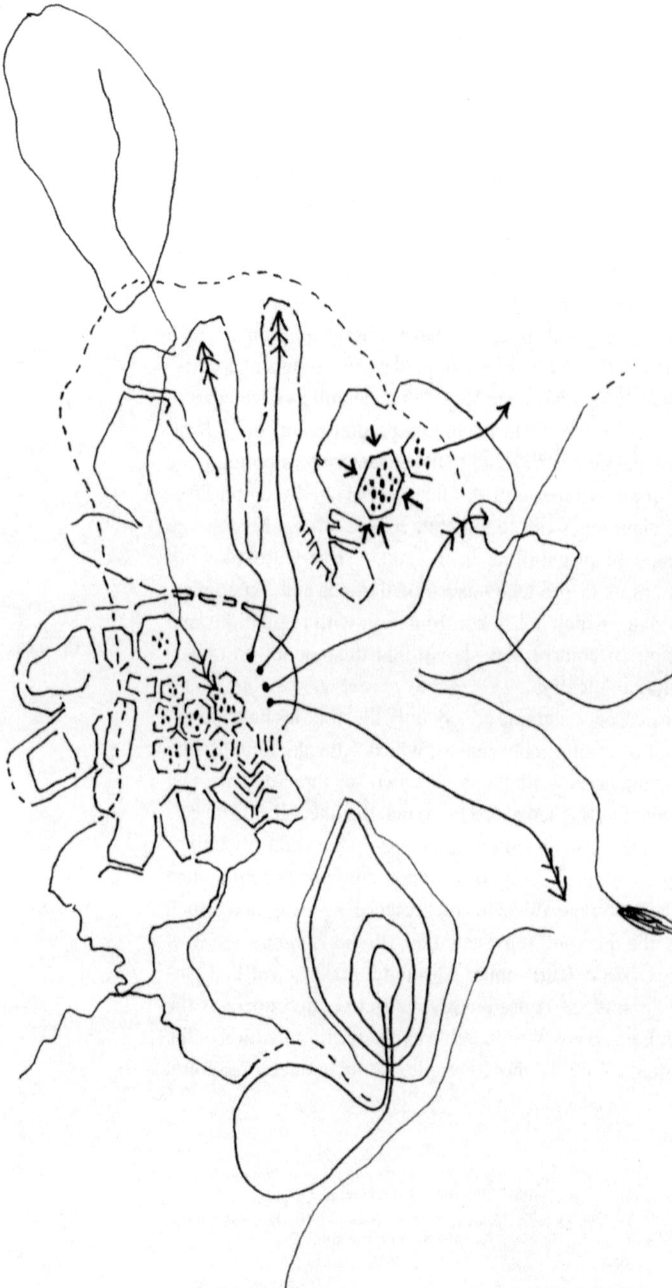

Fig. 06-01

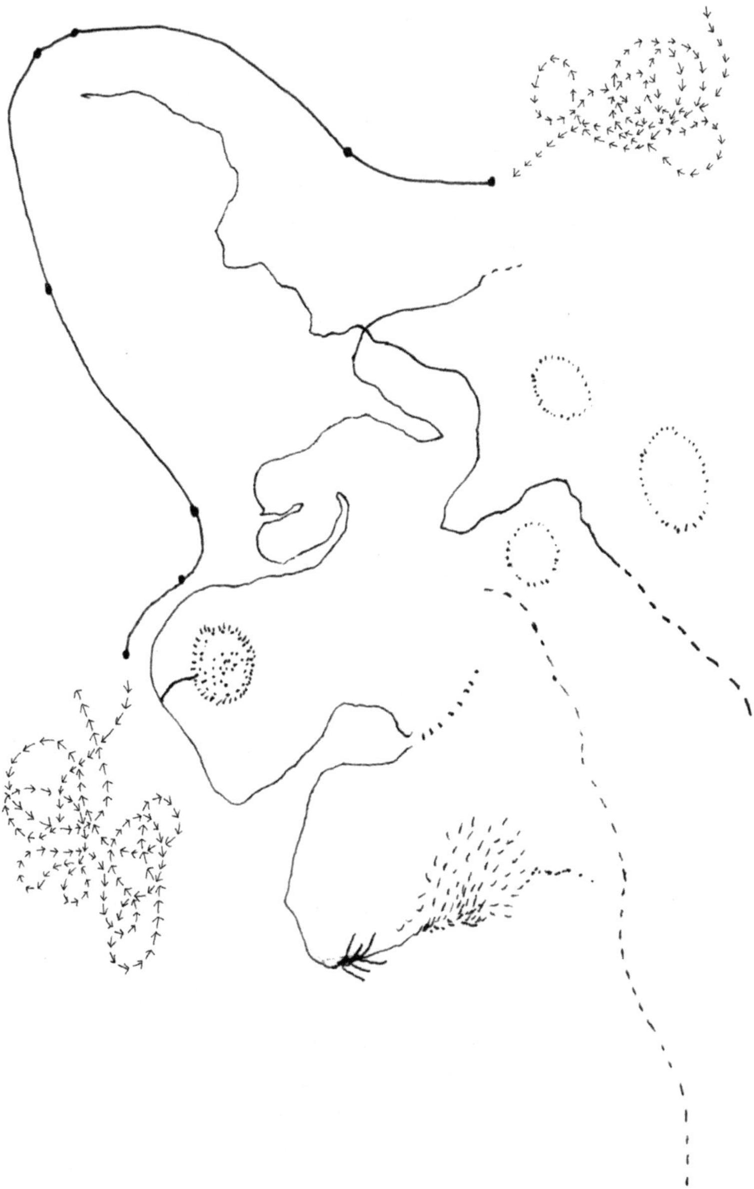

Fig. 06-08

which allows precisely this kind of multiple coding.[13] While the specific nature of diagrams would be overlooked if one were to regard them exclusively as images, without understanding the relations being established with their help, it is only their representative nature which allows one to recognise how lines channel thought in a figurative as well as in a spatial sense.[14] In the art of the 20th century, diagrams turn up in various states: as a work medium in the sense of a specific kind of sketch, which in the 20th/21st centuries has long since ceased to mean only figurative studies or the determining of composition, but also encompasses construction drawing, movement notation, and narrative plan.[15] A second variant can be seen in the appropriation and transfer of economic, statistical and technical diagrams, and also philosophical, spiritual, natural scientific and cosmological diagrams, which systematise knowledge. Here, art mostly breaks with the ideality of form, and runs contrary to a purely semiotic understanding of the diagram, according to which diagrams function independently of their concrete execution.[16] On the contrary, what Deleuze calls diagrams are precisely the material locations, marks, brushstrokes and informal zones that dissolve the established semantics.[17] Consequently, the ambivalence suggested by Deleuze/Foucault can also be found again here; diagrams are constructed around pivotal points and angle points, by means of which non-linear, non-semantic vector connections are constructed.

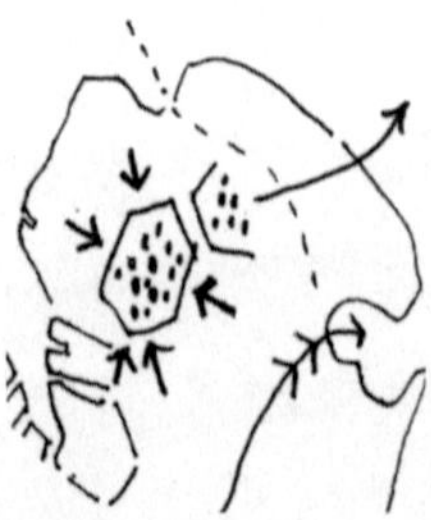

Fig. 06-01a

13) Christopher Alexander, *A City is not a Tree*, in: *Architectural Forum 122*, 1965, pp. 58-61. cf. also the exhibition on architectural theory and urbanism: *Soziale Diagramme* (*Social Diagrams*). *Planning reconsidered* im Künstlerhaus Stuttgart 2008; http://www.kuenstlerhaus.de/wp/wp-content/uploads/2008/08/guide_d_08_07_14.pdf (Stand: 15.3.2010).

14) Here one thinks of the countless forms of diagrams which in specific ways provoke thought independently of their form, such as the Möbius loop as an image of the indifferentiability between inner and outer. cf. Passim. Ubl/Pichler (ed.), *Falten, Knoten, Netze, Stülpungen* (*Folds, Knots, Nets, Reverse Drawing in Art and Theory*).

15) Here one thinks of, e.g. the flux diagram of George Maciunas (cf. Astrit Schmidt-Burkhardt, *Stammbäume der Kunstgeschichte: zur Genealogie der Avantgarde*, (*Genealogy of Art History: Towards the Genealogy of the Avant-Garde*, Berlin, 2005) or of the networks of finance capitalism in the cartograms of Mark Lombardi, Ashley Hunt or Bureau d'Etudes.

16) That the logic of diagrams can be thwarted on a material level can be seen in, the pictures of Alfred Jensen, who painted various diagrams (the Maya calendar, magnetic fields, chromatic spectra) in colours applied extremely thickly.

17) Gilles Deleuze, *Francis Bacon. The Logic of Sensation,* Minneapolis, University of Minnesota Press, 2004. Original French edition p. 66: "Le diagramme, c'est l'ensemble opératoire des traits et des taches, des lignes et des zones."

Although the use of diagrams in the art of the 20th/21st centuries can hardly be reduced to a common denominator, diagram 1 (sketch) and diagram 2 (Deleuze) meet in the concept of the draft as cultural praxis, which pervades all art. John Rajchman explains diagrams as a figure of thought, on this basis of continuing new organisation, when he interprets the architectonic concept of the (draft) plan as a form of thinking: "Then to think would always be to construct, to build a free plan in which to move, invent concepts, unfold a drama".[18] Art, for him, is paradigmatic, since as praxis it continually remakes itself anew and must continually be remade anew, and in this it is rather the opposite of a fixing or identifying thinking.

As tools of thought and forms of representation, however, diagrams in themselves have no status as art *per se*, but they nevertheless serve to crystallise repeated reformulations of the concept of art in the 20th/21st centuries. In the 1990s, for example, they served Marc Lombardi for the reformulation of the image of history, assuming the question of how the narrative can be shaped if the main characters of history are not (individual) subjects but (corrupt) governments, finance groups, consortia and money flows.[19] On the other hand, when in 1966 Mel Bochner collected preparatory diagrams, bills, lists, etc. from various invited artists for the central conceptual art exhibition "Working drawings and other visible things on paper not necessarily meant to be viewed as art", he understood them in an anti-aesthetic sense. It wasn't a question of raising sketches, doodles and bills to the level of art, but of making visible the 'outside' of and the 'before' of what underlies art, and so to reformulate the concept of art. Neither was Bochner the first to make diagrams productive for the discourse about art. As so often in the 20th century, this piece of art history also begins with Marcel Duchamp. Studies of Duchamp view the diagrammatic character of his works, for instance, in the use of technical drawings in the simultaneous transformation of the same into a modern allegory of love (*The Large Glass*), or as he breaks with mathematical axioms such as "A straight line is the shortest distance between

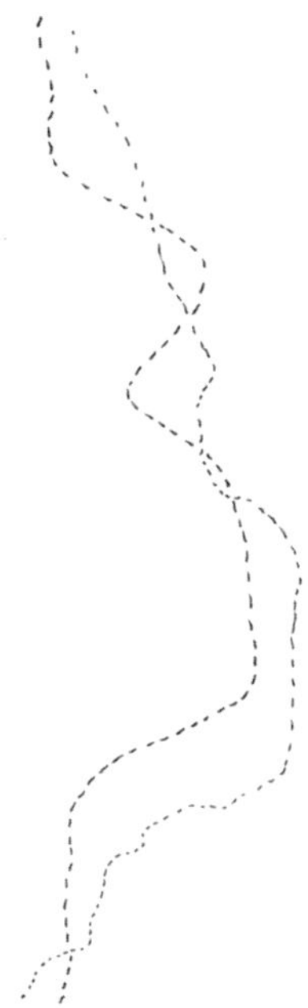

Fig. 06-04a

18) John Rajchman, *Constructions*, Cambridge/MA 2000 (3rd printing), p. 2.

19) Mark Lombardi drew explicitly from the tradition of history painting and on their 'reformulating' by Hans Haacke, "Shapolsky et al. Manhattan Real Estate Holdings, A Real Time Social System, as of May 1, 1971".

two points", as well as the standardisation of the metre by way of three dropped threads (*3 Standard Stoppages*).[20] But to begin with Duchamp is not the only possible 'beginning' for the history of the diagram and modern art; it is only one among the premises of a nominalistic concept of art. For another strand of the diagram, falling foul of the Enlightenment because of its esoteric connection, and more or less left lying there until today, can be found at the same time in the Swedish painter Hilma af Klint. If Duchamp reflects on the fact that the artist has to be a medium, Klint practised this insofar as, from 1900 onwards, she painted large diagrammatic paintings and watercolours at the behest of the voices she heard. With an esoteric women's group dedicated to spiritualism, she stood radically outside of the traditional academic concept of art.[21] Certainly for the ambivalence between the systematisation of knowledge and the opening and production of something as yet unarticulated, 'control' diagrams and their displacement in art have the more central significance, even if many artists are still flirting with the irrational and esoteric and mystical. Such was the use of diagrams in art around 1900 – here both Duchamp and Picabia come to mind – in answer to the question of how the relationship of the body and technology, and individuality to scientification and reification, are created. Buchloh reformulated this question in relation to drawing: What happens if "the conditions of sensory, sensual, libidinal corporeality had become the subject of pure measurement and controlling instrumentalisation, what would happen to those artistic conventions and competences that had traditionally facilitated the sublimating desire of depicting the body?"[22] The art historian Molly Nesbit has investigated precisely this kind of redefining of the role of drawings and drawing with reference to Duchamp's work.

(→PI/03a-c)

20) Cf. the site-monographical work of "3 Standard Stoppages" or "3 Standard Art-Stoppages" of Herbert Molderings, *Kunst als Experiment* (*Art as Experiment*). *Marcel Duchamps 3 "Kunststopf-Normalmaße"* (*"Standard Art-Stoppages"*), Munich, Berlin: Deutscher Kunstverlag 2006. And more specifically, compare with the diagram: David Joselit, *Dada Diagrams*, in: *The Dada Seminars*, ed. Leah Dickerman and Matthew S. Witkovsky, Washington: National Gallery of Art and Distributed Art Publishers, 2005, pp. 221-239.

21) Cf. *3 x Abstraction. New Methods of Drawing, Hilma af Klint, Emma Kunz, Agnes Martin*, ed. Catherine de Zegher, New York, Drawing Center 2005 – an exhibition which applied a feminist transcription of the history and meaning of abstraction.

22) Buchloh, Benjamin H. D., *Hesse's Endgame: Facing the Diagram*, in: *Eva Hesse Drawing*, ed. Catherine de Zegher, New York, New Haven: The Drawing Center, Yale University Press, 2006, pp. 117-150, here: p. 122.

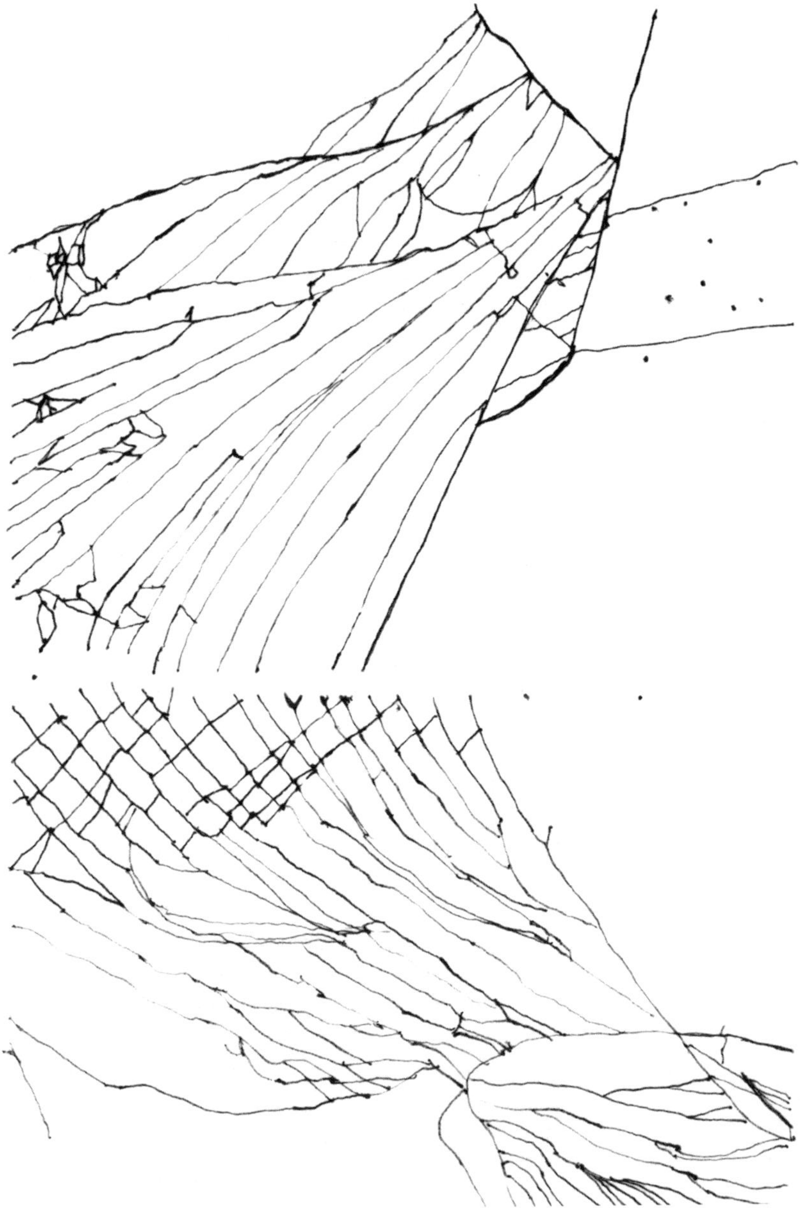

Fig. 07-00

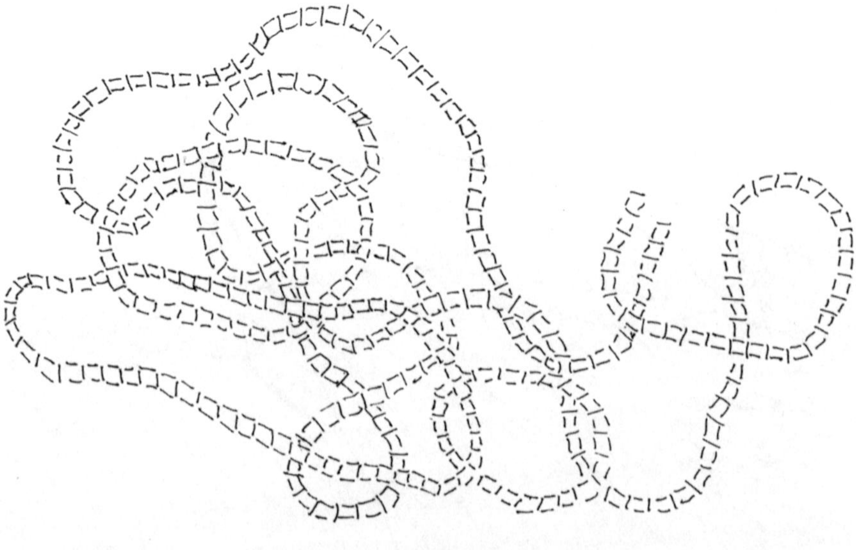

Fig. 10-26

According to her research, the mastery of technical drawing – the 'line', as it was known in French schools of the 19th century – was an activity enabling the development of graphical competence for the process of industrial production.[23] Construction drawings counted as non-retinal, i.e. not confined to the chance appearance of things; instead they were to comprehend this appearance in its constructive-functional principles, a penetrating view reserved for male pupils only. For the question of modern subjectivity this demand was decisive, the demand that technical drawing be trained until it became an unconscious process, "*d'une manière inconsciente, machinale*",[24] – a highly consequential connection of machine and unconscious, reaching from surreal automatism by way of the "machine in the studio"[25] to the abstract machines of Deleuze and Guattari.[26]

23) Molly Nesbit, *Marcel Duchamp: The Language of Industry*, in: *The definitely unfinished Marcel Duchamp*, ed. Thierry de Duve, Cambridge, Mass., London, 1991, pp. 351-394, here: p. 353.

24) Nesbit, ibid., p. 383, fn 24.

25) E.g. Caroline A. Jones' book in which she discusses the "painter machines" of abstract expressionism: *Machine in the Studio. Constructing the postwar American Artist*, Chicago, University of Chicago Press, 1996.

26) Cf. also Rosalind Krauss' text in which she relates Eva Hesse's works to Deleuze/Guattari's "organless body": Rosalind Krauss, *Hesse's Desiring Machines* (1993), in: *Eva Hesse*, ed. Mignon Nixon (= October Files 3), Cambridge/MA, London, 2002.

The sexualised machines of Duchamps or Picabia, but also the biomechanical drawings of Eva Hesse are articulations of the question of how body and technology, desire and scientific rationality cohere, wresting a polymorphous principle of desire from the reality of industrialisation.

How important the normalising, scientific and quantifying diagrams were and are for the question of subjectivity can be gleaned from diagram drawings oscillating between disciplining or self-optimising controls and self-determination. In the process, art itself breaks with the myth of modernity, of the blank page, the white sheet, when artists use pre-prepared material. Thus, there are countless works drawn in and on maps (e.g. Nasreen Mohamedi), on graph paper (Eva Hesse, Agnes Martin, Emma Kunz and many others), in schedules (Eva Hesse) or account books (Morgan O'Hara) – all forms in which a connection is visible between subjectivity and the economy (of time) in the sense of self-administration. This kind of technique also crosses over into the realm of self-regulation, for instance, when the sound artist Stephan von Huene, using neurolinguistic programming and the brain training and memory methods of the British psychologist Tony Buzan, chooses Mind Maps as a form of notation for the theoretical construction of his installations and for his lectures.[27] (→ PI/01)

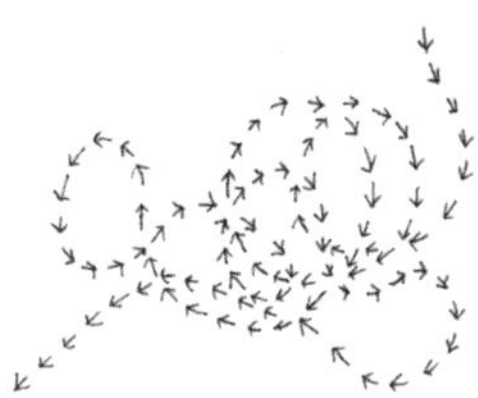

Fig. 06-12b

While diagrams of this kind manifest a specific subject relation which corresponds to the modern invocation to self-administration, a principle of the diagrammatic is found less in a concrete diagram form but rather in loose arrangement and open constellations. This encompasses other arts as well – beyond concrete, material drawing – and allows the diagram to be seen as a tool for channelling the making of relationships and for the abandonment of a rational procedure. One thinks of Öyvind Fahlström, whose installations are conceived as moveable, so that the individual elements always find their way to new constellations; or one thinks of the choreographer Yvonne Rainers with her ephemeral production of a space through movement, and in her changing between rule, arrangement and lapse; or of the absurd performances of the 1970s/80s of

27) Cf. Astrit Schmidt-Burkhardt, *Das Diagramm als Gedächtnisform. Zu Stephan von Huene's Mind-Map-Methode* (*The Diagram as a Form of Memory. To Stephan von Huene's Mind-Map-Method*), in: Irmgard Bohunovsky-Bärnthaler (ed.), *Kunst ist gestaltete Zeit* (*Art is Formed Time*). *Über das Altern*, Klagenfurt, 2007, pp. 105-141.

artist, poet, theatre director and actor Stuart Sherman, in which Sherman handles everyday objects, constantly rearranging them, placing himself in relation to them, producing accidents, collisions and chaos, grouping them over and over again with great seriousness in apparently meaningful constellations;[28] or of the "relational objects" which play a central role in Latin American conceptual art from Lygia Clark to Ricardo Basbaum. As distinct from the diagram as a drawn object, the body draws attention to itself as desiring or (un)controlled, which no longer just inscribes itself in technical drawing but which itself becomes the carrier of diverse thinking and acting. Given this background, Nikolaus Gansterer's *Drawing a Hypothesis* project is thus not diagrammatic because there are indeterminate diagrams, but rather because these, robbed of their function of scientific representation, could be figures of thought or instructions for action whose developing potential places the users under an obligation.

28) Thanks to Amy Sillman for drawing my attention to Stuart Sherman.

HYPOTHESIS #2

I Must Be Seeing Things

Clemens Krümmel

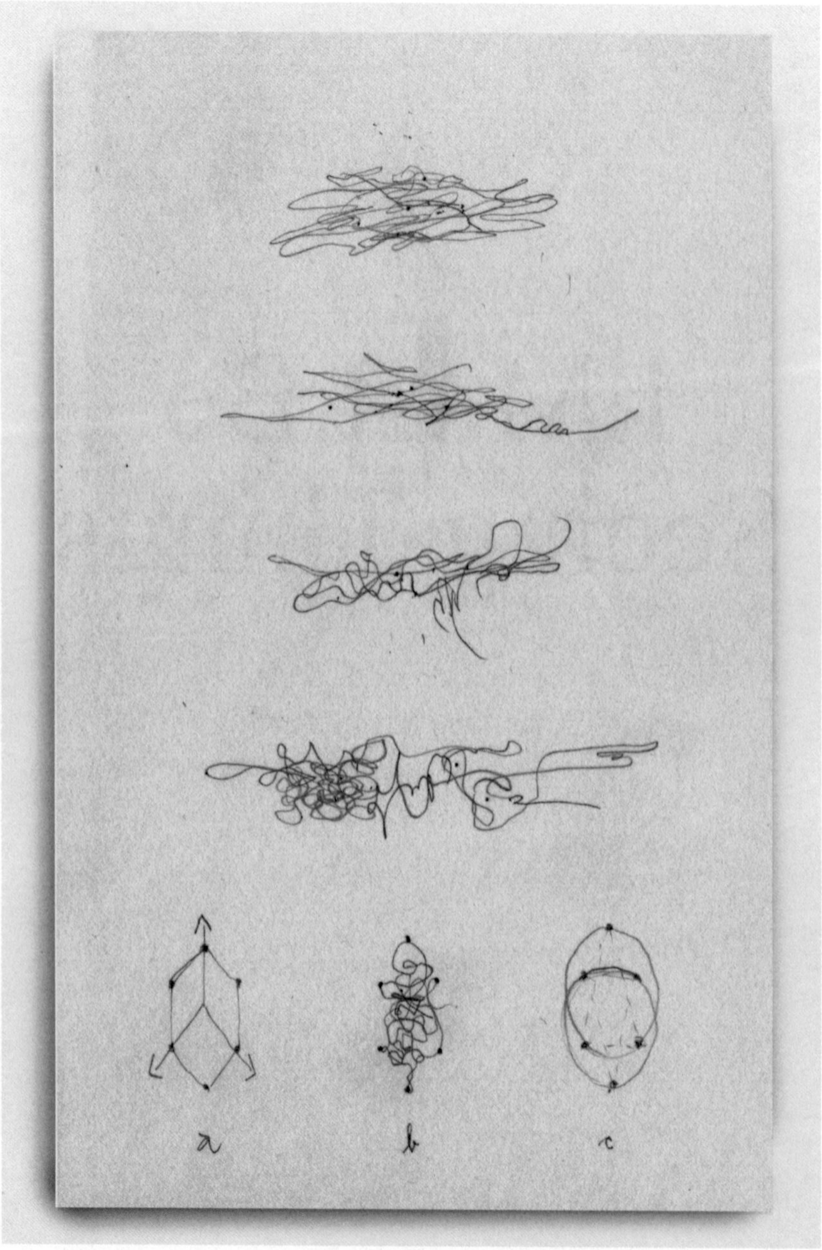

Fig. 11-06

The graphical figures and diagrams on twelve sheets of white paper hanging before my eyes are comprised of black points, and curved and straight lines; they show patterns and series.[1] They are hand drawings, which with very few exceptions appear to have been produced without technical aids. On many sheets, the parts are depicted as something like interdependent reference fields, with more or less obvious centres differentiating them from one another. Even with definite examples of easily recognizable, closed-reference organic or geometric figures, the eye is drawn to other signs:[2] signs, above all arrows, which establish and characterise relationships, indicate relative movements, and create temporality, hierarchy and orientation. Apart from the purely graphical signs, there are also numbers, letters and mathematical symbols, at least on some sheets, which suggests that on these sheets a mixing is taking place, an opening into the sphere and the organisation of written language, which was regarded as necessary by the draftsman and which supports the impression that something is supposed to be explained by these drawings, that they form an ensemble designed to clarify something.

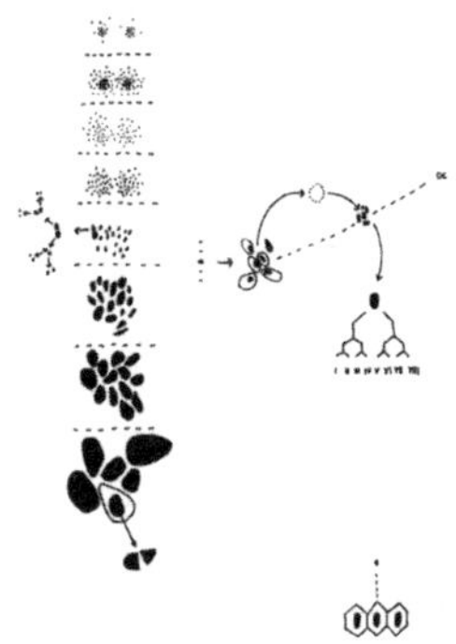

Fig. 02-10

How are we to conceptualise this collection? To begin with, the fact that they are all together does not necessarily imply

1) Initially, I tacked the pictures that had been sent to me onto a bookcase with modifiable shelves, at a distance of about two metres. This means that, for two weeks, the drawings have been hanging right behind my computer screen, where I spend the greater part of my life. Whenever I look up from the monitor and refocus, I see that the sheets look mainly like bright white spots where there used to be coloured book spines with unreadably small writing on them.

2) In order to observe them more clearly, I have to get up and stand directly in front of them. Over the past few weeks and days, I have done this repeatedly; in the end I stopped making changes to the order they were hanging in, since in the meantime I had become used to this washing-line of drawings, parts of which had proved to have curious and amusing links to my daily work. Since, just as there is a peri-artistic tradition of 'doodles', telephone numbers or scribbles parallel to more or less inspiring lectures, the marginal drawings on the white surfaces of more or less opaque textbooks – so during these weeks the drawings have made clear to me that points of concentration arranged in such a way in the visual structure of a living-room or study interfere in a structural way in physical and mental movements, and can provide moments of distraction and concentration. During telephone debates I used to wander through the room, plop myself down on a seat, automatically switch the television on and the sound off, absentmindedly wipe the invincible dust from the edges of the bookshelves. With every emergence from the wandering state I experience my room as a hoard of passive routines and subroutines. In the 'colourful cell' of my room, which furniture and equipment, books and records, CDs and DVDs share in fairly rationally ordered cooperation, the temporary ties of another kind of reasoning are formed by the drawings, of something still open, explicitly still unexplained and perhaps inexplicable, which produce a kind of magnetic effect because of this characteristic but also because of its visual impact – with the comparative emptiness of the white sheets which so brazenly negate the library-like environment.

(→ PII/06)

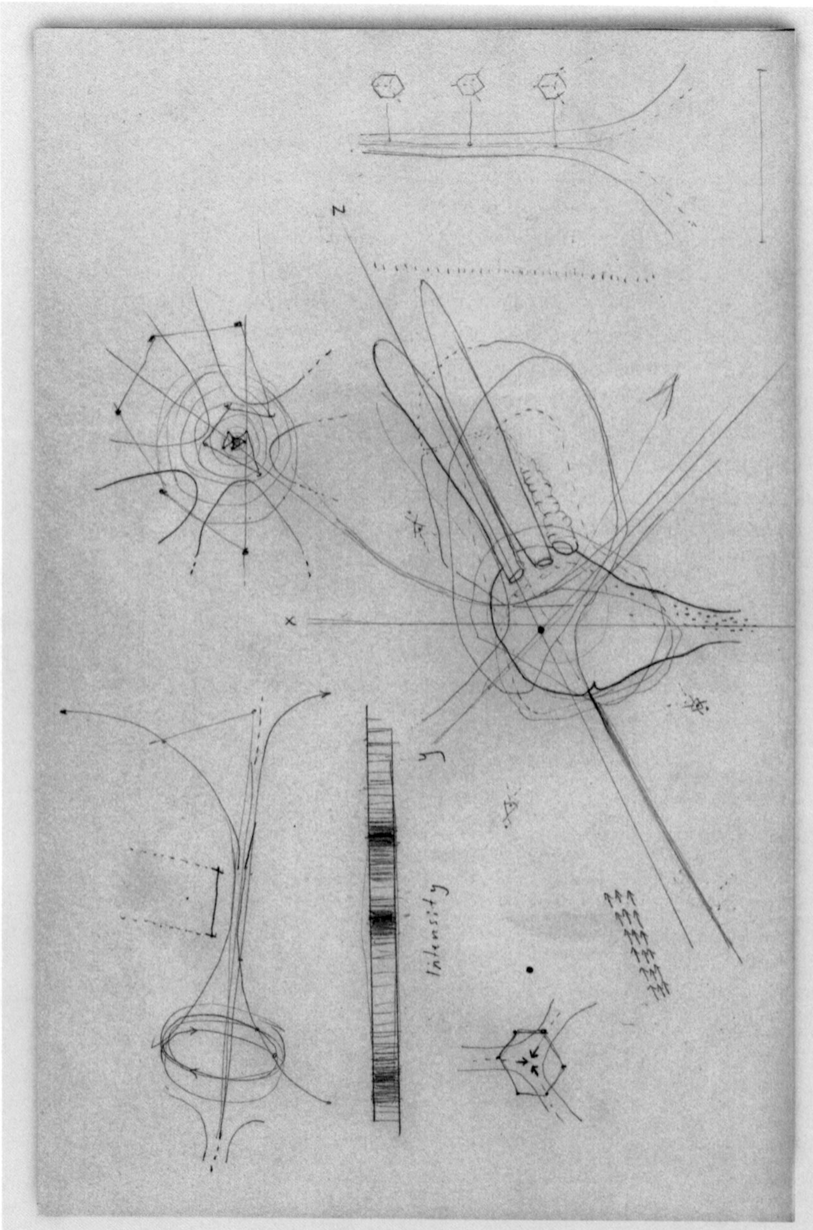

Fig. P01-04

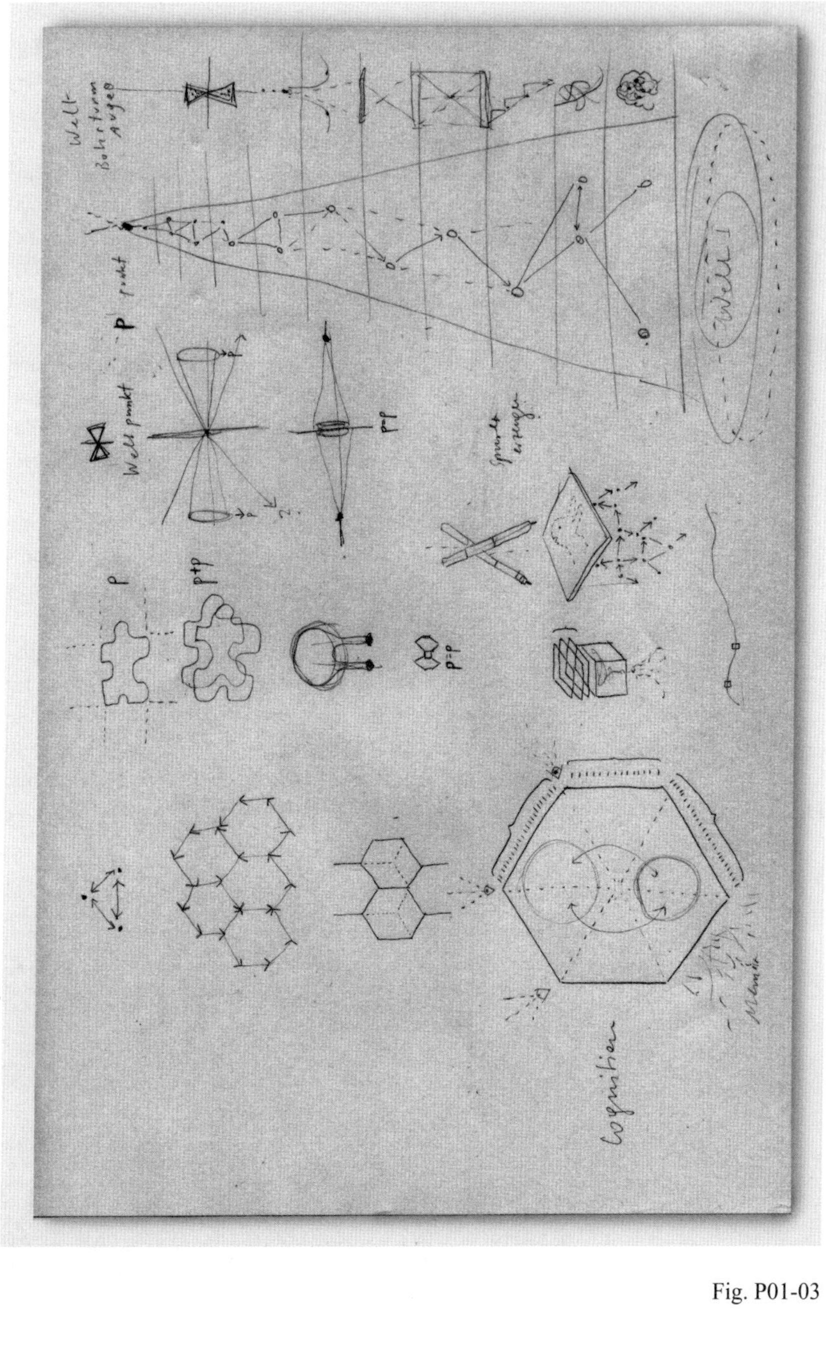

Fig. P01-03

any specific connection between them. Certainly, there are various similarities, and repeated motifs and principles, but without any concrete context these lead to only vague rules of classification. Invited to interpret a collection of drawings that is deliberately only partially organised, I tried to see the openness of the system as a chance to monitor my perception of diagrammatic forms. This collection is marked only by an orientational knowledge not characterised by any kind of specialisation (as one finds the cutlery drawer in a strange kitchen in the night), but instead by the subjective experience of dealing with and interpreting abstract forms.

If – based on the interesting situation of being confronted with a relatively complex collection of drawings – such decisions can be formulated and justified, which form of compilation would be appropriate[3]? Despite the numbering of the sheets (or of the graphical digital documents belonging to them), an order suggests itself to me, which starts from a rather chaotic arrangement and proceeds via various grades of order and complexity until it comes at last to a way of reading them which can at least be described as a *development* from the simple to the complex[4]. One sheet, with looping lines like signatures distributed irregularly in the space, creates a first point of entry for me, for various reasons – and I am conscious of the underlying structure of creation of meaning which brings this decision to light in my thinking. These lines operate associatively for me, reminding me of the well-known graphically running lines, the

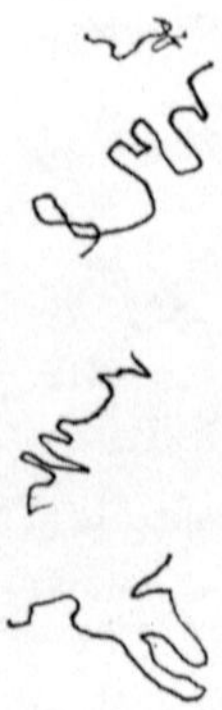

Fig. 10-25a

3) Since the drawings have been hanging on the bookshelves, I have repeatedly caught myself trying to connect them with what's happening on the computer or on the telephone. A flight into a way of associative-visual thinking, which occasionally defies the diurnal, rational aspect of thinking and lures it onto random paths of momentary consonance. This approximates the vegetative side, as it were, of my interaction with the drawings. This allows me to understand the power of abstraction and chance as offering themselves as a 'simple image' in relation to the complexity of my everyday life, characterised by laziness, lack of concentration, memory lapses and lack of imagination. Probably these 'simple images' are not 'archetypes' but unadorned graphical depictions of processes, simple geometric constellations of space and surface, or comparative images attracting, apparently magnetically, the dust of the situational circumstance, on which it can be 'understood'.

4) Without showing me movement mimetically, as a film would do, the drawings draw me into another way of movement, which appears to follow particular laws, like a basic repertoire of chess moves. Like certain books of wisdom, such as the *I Ching*, they are based consciously on the random recombination of the simplest structural elements, and raise an immense potential of associations by their abstract aloofness from the canonical-narrative interpretations, which aim at the supposed 'unchangeability' of the individual's relationship to the world. So it is specifically the structural violence of graphical simplification of the lines in drawings, sketches, diagrams, that furnishes the imagination with the launch pad which our imagination so desperately needs.

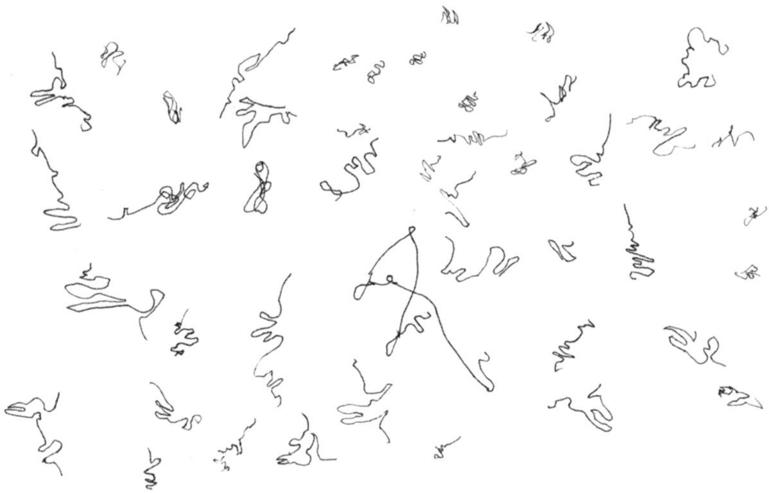

Fig. 10-25

visual writing of the protomodern fantasy novel *Tristram Shandy* which Laurence Sterne wrote before the French Revolution.[5] In this novel, these graphics strewn about establish from the first a different order from that of the written word, and supposedly, for the reader who is so inclined, bring the complicated handling of the previous chapters once again to a simple, pictorial denominator – since here it is not a question of an illustration, nor, as is emphasised, of a precise graphical correspondence. Rather, the capriciously rolling line approaches the authorial allegory of a poetological principle of reflected randomness. It marks a very early moment when the potential of the pictorial and of the drawn line was recognised on the simplest level. More importantly, these scribbled, gesture-like lines, floating 'clumsily' between diagram and writing, such as Roland Barthes discerned in the pictures of Cy Twombly,[6] already exhibit a degree of describable difference. Dimensional differences are already established here, as on other sheets, which produce a weak illusion of space, an imaginative assumption about the profound ordering of forms in an empty space.[7] The forms act

5) Laurence Sterne, *The Life and Opinions of Tristram Shandy*, Gentleman (1769-67); Exhibtion Catalogue *Shandyismus. Autorschaft als Genre*, ed. Helmut Draxler, Secession Wien, Kunsthaus Dresden, Stuttgart, 2007.

6) Roland Barthes, *Non multa sed multum*, in: Cy Twombly, trans. Walter Seitter, Berlin, 1983.

7) The apotheosis of spatial depth in diagrammatic drawings can be found in: Edwin A. Abbott, *Flatland. A Romance of Many Dimensions*, 2nd revised edition, London, 1884.

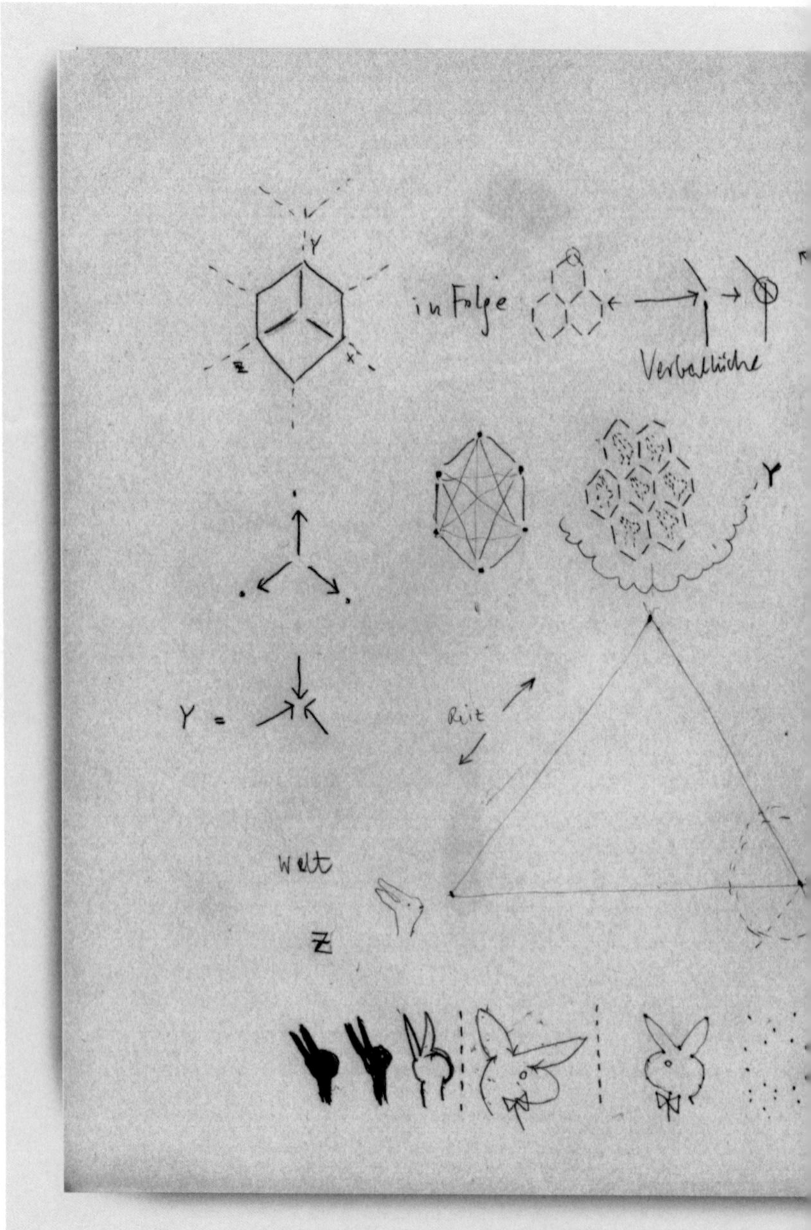

Fig. P01-02

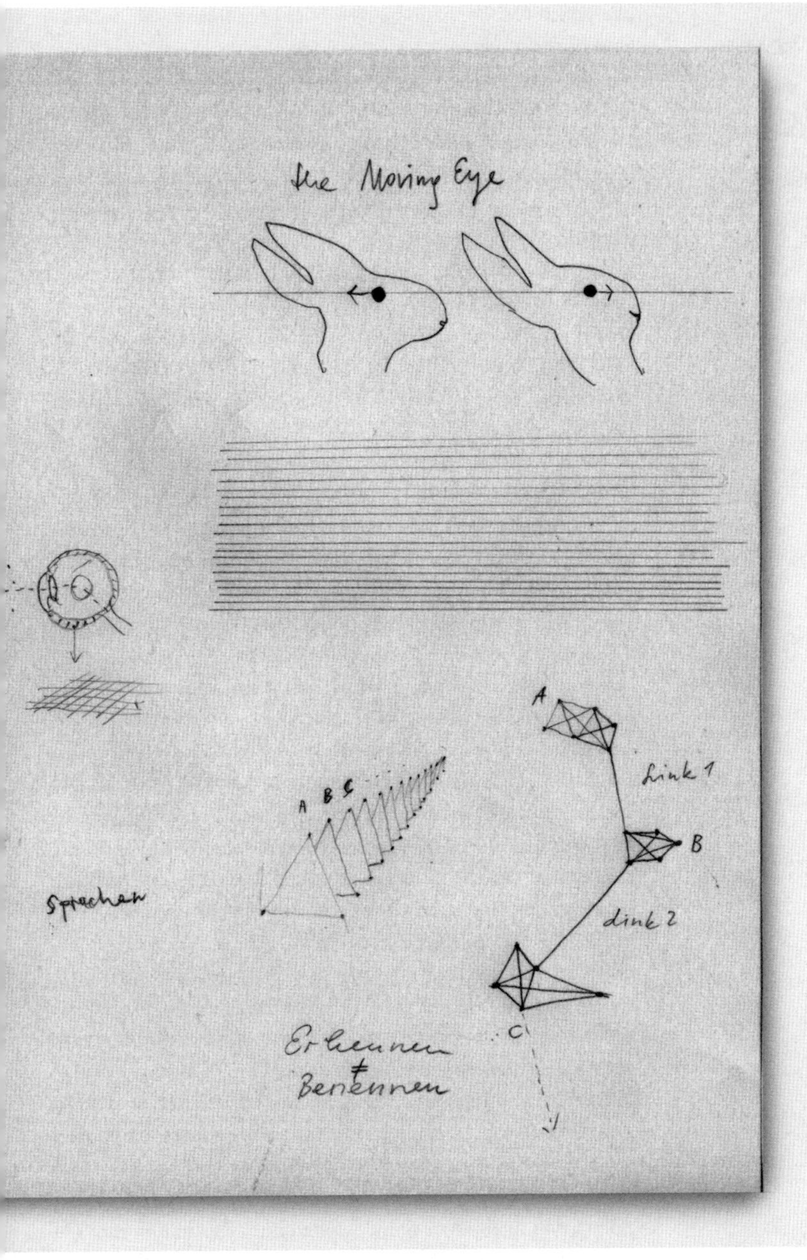
the Moving Eye
A B C
A
Link 1
B
Link 2
C
Sprechen
Erkennen
≠
Benennen

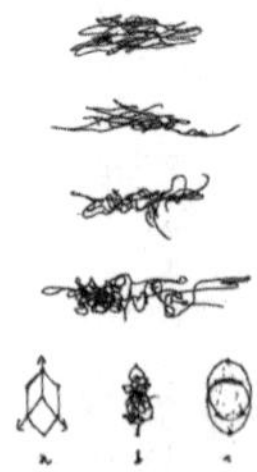

Fig. 11-06

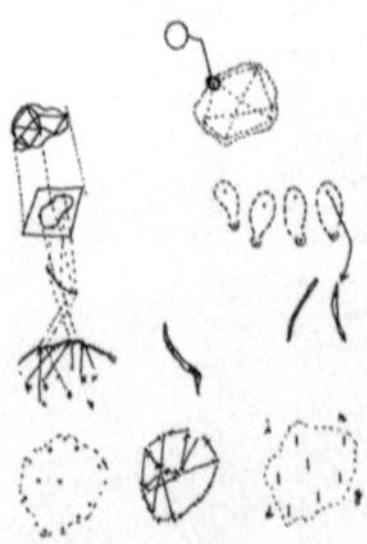

Fig. 09-07

like gestural abbreviations; they overwrite themselves, but do not interloop. On another sheet I see similar overlays of lines arising from rather longer lines to larger areas of the page and executed in four variants (→ Fig. 11-06). Opposite them there are other smaller drawings, only the middle one of which resembles the balls of lines drawn above. What both groupings of shapes share are the emphatically drawn points. These are placed at particular points of the lines; on the drawings below they lead to a coherent pattern which forms a virtual hexagon and which at first suggests that in each of these very different shapes the points touch lines arranged in the same way on each sheet. From this, combined points generate the description. The next sheet (→ Fig. 09-07) would certainly be the one on which the greatest number of shared structural characteristics can be detected: here there are honeycomb or cell-like hexagons; there are clusters of points which expand in dimension, arranged one underneath the next. The most important signs for development and causality appear: the directional and operational arrow and the connecting line of dashes or points. The more dense the organising principle becomes from sheet to sheet, the more the drawings confront me with these kind of assumptions of comprehension. They allow one to think back to the early stages of orientation in the formalities of graphical representation – which in part have maintained themselves with astonishing success from childhood to advanced age: circles of dashes with jagged sides, with text to read inside will forever remind me of the speech bubble asides in comic books. There are further sheets which take up the visual aspiration of the pointed line – particularly prominent on one which places two more broadly executed balls of lines on opposite sides of the format, and again creates references between points of comparison in the formations. Two other sheets also take up the points of comparison again, and out of these develops an interplay of permeable and closed, geometric and organic, simple and complex forms.

One of the drawings shows a cell-like, almost oval form circumscribed by one line in different modalities. Moreover, the open form is penetrated on three sides (→ Fig. 06-16) – once by a stem-shaped structure, then by a slender column of points, and finally by a double dotted line. This in turn runs out into another figuration in which points arising from the double line appear to leak through a square shape into a vase-shaped

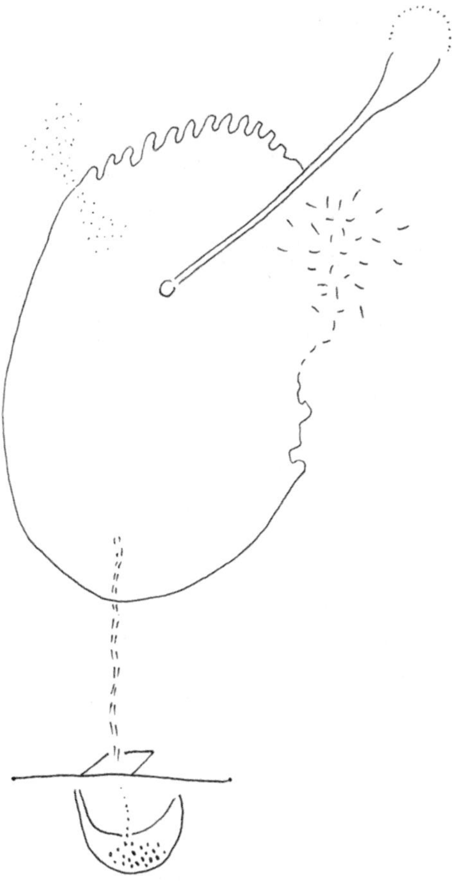

Fig. 06-16

form as if through a filter or a membrane. From a distance I wouldn't recognise the contents of this sketch, but close up it really rather reminds me of the representations of permeability in the biology books of my childhood, and it inevitably assumes the shape of a human head. The lines of waves look incessantly like hair, the steps like stubborn lips, the double line like a scrawny little neck, the cloud of dashes like the bursting out of bitter tears, etc. You might laugh at me here, on the search for orientation (of all things!), fleeing into the fantasy figure of a human countenance. But here at last, on the emotive level, we meet the far side of the cool rationality of the supposedly clear diagram. I must be seeing things. This observation is confirmed in the following sheets, which I assign to the more complex

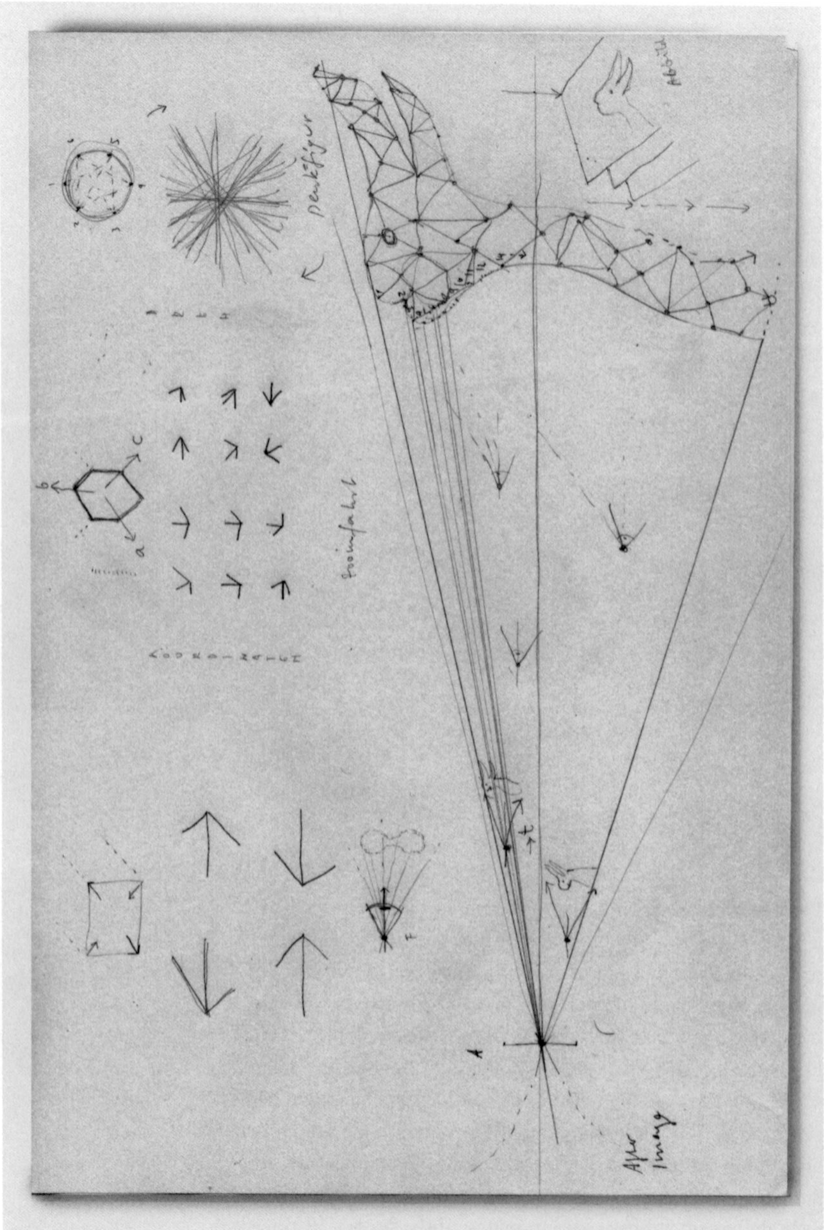

Fig. P01-05

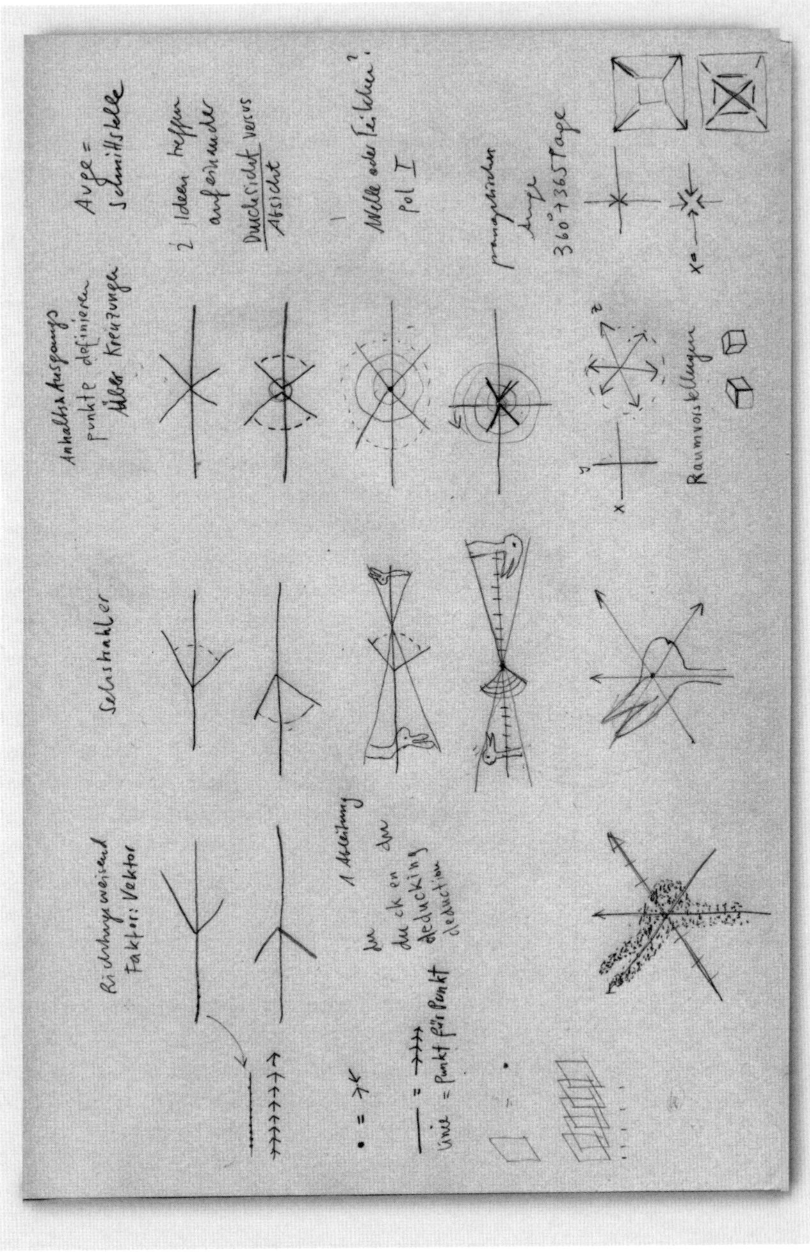

Fig. P01-01

(→ Fig. P01-01 -05)

ones, most of which have a not exactly anthropomorphic but certainly creature-like form as the centrepoint: surrounded by vector systems, connecting lines, progressions and permutations, as well as by the diagrammatic image of optical calculations, we encounter the heraldic animal of the Enlightenment: a composite creature – indeed, how could it be otherwise? It is the popular ambiguous figure of a hare's and/or duck's head, and I no longer know where I saw it first: in a schoolbook? On the games page of a comic book? In the Gombrich classic *Art and Illusion*?[8] The animal's name is ambivalence – and it can take geometric forms or the form of an old man and/or a young woman, among others. It addresses a feature of human perception, or more precisely, the inability to perceive diverging interpretations of a morph, of a profile form, at the same time. Historically, it has been used as an indication of a strikingly deep dimension of the two-dimensionally graphic, and symbolises a direct access to the heights (utopian wish for an unhurried reconciliation of opposites) and also to the depths (rules of expression, skull measurements) of the humanistic worldview. If one liberates illustrative representations, complex graphical systems and symbolic systems from their still to be understood momentary, performative context, as happened in this experiment with 'pictures without words', then the aforementioned composite creatures awaken. Though that isn't quite right, since the sheets of the collection which have not yet been mentioned make use of words throughout. They operate like sketches of ideas, created associatively and supported by writing, whose author appears to have been concerned with the rearranging of an idea of the imagination supported by drawing. 'Recognise ≠ Naming' – I read this on one of the drawings. It is one of the drawings with the composite creature, there, where it mutates into a playboy bunny. Perhaps one sees only what one wants to see. In the diagrams I have lived with in a narrow space for some weeks, I see an erratic compendium of what diagrammatic drawings elucidate, without wanting to elucidate it. A kind of background radiation of the Enlightenment.

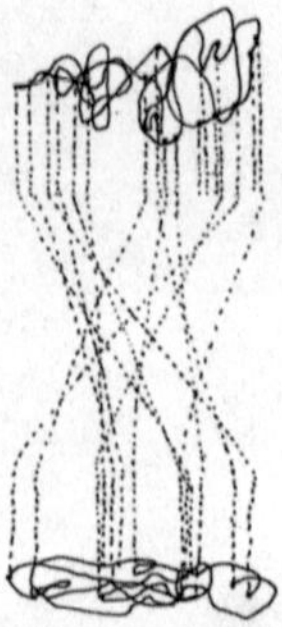

Fig. 05-09

8) Ernst H. Gombrich, *Art and Illusion. A Study in the Psychology of Visual Representation*, 1961.

HYPOTHESIS #3

Objective Subjectivities

Jörg Piringer

Fig. 02-11

After I'd been walking along the path in the forest for ten minutes, I found my way blocked by a barrier put up because of logging work. I went back to a fork in the path and turned off. When this path ended after a while too, I turned round and went back to the point where I'd turned off the original path. I followed this, moving away from the first blocked point, to a new fork. I took the new path, which led gently downhill.
Cockroaches use their feelers to keep an unvarying distance from the wall while they go along it. When they run, they make little body turns toward the wall and away from it, to be able to follow possible wave forms of the wall better. The faster the insects run, the less distance they keep from the wall.

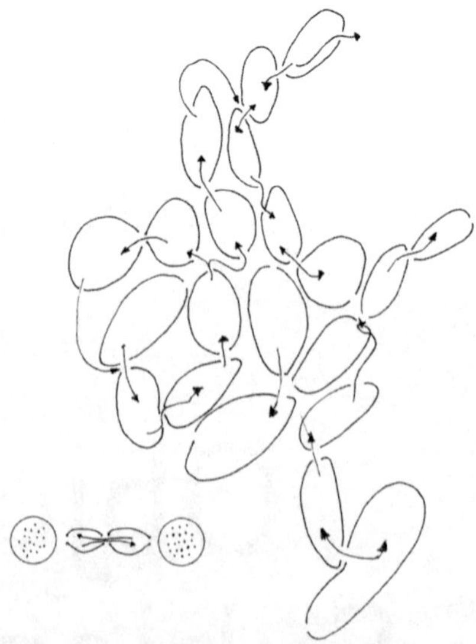

Fig. 02-12

One element has exactly one successor. I take my place last in the queue for the ticket counter. The register of elements can be closed in a loop, by changing the signifier of the last element so that it makes reference to any other one. I ask the first person at the counter whether he'll be much longer, since I'm in a hurry. An algorithm with time complexity O(n) can calculate whether a register possesses cyclical attributes.

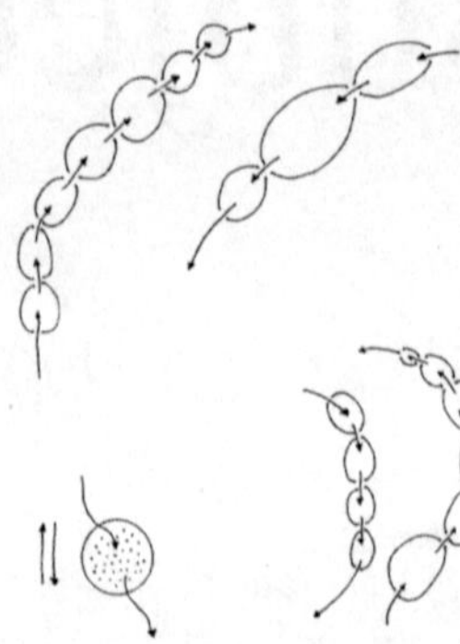

Fig. 02-13

I reserve a table, I lay my towel on the deckchair. In the evenings I draw the curtains, lock the door of the apartment. Pull the bolt across and close the kitchen cupboard.
A room or a surface is broken up by a predetermined number of points or centres into divisions whose point set lies nearer to the given centre than to any other centre. Points of equal distance to several centres constitute the boundaries of the section, they divide the room or surface into cells.

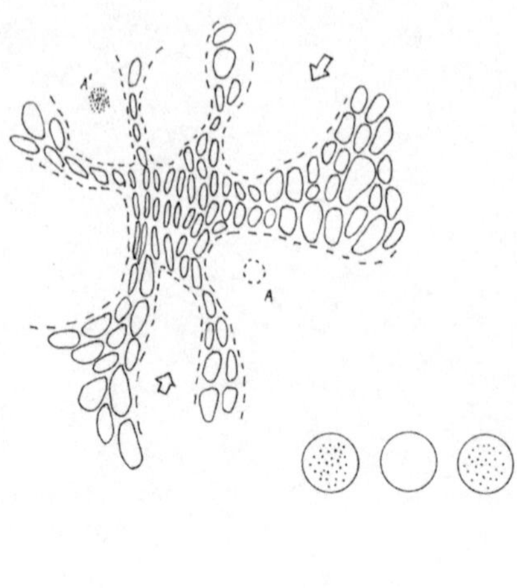

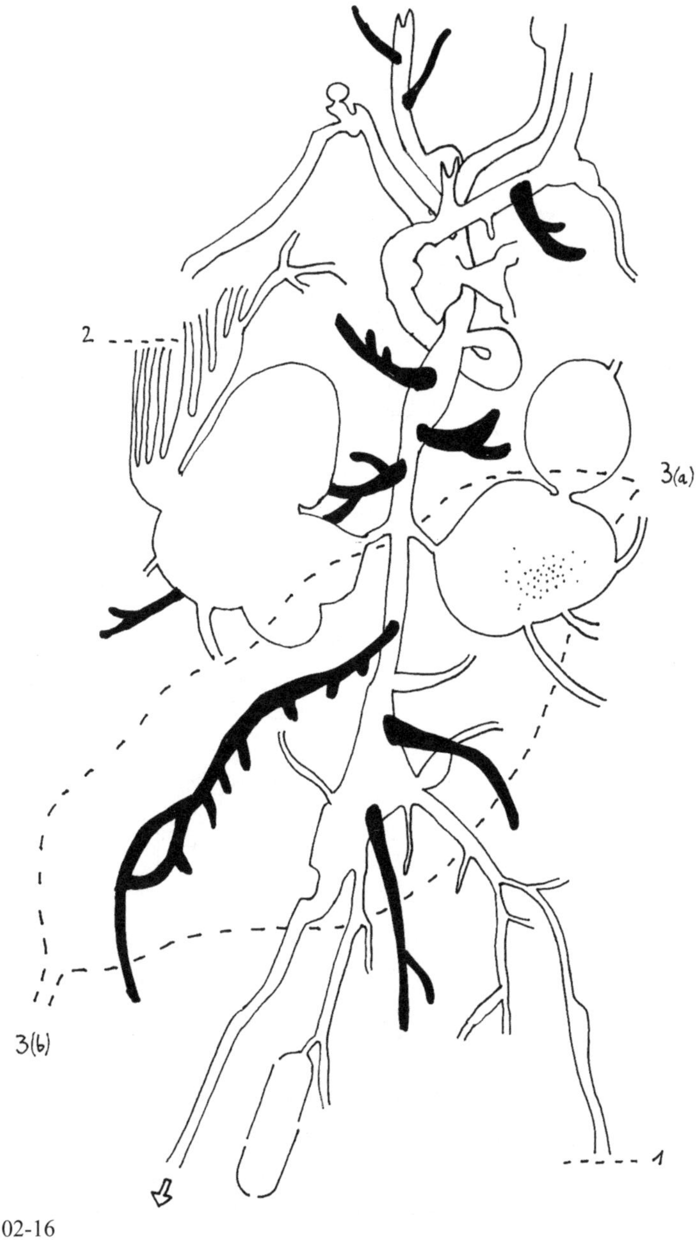

Fig. 02-16

I hold a printout of the programme in my hand. Through the kitchen window, the corridor, the corridor window, the courtyard, the bare tree in the courtyard and between the neighbouring houses, the sun shines onto the sheet of paper, is reflected and warms my stomach into which I pour coffee, sip by sip ...

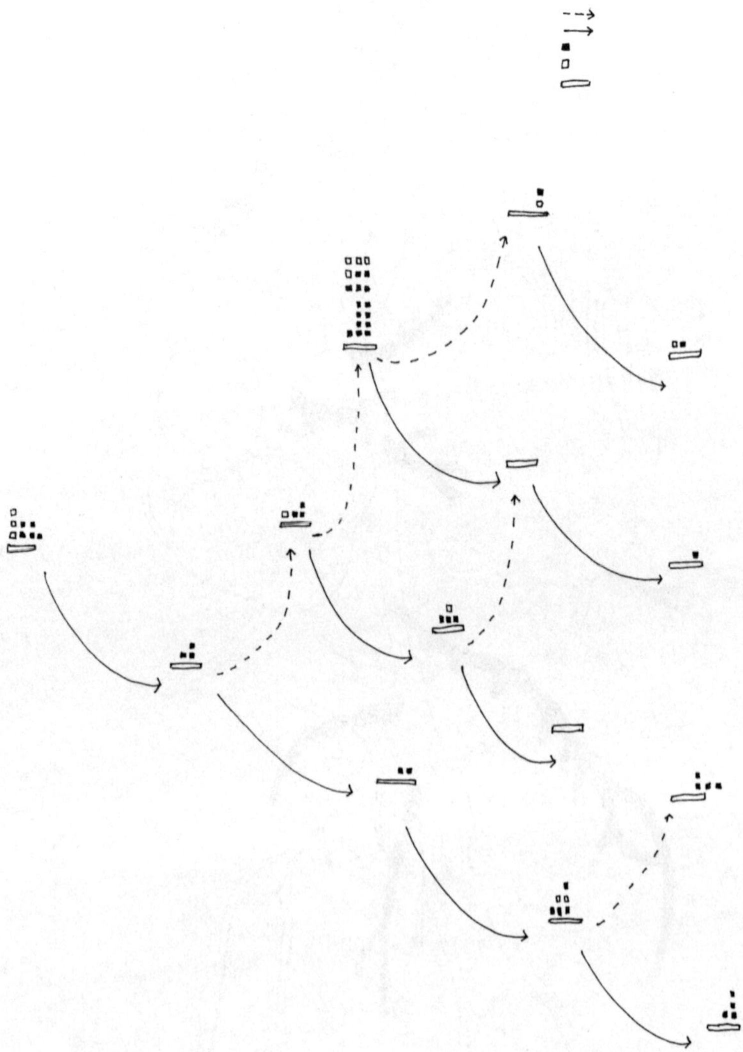

Fig. 02-14

Unfamiliar knots: I have a project. I want to find out about something. I make something up. I fantasise. Familiar knots: when I came out of the underground. When I passed the bakery, closed years ago. When I crossed the street.
Knots conclusively investigated: I close the book. I file the bill. I save the data.
An algorithm is optimal: that means it will always find the best solution, if one exists.

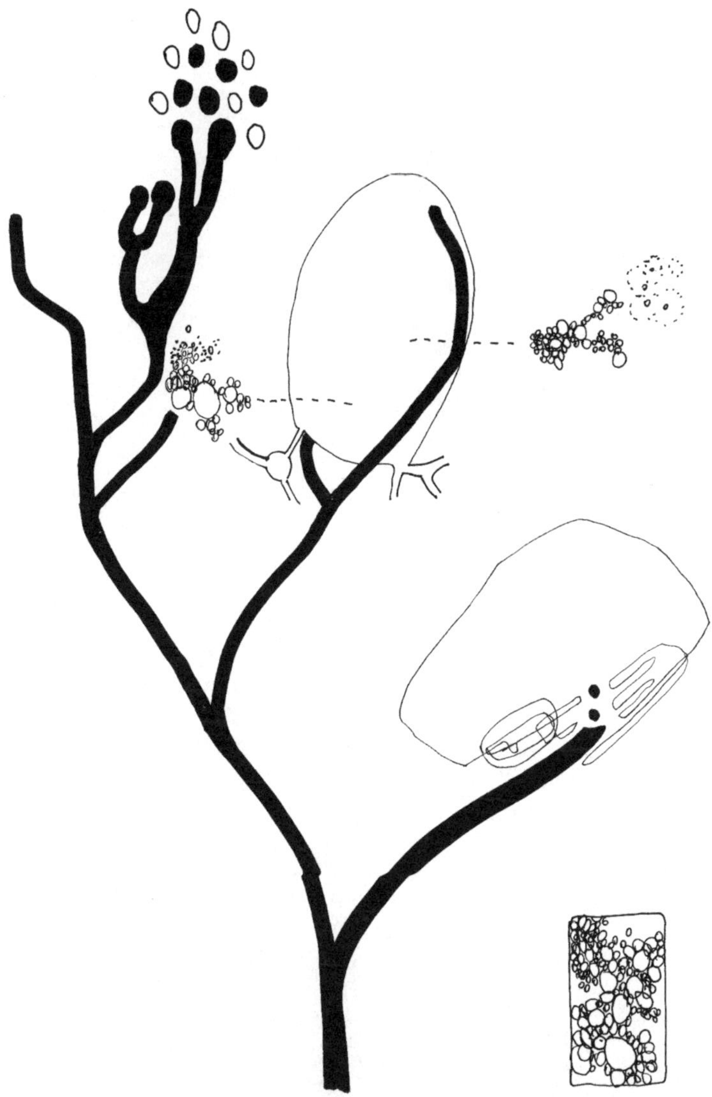

Fig. 02-21

The main programme calls up several routines one after the other, which in turn execute subroutines. Each routine produces one or more results that are combined with the results of other routines. This union forms the end result. (→PIII/05)

When I went past the state opera house at half past ten, the people were streaming out of the building. Some got into little buses, others walked in pairs beneath umbrellas towards the city centre or to the tram stop. Several hailed taxis driving by. I followed some down the escalator into the underground.

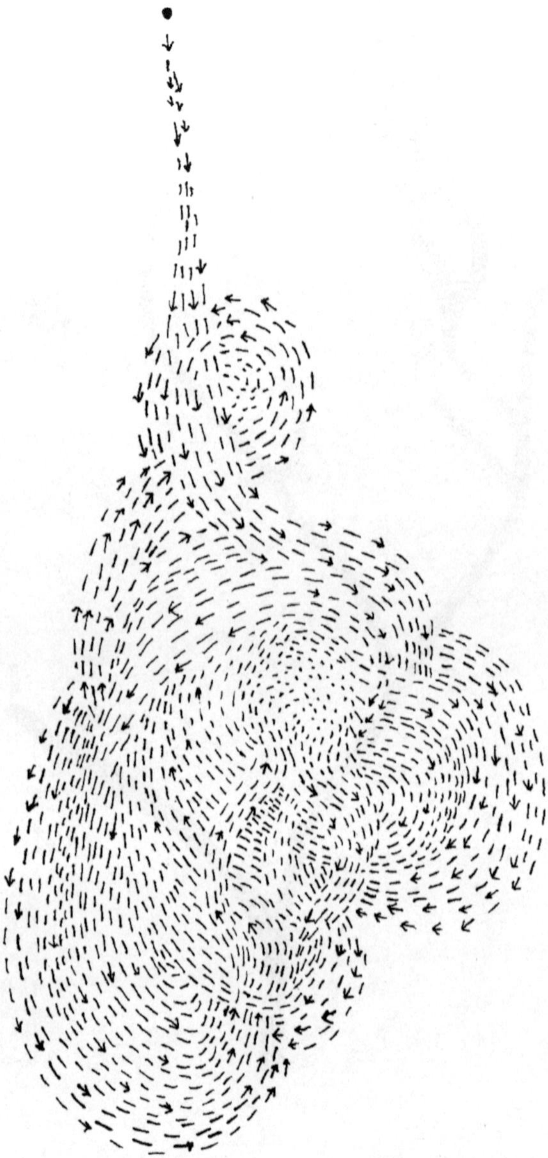

Fig. 02-46

In the dense crowd I take care not to be too hard pressed, I try as much as I can to keep my distance. There's nothing else I can do but go with the flow and I have to keep in step so I don't get pushed over or trip, which on the uneven ground requires some concentration.

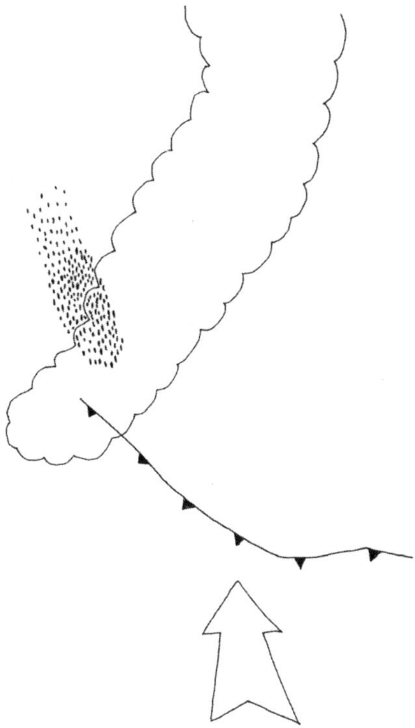

Fig. 03-24

An event can be depicted as dependent on previous events. If a sufficient number of events with their known precedents is registered in time, future events can be predicted.
Yesterday the sun shone at 31 degrees celsius, while the day before yesterday it was 7 degrees and raining. If it snows today at a temperature of -2 degrees, will it thaw tomorrow?

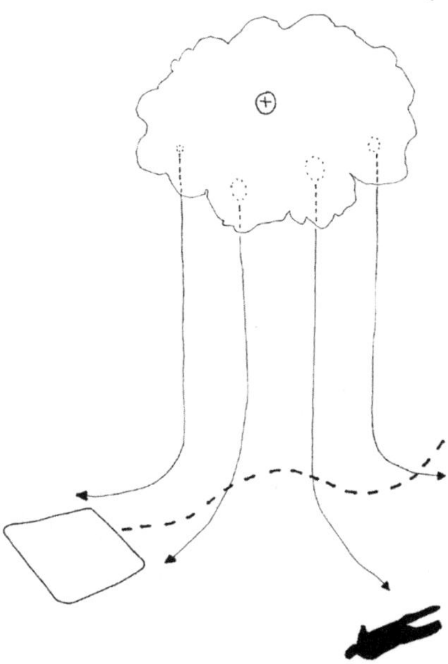

Fig. 03-25

The paving stones in the park are arranged like a chess board. The world looks like a machine.
Passersby move uniformly through the shopping street. The traffic light changes from green to red. At the district office I take a number out of the machine. In the waiting-room it is quiet. Only the steady peeping of a delivery van reversing can be heard from the street. The state is one big company.
I think about last night. Recall an email address I didn't want to forget. A good formulation occurs to me again. The brain is like an organic computer.

HYPOTHESIS #4

Grapheus Was Here

Anthony Auerbach

(→ PIII/02a-f)

Untangling drawing and theory reveals a knot which cannot be undone historically. While cutting it is considered the sign of progress in mathematics, the knot doesn't relinquish its primordial status all that easily. Euclid's first postulate, "To draw a straight line from any point to any point," is the graphic hypothesis on which is founded the notion that there are drawings which may be considered to all intents and purposes equivalent to abstract thought. By literally *drawing a hypothesis*, the postulate at once recruits drawing to the cause of deductive reasoning and furnishes *quod erat demonstrandum* with an image; it warrants a line to draw a conclusion (a theorem) and the *a priori* to compel reality as surely as a geometer constructs figures.

Drawing thus enacted the isomorphism of geometry and its image as a law of nature, and signed the expedients – that is to say, authorised the departures from the strict domain of mathematics – that we associate with the names, for instance, Alberti, Galileo, Newton.

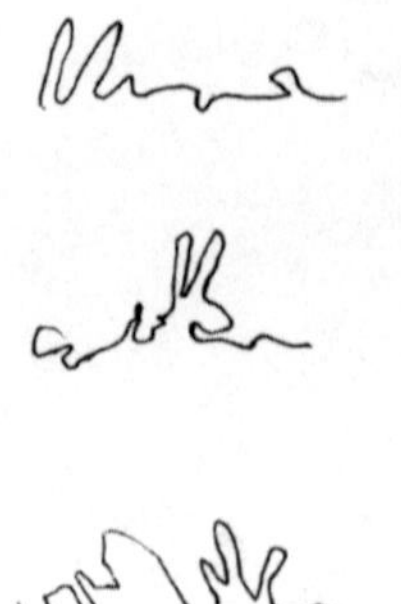

Fig. 15-03a

The point is not to insist on the purity of mathematics, which would be bound to anachronism: the truths which mathematics claims to be timeless remain so, but, whereas the antique fell short of its ideal only by modern standards, the modern refuses to realise antique expectations. Better to note that while mathematics admits no contradiction, in history, contradictions abound. The period when pure mathematics came to be defined by the elaboration of arbitrary hypotheses, free from intuitive and realistic content or meaning, was also the period of the accelerating expansion of the domain of applied mathematics. The types of mathematics that were applied and the fields of knowledge to which they were applied multiplied, along with the number and variety of drawings imagined as embodying *demonstration* on the Euclidean model (*construction* in the Kantian version). Let us call such drawings diagrams. The burgeoning of the scope of mathematics along with its graphic counterparts may also have prompted the revival of interest in philosophising *ad more geometrico*, albeit not according to the old method.

My approach may be called pragmatic because it is concerned with the meaning produced, transferred and transmitted by the *use* of diagrams: content not reducible to the abstractions in which diagrams purport to deal, nor necessarily derivable from the hypotheses on which diagrams rest, more or less

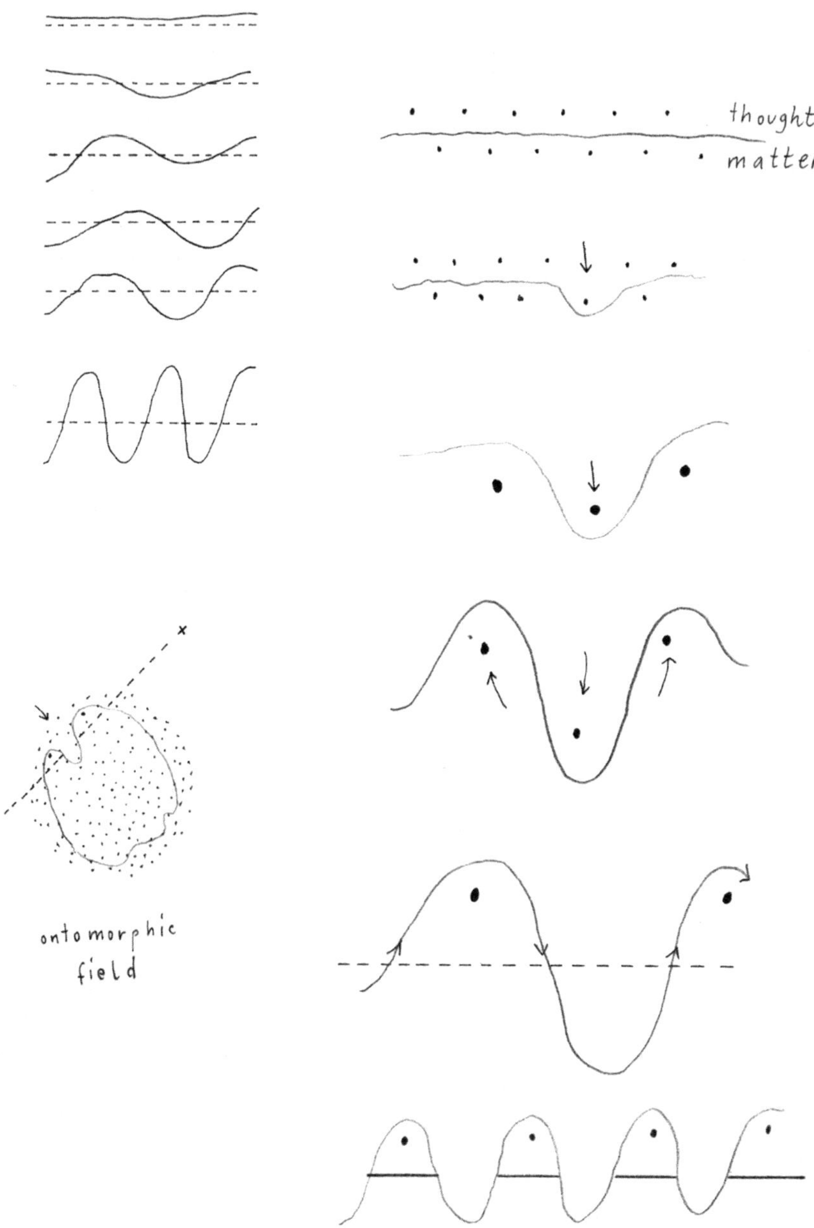

Fig. 15-09

explicitly, more or less consistently. The metaphorical economy of diagrams is a web of exchange in which drawings function not only as tokens but also as agents.

Highlighting some transactions in that network – drawing attention to some of its threads and crossings – is probably as much as can be expected from a short text such as this. While the approach does not promise a fundamental theory of diagrams, nor the format a comprehensive survey, I at least examine the tangle intact.

GASPARD MONGE: GÉOMÉTRIE DESCRIPTIVE

Monge's method wasn't published under the *ancien régime* because it was a military secret. It emerged first in the *Séances* of the shambolic and short-lived École normale de l'an III, the institution hastily contrived for the development of a revolutionary curriculum and the formation of a corps of teachers. Monge's lectures were collected in book form four years later in 1799, and became a cornerstone of the polytechnic tradition that Monge himself helped establish.[1]

Descriptive geometry proposes a universal method of engineering drawing with a double aim: to represent exactly any three-dimensional object – provided it is 'susceptible to rigorous definition' – by means of drawings, and furthermore to derive, from an exact description of any object, everything that follows necessarily from its form. In that sense, Monge adds, it is 'a means of searching out the truth'. It would therefore be 'necessary,' he concludes, for descriptive geometry to be part of a national plan of education, not just for the intellectual benefit of a great people and thereby of mankind, but for the practical benefit of French industry and, by implication, the military capability of the Republic. Monge envisages, on the one hand, the power of nature harnessed by machines determined graphically part by part, and on the other hand, the knowledge of nature, described by geometry, turned to the profit of the arts.

(→ PIII/01) When Monge mentions the construction of perspectives and of shadows as notable applications of the method, it is as if he

1) Gaspard Monge, *Géométrie descriptive*, Paris, Baudouin, 1799.

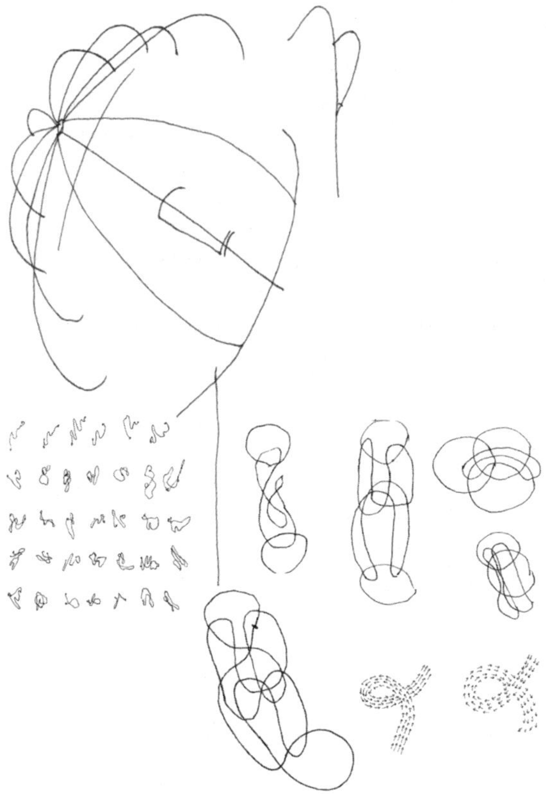

Fig. 09-05b

is simultaneously aligning descriptive geometry with the Vitruvian canon while differentiating them. And indeed, he assert the priority of descriptive geometry – both logically and pedagogically – over the methods taught in the academies; which is to say, Renaissance methods that had been invented in honour of the antique.

Descriptive geometry distinguishes itself from the perspective inherited from Alberti in several important ways. Above all, descriptive geometry is not optical: its notional rays do not converge in an eye. Instead of a bundle, descriptive geometry supposes parallel projectors – like the sun's rays that project shadows, although Monge himself avoids such metaphors. Descriptive geometry does not produce a picture: not one, because more than one drawing is required to describe an object, and no picture, as long as Alberti's intersection of the visual pyramid defines the very idea of a picture. Whereas perspective rests on the theory of proportion (expressed geometrically by the similar triangles that encompass base and intersection) and pays homage to Euclid, descriptive geometry is conceptualised in terms of three-dimensional Cartesian analytic geometry, with which, Monge says, it has 'the most intimate relations'.

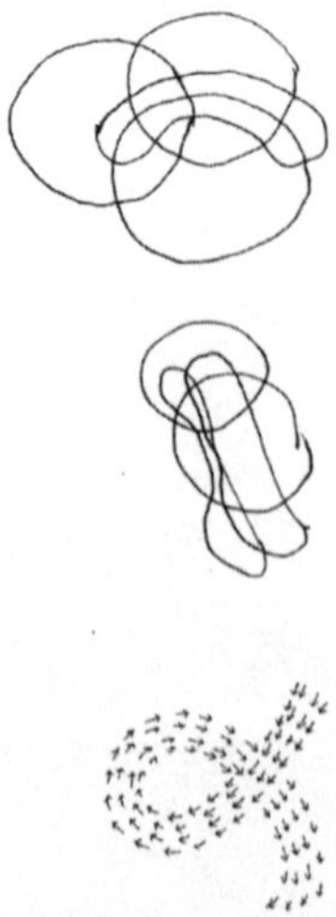

Fig. 09-05c

The *correspondance* between geometry and algebra (which Monge inherits from Descartes) means that "every analytical operation can be regarded as the script for a play (*l'écriture d'un spectacle*) in geometry," and reciprocally, there is "no construction in descriptive geometry which cannot be translated into analytic form," the *évidence* of drawing complementing the *généralité* of algebraic expression.

Monge conceived of drawing as a rational machine, responding efficiently to the tasks appointed by mathematics as well as to practical engineering problems. Although descriptive geometry's mathematical credentials lent it prestige and supported institutional hierarchies of knowledge, the method was mainly transmitted as technical drawing: as a repertoire of graphic gestures taught and learned mechanically, producing signs standing not only for their intended objects but for rational form as such – just as perspective constructions had earlier come to signify the authentic trace of appearance, and schoolbook geometry stood for reason itself.

C. S. PEIRCE: EXISTENTIAL GRAPHS

> "Come on, my Reader, and let us construct a diagram to illustrate the general course of thought."

This opening sentence of the *Prolegomena to an Apology for Pragmaticism*[2] is the gambit Peirce offered at the outset of the philosophy he distinguished for himself. Peirce's enthusiasm for diagrams goes, on the one hand, with his insistence on the purity of mathematics, and on the other hand, with his receptivity to metaphor, but it has still one more preliminary: a *semeiotic* adequate to diagrams, which will state clearly Peirce's

2) Charles S. Peirce, *Collected papers of Charles Sanders Peirce*, Harvard University Press, Cambridge, 1931, 4.530. Additional references from this and other published and unpublished papers are given by volume and paragraph numbers in the text.

hypothesis. "Not that the particular signs employed *are* themselves the thought! Oh no; no whit more than the skins of an onion are the onion. (About as much so, however.)" (4.6).

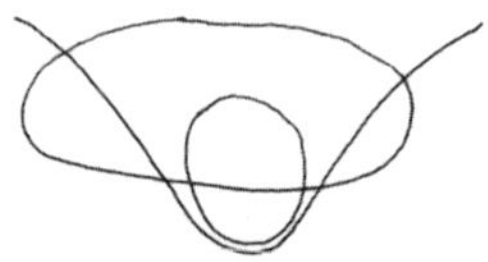

Fig. 15-03b

While Peirce's semiotics is widely accepted (like Monge's geometry, usually in simplistic form), his system of diagrammatic logic, the Existential Graphs, as he called them, are regarded as something of an eccentric curiosity. For Peirce, the effort he devoted to elaborating the system promised "moving pictures of thought" (4.8), "rendering literally visible before one's very eyes the operation of thinking *in actu*" (4.6). Peirce's imagination, however, wasn't quite the same as that of Kant, for whom necessary reasoning was performed by constructing geometric figures; nor quite like that of Monge, whose geometry traced the *spectacle mouvant* predicted by analysis. Existential Graphs were to be understood, under the strictest regime of abstraction, as expressions concerning a hypothetical universe, "perfectly definite and entirely determinate, but the arbitrary creation of an imaginary mind" (4.432).

Peirce's notion of Existential Graphs suggests both a meta-logic and a meta-image, since he already regarded deduction, exemplified by mathematical reasoning – which set the standard for exact logic – as none other than "*diagrammatical*, or, *iconic*, thought" (3.429). Whereas Peirce often cites algebra as iconic thinking *par excellence* (3.364) – since algebraic formulae display relations and, further, open them to experiment and observation – he was convinced Existential Graphs would amount to a "far more powerful method of diagrammatisation"(3.418).

Wittgenstein's reflections on logic (Wittgenstein once imagined his own book "might well be equipped with diagrams"[3] – though it was not) could suggest why Peirce's diagrammatic system did not, after all, catch on. The problem with Existential Graphs is not that there are more efficient methods of notation. Peirce preferred a more complex (not to say unwieldy) style in so far as it disclosed the structure of thought in more detail. Still – despite Peirce's pains to generalise the relations between "the grapheus", out of whose imaginary mind a hypothetical universe is continuously developed, "the graphist", whose graphs, or rather, whose successive modifications of "the entire graph",

3) Ludwig Wittgenstein, *Notebooks 1914-16*, Basil Blackwell, Oxford, 1961.

assert something about that universe, and "the interpreter" who is to make sense of the graphs – despite all that, the system is probably too heavily burdened with (sometimes bizarre) metaphors (like the heraldic "tinctures" applied to the figures) for most logicians' taste, and remains much too abstract for most literary philosophers.

The problem is, Existential Graphs do not elucidate the question which mobilised Peirce's effort and which would justify it, namely, "how the diagram is to be connected with nature"(3.423): in short, the question of representation. Peirce does not need to be told that this is not a question for logic, but he insists that thought is not just a mental thing. That "there cannot be thought without Signs" (4.551) is not *more* evident from Existential Graphs than from any other notation. The boldest hypothesis of semeiotic, however, goes beyond what logic can demonstrate, for the means by which "Reality ... contrives to determine the Sign to its Representation" (4.536) is not the force of reason. In other words, if we agree with Peirce that *all* signs are ultimately Indices – as typified by physical traces, pointers and interpellations – then no line can be drawn between thought and matter.

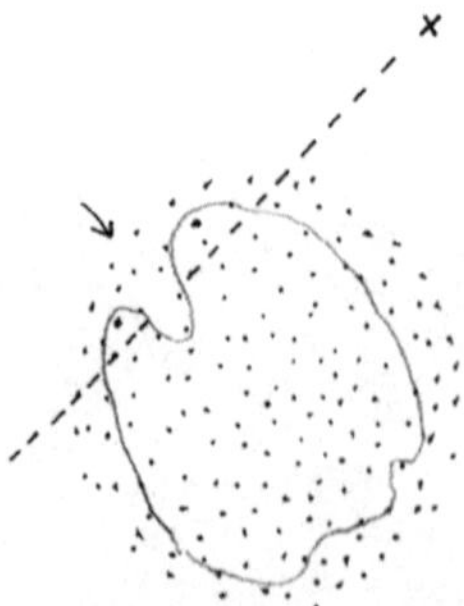

Fig. 15-09a

FRANCIS PICABIA: CE QUI DÉFIGURE LA MESURE

Picabia's drawings would certainly qualify as diagrams on Peirce's criteria: as experimental devices for investigating and demonstrating the structure of reason. The title imprinted on the first drawing in *Poèmes et dessins de la fille née sans mère*[4] reads "VIS-À-VIS": an icon of relations, as Peirce would say. The combination of more or less abstract graphic gestures with more or less abstract verbal labels gives Picabia's drawings all the appearance of diagrams familiar, or half-remembered, from a variety of didactic contexts: perhaps mechanics, biology, geography, philosophy. Yet they have no such context to lend continuity to what Peirce would call "the sheet of assertion", nor any hypothetical grid to map each gesture – each discrete sign – to a field of knowledge. These "Witticism Machines"

(→ PII/07a-c)

4) Francis Picabia, *Poèmes et dessins de la fille née sans mère*, Imprimeries Réunies, Lausanne, 1918.

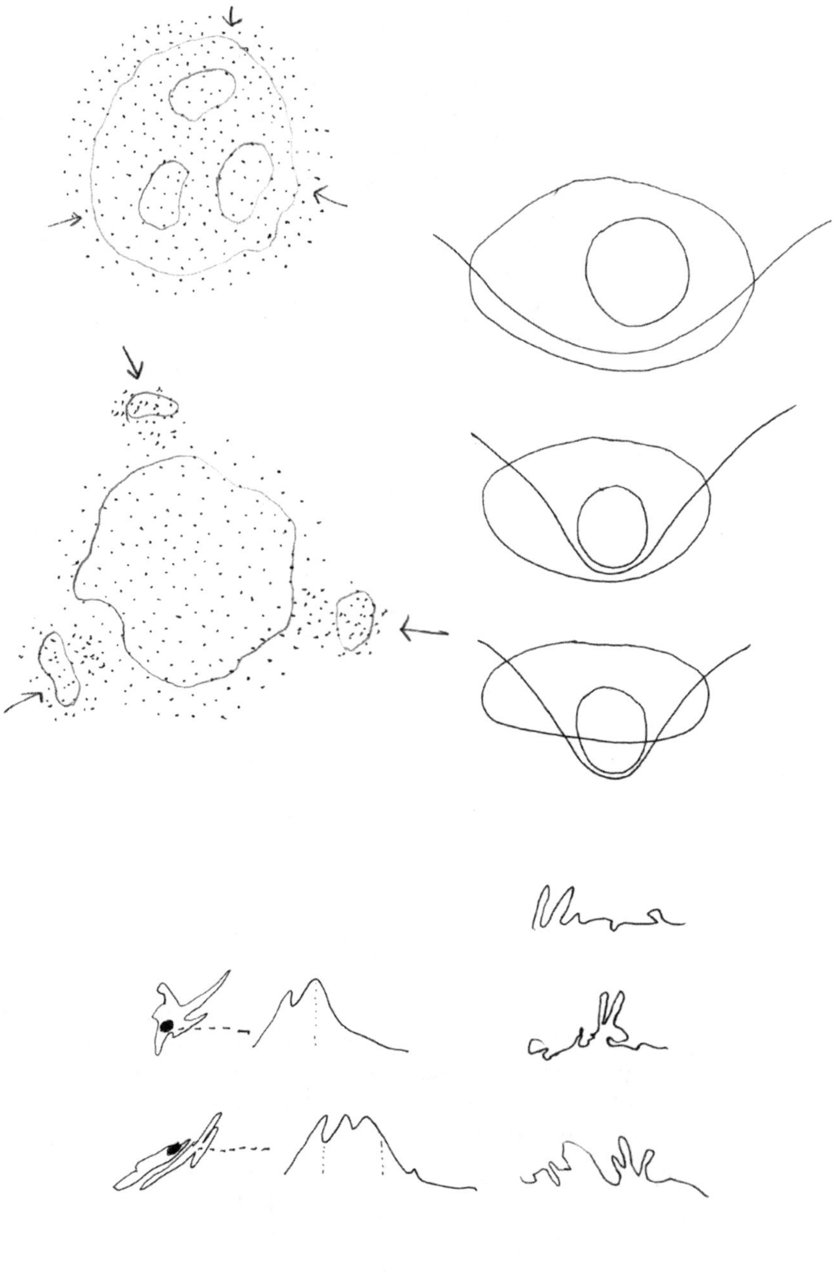

Fig. 15-03

feed on ardour, Madagascar, hermaphroditism, truth, error, madman's hands, limpidity, vernal vagina, to cite only a few of Picabia's indices. They are vivid in the context in which they appear: a book of dull poems exhibiting the Dada strategy in its pure form: sabotage meaning! (Not that Dada has no cargo of meaning, only that it is going to explode.) Half image, half sentence, the drawings by "the girl born without a mother" are no image and no sentence. The blanks which reason does not leap gape for association, the tentative and anxious web spun by the interpreter who exists to make sense of signs.

VIS-À-VIS is inscribed, "That which disfigures measurement". Even as it appears to discredit and deform reason, Picabia's drawing hints at a discipline. The line of reasoning which can be traced through projective geometry (the science of properties and relations preserved under projective deformations), and which finds its most general expression under the term *topology*, could be called geometry without measurement. Topology stands for thinking from which all constraints of measure and matter have been rigorously subtracted,

(→ PII/04a-d)

and hence preserves (in altered form) the promise of necessity that made Euclidean geometry so compelling. While Picabia's drawing, in a book dedicated to "tous les docteurs neurologues en général" and to his own psychotherapists in particular, is a comic play on the script of analysis (to distort Monge's terms a little), it is Lacan's affectation for diagrams which draws the consequences, in all seriousness, of Dada logic.

JACQUES LACAN: LA LOGIQUE DU FANTASME

(→ PIII/02k)

It is as if the headline "Dada signifies nothing", which interrupted Tristan Tzara's manifesto[5] with a typographic pointing finger, were condensed into twenty years of weekly seminars in front of the blackboard of the École normale. Lacan posits his geometric origin at a double crossing: a hybridisation and a crossed purpose. His zero-setting of subjectivity identifies a supposed Freudian subject with a subject he claims originates with Descartes. "What does that imply?" Lacan asks rhetorically,

5) Tristan Tzara, *Manifeste dada, Dada, 3*, 1918.

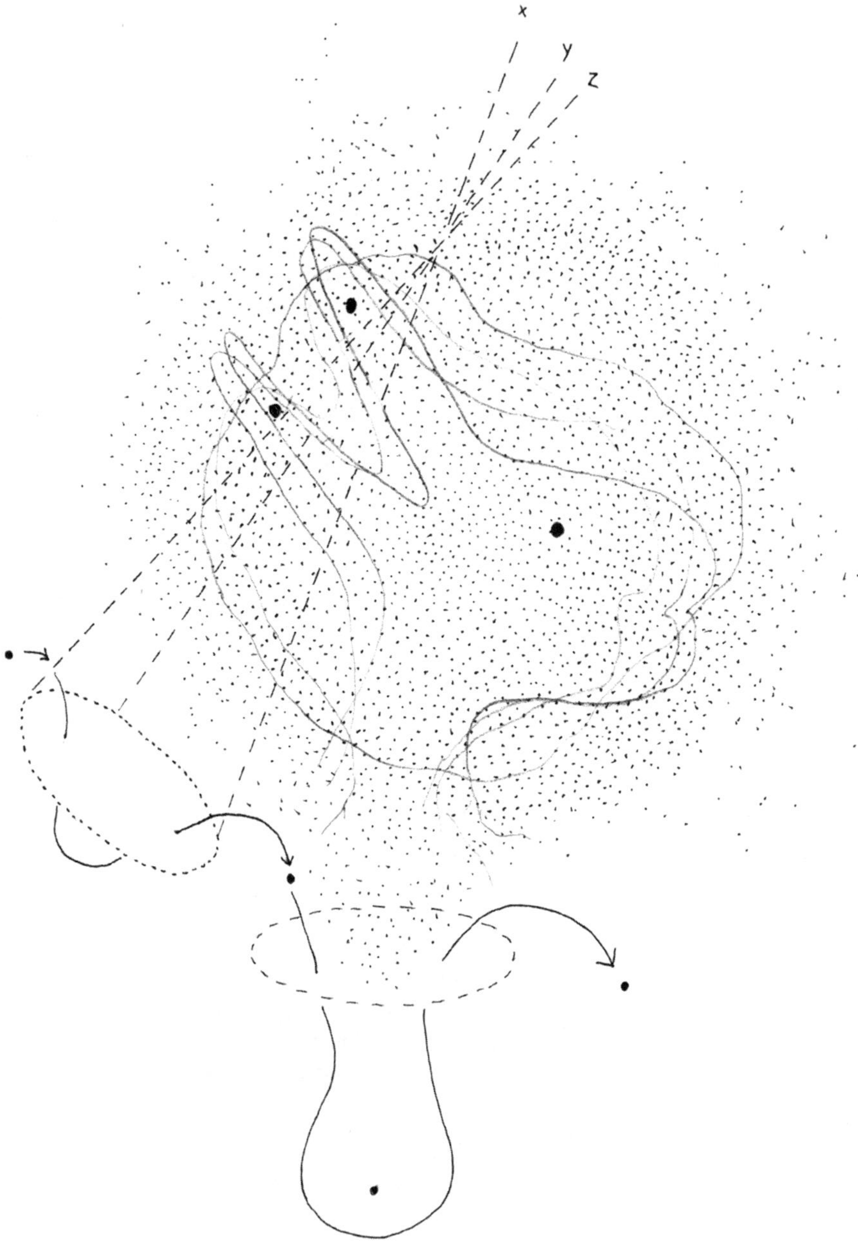

Fig. 15-04

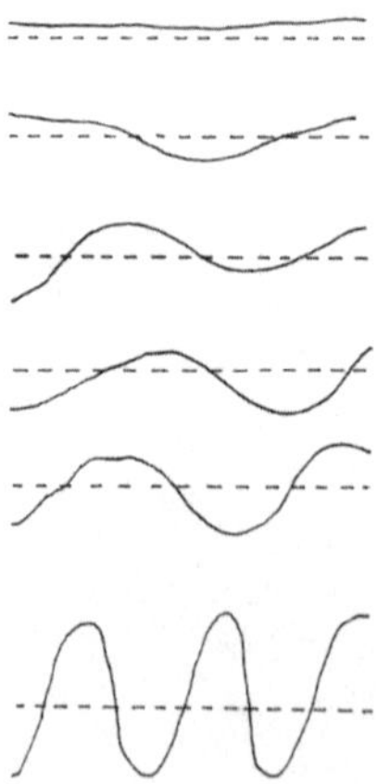

Fig. 15-09b

"if not that we are going to be able to start playing with the little letters of algebra, which transform geometry into analysis [...] – that we can allow ourselves everything as hypothesis of truth."[6] The geometrisation of psychoanalysis, Lacan believes, will secure its constitution as the "science of the unconscious". From a likeness to the structure of the unconscious, he professes to have "deduced a topology whose aim is to account for the constitution of the subject" (27 May 1964). A repertoire of quasi-algebraic formulae and quasi-geometric diagrams will therefore prove indispensable to a teaching in which such figures are assigned the duty of demonstration, despite being deprived of any consistent premise or rule of transformation that would allow anything to be deduced independently – any premise or rule, that is, other than that language-world, that law of semeiosis, in which everything is permitted – Lacan's diagrams are no autonomous machines.

(→ PI/04e)

When there is no difference between metaphor and theory, apodeixis is reduced to a didactic gesture that would command reality like an abracadabra. The performer's flourish, not to say sleight of hand, masks a schoolmaster's charisma with ecclesiastical authority. Lacan did not fail to remark of one of his favourite *objets trouvés* – a drawing sometimes used to illustrate a kind of surface that crops up in topology and nick-named "the mitre" or cross-cap (though topologically speaking, the figure has no particular form) – that it is worn by bishops.[7]

The ambition of constructing the science of the unconscious after Descartes (E. F. P., the school Lacan founded and dissolved, stood briefly for the French School of Psychoanalysis before it was altered to the Freudian School of Paris) stumbled on no obstacles among its empirical data (supposedly the practice of psychoanalysis) nor amid the abstractions it borrowed from philosophy and mathematics. It turned out, indeed, very like a language. The knots in which the project finally became embroiled were the result of tangling with drawing.[8]

6) Jacques Lacan, *Les quatre concepts fondamentaux de la psychanalyse*, Seuil, Paris, 1973), 29 January 1964. Further references to the seminars collected in this book are given by date.

7) Jacques Lacan, *L'étourdit*, *Scilicet*, 4, 1973.

8) "Bon c'est ennuyeux que je m'embrouille, mais je dois dire que je dois avouer que je m'embrouille. Bien. Ça sera assez pour aujourd'hui." ("It's annoying, but I'm confused. I have to say that I have to admit that I'm confused. Well, that will be enough for today.") Jacques Lacan, *La topologie et le temps*, 16 January 1979, unpublished transcript.

HYPOTHESIS #5

Asynchronous Connections

Kirsten Matheus

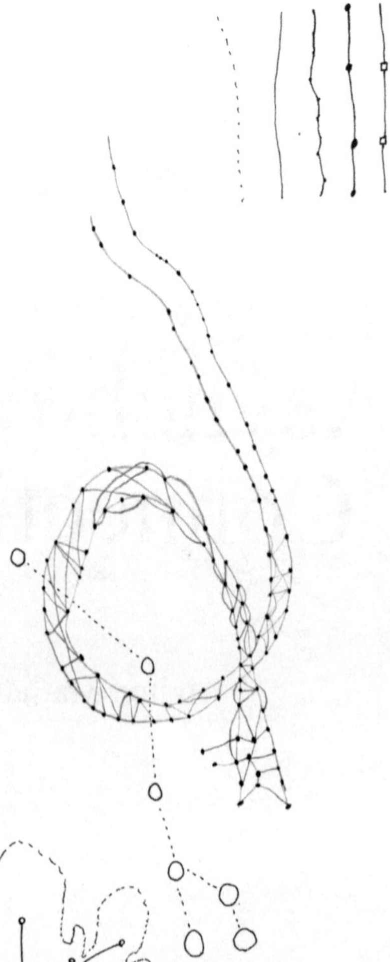

Fig. 10-06

Interrelations in a sensor cluster having just gauged an involuntary 360° turn. Standard relations (see dashed line). Variants of occurring output within (see other line forms).

Fig. 02-37

Real connectivity traces in an arbitrary possibility cloud. The symmetric appearance of the traces is caused by the seemingly symmetrical possibility cloud. The deviations from the exact symmetry are caused by asymmetrical effects of multipath propagation and Doppler effects.

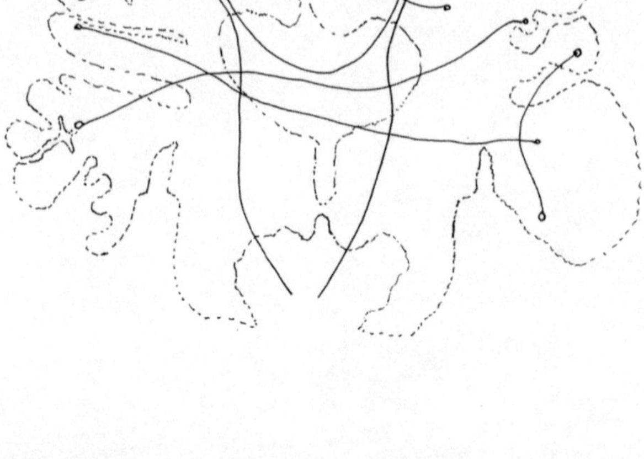

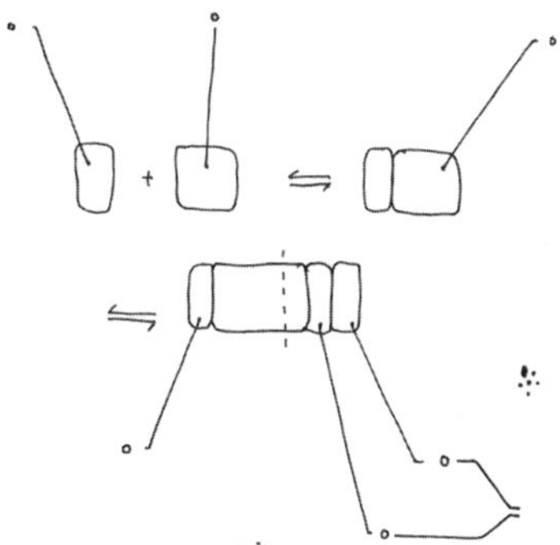

Fig. 03-05

Typical visualisation of the functioning of synergetic effects. Whereas in a normal additive operation (see top half of figure) the summing up of parts (see left side) simply results in the parts added up (see result on right side), the case of synergetic effects leads to supplementary parts (see lower half of figure). In this example, the synergetic surplus enlarged one of the original sum's parts and caused the addition of two new pieces of similar origin.

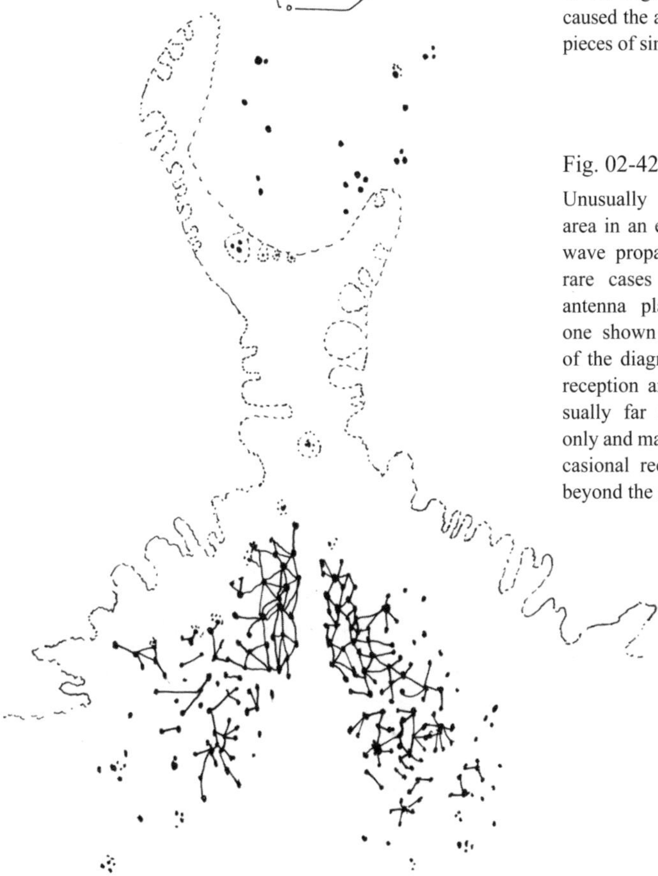

Fig. 02-42

Unusually shaped reception area in an extreme case of air wave propagation overlap. In rare cases an uncoordinated antenna placement (like the one shown in the lower half of the diagram) can cause the reception area to extend unusually far into one direction only and may even result in occasional reception islands far beyond the main area.

PLATES I

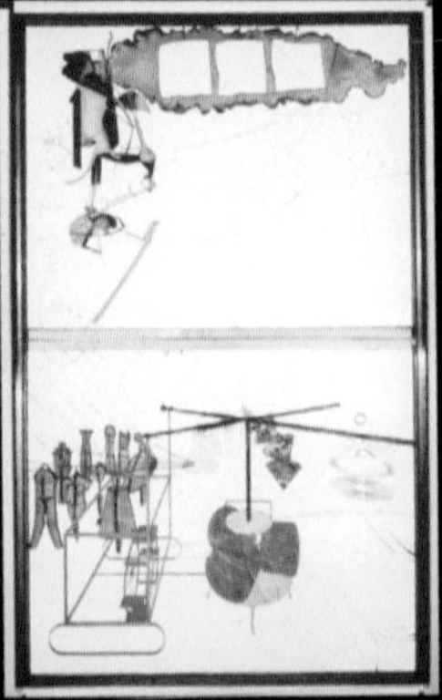

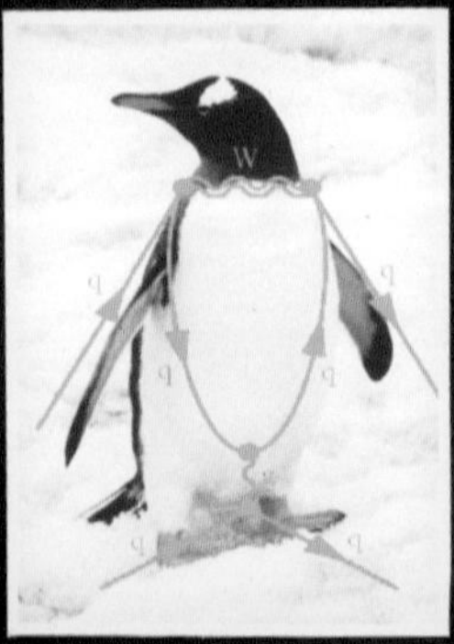

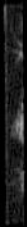

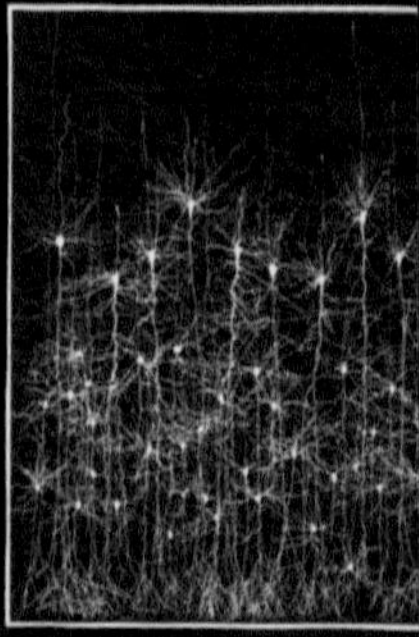

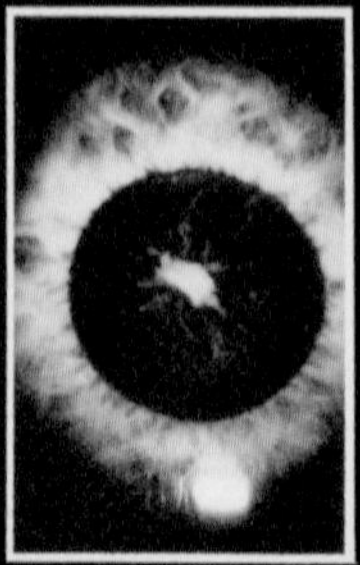

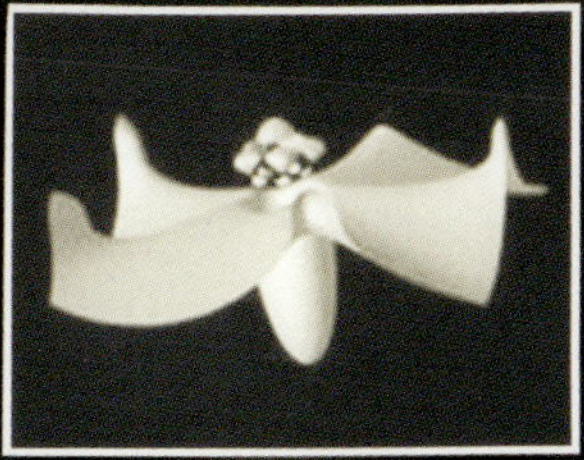
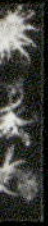
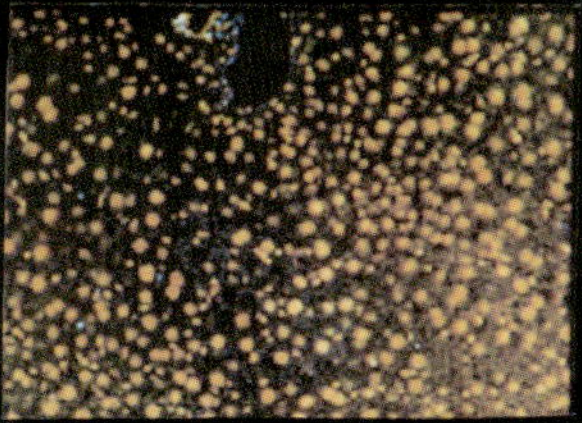
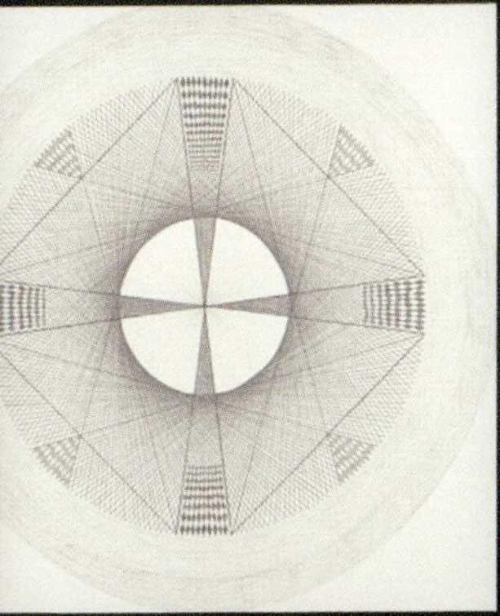
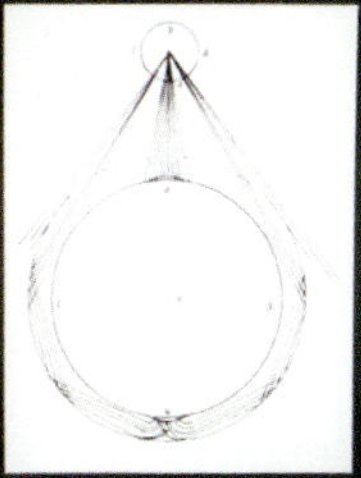
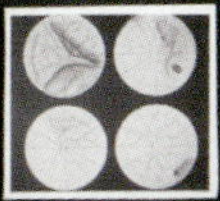

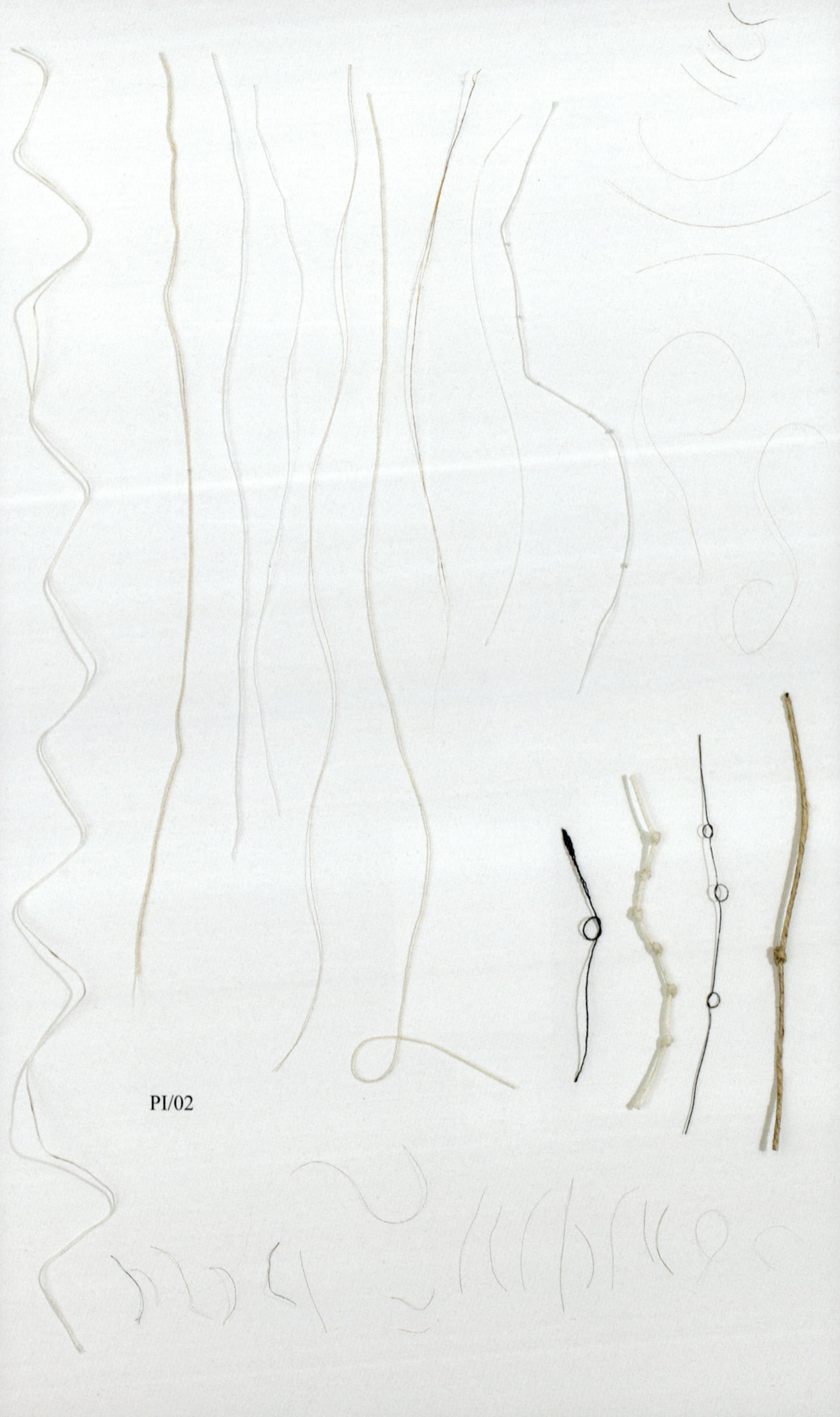

PI/02

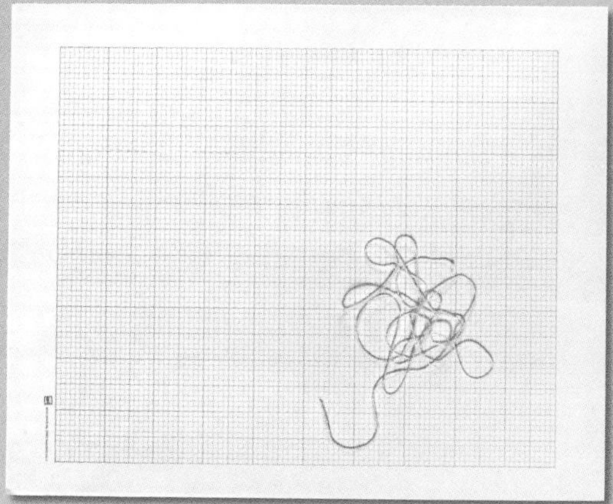

PI/03a

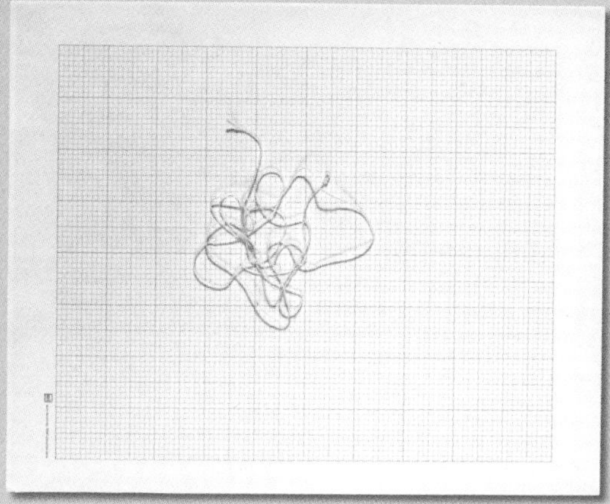

PI/03b

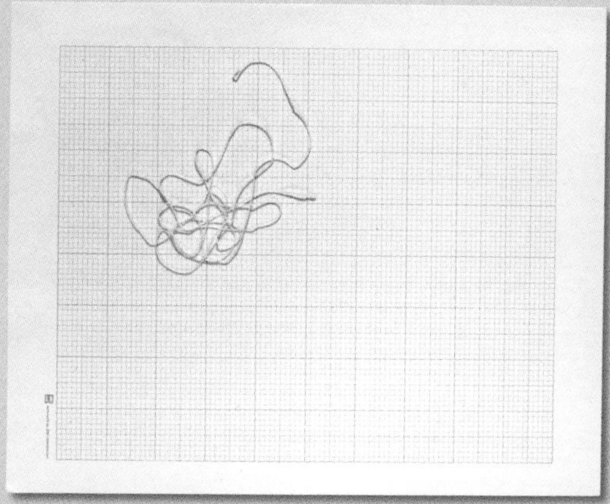

PI/03c

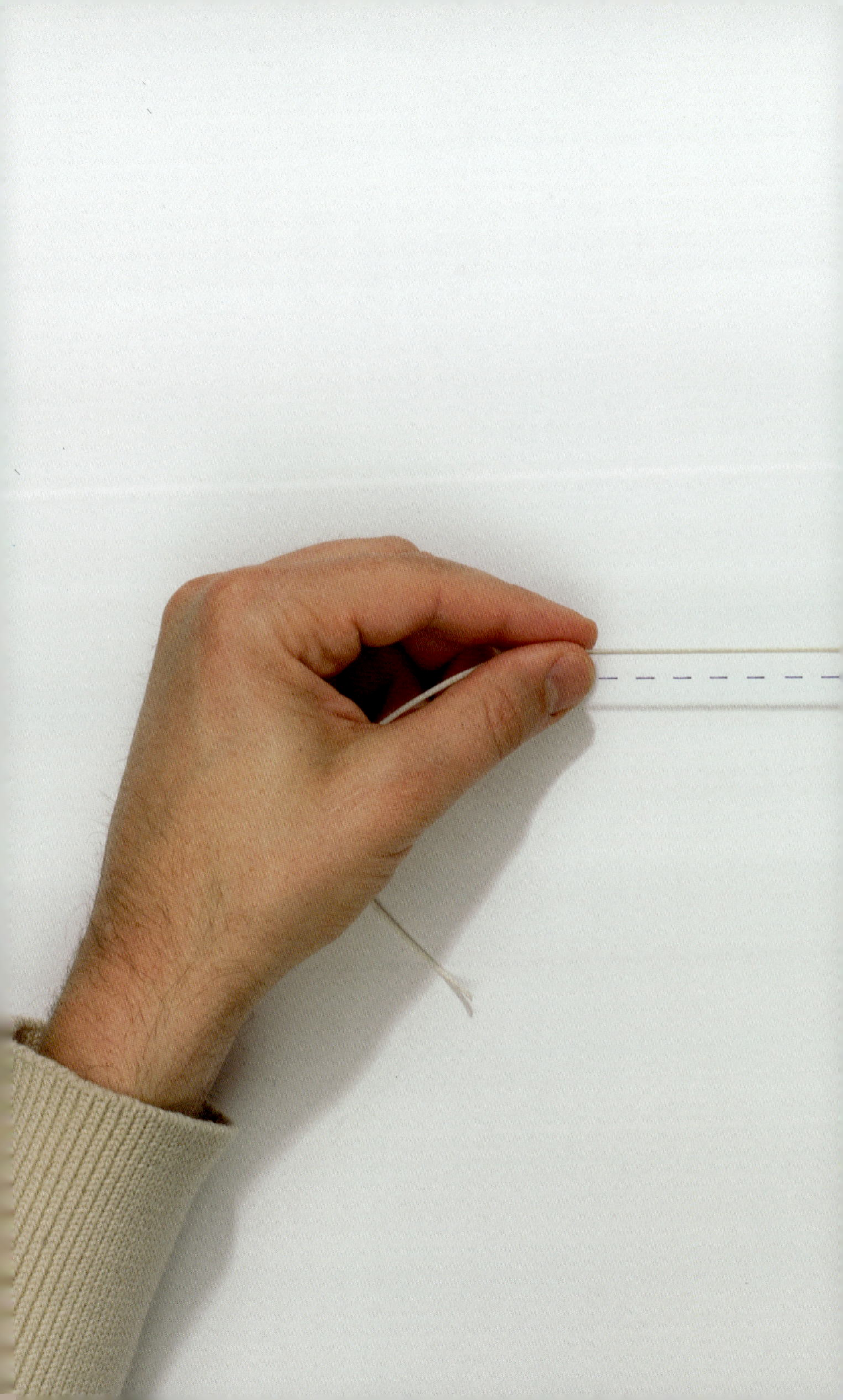

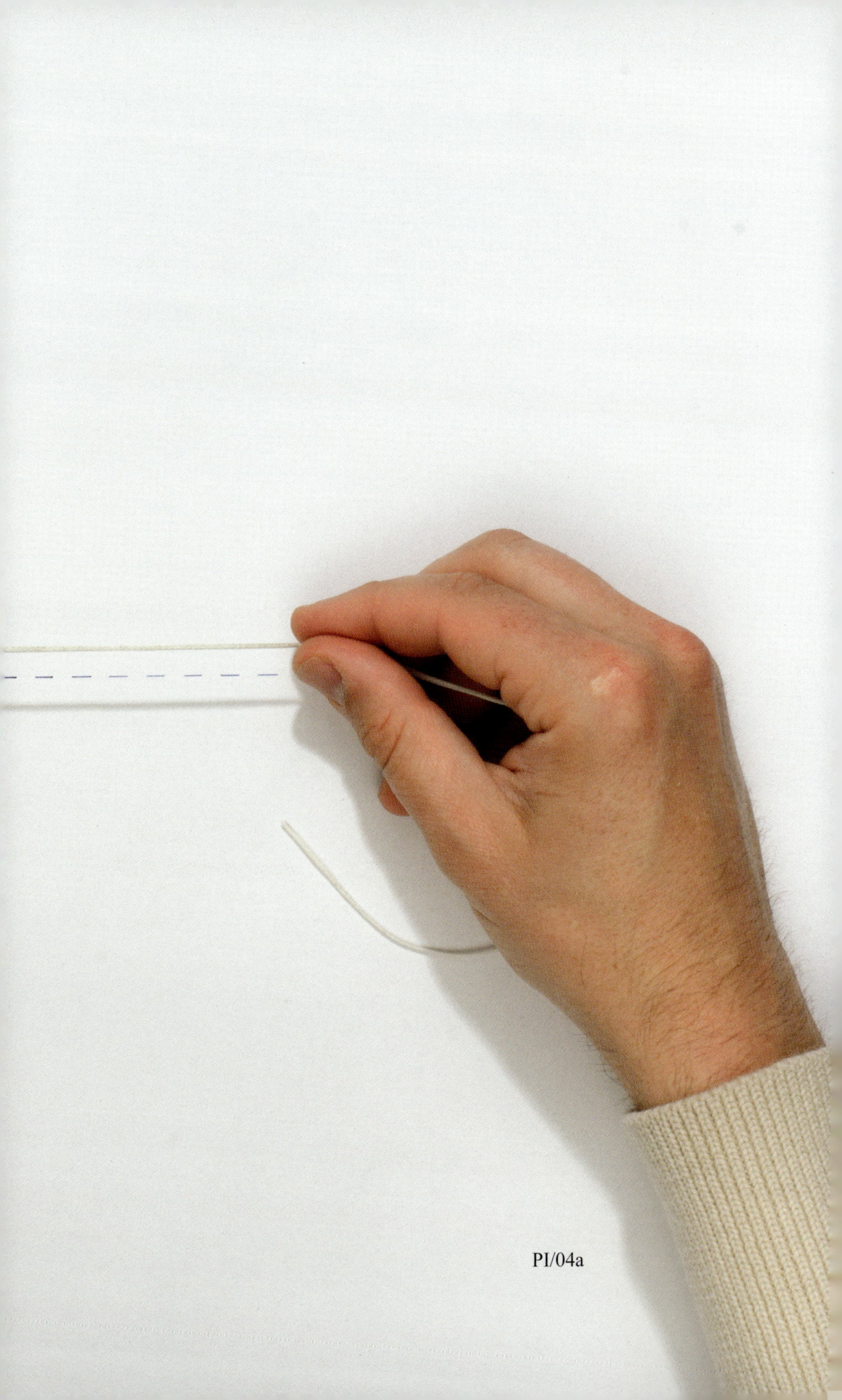

PI/04a

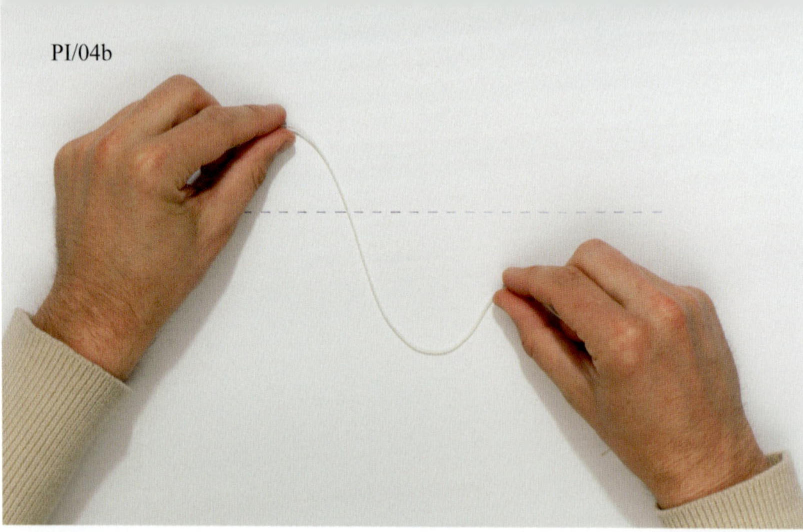
PI/04b

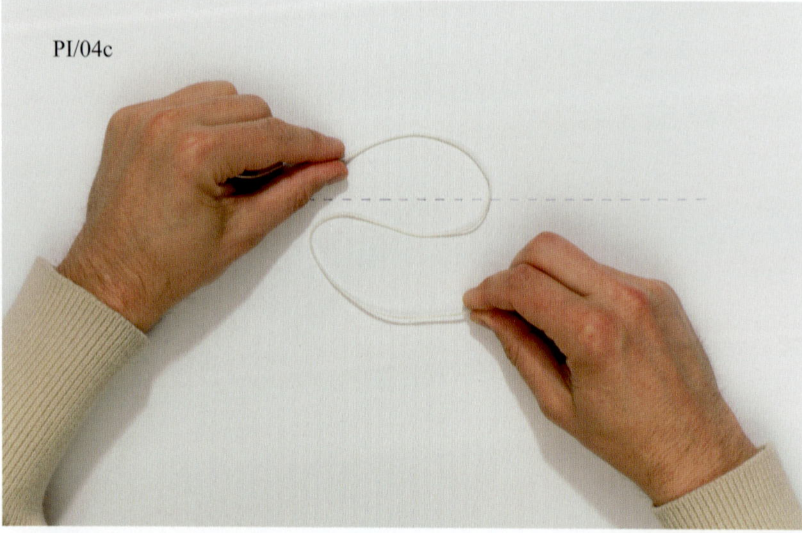
PI/04c

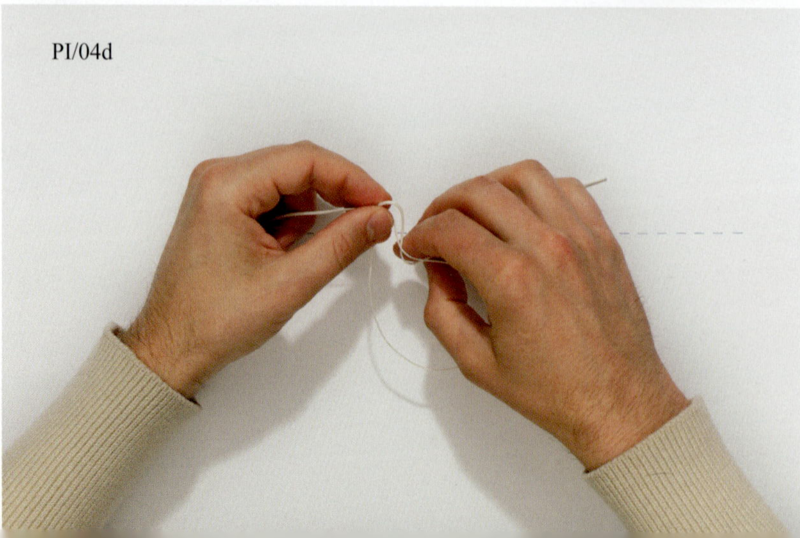
PI/04d

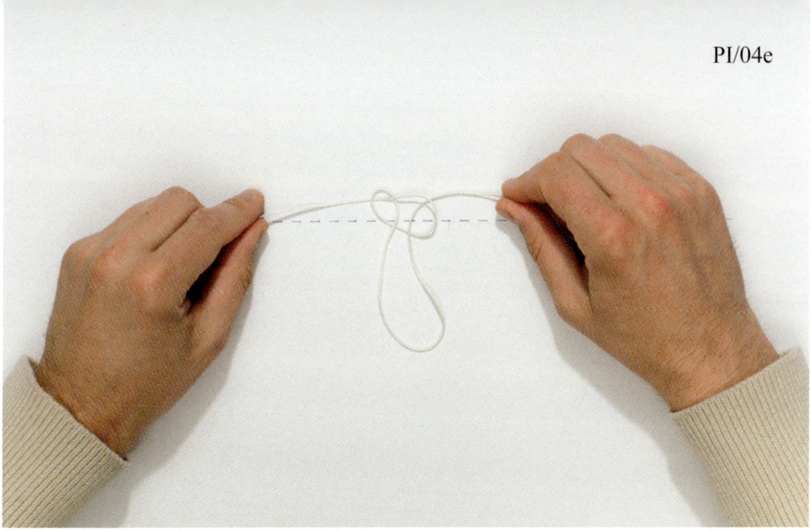
PI/04e

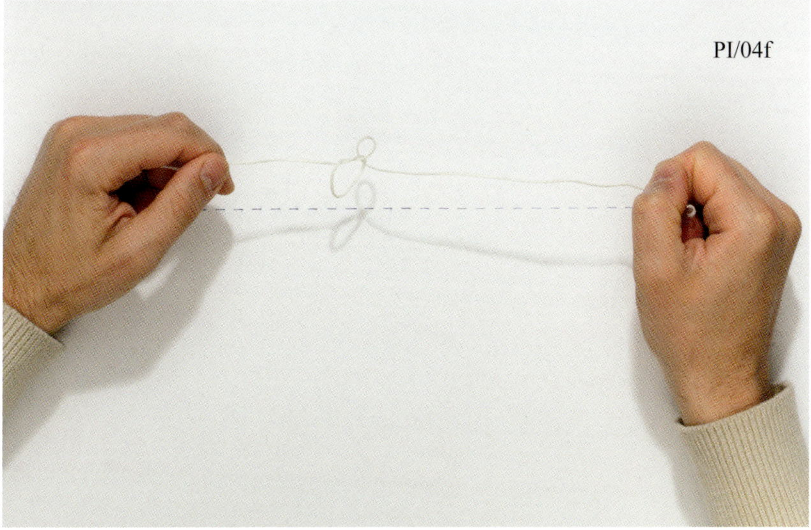
PI/04f

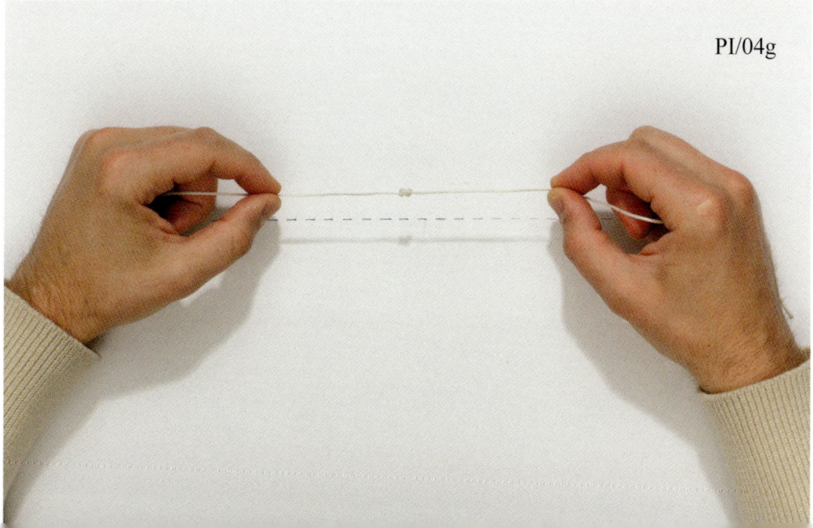
PI/04g

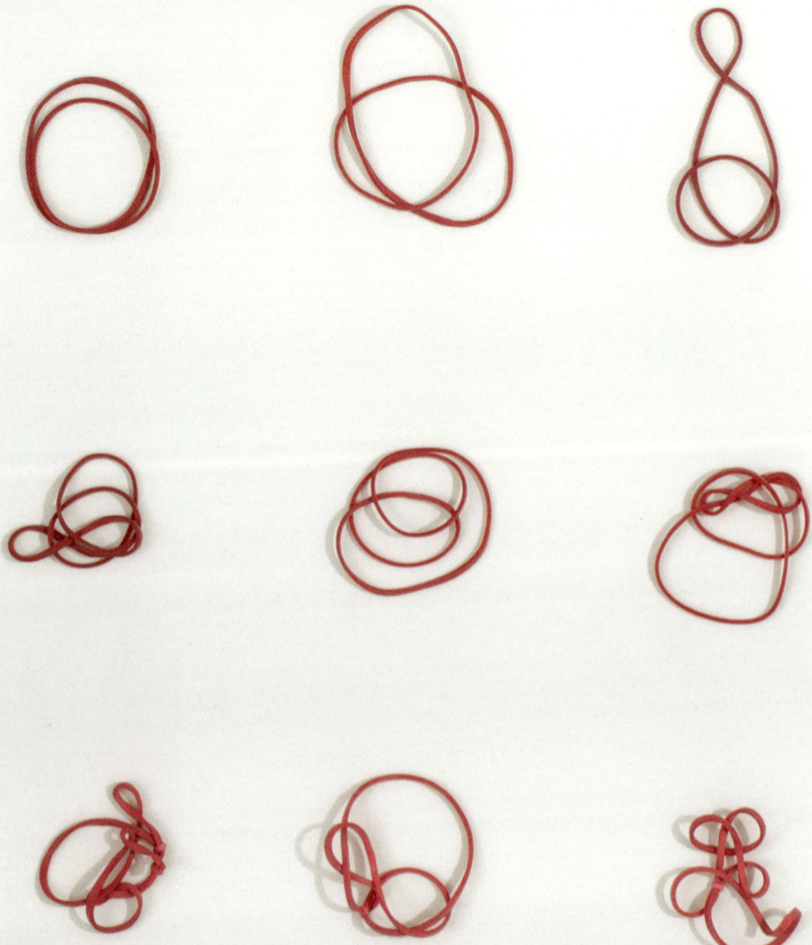

PI/05

PI/06a

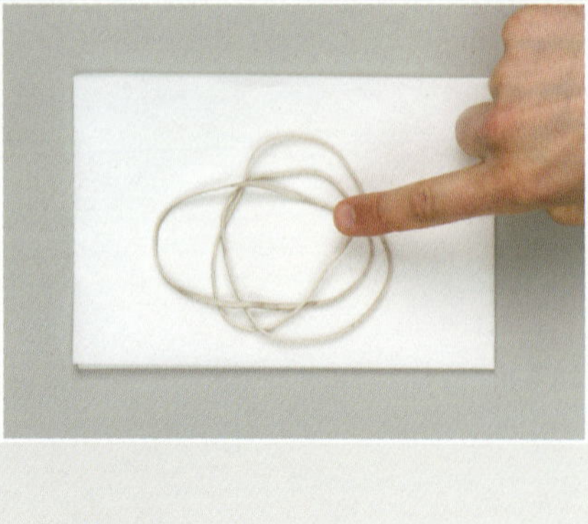

PI/06b

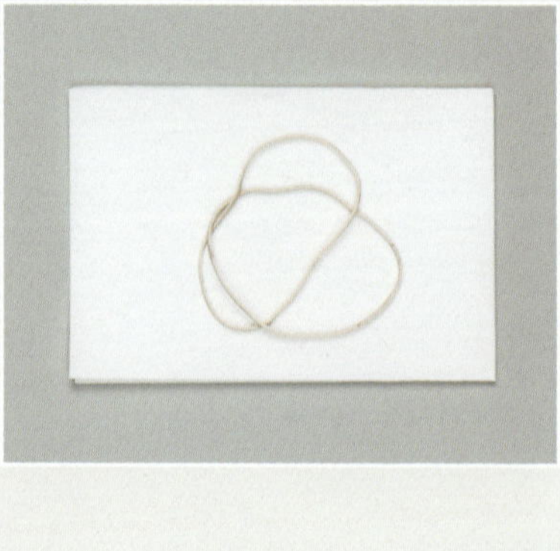

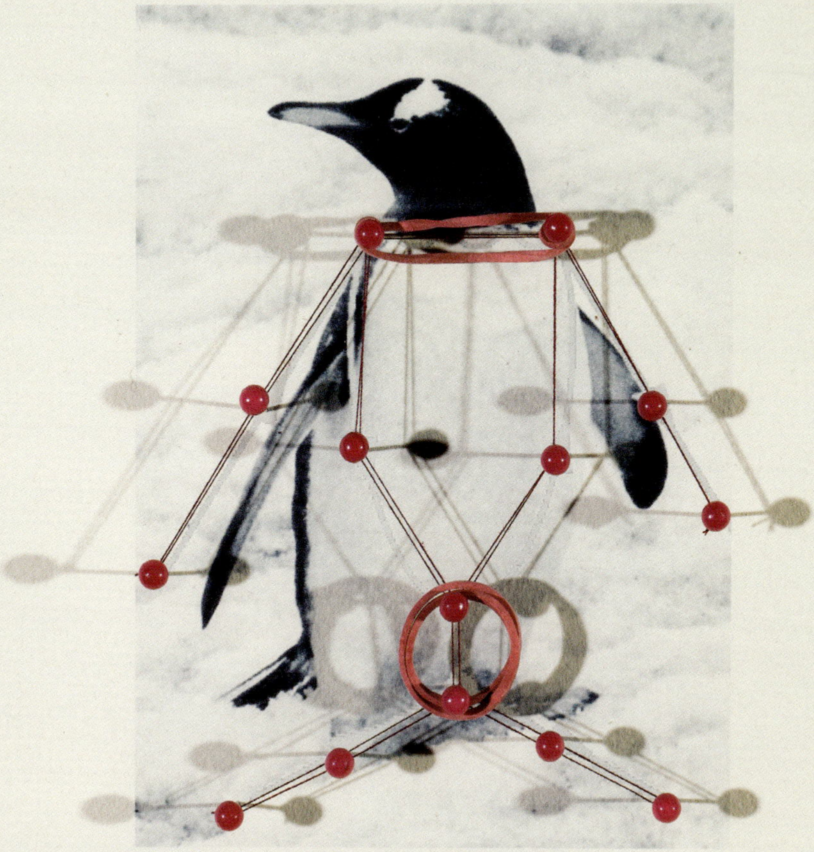

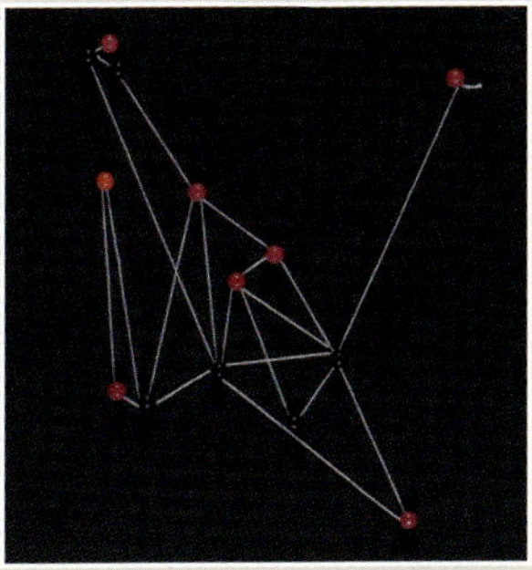

PI/07

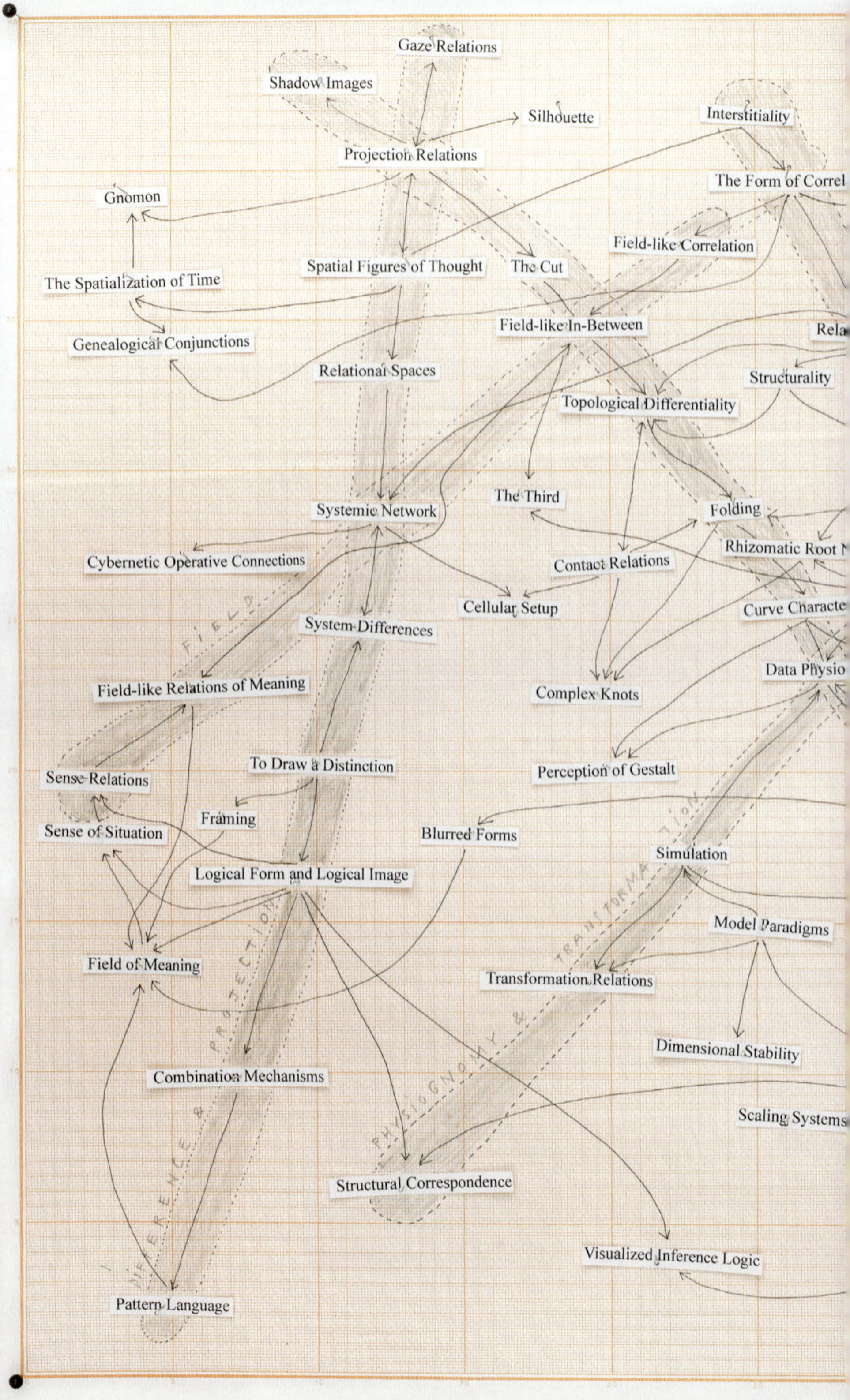

Gaze Relations
Shadow Images
Silhouette
Interstitiality
Projection Relations
The Form of Correl
Gnomon
Field-like Correlation
Spatial Figures of Thought
The Cut
The Spatialization of Time
Field-like In-Between
Genealogical Conjunctions
Relational Spaces
Structurality
Topological Differentiality
The Third
Systemic Network
Folding
Cybernetic Operative Connections
Contact Relations
Cellular Setup
Curve Characte
FIELD
System Differences
Data Physio
Field-like Relations of Meaning
Complex Knots
Sense Relations
To Draw a Distinction
Perception of Gestalt
Framing
Sense of Situation
Blurred Forms
Simulation
Logical Form and Logical Image
TRANSFORMATION
Model Paradigms
Field of Meaning
PROJECTION
Transformation Relations
Dimensional Stability
Combination Mechanisms
PHYSIOGNOMY &
Scaling Systems
DIFFERENCE &
Structural Correspondence
Visualized Inference Logic
Pattern Language

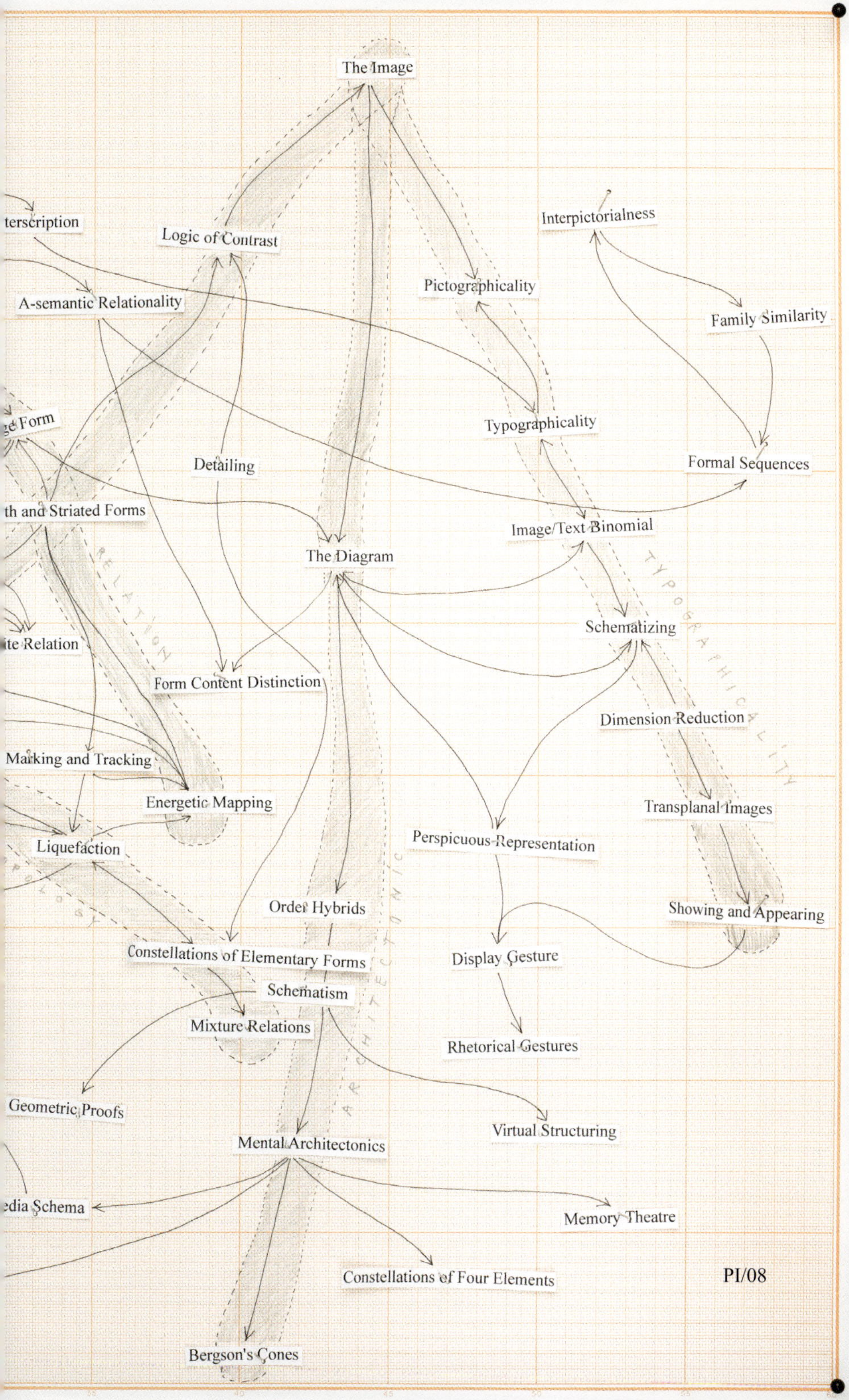

The Image
terscription
Logic of Contrast
Interpictorialness
A-semantic Relationality
Pictographicality
Family Similarity
ge Form
Typographicality
Detailing
Formal Sequences
th and Striated Forms
Image/Text Binomial
The Diagram
RELATION
TYPOGRAPHICALITY
Schematizing
ite Relation
Form Content Distinction
Dimension Reduction
Marking and Tracking
Energetic Mapping
Transplanal Images
Liquefaction
Perspicuous Representation
Order Hybrids
Showing and Appearing
ARCHITECTONIC
Constellations of Elementary Forms
Display Gesture
Schematism
Mixture Relations
Rhetorical Gestures
Geometric Proofs
Virtual Structuring
Mental Architectonics
edia Schema
Memory Theatre
Constellations of Four Elements
PI/08
Bergson's Cones

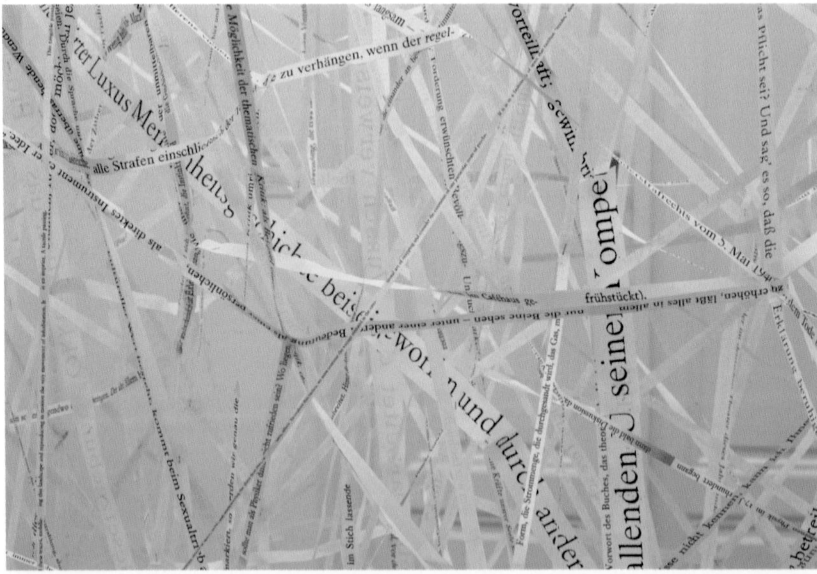
zu verhängen, wenn der regel-
alle Strafen einschli
Pflicht sei? Und sag' es so, daß die
frühstückt).

PI/09a

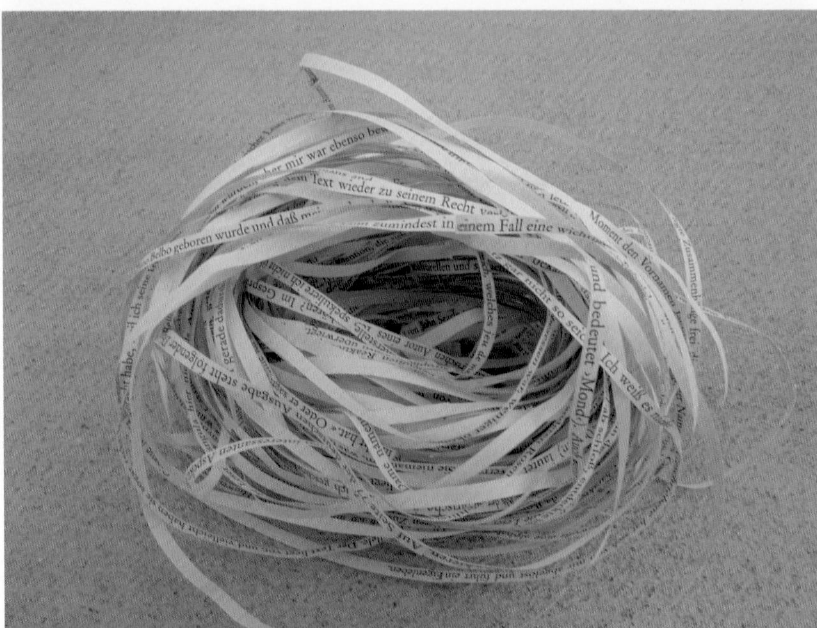
mir war ebenso be
Text wieder zu seinem Recht
geboren wurde und daß
zumindest in einem Fall eine
und bedeutet
Ich weiß es

PI/09b

SAMMLUNG VON DENKFIGUREN II

(Collection of Figures of Thought)

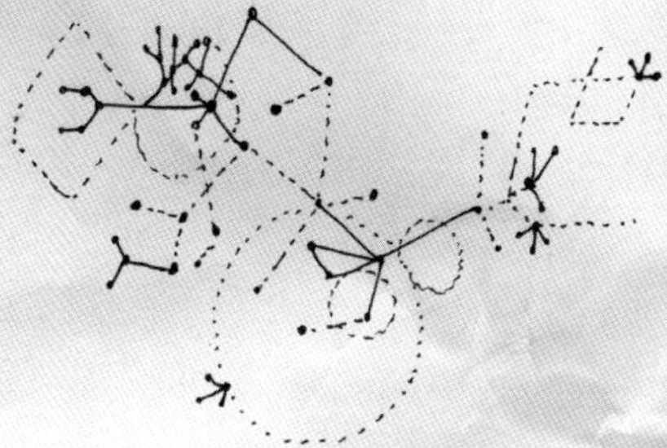

M-22-28-R5870

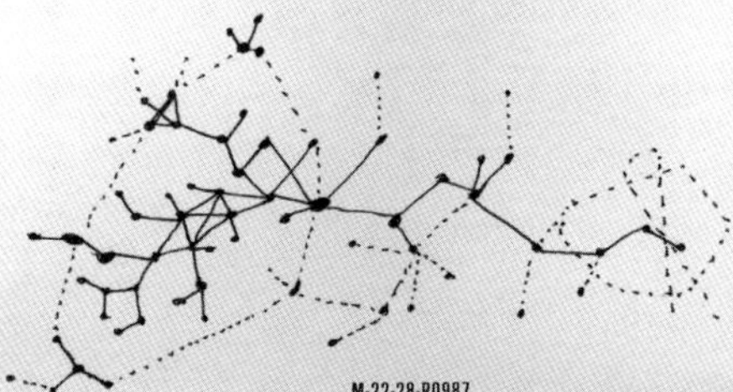

M-22-28-R0987

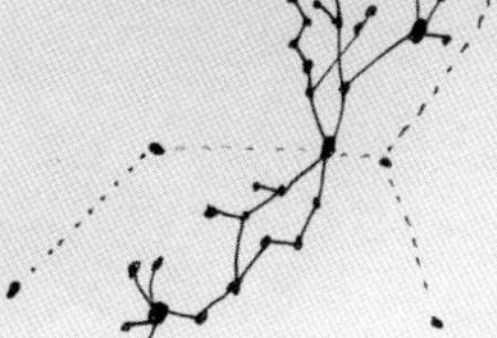

M-22-28-R2224

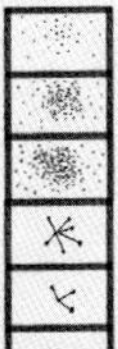

NOTES ON PLATES I

PI/01: Atlas of correlations – Plate I/similarity – difference study
(The broken multi/dimensional/eye/space/pinguine/memory/complex)

PI/02: Collection of Lines I-III (striated/curved/discreet)

PI/03: Fallen experiments study a-c

PI/04a: Phase I: A line is a line. High tension act.
PI/04b: Phase II: The wave/sign/particle question
PI/04c: Phase III: The reflexive curve position
PI/04d: Phase IV: The intersection tangent
PI/04e: Phase V: The grapheus knot (a)
PI/04f: Phase VI: The infinity loop hole
PI/04g: Phase VII: The nodal point record

PI/05: Collection of curved complexities

PI/06: Special vis-à-vis constellations (a, b)

PI/07: Diagram of probability study (animal discontinuity)

PI/08: Collection of figures of thought (wall chart I) after Gerhard Dirmoser

PI/09: Mnemocity: Figures of Thought (a+b)
Two states of intertextuality (installation view)

PI/10: Collection of Figures of Thought II
(Mnemoseum index card – www.memoseum.net)

HYPOTHESIS #6

Distancing the If and Then

Emma Cocker

The term hypothesis describes the gesture of supposition, the event of supposing. Taken as a suggestion, it is a proposal towards the possible but not yet known, towards that which is conceivable but still unverified. It is an act of thinking, believing or imagining something about the world in the absence of having the available evidence or facts to hand, a provisional statement served to the inquisitive as provocation for further exploration or investigation. A hypothesis is the leap of an idea performed by the curious when existing explanations no longer suffice. Like the pioneer who pushes at the edges of territorial frontiers, its statements skirt the boundary or limit of existing knowledge(s), the point at which a known reality slips towards the indeterminacy of unchartered waters. Akin to the returning traveller, the hypothesis offers a tentative account of those phenomena witnessed along the borderlands of the encyclopedia or map; its explanations remain as the line drawn in wet sand – indefinite, susceptible to change. In the realm of scientific method, the hypothesis would seem to be considered potentially suspect; it must be tested through experimentation, subjected to rigorous review. Here, perhaps, the hypothesis reveals the location of a troubling grey area – or *terrain vague* – disturbing the smooth landscape of what is already named and known. It is the site of some uncertain doubt. The hypothesis sets in motion a process of enquiry that hopes to clarify matters by settling things one way or the other. The unknown or unexplored situation that the hypothesis identifies as its subject is taken as an inhibitory rupture or break, which needs to be carefully filled or bridged by the production of new knowledge. It is an invitation towards decisive action, where frontiers are extended, gaps closed.

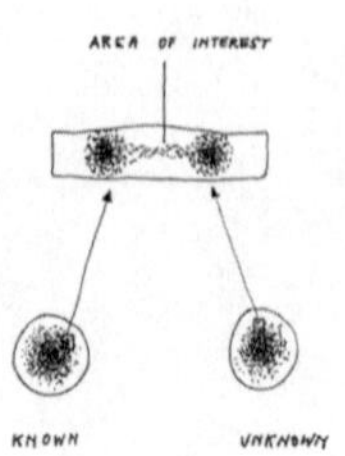

Fig. 01-01

The hypothesis is often considered as a preliminary or preparatory phase within a given enquiry; it creates the premise for something to follow, where it is perceived as being always antecedent to something else. However, the hypothesis may also be considered preliminal, since it marks the entrance of a threshold zone between the known and the unknown. The hypothesis signals a transitional state of being between, where things are neither yet proven nor disproved. It is a double-headed arrow. Like Janus, its glance is double-facing, for it always looks towards the conditions of the present-past for stimulus, whilst gesturing forwards to the future, to the (imagined) arrival of clearer understanding, towards the moment of realisation. For

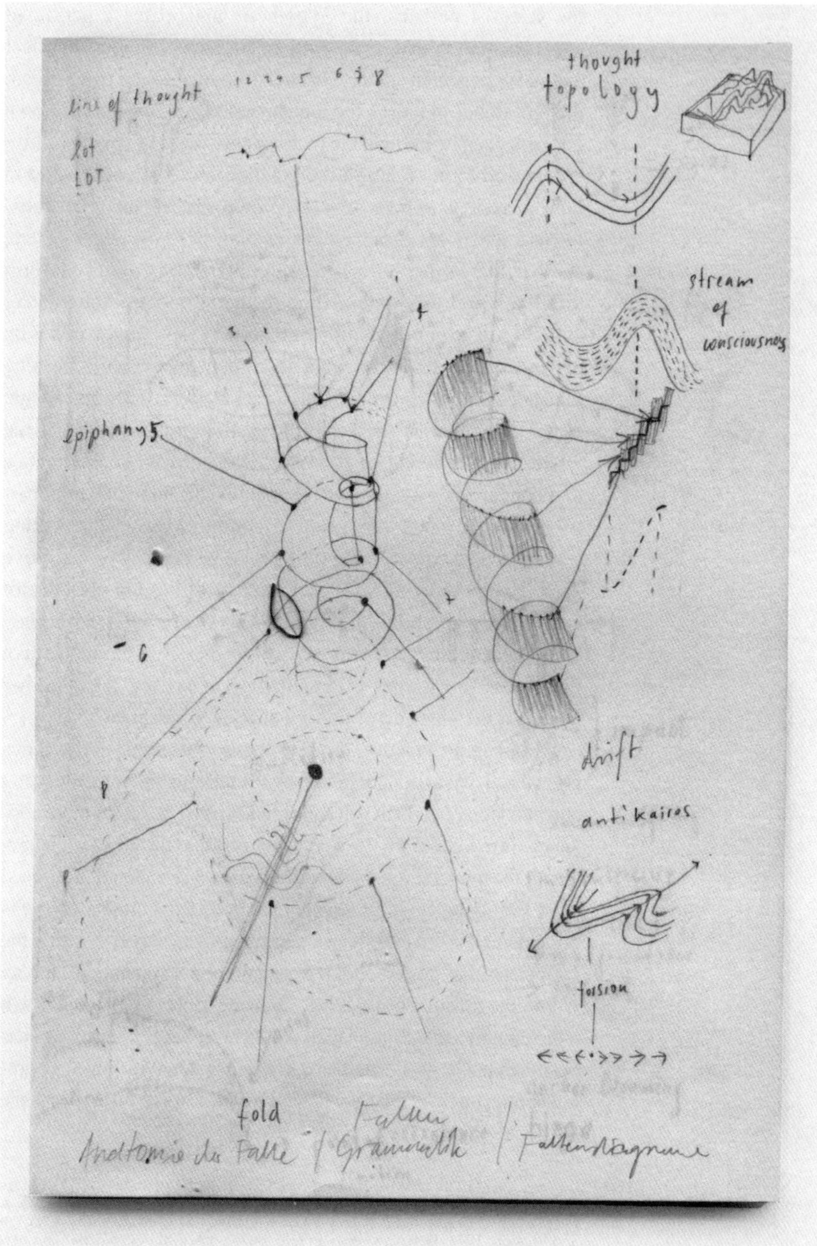
line of thought
lot
LOT
thought
topology
stream
of
consciousness
epiphany 5
drift
antikairos
torsion
fold
Falten
Anatomie der Falte
Grammatik
Faltendiagramme

Fig. 12-21

the scientist perhaps, the hypothesis anticipates a period of experimentation that – like a rite of passage – attempts to affect a transformation in status. Through the ritual of the experiment, the researcher practises the alchemical turning of the unknown into what can be known, the making consistent of what has hitherto lacked form or definition. Yet, thresholds can be crossed in both directions, where what is known can as easily be transformed into what is no longer recognizable or certain. Here, another logic emerges wherein the hypothesis might perform differently, operating according to the terms of an alternative structure of experimentation and enquiry, less concerned with expanding the limits of what is known than with increasing the spaces of indeterminacy along its borders. This other logic is not a critique of the scientific method but neither is it the wholesale borrowing of its terms. Rather, it is the emergence of a concurrent way of knowing that reveals moments of porosity or elasticity within existing structures of knowledge, taking a certain pleasure in inhabiting these perceptual or cognitive gaps. Here, the hypothesis no longer identifies the presence of a temporary glitch in the fabric of knowledge such that it may be apprehended and its run stalled. Rather, it is the inquisitive finger that finds holes in anticipation of teasing them further open, for the pleasure of pulling at their loose threads.

(→ PI/06a)

Within an art practice, the hypothesis emerges as autonomous critical activity, no longer bound by the repetitious cycles of testing and validation to which is it subjected in other fields. Its mere conjecture is rescued from the pejorative, recast as the pleasurable reverie of the thinking mind engaged in nascent speculation. Released from the stranglehold of teleological knowledge production, it is possible to discern specific properties or characteristics within the hypothesis that, in turn, point to certain critical operations at play within the practice of drawing. Drawing is the language through which the hypothesis is shaped within art practice, since it too has been habitually designated as a preliminary activity, always coming before, rarely taken for what it is in itself.[1] Like the hypothesis,

1) The idea of drawing as the 'hypothesis of sight' is explored by Jacques Derrida in *Memoirs of the Blind, the Self Portrait and other Ruins*, trans. Pascale-Anne Brault and Michael Naas, University of Chicago Press, Chicago and London, 1993. Derrida's ideas around the hypothetical or conjectural properties of drawing are further explored in *Drawing Now, Between the Lines of Contemporary Art*, Downs, Marshall, Sawdon, Selby and Tormey, I.B. Tauris (eds.), London and New York, 2007.

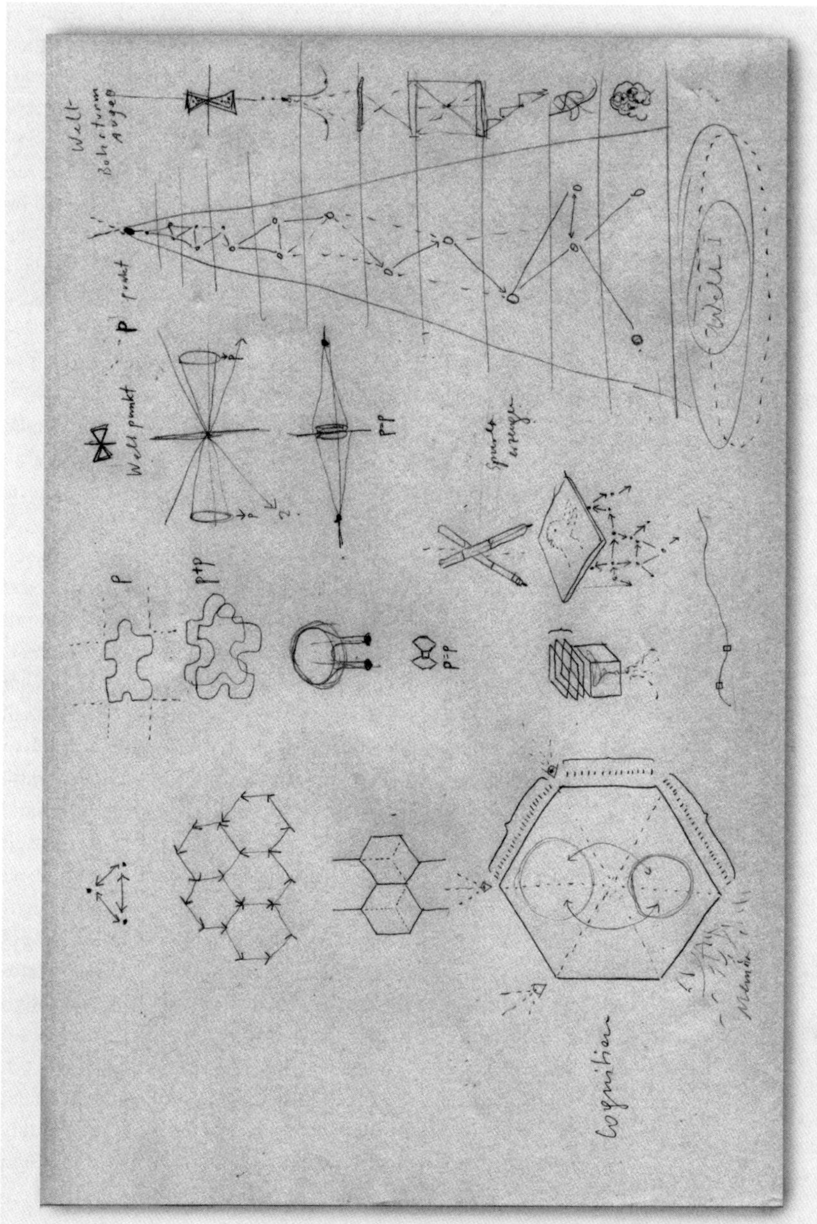

Fig. P01-03

drawing is a conjectural operation, the tentative manifestation of an insurgent *if.* The hypothetical *if* is typically understood as a conditional statement, closely followed by the consequential or predictive *then*. Whilst *if* is the opening of innumerable possibilities, *then* grounds, returning the flight of the imaginary back to the realm of measurable affect. Paul Klee notes, 'In the world of physical reality every ascent must be followed by a descent at the moment at which the gravitational pull of the earth overcomes the ascending energy of the rudder'.[2] He signals this as (⟶ Fig. 12-81) a drawn curve, whose rise falls as surely as Newton's apple. An ascendant (and affirmative) *if* is thus habitually subjected to the descendant or negating pull of logic, the gravity of the consequential *then*.

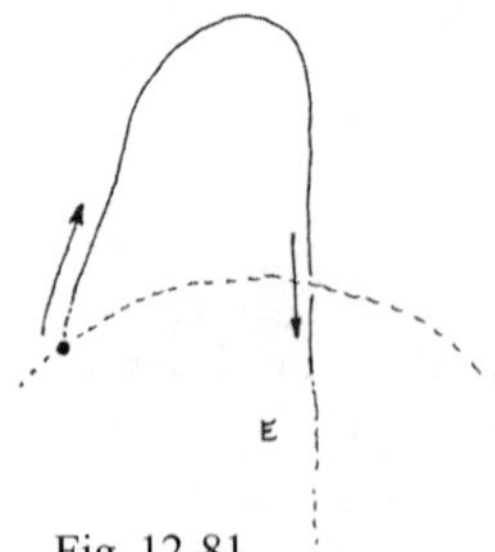

Fig. 12-81

Conjecture is a practice for scarifying a conceptual terrain, unsettling its surface to create the germinal conditions within which further thought may take root. The drawn hypothesis attempts to extend the space of the conjectural, deferring or delaying the effects of consequential thinking in order to keep the *if* in flight. Comprehension remains suspended between one mode of thinking (as *if*) and the beginning of another (*then*). Suspension delays the logic of cause and effect, creating hesitation between stimulus and response. Stalling disturbs rhythm and unsettles familiar patterns by creating the space of a missed beat, an affective gap or form of creative attention in which to consider things differently to what they already are. Here, drawing produces the possibility of (⟶ Fig.12-82) Klee's 'cosmic curve', the trajectory of a line (of thinking) that 'frees itself more and more from the earth in infinite motion, to fulfill itself freely in a circle or at least an ellipse'.[3] Propelled by the invitation of the drawn hypothesis, thinking momentarily escapes the pull of gravitational logic, for drawing not only complicates the production of the consequential *then*, but also encourages the generation of further *ifs*. If is like the wind, an auspicious force whose energy keeps the arrow air-bound, buoyant. Yet, too many ifs and the arrow's flight collapses impotently under the weight of its own potential or against the pressure of unruly turbulence, its hypothetical properties lost within the realm

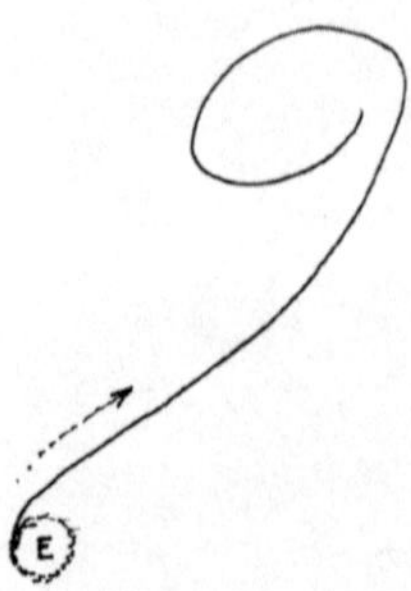

Fig. 12-82

2) Paul Klee, *The Pedagogical Sketchbook*, Faber and Faber, London, 1953, p. 56.

3) Klee, *The Pedagogical Sketchbook*, 1953, p. 56.

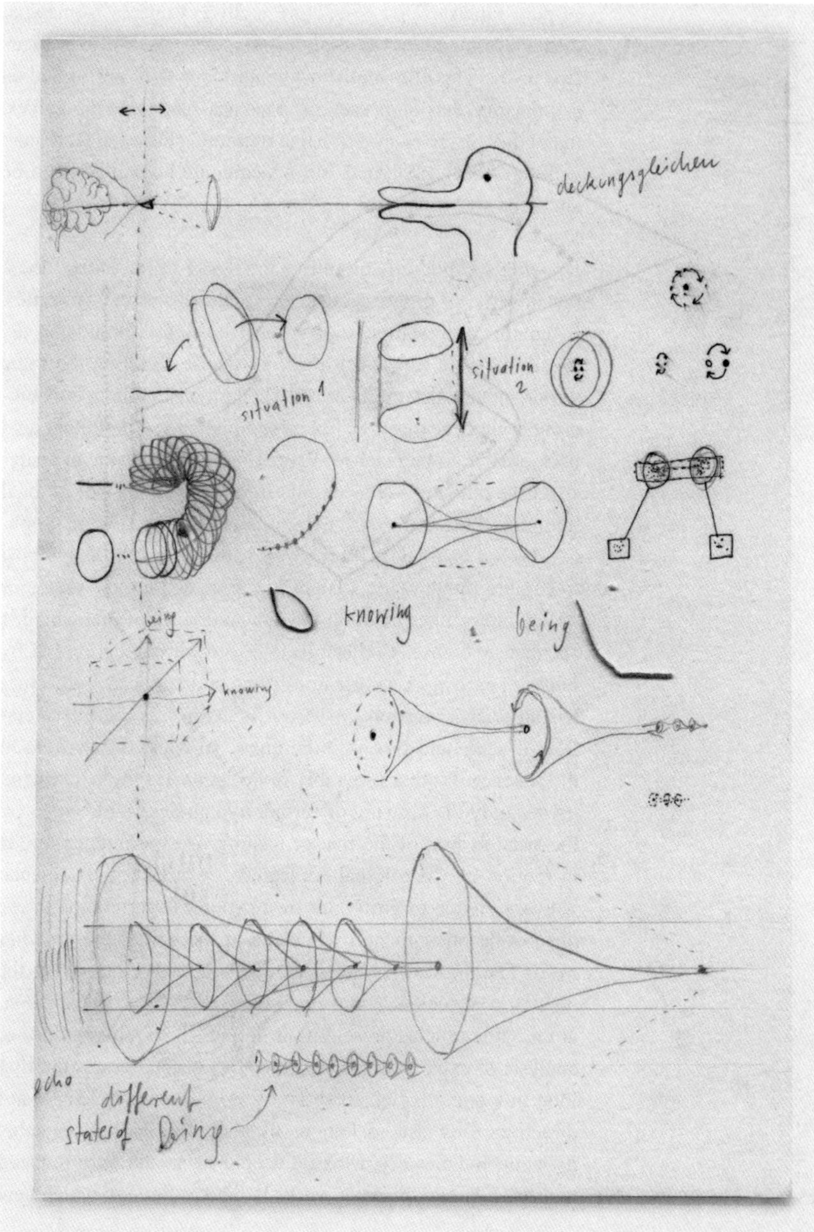
deckungsgleichen
situation 1
situation 2
knowing
being
being
knowing
echo
different
states of being

Fig. 12-27

of pure fantasy. True conjecture is always uneasy, somewhat difficult to maintain.[4] Without caution it is possible to get carried away. The drawing of a hypothesis is thus performed as a trajectory that harnesses the tensions of competing forces, maintained as an ever-active line oscillating between what may well have been imagined, but which could be perceived to be anchored within the real.

Drawing's hypothesis mobilises the desire of the logical then, but thwarts its progress such that a conclusion never comes. It remains an incomplete or unresolved figure, promising the possibility of a revelatory moment whilst disabling the logic through which this might occur. Thought is brought to the quivering brink of realisation, but its summation is indefinitely held back, unable to be reached. Predictions formed from an analysis of the drawing's conjectural efforts are not those of rational reasoning but seem more akin to acts of divination or prophecy. Occult methods are borrowed as the means through which to conjure the drawing's latent meaning, as familiar strategies of reading or interpretation fail to make sense of that which is abstract or obtuse. Conjecture is a form of perception led by intuition or insight, a portentous occupation. Indeed, conjecture has an archaic meaning, where it is defined as the interpretation of signs and omens – the quest, perhaps, for answers in the absence of other (arguably more rational) means. Drawing invites only the drawing of further hypotheses, made either by the artist as part of the line of enquiry or experimentation set in motion by the original conjecture, or else by the audience who are invited to form their own hypothesis in relation to the observable phenomenon witnessed at the site of the drawing itself. The drawn hypothesis is thus both a speculative act for making a statement about one set of observable phenomena, at the same time as presenting it as one which requires further analysis or explanation. The drawn hypothesis creates the first loop in a cognitive chain stitch of an interminable length and direction. This lasts as long as the thread of thinking remains dynamic and aleatory, where it is neither cut short nor reduced to snarled knots. Drawing works loopholes through which new

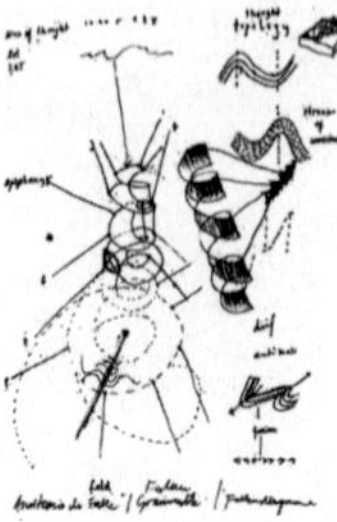

Fig. 12-21

4) Indeed, the presence of these 'evidentiary' footnotes attests to the difficulty of remaining truly conjectural.

thought may make its escape. Yet, opportunity (or *kairos*) is only so if taken.[5]

The encounter with art provides the conditions – of potential indeterminacy – from which a hypothesis might be drawn, where the task becomes one of drawing the hypothesis in a way which remains faithful to the terms of the original stimulus (art).[6] Significantly, the testing of the hypothesis must also be undertaken without simply reducing matters to the realm of the determinate, without simply making things at once stable. Drawing is the hypothetical figure deemed capable of describing the unfolding phenomenon encountered at the very site of drawing itself. In these terms, drawing is the kairotic event of creating an adequate epistemology simultaneous with the experience it attempts to describe, the restless instant where naming and the thing named attain co-existence (in time).[7] It is the optimal means through which to communicate the nature of the observable – if somewhat intangible – phenomenon of drawing (and also perhaps of being) whilst demonstrating fidelity to its terms. Drawing is a form of hypothesis which attempts to account for its own coming into being, a reflexive practice performed as the infinite loop of observing itself observing, ad infinitum. It is the hypothesis folded back to regard its own making, this being analogous to thinking about thinking – a Foucauldian inversion.[8] Or rather it is that which is produced through the process of attending to and documenting the process of its own production. Drawing is thus not only the observational record or explanation of those occurrences belonging to the

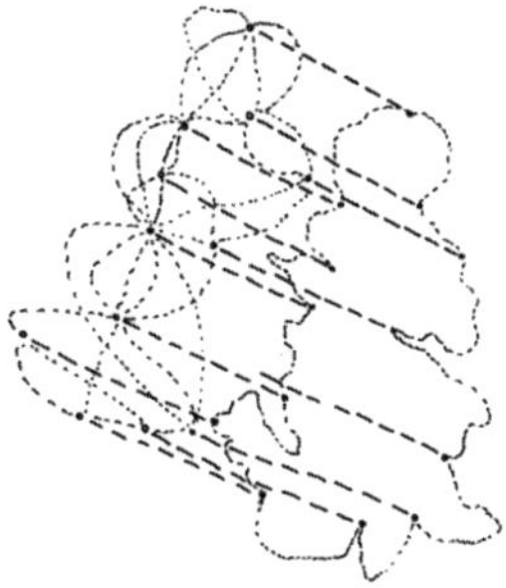

Fig. 05-08

5) *Kairos* is an ancient Greek word meaning an opportune or fleeting moment whose potential needs to be grasped before it passes.

6) A series of 'figures' provided by the artist provided the 'conditions' that prompted the production of this particular written hypothesis. However, the nature of its conjecture has been encouraged by other encounters with art practice also. I would especially like to thank artist Lee Triming for the provocation offered by his work and for his insights into the conjectural nature of drawing.

7) Here, the reference to kairós is more specifically made in relation to how the term is used by Antonio Negri in *Time for Revolution*, trans. M. Mandarini, Continuum, London, 2003. For Negri, 'Kairós is the modality of time through which being opens itself, attracted by the void at the limit of time, and it thus decides to fill that void', Negri, 2003, p. 152. Here, suggests Negri, 'the thing, on the edge of being, calls on the act of naming to augment being, in the same way as the name calls the thing to a new singular existence,' Negri, 2003, p. 154. My hypothesis then is that the act of drawing may equate to both the 'thing' and the 'name'.

8) Gilles Deleuze further conceptualises Michel Foucault's 'fold' of subjectivization in *Foldings, or the Inside of Thought (Subjectivation)*, in *Foucault*, trans. S. Hand, University of Minnesota Press, Minneapolis, 1988.

(external) world but also an attempt to account for or make manifest experiences that exist along another plane of reality. This zone of experience extends from deep within the body outwardly towards the newly emergent and indeterminate spaces opening out into and beyond the surface of the paper upon which the drawing works. Within the drawn hypothesis, internal and external realities are conceived as a continuum, where the body's skin no longer keeps the individual distinct from the world but rather is considered a precarious threshold through which they merge, becoming inseparable. Here, thought can be observed in the same way that a tree might be. Distances cannot be measured by a ruler's yard, for within the reality of the drawing spatial proximities remain unstable, shifting. Scale fluctuates. Dimensions waver. Shapes appear solid in one instance and then disappear in the next. Flat surfaces give way to vertiginous voids. Lines shimmer along their axis, turning. Concave forms bulge forward suddenly into unexpected protrusions. Cuboids worry themselves inside out. Receding objects make an unlikely return. Edges seem undecided about which entities they delineate. Movement occurs even whilst remaining still.

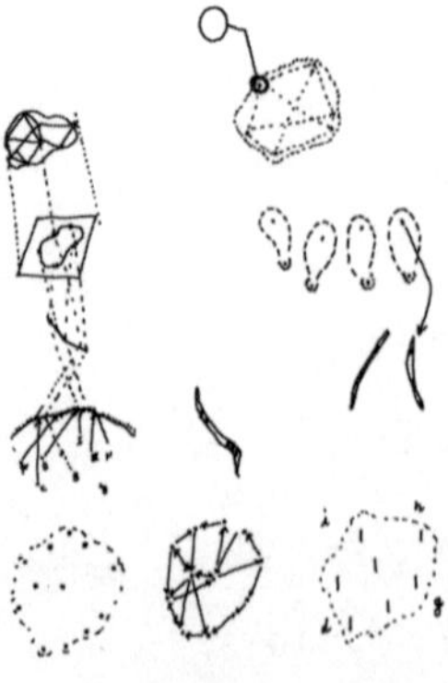

Fig. 09-07

The supposing drawing is in the world but not quite of it, it remains at the level of suggestion. Suggestion is the practice of inducing or guiding thought without recourse to rhetorical ruse or rational reasoning, the bringing forward of ideas in the absence of intervening sense. Suggestion draws thought. Those susceptible to its powers may encounter a change in perceptual experience whilst under its spell. An older meaning links the term to the prompting of evil, a turning to the left-hand path. Here, the left is that which is out of order, out of line, out of sight. If right is to tighten, then left is to loosen – it is a politics of undoing, of allowing things to unravel. Left is to operate anticlockwise. It is also a lover's language, being closest to the heart. The tendency towards suggestion is also a move towards the improper or unseemly, a deviant form. Suggestion is thus both a cloaked and immodest practice, the offering of a hint. At one level, the hint can be considered a form of intimation; however, it also describes an occasion of opportunity, a kairotic moment waiting to be seized. To hint is to offer invitation towards another's thinking; it is the leaving of a sufficient gap. The supposing drawing is that which belongs to the world, but

(→ PII/07a-c)

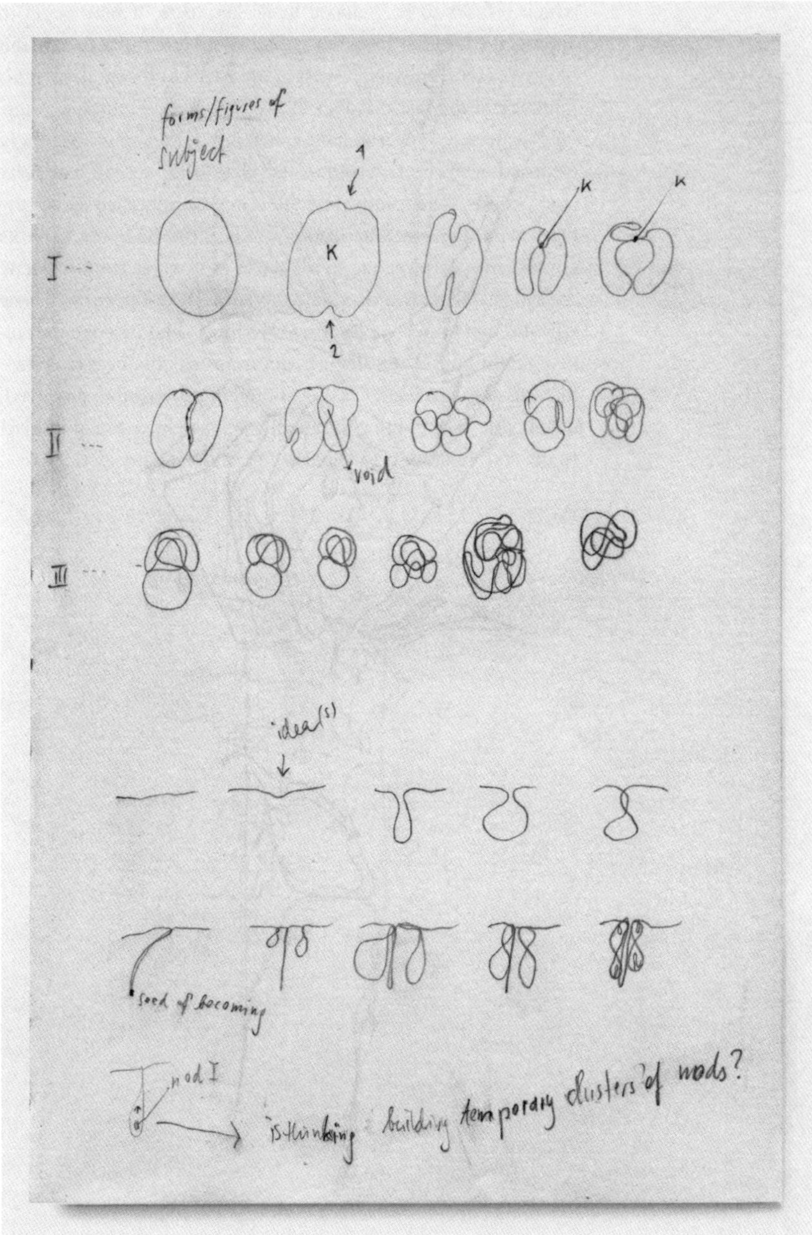
forms/figures of subject
K
void
idea(s)
seed of becoming
temporary clusters of wods?

Fig. 12-23

which refuses to be reduced to its language. It may begin to approach a familiar form but will always stubbornly remain out of grasp. Here, drawing hovers at the edges of recognition, pulling back at the last moment to stay beyond definition's range. Or else, it may appear to have fallen out of meaning, seemingly cleansed or even exorcised of its relationship to any particular signification. The removal of the frame of reference leaves the mark wild. Decontextualization extracts the fragment from its context, in turn evacuating all sense of context from it. Here, drawing aspires towards a state of neutrality or openness. Those who attempt to decode its structures must acknowledge the status of their guesswork; their hypothesis can only ever operate – like the drawing itself – as a contingent proposition, unsolved, unsolvable. The contingent hypothesis is neither true nor false. In the end, to draw is to leave things undecided.

HYPOTHESIS #7

Drawing Interest

Recording Vitality

Karin Harrasser

DRAWING INTEREST

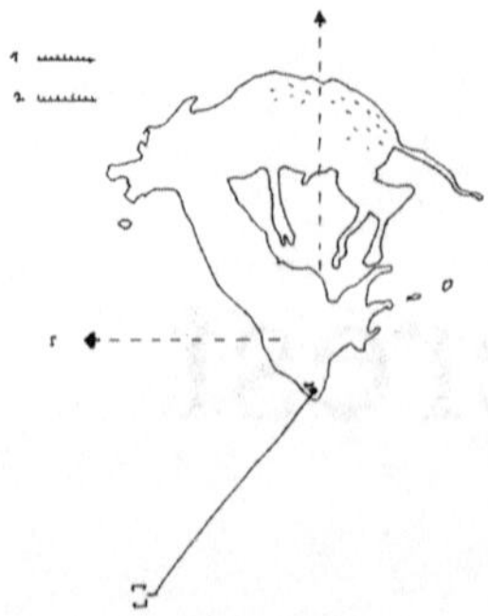

Fig. 01-20

Contemporary experimental systems (Hans-Jörg Rheinberger) are not only technically more complex then older ones, they are also epistemologically more fragile: They can no longer claim to be disinterested and hence free from structures of desire and dominance, free from culturally determined requirements. This insight owes as much to the history of science and to the study of science and technology as to internal scientific reflection: we owe to theoretical physicists (Einstein, Schröder, Heisenberg) the insight that the role of the observer is a critical factor in the question *what* is observed in a research setting. In addition, since the beginning of the 20th century, philosophers have understood the production of scientific and other knowledge to be based on language, and with cybernetics a radical constructivist approach has gained ground. Furthermore, historical epistemology and science and technology studies have addressed the permeation of scientific endeavoure by professional and societal interests. Such interests are not only factors external to research (lobbyism funding structures, political or economic control, institutional structures), but important also internal to science: they are crucial to communication processes within science in terms of research methods chosen, but also in the media images that are used. The act of drawing, the very production of a sketch or diagram in the context of scientific work is not free of cultural values and norms. It is a high-tension act, an act which demands the focussing of attention as well as a whole range of intellectual and practical techniques. It is an act which is communicatively embedded and yet not entirely determined: Every stroke is the surprising result of an interested navigation within an area of possibilities.

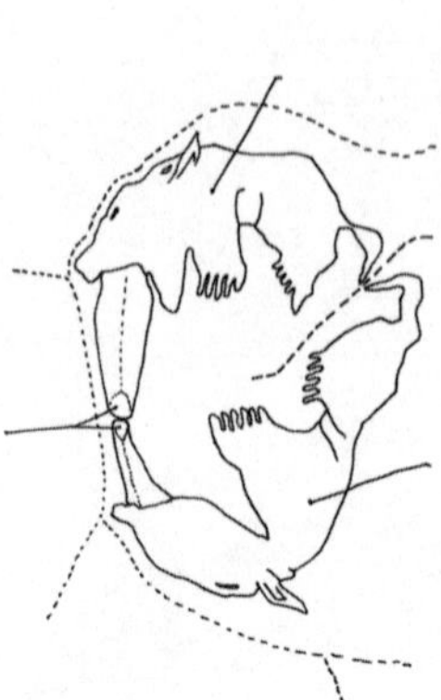

Fig. 06-06

How can these visual artefacts be comprehended? I would suggest, following Roland Barthes, that they be conceived as "figures". In the preface to *A Lovers Discourse: Fragments* (German ed. 1984), he writes: "We can call these fragments of speech 'figures'. The word is to be understood, not in its rhetorical sense, but rather in its gymmastic or choreographic acceptation; in short, in the Greek meaning σχήμα ['sçima] is not the schema, but, in a much livelier way, the body's gesture caught in action and not contemplated in repose: the body of athletes, orators, statues: what in the straining body can be immobilised." Consequently, the drawing is only a fragment in the research process. It is the moment in research which can be captured and fixed, if only momentarily.

Figures are thus snapshots of a process of knowledge production; they sort results and interpretations, and emphasise one direction of thought out of the pool of ideas and of ways of thinking. In addition, their material aspects provide contextual hints about the social and cultural embeddedness of research. What kind of paper is used? What kind of pen? What status do the drawings have for communication within the research community? Are they a means of communicating so-called interim results for internal use, or do they serve to illustrate knowledge for people outside the scientific community? (→ PIII/07)

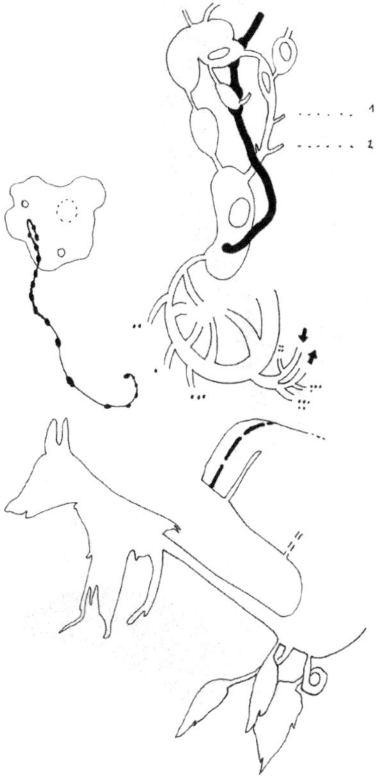

Fig. 02-15

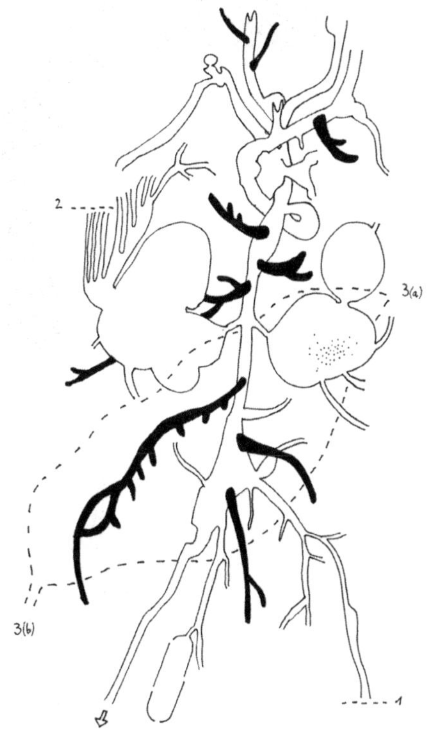

Fig. 02-16

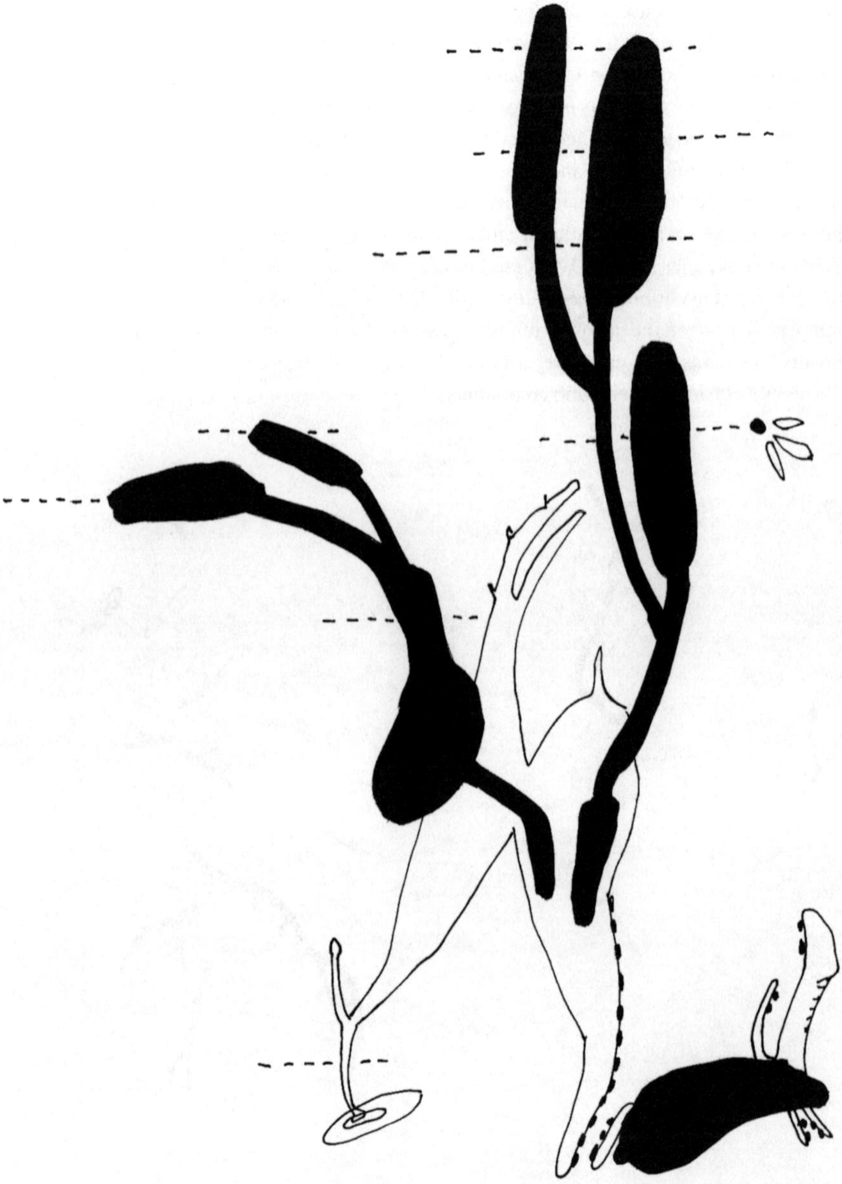

Fig. 02-19

Horst Bredekamp has described the interconnection of styles of drawing, the reproduction of images and the formation of scientific theory in detail with reference to Galileo Galilei. In his book *Galilei der Künstler. Die Zeichnung, der Mond, die Sonne* (*Galilei the Artist: The Drawing, the Moon, the Sun*), 2007, he suspends the distinction between the symbolic and cognitive image, and shows that Galileo's theory of the solar system is interdependent with his abilities as a draughtsman and his interest in contemporary art: aesthetic preferences and theory formation are bound in one 'visual way of thinking'. Though contemporary researchers are seldom artists, they still use visual strategies: e.g. image comparison or series formation. However, most likely technical images are compared, and often not by human eyes, but as differential series for machine calculation. This is a stark contrast to the notion of the "figure": It is not by chance that Roland Barthes' concept of the figure was bound up with the human form and the vitality of the body. It was the scale of the human body and perception that counted for him.

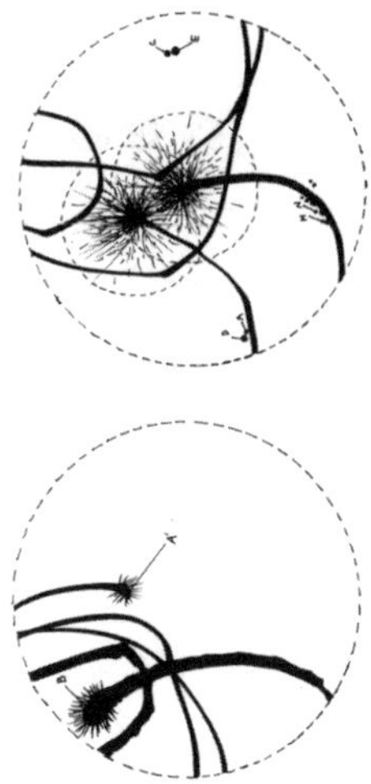

Fig. X03

But perhaps our machines have been producing figures for some time now, without us being able to recognise them. And it is not yet known whether machines have interests and desires. Without desire – what the history of science taught us – there can be no knowledge, but only data. That would mean the definitive end of drawing as a cultural technique.

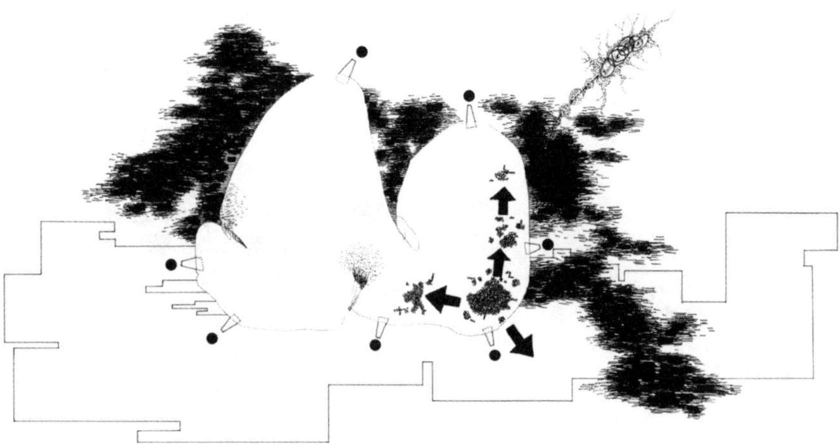

Fig. X08

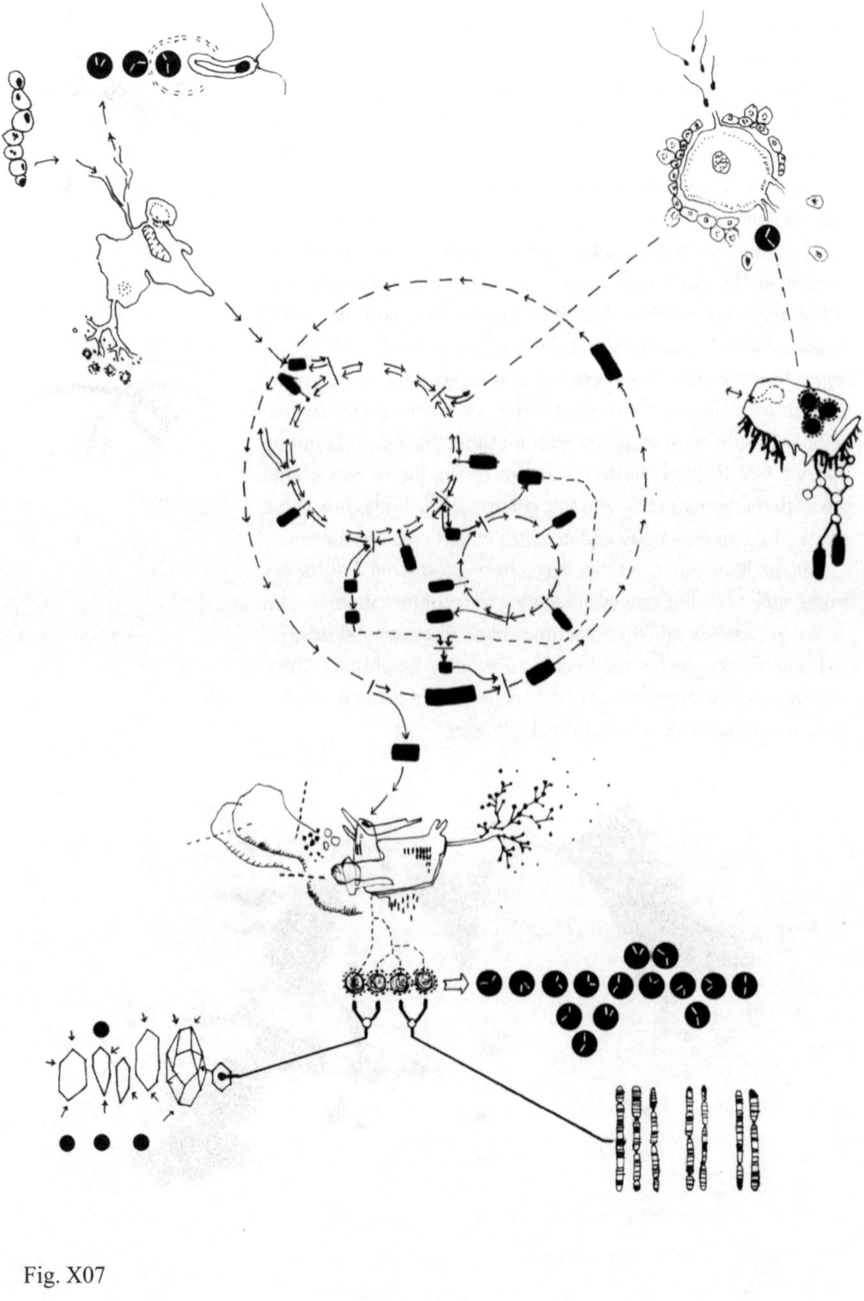

Fig. X07

RECORDING VITALITY

With the discovery of life as an object of research, questions of representation shifted: how can something be recorded if in its nature it is permanently changing? Techniques which facilitated the mapping of, for example, the human body, originally relied for that very reason on corpses: only corpses remained still long enough to be captured on paper. In this way, anatomical drawing developed parallel to embalming techniques until the eighteenth century, when techniques were developed to sculpt wax cast replicas of alive bodies. Nonetheless, this was not enough to visually reproduce the specific vitality of bodies: movement sequences or progressions of development and growth could only be depicted as discrete states shown one after another. Time-lapse photography (e.g. Muybridge's and Marey's motion studies) is the high point and the turning-point of documentation techniques of this kind, since film allowed the discrete states to be merged back into a moving image. It is the point when it is necessary to turn to different technique for representing vitality, which represents the vital processes not through moving images but through vectors and the technical alienation of perception.

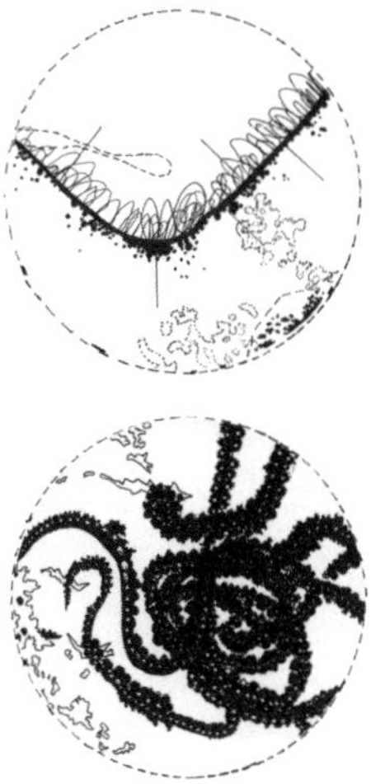

Fig. X04

Since Lamarck and Darwin, biologists have understood vitality as a specific relation of the life-form to its environment. In contrast to, for example, a stone, a living being behaves flexibly in relation to its environment: it adapts to environmental conditions. It maintains an active relationship to its environment. In the 1920s, in his *Theoretical Biology*, zoologist Jakob von Uexküll developed an idiosyncratic vocabulary for this: he developed a theory of animals' relationship to their 'Umwelten' (environments): their directedness, interestedness, and functionality within it. He developed a schema whereby animal behaviour could be interpreted as a feedback system of organism and environment, of the world as perceived and the world as acted on. Uexküll conceptualised the organism's relationship to its environment as a process of meaning-making: within its surroundings, the organism interprets what it perceives and modifies its behaviour accordingly. 'Meaning' is thus above all functional. Organisms assess their surroundings according to four functions: is the environment a facilitator/a medium, a friend, food or a sexual partner? Uexküll depicts the circular

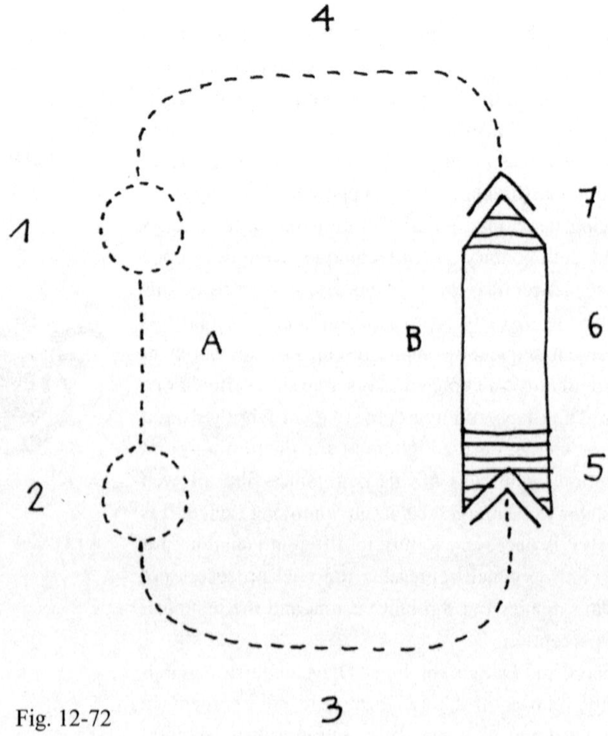

Fig. 12-72

	FUNKTIONSKREIS = FUNCTIONAL CIRCUIT
1	Merk-Organ = Sensor
2	Wirk-Organ = Functor
3	Wirkwelt = World as Acted On
4	Merkwelt = World as Perceived
5	Wirkmal-Träger Effektor = Functional Trait Carrier Effector
6	Gegengefüge = Opposing System
7	Receptor Merkmal-Träger = Receptor Trait Carrier
A	Innenwelt des Subjektes = Subject's Inner World
B	Objekt = Object

Table 1

decision-making processes of perception and readjustment with the help of forces a.k.a. vectors.

On the one hand, Jakob von Uexküll conceived of animal bodies, in the physiological tradition, as assemblages composed of smaller entities which fulfill a particular function: perception follows from the sensor, physical movement from 'walk-drivers' (*Laufwerke*); generally speaking, the organism's relationship to its environment is determined by its 'act-drivers' (*Wirkwerke*). This vocabulary refers explicitly to the motor and mechanical aspects of the organism's physical organisation. But Uexkülls theory of a radically subjective relation of organism and 'Umwelt' also makes him a neovitalist. He assumes that the relation of a living body to its environment is a process of meaning-making, and that vitality exists precisely in the flexible fit between organism and environment, that organ and environment create each other reciprocally: "On the one hand, the body is the creator of meaningful symbols, populating its garden, and on the other hand it is the creation of the same symbols which influence the body's own construction."[1] In Uexküll's conception, the mechanical thing, the machine, the single organ have only one limited, specific, goal-oriented function; the different 'subroutines', as it were, cannot adapt to an environment, while the organism is conceptualised as a control unit ('the machinist') which prompts the whole body to continually reassess its environment and imbue it with meaning. Living things adapt to their environment and mould themselves to it, making use of continually changing conditions to develop or lose organs: "It is tempting to assume that an animal is nothing but a selection of adapted sensors and tools bound into a whole by a control apparatus, which remains a machine despite being adapted to execute the living functions of an animal. Indeed, this is the view of all machine theorists, whether they think along the lines of rigid mechanisms or plastic dynamic entities. By this reasoning, animals are regarded as pure objects, and it is forgotten that from the very beginning the most important thing has been suppressed, namely the subject that is served by these means, which perceives and acts with them." (p. 21)

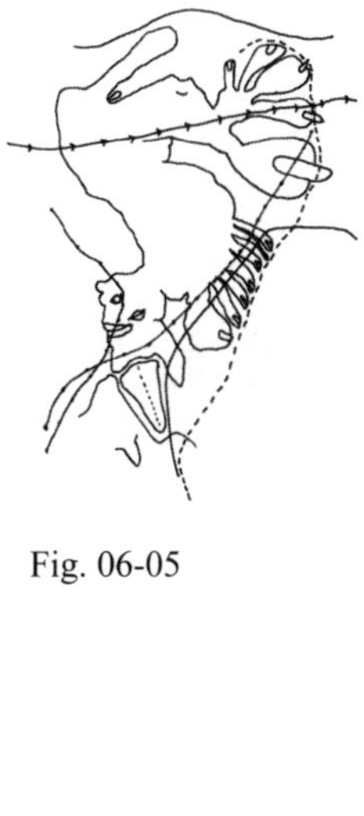

Fig. 06-05

1) Jakob von Uexküll & Georg Kriszat, *Streifzüge durch die Umwelten von Tieren und Menschen. Ein Bilderbuch unsichtbarer Welten. Bedeutungslehre*, Rowohlt, Hamburg, 1956, p. 158.

Environment and organism are related and mediated by processes of regulation, and even more then that: organism and environment are subject to a mutual formation process. One example given here by Uexküll and later quoted by Deleuze/ Guattari, an example similar to the prominent role of Uexkülls tick in Georgio Agamben's work, is the body shape of the bee and the calyx of the flower. Uexküll presents the coproduction of meaning by environment and organism (every organism, including the researcher, can be seen as environment for any other organism and is both subject and object of the process of generating meaning) as well as different organisms' subjective relationship to the environment with artistic-experimental methods, which are nowadays common practice in biology textbooks. To present the animal environment more vividly, he experimented with grid photography and watercolours, and even dabbled in poetry, adapting Goethe's famous poem on the relationship between the sun and the eye to the bat's sonar and the moth:

> "Were the eye not like the sun,
> The sun could it never glimpse; (...)"
> (Johann Wolfgang von Goethe)

> "Were the moth not like the bat,
> Its life would soon be ended."
> (Jakob von Uexküll)

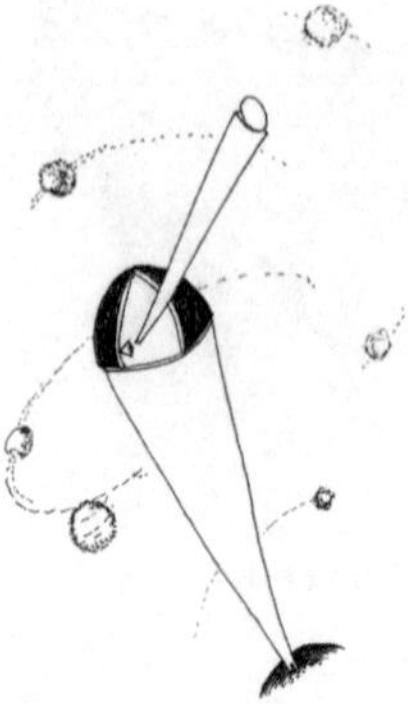

Fig. 12-80

Without doubt, Uexküll's radicalism consists in the nonchalance with which he negates the special status of the human worlds of perception and action, which is a kind of preview into radical constructivism. This becomes obvious in the final chapter of the *Streifzüge durch die Umwelten von Tieren und Menschen*, in which the astronomer's environment is depicted according to the same schema as the environments of ticks, toads, flies, dogs, paramecia, grasshoppers, sea urchins, etc., and which ends with the succinct comment: "On a high tower, as far as possible above the ground, sits a human being, who with the aid of giant optical devices has so transformed his eyes that they are able to penetrate space to the most distant stars. (...) And yet the whole environment is only a tiny fragment of nature, tailored to the capacities of a human subject."

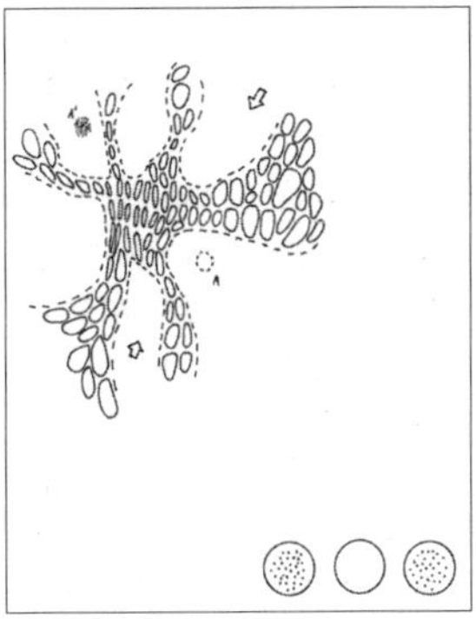

Fig. 02-13

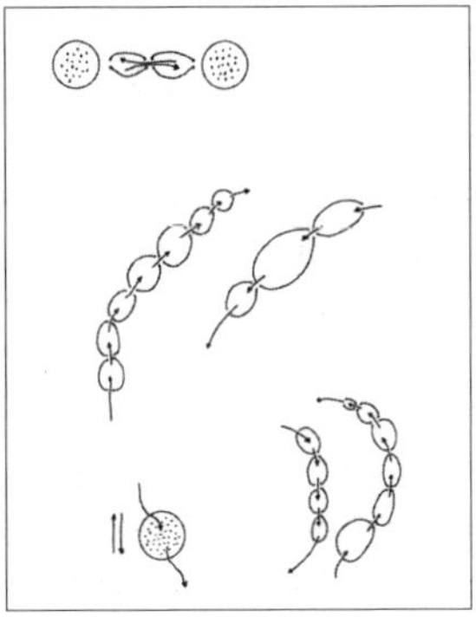

Fig. 02-12

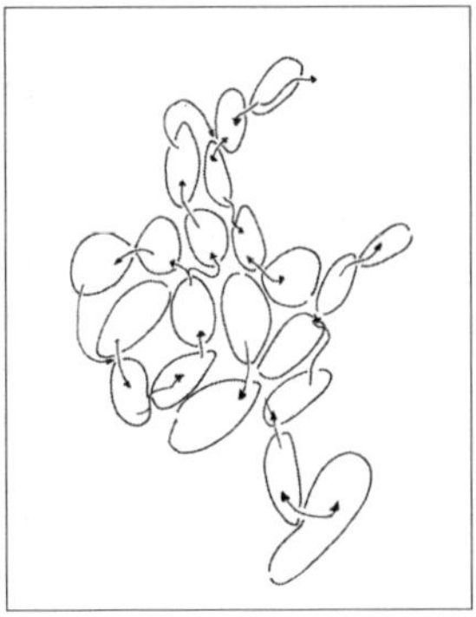

Fig. 02-11

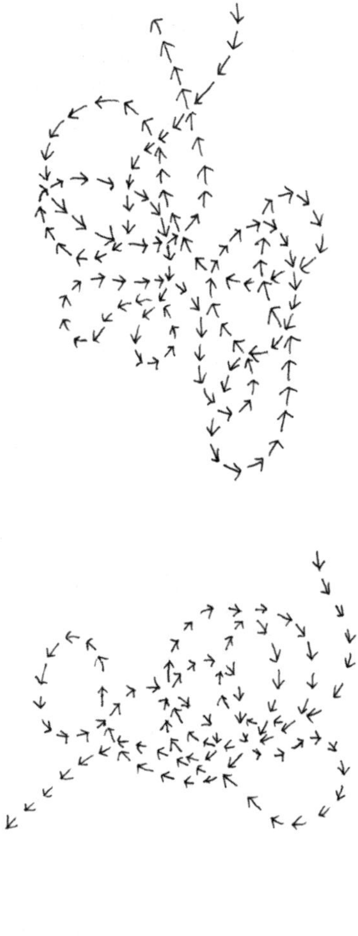

Fig. 06-12

(Ibid., p. 100). It is this decentralisation of Man as the subject of knowledge that makes Uexküll an important testimonial for (anti)anthropologies.

Besides these special methods of presentation, which denotes Uexküll's *Theoretical Biology* – besides other things – as some kind of Science Fiction, it is clear that in the organism's equally adapted and flexible relationship to its environment, in its ability to fit, Uexküll recognises what Claude Bernard had located in the organism's system: the organism's fundamental capacity for realising its potential and for self-regulation. In retrospect, a further aspect makes Jakob von Uexküll, look like a cyberneticist (and indeed he was rediscovered by Ludwig von Bertalanffy in the 50s): his functional circles can be represented as electrical circuits, and consequently they were one of the preconditions for the successful transfer of biological knowledge to the technical sciences, providing an argument and an image for the universality of feedback control mechanisms. Consequently, Uexküll's sketch of the functional circuit (→ p. 116) has to be viewed as one of the most effective drawings ever.

HYPOTHESIS #8

Nonself Compatibility in Plants

Monika Bakke

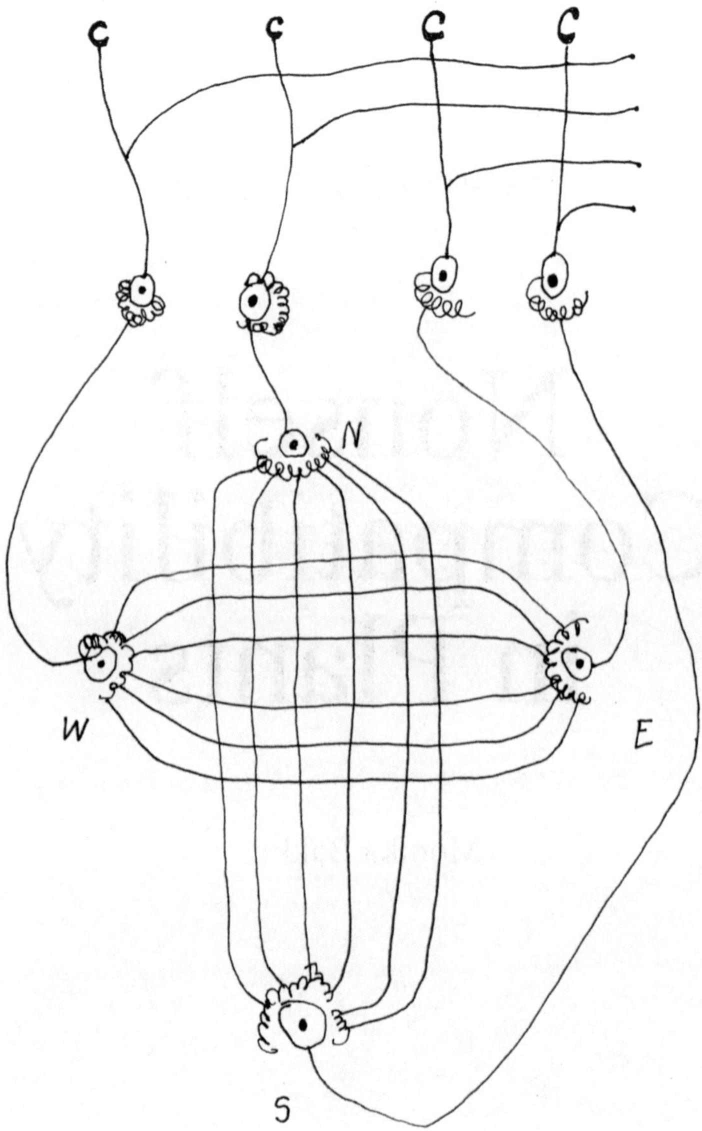

Fig. 01-38

Airborne volatiles of plants serve communicative purposes and can be detected and picked up by other plants and animals. Flowers produce volatiles to attract pollinators and yet volatiles emitted from leaves can either have a direct toxic impact on pathogens or serve as signals in a socalled transmutagenic interaction.

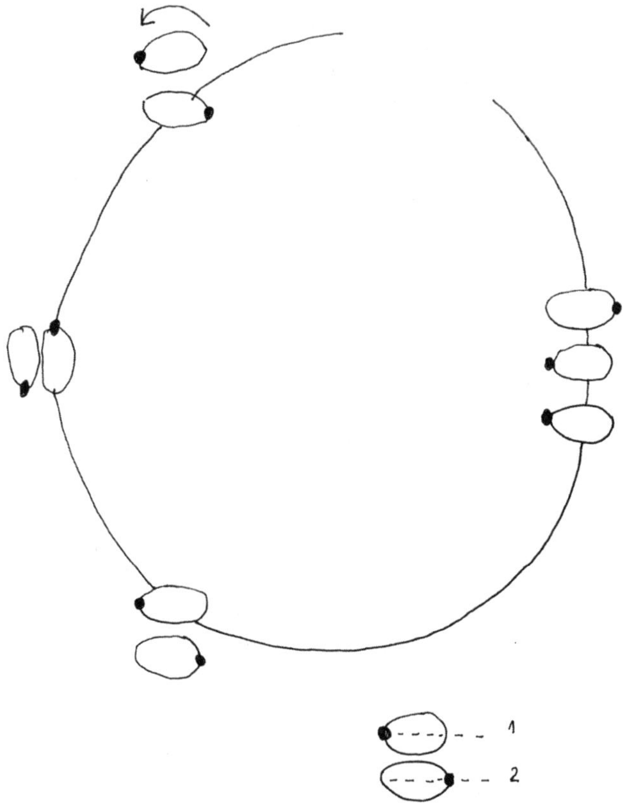

Fig. 01-33

Some of the volatile signals of various biochemical functions may get fused again and again therefore the original stream of data gets altered and the possibility of 'hacking' this system of communication by other life forms increases. Moreover, in a sense, some airborne data become contageous. Once the information enters (infects) the system of some life form, it cannot be "forgotten" or removed.

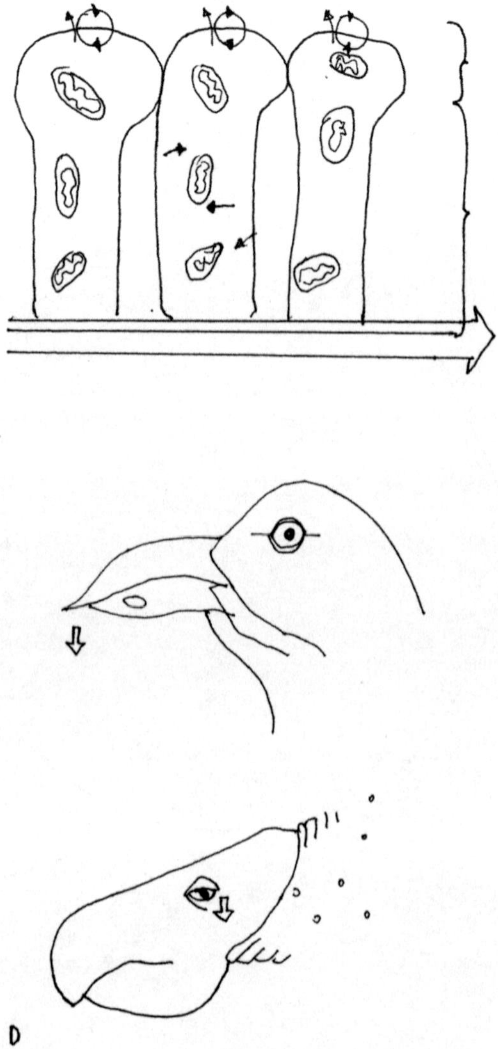

Fig. 01-12

Volatiles' production plays an important role for defense mechanisms as some plants emit a broad spectrum of volatiles after being infected by herbivores or treated with high- or low-molecular elicitors. But less known is the fact that plant volatiles may induce transformation of some non-plant life forms for reasons not directly related to their survival strategies. These plants also possess extra floral nectaries, which may as well play a role as an induced indirect defense or, possibly, as a product and tool of attraction towards the animal life forms. It is a form of zoothropism (zoophilia) observed also, on another level, in carnivorous plants.

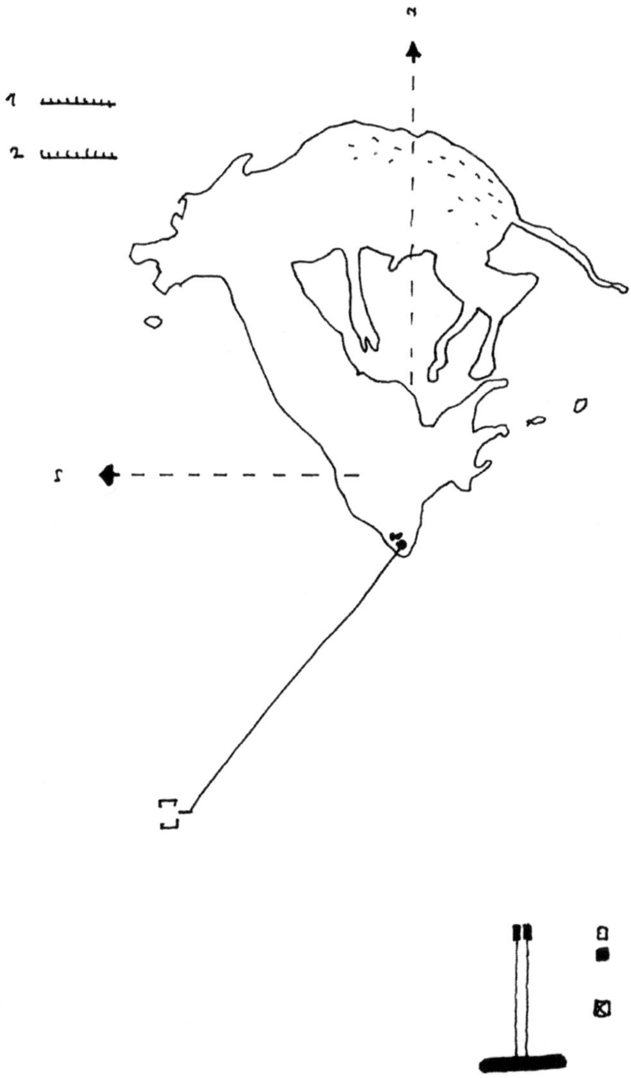

Fig. 01-20

Elliot's hypothesis of plant zoothropism explains very rare cases of non-functional floral-like structures developing from the body of animal as the first stage of this peculiar grafting process. As one well-documented case implies, it is possible that, eventually, an arboreal structure may take over the animal life form. This may explain a case of a still living, although highly mutated, fox found growing off a branch of a fully developed elm tree.

HYPOTHESIS #9

Hypotheses Non Fingo or When Symbols Fail

Andreas Schinner

"For whatever is not deduced from the phenomena must be called a hypothesis; and hypotheses, whether metaphysical or physical, or based on occult qualities, or mechanical, have no place in experimental philosophy. In this philosophy particular propositions are inferred from the phenomena, and afterwards rendered general by induction."
(Isaac Newton, *Philosophiae Naturalis Principia Mathematica, General Scholium*; translated by Bernard Cohen and Anne Whitman)

"Everyone wants to understand art.
Why not try to understand the song of a bird?"
(Pablo Picasso)

Imagine a medieval book, written in an elegant, unique script that has puzzled scholars, cryptanalysts and historians for centuries. Imagine an incomprehensible book, illustrated with figures of unidentifiable plants, magical symbols and what seem to be sketches depicting bizarre rituals. Now you will have a faint idea of how hypotheses sometimes grow into legends.

That book is called *The Voynich Manuscript*, named after the antiquarian book dealer Wilfried Voynich, who rediscovered it in 1912.[1] It may serve as a paradigm for an object prompting analysts to generate wild hypotheses: these range from absurd speculations about the "lost civilisation of Atlantis" to the *hoax hypothesis*, confirmed (but not proven) by contemporary computer-aided pattern matching analysis. However, this is not an article about the Voynich manuscript, although its intriguing properties may provide the proper starting point for focusing on a question of much higher impact: what is a hypothesis?

In 1799, Napoleon Bonaparte is said to have asked the famous French mathematician and astronomer Pierre Laplace why his new book *Mécanique Céleste* made not a single mention of God. Laplace replied: "Sire, I had no need of that hypothesis." As always, mathematicians give the most precise answer: a hypothesis (a *conjecture* as they call it) is a logical statement for which neither a proof nor a counterexample has yet been found. As soon as a conjecture is proven it becomes a *theorem*, and then the true magic of pure mathematics unfolds: *theorems* are valid, literally,

1) Gerry Kennedy and Rob Churchill, *The Voynich Manuscript*, Orion, London, 2005.

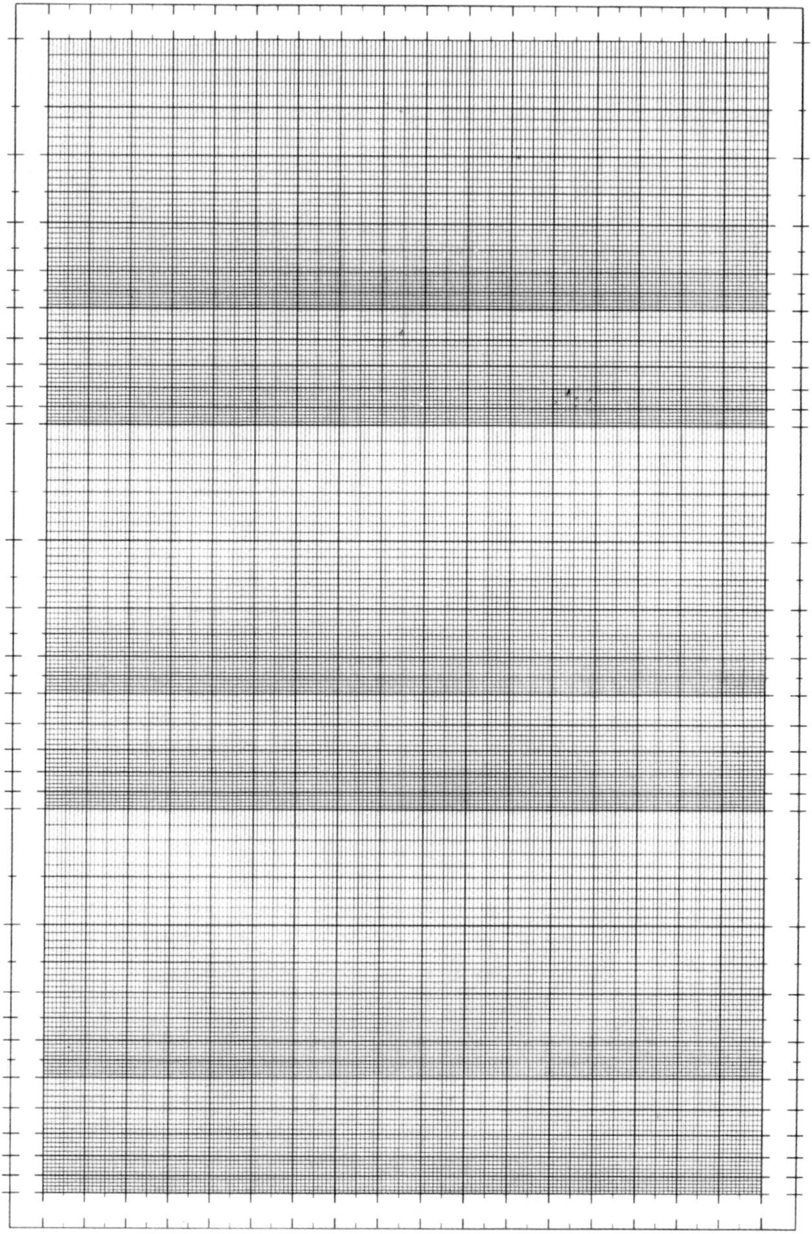

Fig. N01-03

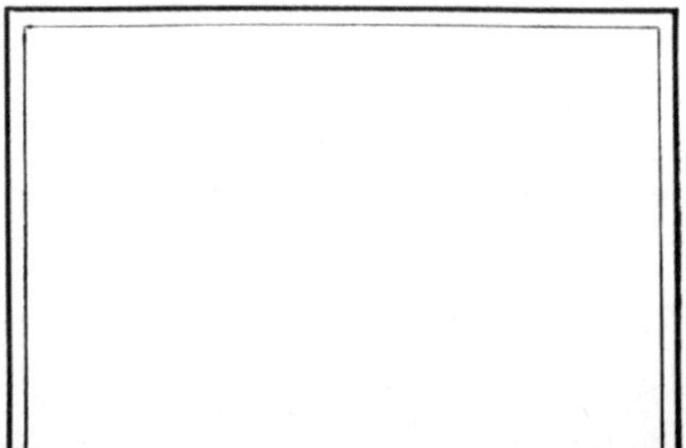

Fig. N01-00

forever. Nevertheless, even in the most perfect world of all, the world of mathematical objects, inherent inconsistency is lurking in the dark: the famous *incompleteness theorems*, proven by Kurt Gödel in 1931, state the impossibility of proving all arithmetic truths in non-trivial axiomatic systems. These theorems are very important in the philosophy of mathematics; however, they cannot devalue the basic principle of mathematical methodology: a conjecture is nothing, a theorem is all.

But what is the situation in the 'real' world, the world of physics, chemistry, biology? A never-ending dispute is going on among philosophers as to whether the objects of mathematical research are *discovered* or *invented* by mathematicians. However, this controversy is decided, in the field of natural science, obviously, an additional key aspect turns up: the *experiment.* For physicists a hypothesis is the conceptual assumption of particular phenomena, formulated in the language of mathematics. Combine several hypotheses, subject them to mathematical formalism to ascertain their logical consequences, and what you get is called a *theory*. Now the most exciting part takes place: do the predictions of your theory coincide with the observations, the experiment? If not, at least one of your basic assumptions must be wrong, and the process restarts for the next iteration cycle.

But even if the theory satisfactorily describes that part of 'reality' it has been constructed for, there may (or most probably will) exist a superior theory: one that addresses more phenomena and/or needs fewer hypotheses. In fact, this methodology is just a reformulation of the well-known, very useful scientific principle called *Occam's razor: entia non sunt multiplicanda praeter necessitatem.*[2]

2) "Do not multiply entities (i.e. hypotheses) beyond necessity." Also known as lex parsimoniae, attributed to William of Ockham, a 14th-century English scholar.

This basic line of attack is the key principle of modern post-Aristotelian science, in contrast to the intuitive hypothetic-deductive method of ancient natural philosophy. It is closely connected with the concept of falsifiability, investigated in detail by the Austrian philosopher Karl Popper:[3] Unlike mathematical conjectures, a theory in the context of natural science cannot be verified. It is not possible to prove that the speed of light cannot be exceeded under any circumstances. However, as a "good" scientific theory, the Theory of Relativity is falsifiable: you can always try to accelerate particles through the light barrier. Consequently, not even a key theory of modern physics like Einstein's work is 'immortal' as is a mathematical theorem, but it will surely survive forever as a special case or approximation within a more general model (as Newton's equations of motion are still a limiting case to their relativistic counterparts).

How do you construct a cube? Well, you could start from a line; add another of equal length perpendicular to it, and, finally, a third line perpendicular to the others. Close the planes in the most symmetrical way you can imagine, and what you get is the skeleton of a cube. Simple, isn't it? However, why should we stop at just three base lines? We could try to add at least a fourth, perpendicular to *all the others*. Impossible? Yes – and no!

Our species has evolved in an environment that seems to possess exactly three dimensions of space: *length, width, height*. And our brains have evolved with us; in fact, they still are the brains of hunter-gatherers: well adapted to aim arrows at our prey, or to estimate the distance to a potentially dangerous predator. Consequently, no human brain is able to mentally depict more than three lines perpendicular to each other. Even when we leave this tiny grain of sand we call 'Earth', at first glance we are confronted with three-dimensional physics: planets are orbiting the sun, solar systems coagulate to galaxies, galaxies form even bigger super-structures – nevertheless, everything seems to fit nicely into (extremely stretched out) *boxes*.

It is still an open question why the universe we live in has exactly three 'easily observable' spatial dimensions. The answer most probably is that life as we know it would not be possible in

3) Karl R. Popper, *Objective Knowledge*, Clarendon Press, Oxford, 1972.

fewer than or more than three-dimensional space[4] (and, following the *weak anthropic principle*, we would not be here asking questions in such a case). However, this universe *is* much stranger than our limited brains will ever be able to actually *visualise*: our planet, our sun, like all matter, bends three-dimensional space within a 'surrounding' fourth dimension;[5] this is what we call *gravity*. And furthermore, in the world of subatomic particles, where the mind-twisting laws of quantum mechanics replace the macroscopic view our brains are familiar with, this universe most probably possesses no fewer than *ten* spatial dimensions (with all but three being 'hidden' from macroscopic objects such as ourselves).

(→ PI/07)

What imposes an impenetrable barrier to our *visualisation* capabilities is no great challenge for mathematical formalism: conjectures and theorems frequently operate with multi-dimensional abstract objects, embedded in vector-spaces of arbitrary or even infinite dimension. The self-esteem, however, of our species appears to be suffering deeply from the fact that the better we understand the universe surrounding us, the less we are able to, literally, *grasp* it, as a child wants to grasp a stone before skimming it across the water. That is why modern science has successfully abandoned the intuitive viewpoint of natural philosophy; *visualisation* is no longer an inherent part of scientific methodology. A blind physicist can also understand the laws of refraction, although he or she will never be able to actually see a rainbow.

It is the tragedy of contemporary science that this strict separation of hypothesis from theory, and of theory from visualisation (as demanded by Isaac Newton) is weakening again, even among some scientists, though more frequently in the public view represented by modern mass media. A diagram, even a formula, is completely worthless, containing no useful information unless its exact context is known. And the interpretation of scientific results out of their respective (limiting) context necessarily leads to 'intellectual anarchy' and epistemological disaster. Unfortunately, the human mind has a fatal tendency

4) Two dimensions cannot provide enough 'variety' to allow the evolution of complex life forms. In four and more dimensional space, for example, planets do not have stable orbits around their suns.

5) More precisely speaking, mass and energy cause a curvature of the four dimensional space-time continuum.

to prejudicially look for 'simple answers': this is, for example, how religions are born.

My own close encounter with the irrational world of over-simplification took place a few years ago: having had my mathematical analysis of the *Voynich Manuscript* 'cipher' text published in a cryptology research journal,[6] I was almost immediately confronted by literally hundreds of interpretations and re-interpretations of my work. Even today I still occasionally receive e-mails from *soi-disant* experts, ranging from the tragicomic dreamer (who wants to discuss the lost library of Atlantis) to conspiracy theorists ("How dare you denigrate this elaborate book as a hoax?!"). Obviously, very few of them go to the trouble of looking up my original article, and most of those who do just pick a diagram or two, seeing within the curves whatever pleases their expectations and dreams. I think it is this aspect of the *Voynich Manuscript* that may really mark its importance beyond merely representing an intellectual curiosity: it appears to be of marginal historical relevance, and even if the cryptic symbols forming the text should conceal linguistic information (which, from my point of view, is very unlikely), then that text would most probably just consist of medieval magical incantations and alchemy recipes. Nevertheless, the strangely shaped empty symbols, the meaningless diagrams, do hold up a precious mirror to the nature of human reasoning.

Imagine two scholars in two distant cities, arguing about a complex diagram of unknown origin. Much as in a game of correspondence chess, they exchange short brainstorming messages containing hypotheses in the form of spontaneous ideas. Perhaps the texts may sometimes appear to be a bit disjointed: after all, neither scholar really knows how to interpret this (presumably very important) out-of-context figure, and, worrying about their respective academic reputations, they try to avoid saying something really concrete. Perhaps this aimless game finally becomes boring to one of them, but instead of frankly admitting this he orders his apprentice to simply look up arbitrary but seemingly appropriate paragraphs in an encyclopaedia, transmitting them as 'novel ideas'.

(→ PIII/021)

6) A. Schinner, *The Voynich Manuscript: Evidence of the Hoax Hypothesis*, Cryptologia 31, 2007, p. 95.

Fig. N01-02

Of course, the apprentice's easy task could also be carried out by a simple computer programme, which any student in a beginner's class for software engineering should be able to design. Is there a chance the other scholar will not notice that he is no longer communicating with an educated, intelligent, feeling human being, but is mulling over automatically generated replies instead?

Such programmes have existed almost as long as transistor-based computer hardware. Traditionally, they are called *Eliza programmes*, and it is great fun to write one. The name originates from the first 'personality mimicking software' (entitled ELIZA), which was presented in 1966 by Joseph Weizenbaum. He designed his programme to simulate the behaviour of a psychotherapist: the (astoundingly simple) algorithm examines the 'patient's' input sentences for several keywords; each of them triggers a rule that transforms the respective sentence into an appropriate reply. If a keyword cannot be found the programme returns either a randomly selected predefined phrase, or repeats previous output. Most surprisingly, extensive experiments have shown that many people are easily fooled by ELIZA into believing that they are communicating via telex machine with a real person. Obviously, this is telling us a lot about how little personality you need to successfully take up a career as a psychotherapist …

Besides other important philosophical implications[7] these experiments should be seen as a clear warning of how easily a scientific methodology may result in epistemological disaster, as soon as it becomes infiltrated by the (natural) human desire to oversimplify, and to visualise. Unfortunately, the extremely powerful pattern-matching capability of the neural networks in our brains also has a dark side: without the clear separation of perception from imagination we might come to a bad end like the scholar in Edgar Allan Poe's famous poem: *The Raven* is uttering nothing but the single word 'nevermore', which, interpreted as the revelation of a depressing truth, destroys the scholar's mind until his "soul from out that shadow that lies floating on the floor shall be lifted – nevermore!"

Perception and *imagination*[8] are the two strategies the human mind employs to map (its) 'reality'. You could also call them

7) Eliza programmes are intimately connected with the complex of problems addressing *artificial intelligence*, in particular the so-called *Turing test.*

8) These terms should be understood here in the wider sense of scientific thinking (analysis) versus empathic (artistic) description.

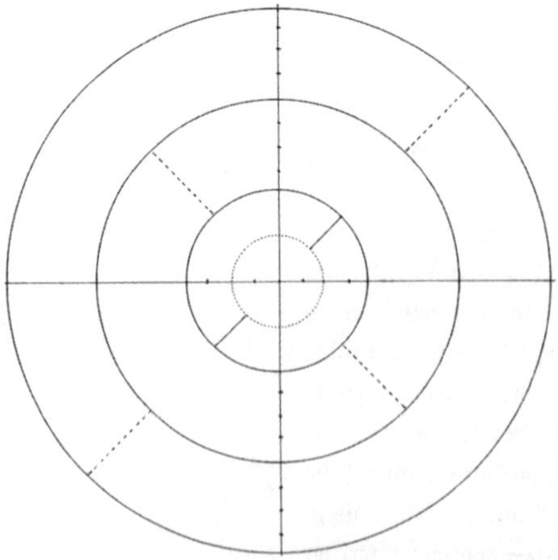

Fig. N04

science and *art*. So far we have taken a closer look at the scientific methodology, at its strengths, but also at the inherent danger of confusing hypotheses with theories, facts with interpretations. In the world of *perceptual thinking*, hypotheses – although indispensable starting points – are the unloved ancestors of theories, something you would like to reduce in number to the absolute minimum possible. Hypotheses non fingo! This stringent corset of intellectual discipline loosens rapidly as soon as you leave the field of the so-called 'hard sciences' (physics, chemistry, biology, etc.). Historians, sociologists and psychologists, for example, confuse hypotheses with facts much more commonly (contemporary psychology is as far from being science as was medieval alchemy compared to modern chemistry). Does the concept 'hypothesis' completely cease to exist when we finally enter the world of 'pure' *imaginative thinking*, the world of art?

To answer this question we first have to address another: what is art? This innocent looking three-word phrase stirs up a hornet's nest. Philosophers and artists, historians and art critics have long struggled for a 'grand unified theory of art'. Obviously, the problem of understanding art is closely connected with the enigma of human *consciousness*, since we are the only species on this planet expressly inclined to aesthetic concepts (although, most probably, all aesthetics has its distant roots in the florid mating behaviour of species reproducing sexually). As I am typing these words into my laptop, I wonder whether electronic circuits might be hardwired to be artists. Can computers, apart from technical limitations such as memory capacity or processor speed, in principle be programmed to replicate the higher functions of the human neo-cortex? Can they have *consciousness*?

The two primary answers, 'yes' and 'no', correspond to the two long-existing philosophical schools of thought, *materialism* and *dualism*: a dualist assumes an additional entity beneath the obviously visible (the connected neurons) to be responsible for our special kind of self-awareness; you may, for example, call it a soul. Consequently, no material 'man-made object' will ever be really able to replicate human consciousness. All we can ever hope to achieve is to mimic personality (as Eliza programmes do on a very primitive level).

Is the dualistic viewpoint a 'good' theory? Is it a theory at all? I do not think so. First, it confuses hypothesis with *theory* (we have already discussed the potentially disastrous consequences of this procedure): the dualist *desires* to be more than "just a lump of protein" – and postulates are constructed simply to satisfy this urge (despite the fact that there is not the least evidence to support them). Applying Occam's razor, such a hypothesis clearly has to be 'eliminated'. On the other hand, modern brain mapping already allows us to observe something of the brain's basic operational principles. Innovative theoretical models attempt to establish an understanding of consciousness as the effect of information feedback loops across different levels of abstraction, possibly even the so-called 'strange loops' involving *self-reference* of the same type that centres on the basic idea of Gödel's incompleteness theorems.[9] And, finally, contemporary ethology is rediscovering more and more key aspects of human consciousness (more or less rudimentary) in the social behaviour of animals. Do they have souls, too, perhaps 'tiny souls'?

The concepts of souls and gods (and a universe that is taking any notice of us) are part of the world of *imagination*. They are appropriate *objects* of artistic expression and cannot serve as an explanation of the principles of art. There is nothing like a divine spark 'out there' (or within us). What is art?

The oldest recorded (and, surprisingly, still widely held) view of the nature of art is Plato's *mimetic theory*: art is simply mirroring what we call 'the world' (even that, according to Plato, is only the faint shadow of the intellectually unreachable 'true world'). Consequently, art is useless. Even worse, it is potentially dangerous: deceptive, mainly concerned with sensual pleasures, easily leading to immorality, and a political threat to the common good. Plato's famous student Aristotle, obviously, was less averse to sensual pleasures: he agreed with the doctrine of reducing art to bare mimesis, while still emphasising the

9) Douglas R. Hofstadter, *I Am A Strange Loop*, Basic Books, New York, 2007.

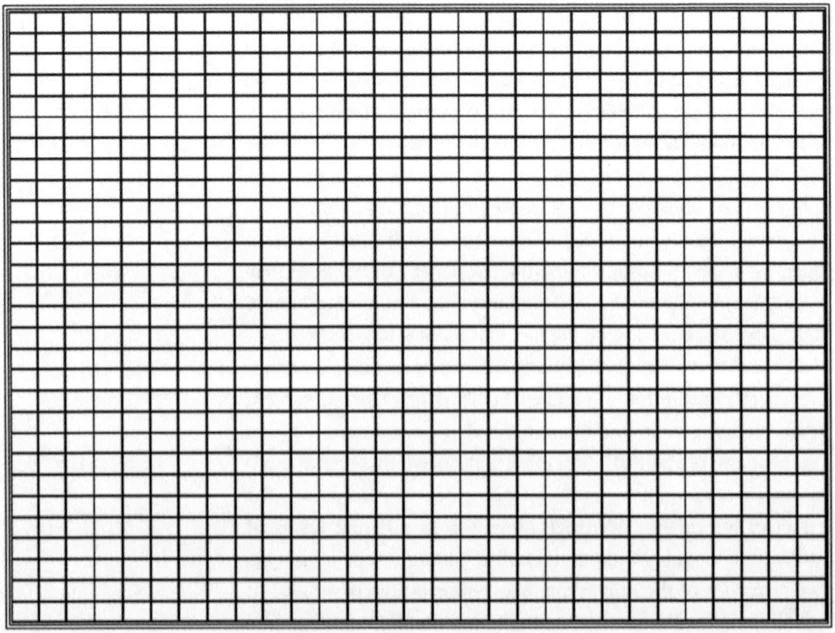

Fig. N01-01

beneficial aspects of what he called 'good art'. This, more or less, remained the common viewpoint for the next two millennia.

In 1964, the first *institutional theory* of art was outlined by Arthur Danto.[10] What is it that makes Andy Warhol's *Brillo boxes* an artwork, which hundreds of boxes stacked in grocery stores 'obviously' lack? Danto tried to solve this paradox by introducing an additional (immaterial) entity separating art from triviality: the *artistic context*.[11] The very essence of institutional art theories was cast into a famous compact formula by George Dickie: "A work of art in the classificatory sense is (1) an artefact, (2) a set of the aspects which has had conferred upon it the status of candidate for appreciation by some person or persons acting on behalf of a certain social institution (the artworld)."[12] Other art theoreticians such as Marcia Eaton[13]

10) Arthur Danto, *The Artworld*, Journal of Philosophy 61, 1964, p. 571.

11) Danto called it "the artworld".

12) George Dickie, *Art and the Aesthetic*, Cornell University Press, Ithaca, 1974.

13) Marcia Eaton, *Art and Nonart*, Associated University Presses, East Brunswick, 1983.

added historical and aesthetic criteria to this definition: the history of the production of an artwork has to "direct the viewer's attention to properties which are worth attending to."

At the end of the twentieth century the first promising attempts were made to understand art and aesthetics on a purely neurological-theoretical basis. The neurological theory of aesthetic experience by Ramachandran and Hirstein[14] formulates eight laws of artistic experience: (1) *the peak shift principle* (art captures and amplifies the essence of something; "all art is caricature"); (2) *isolation of a single visual modality* (art amplifies the limbic activation feedback); (3) *perceptual grouping*; (4) *extraction of contrast*; (5) *perceptual problem solving* (artworks are puzzling); (6) *an abhorrence of unique vantage points* (the visual cortex automatically selects the "optical interpretation" with the highest probability); (7) *metaphors*; and (8) *symmetry*.

What today must be seen as the early outline of a tentative scientific approach to the phenomenon of "art" may, or most probably will one day lead to a first-principles-based neurological description, compatible with the fundamental requirements of any true scientific theory: experimental falsifiability, and a minimal set of well-defined hypotheses. Nevertheless, some key aspects can be extracted already from the various philosophical viewpoints: art, much like any language, operates with symbols to transfer information. And, as in any language, whether natural or artificial (such as a mathematical formula), symbols *without context* are useless. That is why the proponents of institutional theories have been forced to introduce the concept of artistic context into the intellectual puzzle 'art versus non-art'. The artist (consciously or unconsciously) utilises special techniques, a particular 'language' or 'formalism', to present associative ideas about 'the world' in a stimulating, puzzling, contradictory (sometimes even provoking) way. In a wider sense, this has a strong resemblance to *proposing a hypothesis*; however, unlike hypotheses in scientific methodology, *artistic concepts* or *premises* are end points[15] of the intellectual process generating them, rather than starting points.

14) V. S. Ramachandran and W. Hirstein, *The Science of Art, Journal of Consciousness Studies* 6, 1999, p. 15.

15) Although an artwork is the end point of a particular intellectual process, it, nevertheless, may inspire other artworks, or even scientific theories. For example, the theory of quasi-crystals has drawn inspiration from the work by M. C. Escher.

A 'scientific' theory based on wildly imagined hypotheses, working with incoherent symbols, is inescapably doomed to fail. At best its results will be merely ridiculous, but if they are taken seriously, the consequences may be fatal: the simple, naïve, childlike belief that some supernatural, omnipotent entity is watching and, finally, judging our every move has already taken a heavy toll on human life. Not to mention the hecatombs yet to come. *Abyssus abyssum invocat!* How much would our species improve if at last we realised that religion is part of the world of imagination, an artwork, not at all part of the world of *perception*?

Imagine a book filled with indecipherable symbols. Could it be an artwork? Most probably the *Voynich Manuscript* 'cipher' does not conceal any interpretable clear text. Most probably the enigmatic figures are nothing more than empty puzzles that subtly catch the eye. It is an as yet unanswered question who has written the Voynich manuscript, and, in particular, why. After all, it must have taken a remarkable amount of time, not to mention the expenditure for vellum and ink. The most obvious explanation is as old as human nature: greed and fraud.

But this is not the only conceivable interpretation. In 1980, the Italian architect and industrial designer Luigi Serafini wrote and illustrated his *Codex Serafinianus*, which looks like a visual encyclopaedia of an extraterrestrial world, completely written in an incomprehensible 'language' with a strange curvilinear script. It is a comforting idea (and, to close the circle, an interesting *hypothesis*) that, perhaps, the Voynich manuscript, this fascinating, beautiful mirror to human reasoning, might also have been originally created as an *artwork*.

HYPOTHESIS #10

Wiry Fantasy

or the electronic line is also a handwriting and itself effects the overcoming of its system, which it draws, constructs and leaves: into the poetical eye, too, which has dreamed its original state of pure perception and launches itself into the dialogue as source.

Ferdinand Schmatz

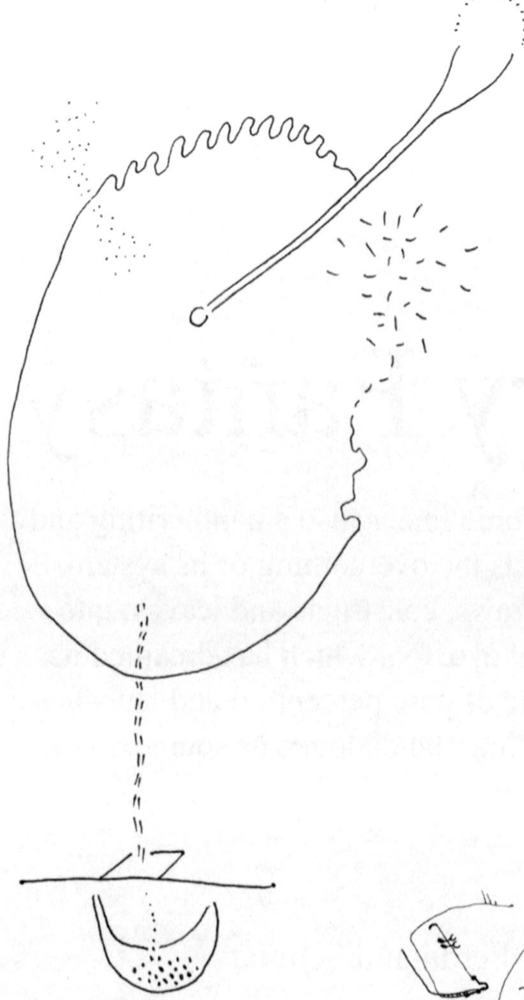

Fig. 06-16
the mouth moon
pollinates eyes
smiles

Fig. 09-08
the pollen flight
strews blossoms
the leaves seem
morsed

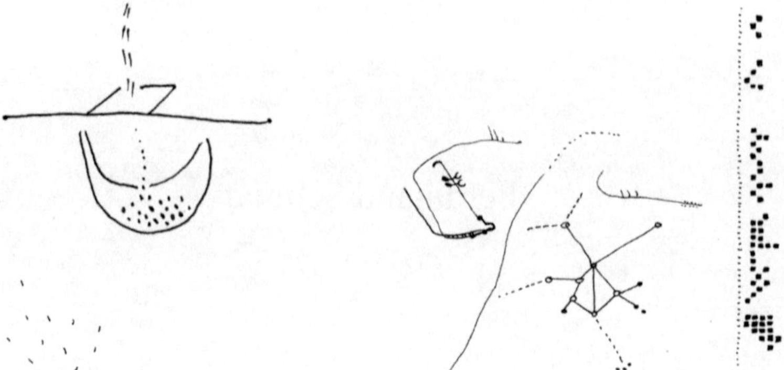

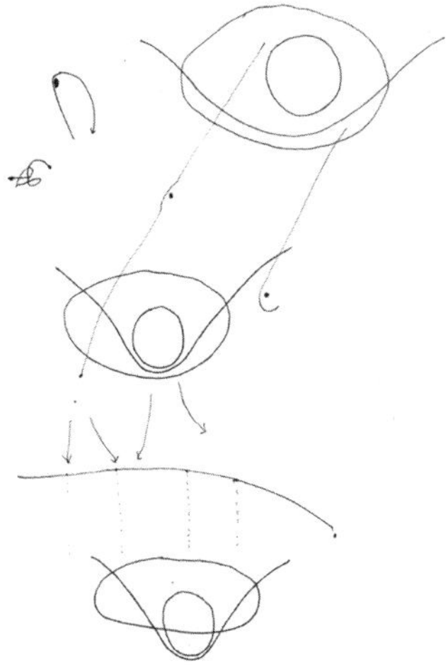

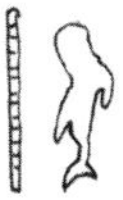

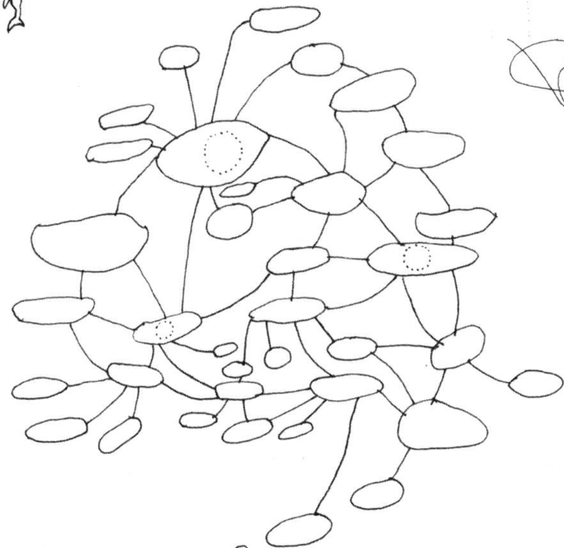

Fig. 09-17a
the head earth
balances out
the eye

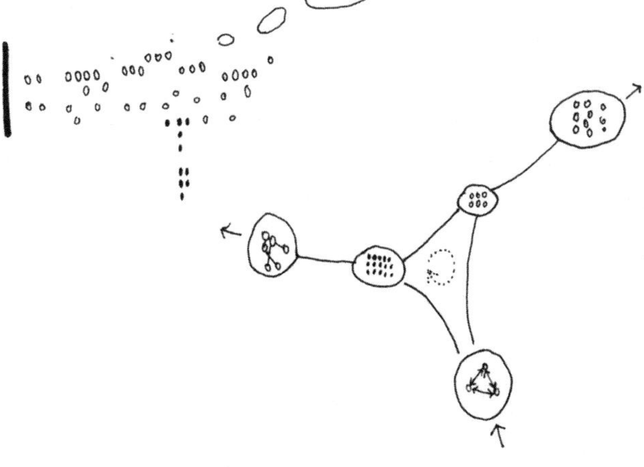

Fig. 09-11
where should it
go to
“i want
an unworkable
anarchy”

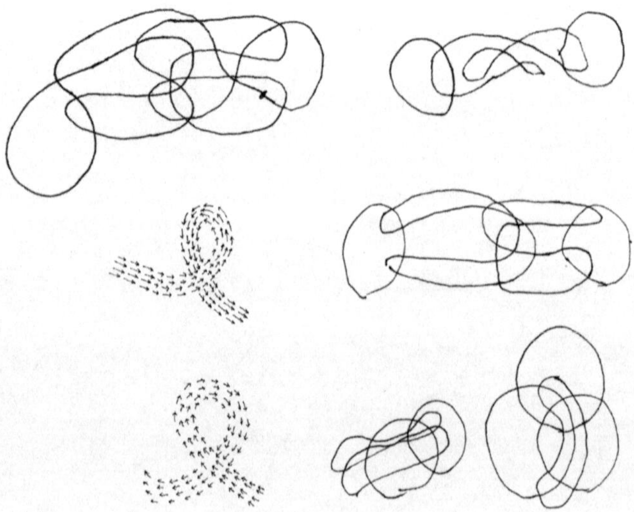

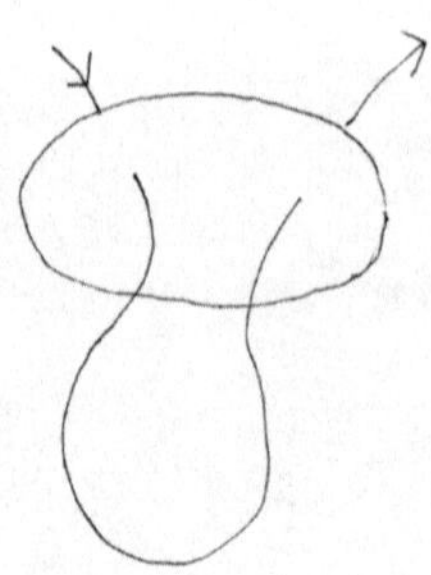

Fig. 09-15
the loop solution
brings blossoms
punctually
in
the spin binds
itself in its
self
(fading)

Fig. 09-03

one two three four
the symmetrical currency
of the careening
circles
(elipse brides)

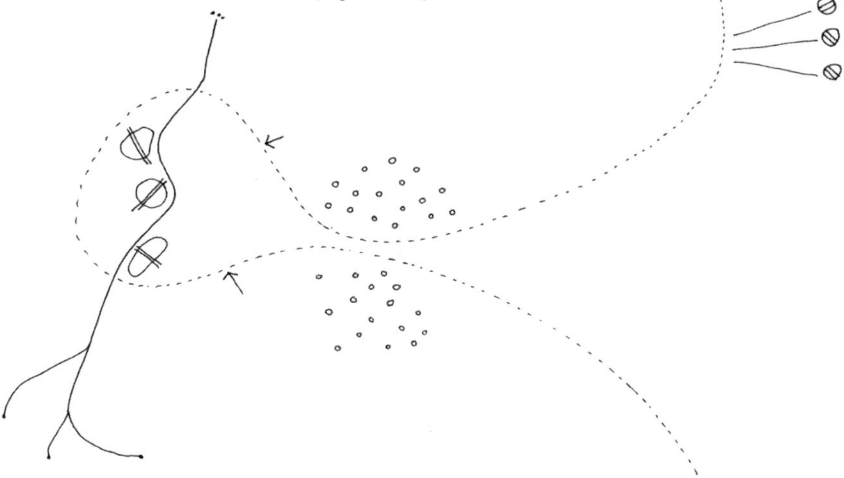

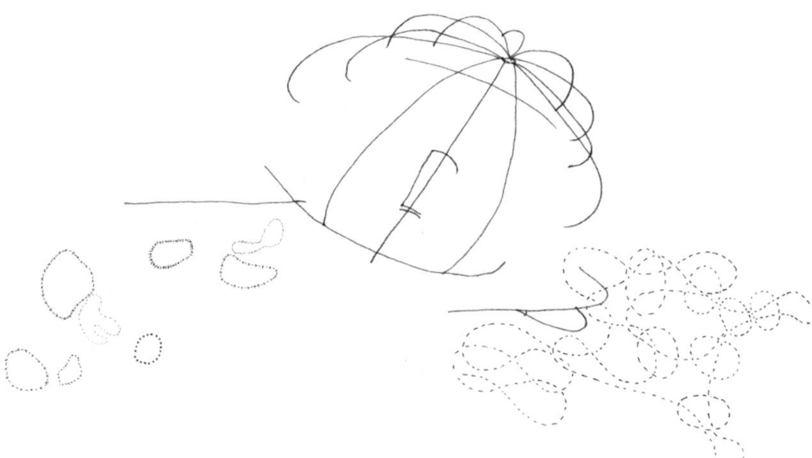

Fig. 09-05a

the core
or the bubbles
do not go into the net
of the spin

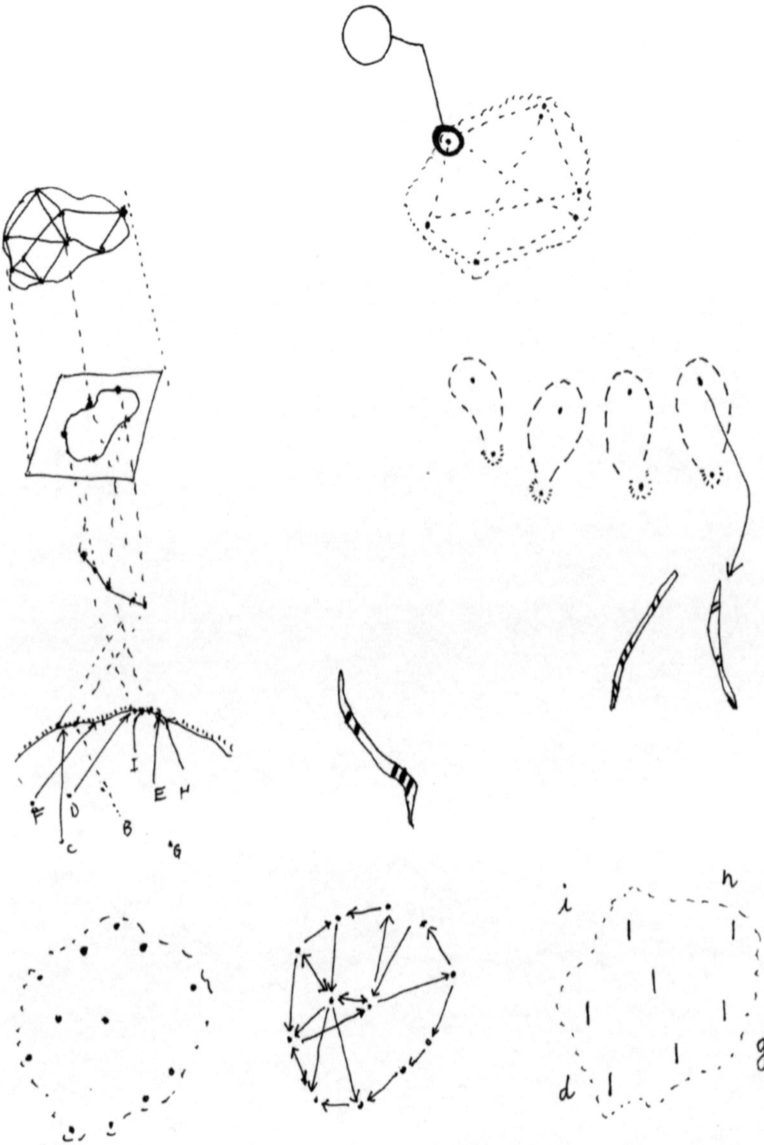

Fig. 09-07
picnic
in the open
all greet each other
the serviceable
anarchy

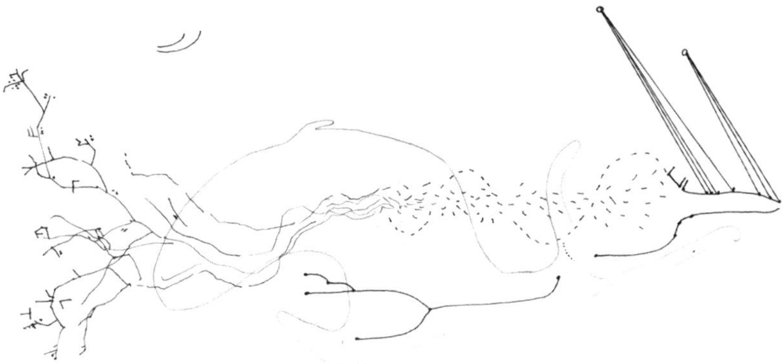

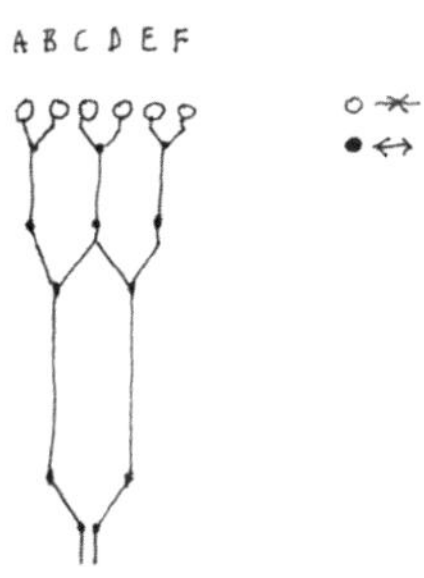

Fig. 10-08

go west
those who were left behind
are rooted loosely
in the light of the conquerors
(steel stars)

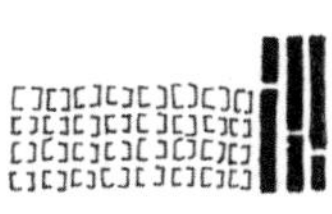

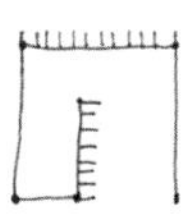

Fig. 01-29

finally at
home
the light is switched to
head eye mouth
plan the loose
anarchy
(in concert)

HYPOTHESIS #11

Reading Figures

Helmut Leder

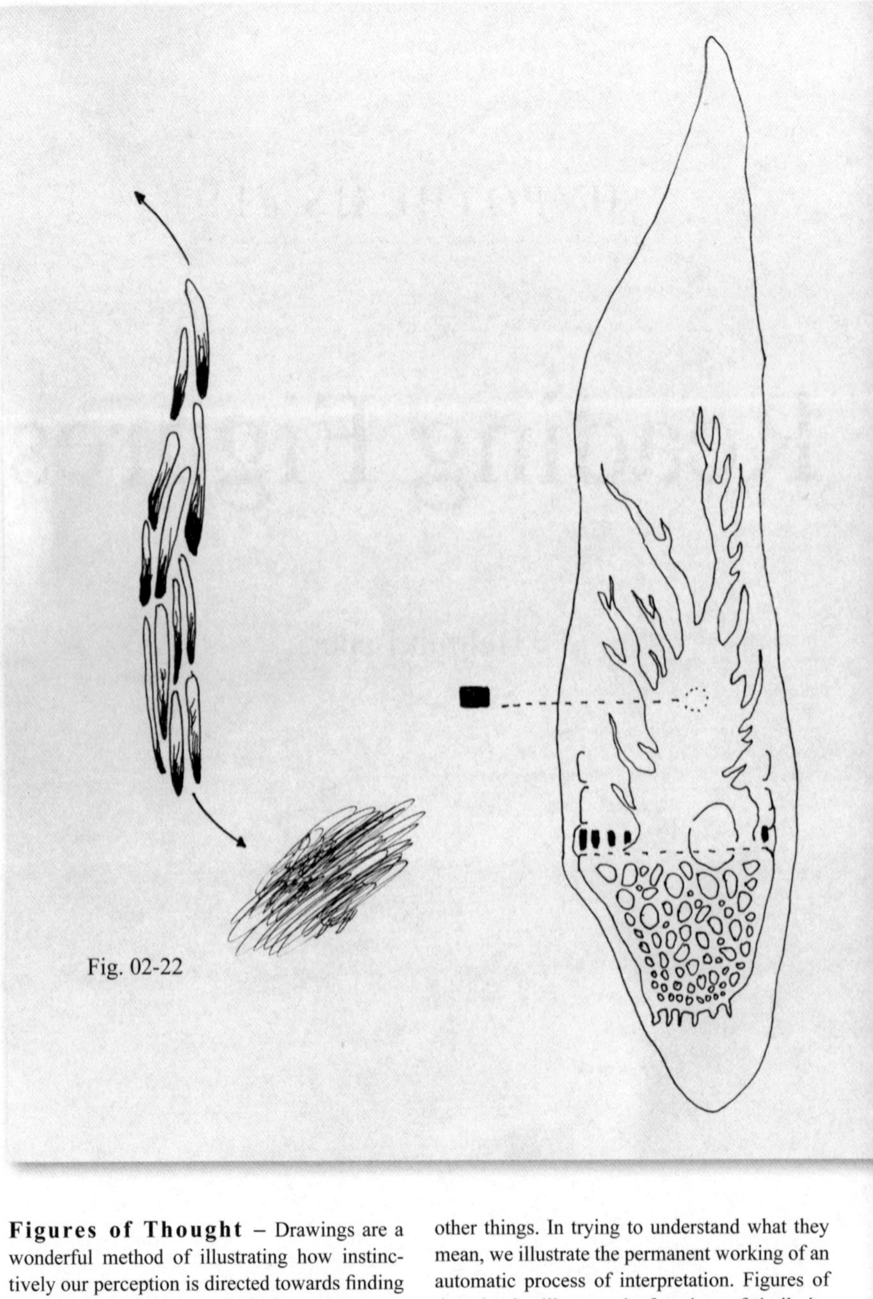

Fig. 02-22

Figures of Thought – Drawings are a wonderful method of illustrating how instinctively our perception is directed towards finding meaning in things. Each of the individual visual elements stands for something else, representing other things. In trying to understand what they mean, we illustrate the permanent working of an automatic process of interpretation. Figures of thought also illustrate the functions of similarity which we constantly use in recognising things.

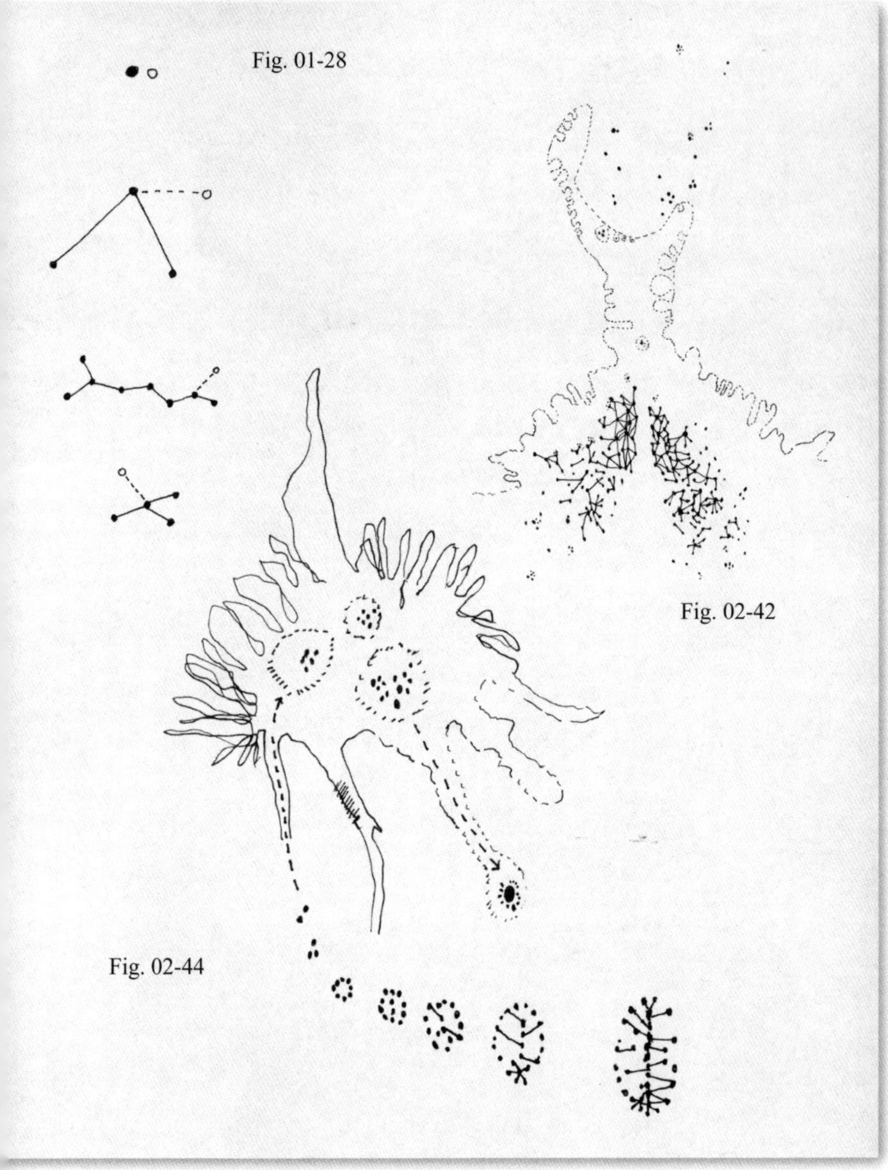

Fig. 01-28

Fig. 02-42

Fig. 02-44

Since hardly any two things look exactly alike, we have to work from similarity to recognition to test hypotheses of what an image could be. Certain rules help us to do this: natural, organic things are rarely rectangular, so that we interpret right angles and straight lines as an illustration of abstract relations. However, if the drawing can't be identified, then it seems likely to be a case of something schematic, or possibly even artistic.

HYPOTHESIS #12

Figures of Thought

The Use of Diagrams in Science and Art

Gerhard Dirmoser

The term 'figure of thought' is found in the most diverse disciplines.[1] In a sense, figures of thought unlock the toolbox of a discipline. This article is intended to explore the toolboxes of image sciences and, in particular, of diagrammatics/graphematics. In the context of research on 'diagrammatic thinking' and how diagrams are concretely implemented in drawing, the term 'figure' of thought appears in an expanded field of meaning. To begin with, I would like to briefly explain how the term 'figure of thought' came to be productive in my studies.

USE OF THE TERM IN THE DIAGRAMMETICS STUDY

The term 'figure of thought' is already found in my diagrammatics study *On the Benefits of Schematic Drawings* (2004) on the first page of the introductory chapter.[2]

For over two years, I had attempted to base my diagram collection on a manageable group of basic types. Degree of order and explicitness of order were defined as the coordinates of order. Then the term 'forms of order' developed from this and subsequently the term 'figure of order'.

Quotation from the study: "These non-mimetic forms of order can be seen in the most diverse questions of content as a foundation from the perspective of representation technique. From the perspective of content, they are generally quite neutral, even though certain content-defined figures of thought have proven useful in terms of an ordering technique within the framework of application."

From the 'forms of order' to the 'figure of thought': It was certainly the development of the diagram with the title 'Form Questions – as Questions of Order' (August 2004)[3] that provided

1) Several variations to exemplify this include: epistemological figure of thought, philosophical cognitive theory figure of thought, hermeneutic figure of thought, difference theory figure of thought, figure of thought in Modernism, Kantian figure of thought, psychoanalytical figure of thought, … etc.

2) www.servus.at/kontext/digramm

3) http://gerhard_dirmoser.public1.linz.at/art/Formfragen_Denkfiguren.pdf

the background for the choice of the term 'figure of thought'.[4] In this diagram (on the form question), an attempt was made to compile all the figures of order that can also be grasped well in verbal terms. These include, for instance: row, network, tree, rhizome, matrix, album, atlas, collage, … etc.

The central idea in this collection of terms was that it had to deal with patterns or figures that could also be implemented in drawing (or gesturally), in other words, illustratively. Hence there was no room in this collection for metaphors, or they were only allowed as an additional reading. Quotation from the study: "In a further diagram *(Form Questions – as Questions of Ordering)*, an attempt was made to arrange a collection of illustrative figures of thought. In this way, it is possible to show how deeply diagrammatic figures of order in thinking are also verbally anchored." In the quoted excerpts from the study, one thus finds the formulations 'content-determined figures of thought' and 'illustrative figures of thought'. Even though the diagrammatic patterns of order were intended to be open to any content and were therefore consistently imagined a-semantically, it was clear from the beginning that, for example, in treatments of politics of power terms like hierarchy and centrality were usually visualised with tree structures and concentric circle forms. It is important to take these content-related preferences and special application contexts into consideration from the beginning, in order to learn to assess spontaneous associations and application advantages. This approach is to be covered in more detail elsewhere in *Rhetorics of Graphical Elements*.[5]

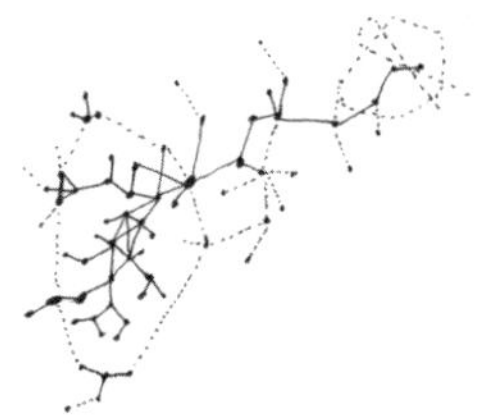

Fig. DF-R0987

(→ Pl/10)

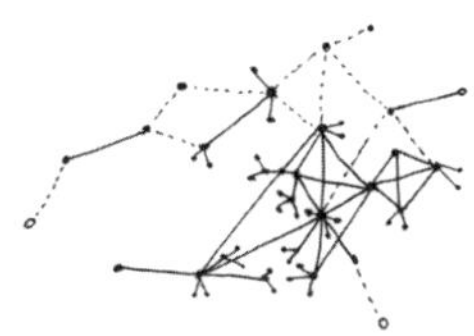

Fig. DF-A2231

A closer analysis of the last two quotation sentences indicates that in these initial considerations in 2004, the relationship between 'illustrative figures of thought' and 'diagrammatic figures of order' was not yet really clarified.

The majority of forms assembled on the diagram deal with designations of figures of order. Clarification is still needed on how figures of thought are related to the figures of order.

4) In her letter from 24 August 2004, Astrit Schmidt-Burkhardt commented on this diagram with the words "elementary … fundamental … inexorable", and she continued: "form questions/figures of thought, these must been seen together." From my response, it is clear that I owe the term 'figure of thought' to this commentary.

5) Gerhard Dirmoser, *Rhetorik der graphischen Elemente*, http://gerhard_dirmoser.public1.linz.at/FU/strukturale_Rhetorik_V3.pdf, 2009.

TERMS OF THOUGHT IN NETWORKED FORM

In addition to the diagrammatic studies, there is also another reason why I am so fascinated by the concept of the 'figure of thought'. From 1996-1998 I developed a collection of concepts of thought and assembled them in a networked form (with 7000 edges) on thematic plateaus. Since 2004, this networked structure has also been available (thanks to Pajek software) as an integral diagram[6]. This attempt at conceptual clarification led to a paradoxical insight: with every further finding (600 were found in book titles alone), the verb 'thinking' dissolved into increasingly detailed aspect variations. What ultimately remained was the fascination with the semantic range of the adjective-supported field of meaning and the certainty that that we do not really know, even in the age of AI research, how thinking could be grasped in the operative sense. Therefore, the question arises for me as to whether the concept of the 'figure of thought' now presents a reasonable chance of coming closer to 'diagrammatic thinking', or whether we have again wandered into the mists of a gigantic field of meaning.

(→ PI/08)

FIGURES OF THINKING IN RHETORICS

Perhaps design theory will help us develop a pragmatic approach: in his study *Visual Verbal Rhetorics*, in the section *Rhetorical Figures*, Gui Bonsiepe introduces the concepts 'word figures' and 'figures of thinking'. "The defining characteristic of a rhetorical figure is – according to conventional understanding – the deviation from normal usage to increase the communicative effectiveness. The figures can be divided into two classes:

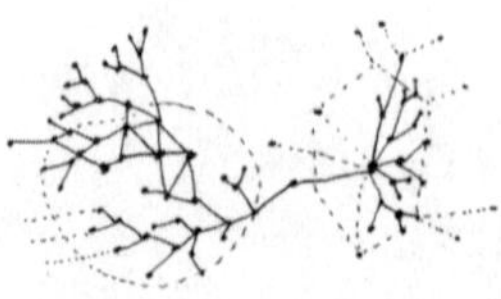

Fig. DF-C4443

- word figures that relate to the meaning of a word or the positions of words in a sentence;
- figures of thinking that relate to the forming and organisation of information."

6) http://gerhard_dirmoser.public1.linz.at/art/ARS_denken_Pajek_1_2.pdf; The diagram includes concepts such as: networking thinking, rhizomatic thinking, system-oriented thinking, ordering thinking, geometrical thinking, logical thinking, typographical thinking, topological thinking, conceptual thinking, pictorial thinking … and also the diagrammatic thinking that is to be found in this collection: http://gerhard_dirmoser.public1.linz.at/FU/Knoten_Denknetz.xls

In rhetorics the ‘figure of thought’ serves to structure the thought process. These figures of thought are recognizable by a certain syntax. In his compact representation of the concept of the figure of thinking, Bonsiepe manages to make it diagrammatically useful through the aspect of organisation. In addition to the ‘figure of thought’, the concept of the ‘figure of thinking’ is also available to us. It thus remains to be clarified how the structuring of the thought process (i.e. the figure of thinking) can be reflected on paper in concrete application as an ‘ordering figure’.

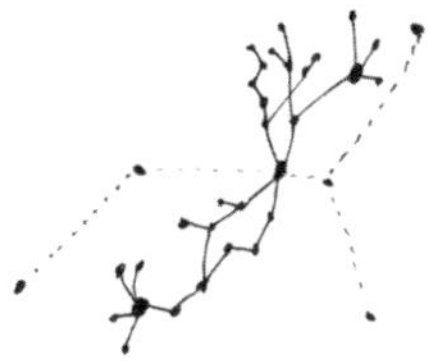

Fig. DF-R2224
(→ PI/10)

Of course, everything would be much simpler, if we could already formulate (with C. S. Peirce) what is to be understood as ‘diagrammatic thinking’ in detail. For now, however, we must make do with the analysis of forms of the figures of order that can be grasped (on paper). In his formulation, “figures of thinking that relate to the forming and organisation of information”, Bonsiepe elegantly evades the question of implementation as well. This relatedness of the figure of thinking – to concrete organisation (as a pattern of order) – is not explained in more detail.

FIGURA, FIGURE, FIGURATION

The concept of the ‘figure’ or ‘figuration’ and the case of conceptual thinking are similarly colourful. A first insight into this is conveyed by the essays in the book *Figure and Figuration – Studies on Perception and Knowledge*, 2007.

In his article *The Iconic Figuration*[7], Gottfried Boehm focuses in the introduction on the flexibility of figuration in relation to form and schema: “The new concept of figuration reinforces aspects that are already found in the old word ‘figura’, first found in the 2nd century BC in the writings of Terence.

In his seminal analysis, E. Auerbach investigated Greek preconcepts and their further semantic development until the end of the Middle Ages. Along with the plastic, he especially emphasises the dominant flexibility of the figura. They are clearly distinguished from statically conceived concepts like ‘forma’, including the Greek word formations ‘schema’, ‘morphé’, ‘typos’ or ‘eidos’.

7) Gottfried Boehm, *Die ikonische Figuration*, in: *Figur und Figuration: Studien zu Wahrnehmung und Wissen*, Fink, 2007.

He could not even have dreamed of the current rediscovery of this latency and its eminent rise. This is because it is based on specifically modern or postmodern premises, most recently on the topicality of the performative. This also circumscribes the orbit, in which the most recent debates about figuration have moved." This aspect of flexibility is, in any case, helpful for further clarification.[8]

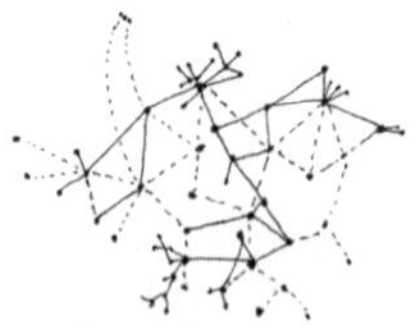

Fig. 22-R6565 (→ PI/10)

Diagrammatic 'Figurations' and 'Figural Means'

The concept of the 'figure' (as 'figure of thought') cannot easily be grasped in the central art historical texts on diagrammatics either. The formulations leave unanswered, whether a mental figuration or a drawn/painted figuration is involved. Compare this with the statement from S. Bogen and F. Thürlemann[9]: "Because diagrams conjoin together linguistic and figural means, …." Similarly H. U. Reck: he regards 'diagrams as figurative organisation'.

Figura as a Means of Expressing an Assemblage of Thinking

A. Patschovksy's approach of understanding diagrams as a "medium of the intellect" suggests the idea of reading the 'figura' as a figure of thought. Yet Joachim of Fiore brings the concept back to the material level of the drawing paper again: A. Patschovsky[10] on the image world of Joachim of Fiore's diagrams: "The focus is more on the question of the specific 'cultural dimension' of Joachim's mental construction, which takes shape in the diagrammatic media form typical for Joachim. Joachim himself calls this means of expressing a complex assemblage of thinking the figura. What remains to be clarified is therefore what the diagram as a medium of the intellect provides for conveying Joachim's construct of history."

8) Another form of flexibility is addressed in the picture caption for the project *Memoseum* (N. Gansterer, 2009): "The Vienna Technical Museum, rearranged according to 'figures of thought in the process of their hardening'." This turn of expression is based on a formable or fluid figure.

9) Steffen Bogen, Felix Thürlemann, *Jenseits der Opposition von Text und Bild – Überlegungen zu einer Theorie des Diagramms und des Diagrammatischen* in: *Die Bilderwelt der Diagramme Joachims von Fiore, in: Die Bildwelt der Diagramme Joachims von Fiore. Zur Medialität religiös- politischer Programme im Mittelalter*, Patschovsky, Alexander (ed.), Thorbecke, Stuttgart, 2003. S. 1-22.

10) Alexander Patschovsky, *Die Bilderwelt der Diagramme Joachims von Fiore: Zur Medialität religiös-politischer Programme im Mittelalter*, Thorbecke, 2003.

Graphical Figures

In this consideration, I principally want to avoid mixing together questions of the 'figure of thought' with a breakdown of basic types of diagrams. However, Ch. Meier's use of language (on 'figuration') makes it seem meaningful to quote this (one) typisation approach from Medieval diagrammatics.

Ch. Meier *The Quadrature of the Circle – Diagrammatics of the 12th Century as a Form of Symbolic Thinking and Representation*[11]: "Based on formal criteria, basically four types of diagrammatic figurations can be distinguished:

1. Geometrically and mathematically defined figures, such as circle, rectangle, triangle, cube, sphere, etc.
2. Figures that are natural or man-made objects, but can be stylised into diagram forms due to specific forms and characteristics, such as tree, ladder, wheel, wagon, building, human form, cherub, etc.
3. Figures that assemble a selection of concepts and relate them to one another with the help of a regular graphical form, i.e. as relational figuration, e.g. Ten Commandments or ages of life in a circle, four or twelve winds in a quadrant, etc.
4. Graphical Figures, in which logical operations or relations are illustrated."

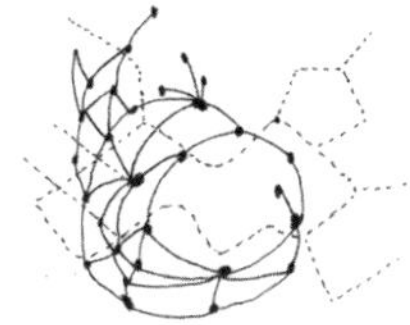

Fig. DF-K8922

ON THE RELATIONSHIP OF THE FIGURE OF THOUGHT TO THE FORM OF ORDER

To avoid further complicating the issue, I will simply assume (with G. Boehm) that the (dynamic) figure of thought to be mentally carried out cannot only be a (static) form of order. The figure of thought thus becomes an operative figure of process that is applied in a (diagrammatic) performance. The illustrativeness of a figure of thought can be grasped in different ways. I will start from operations that can be executed in space (or spatially imagined), whether through drawing, mentally tracing, mentally drafting or algorithmically simulated (shifted to virtual space, so to speak). This basically involves a strange experiment: To assess the illustrativeness of a thinking process

11) Christel Meier, *Die Quadratur des Kreises – Die Diagrammatik des 12. Jahrhunderts als symbolische Denk- und Darstellungsform,* in: *Die Bilderwelt der Diagramme Joachims von Fiore*, Thorbecke, 2003.

that is hard to grasp (= not illustrative), we shift this process (to the outside) to a piece of paper and now observe this decelerated thinking process in a drawn implementation. In a sense, we watch ourselves over our own shoulder while 'thinking in drawing'. Cf. C. S. Peirce[8]: "In his diagrams he sees means for slowing down, controlling and revealing the motion of thinking."

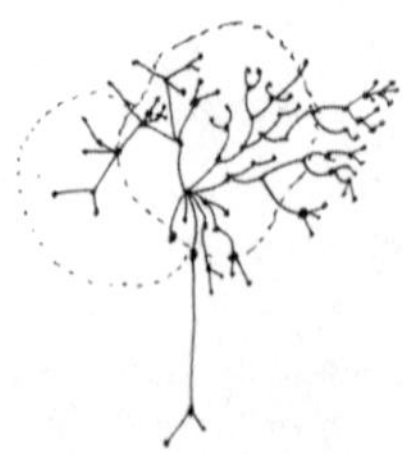

Fig. DF-D4450

Figures of thought can be located in different layers of abstraction. I do not want to start here from mathematically abstract operations of thought or those that can be followed purely verbally, but rather only include formulations that can also be grasped in a drawn implementation as a concrete description of the operation (or description of the procedure). At the same time, familiar entities (such as framework, relations, fields, cuts, knots …) should be addressed to enable an illustrative implementation or mental visualisation. The use or application of these figures of thought (as specified earlier) thus leads to forms that can be grasped (in drawing).

(→ Folding Map)

What does this mean for the study cited in the beginning? The concrete result forms (i.e. order forms, order shapes, order figures, order formations or order patterns) are assembled in the diagram study *Form Questions – as Questions of Ordering*. The forms named in the diagram are the result of operatively applied figures of thought. In their application, or as they are captured in drawing, these figures of thought lead to diagrams. This is also congruent with A. Reichert's approach: "… It is the reality of movements of thought and figures of thought. They can be recorded in diagrams …"

Figures of thought are also applied in the visualisation of measurement data in the conception (and programming) of measurement arrangements. The (measurement data) graphs resulting in the course of measuring or simulating can be called data figures. In general, the figures of thought applied can no longer be directly comprehended in these data figures. I think the field is now sufficiently prepared that a set of figures of thought can be discussed in detail.

Thanks to A. Schmidt-Burkhardt, S. Krämer, D. Mersch, E. Schürmann, D. Offenhuber, G. Hasenhütl, K. Mayer, A. Reichert, S. Bogen and N. Gansterer.

COLLECTION OF
Figures of Thought

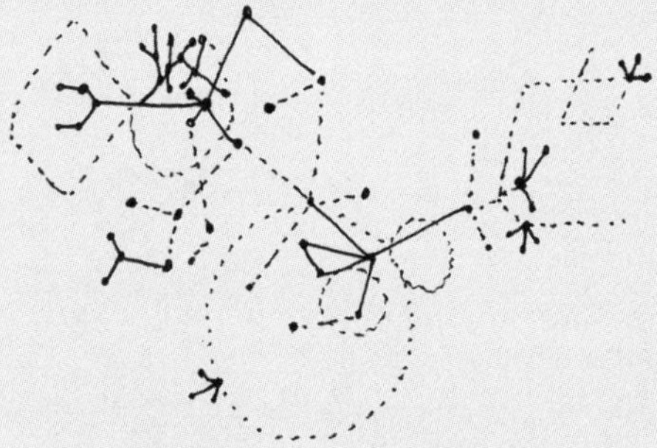

Gerhard Dirmoser

(→ This collection is related to PI/08)

A-semantic Relationality
as a Figure of Thought
(G. Dirmoser, D. Mersch, G. Kubler)
In analyzing diagrammatic and graphemic formations, it was previously very fruitful to take a-semantic positions for as long as possible. It is only in this way that the structural aspects come into view which are too often covered up by semiotic/symbolic approaches. G. Kubler: "Structures can be perceived independently from meanings."

Blurred Forms as a Figure of Thought
(G. Gamm, W. Ulrich, P. Garnier)
In some technical/natural science disciplines, fog-like structures are studied and visualised. This involves the visualisation of density relations and the calculation of artificial entities by smoothing or calculating artificial surfaces. In the course of considering these transient forms, it becomes clear that these dynamic, fluid, fog-like structures can facilitate key questions in terms of perception. Briefly outlined: Our perception evinces a tendency to 'produce' forms. Every 'correlation' prompts us to see forms. Our perception evinces a tendency to 'spatially comprehend' visual offers. In detail, see the experimental arrangements described by G. Bateson.

Cellular Setup as a Figure of Thought
See: **Systemic Network / Cellular Setup**
as a Figure of Thought

Combination Mechanisms
as a Figure of Thought
(R. Lullus, A. Kircher, C. Alexander, G. W. Leibniz)
Olaf Breidbach: Athanasius Kircher developed "... the principles of an art of combination, which is to be found through the depiction of all possible references of the basic terms he found for describing the world." Even before Athanasius Kircher, it was Raimundus Lullus in his *Ars Magna*, who laid the foundation for an *ars combinatoria*, which was consequently taken up by others, including G. W. Leibniz in his *Dissertatio de Arte Combinatoria*. Leibniz wanted to create (following Rene Descartes) an alphabet of human thinking. For the field of architectural design, Christopher Alexander developed a 'pattern language', which as an elementary system was intended to serve the parameterisation of every kind of useful architecture. This concept inspired computer scientists to develop object-oriented programming languages and database concepts.

Complex Knots as a Figure of Thought
(J. Lacan, M. Epple)
A very special concept of knots is pursued within the framework of knot topology. Knots are found visualised in specialist literature, which belong to the same knot group or are topologically equivalent, but which are visually dissimilar to a degree that an amateur can find no basis for comparison and becomes more uncertain about the form question as well. For details, see Moritz Epple: *The Emergence of Knot Theory*. From the view of the form question, we can expand the list of rows, chains, trees and networks with topological knots, plaits and stitch structures, even though they often only serve to visualise the theme of 'complexity' as such in concrete diagram application. (→ PI/05)

Constellations of Elementary Forms
as a Figure of Thought
(R. Descartes)
Descartes' form theory is the foundation for his theory of matter. See: C. Zittel *Theatrum philosophicum*. A highly contemporary form of the treatment of visual data is described in Bela Julesz' *Texton Theory*. Through the application of elementary primal text fragments, any amount of image data can be transferred to contour drawings. These algorithms also make it possible to calculate spatial constellation through lines of flight following the calculation of object contours.

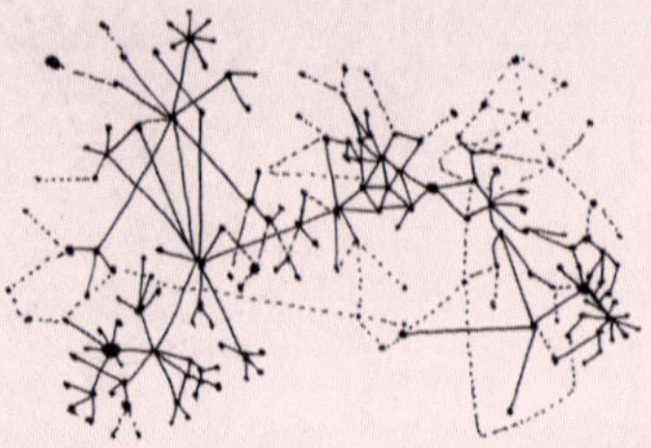

Fig. DF-S4587

Constellations of Four Elements
as a Figure of Thought
(Empedocles / four-element theory)
The semantic exception (to the a-semantic limitation rule) is listed here to represent many other figures charged with the history of culture. This figure has been used (independently from content) in countless variations.

Contact Relations as a Figure of Thought
(G. Dirmoser)
Topology as contact relations: "I first realised the power of the contact view in treating the topology concepts. Through the analysis of foldings, I noticed that the concept of 'contact' (or 'touching') can be considered as the counter-pole to 'interstitiality' (contact thus as an extreme case of interstitiality). In topology, the 'touch' relationship is also addressed as 'meet'. 'Touch' also forms the founda-

tion for 'connectedness'. Overlaying, superimposing and permeating, in other words 'overlap' and 'cross' are also based on touch or contact. This also applies to many cases of encasing, as long as the casing touches what is encased."

Contextuality as a Figure of Thought
See: **Sense of Situation / Contextuality** as a Figure of Thought

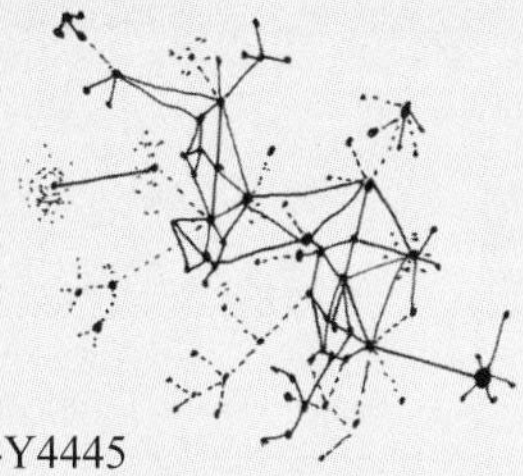

Fig. DF-Y4445

Curve Character as a Figure of Thought
(G. Lynn, G. W. Leibniz)
Since continual lines and complexly curved planes do not (may not) have any instability at their disposal, the question arises of how "continual correlation" can be used in terms of techniques of representation. Here it should be briefly mentioned that maxima, minima, zero crossings, turning points, curvatures (as a character of the curve), saddle points, etc. have a number of things to offer for scientific visualisations. Looking at the 'curves discussion' in mathematics, the view of folds (and clothoids) becomes even more fascinating. The first derivation of differentiation provides the minima and maxima of continual implementations. The second derivation of differentiation provides the turning points. The third derivation enables grasping the character of the curve. This means that there is a powerful approach to the view of turning points and clothoids that can be mathematically described.

The Cut as a Figure of Thought
(Relations of overlaps)
(B. Nieslony, G. Dirmoser)
This approach involves grasping diagrammatics and graphematics as the art of cutting (this approach covers topology and projection). "It is not the topological detail observation that first makes it clear that the view of cutting has something to offer for diagrammatics. When different media come together (touch, overlap or permeate one another), then visually comprehensible borderline processes occur. Purposely placed framework positionings and cuts mark an inside and outside. With virtual cuts one imagines landscapes dug out and marks each position as a contour line. Or one imagines the contour lines as marking a water table (as though a river were flooding a valley)."

Cybernetic Operative Connections
as a Figure of Thought
(S. Krämer)
Sybille Krämer writes in her thesis paper *Travesties of Cybernetics* ...: "Just as the early modern quantification is unimaginable without the conjunction of scripturality and visualisation (of the invisible: e.g. null), cybernetics is rooted in the conjunction of diagrammatics and visualisation (of the invisible, e.g. the black box). What the lacuna made representable through visualisation means for early modernity (vanishing point, central perspective, null, vacuum), is disruption, white noise for the cybernetic flow diagrams of communication. Cybernetics is thus also a field of realisation of the – as yet still unrecognised and neglected – role of the diagrammatic. Can cybernetics be reconstructed as diagrammatology?"

Data Physiognomies
as a Figure of Thought
In conjunction with the complex curved smooth forms, it is meaningful to speak of physiognomies. Our perception tends to grasp physiognomies as expressive entities. This results in issues that are interesting for scientific visualisations (e.g. the emotional effectiveness of data figures and the aesthetic consequences of colour attribution).

Detailing as a Figure of Thought
(W. Pichler) ("figures of the details")
Wolfram Pichler addresses "discontinuities that found meaning", which provide starting points for semantic interpretations in complex images. He describes the etymological connections between 'cut' and 'detail' in a way that is diagrammatically informative. See his article *Details of the Image* in: *What Falls out of the Picture – Figures of Detail in Art and Literature*

The Development of Graphematics
as a Figure of Thought
(side by side with diagrammatics)
In conjunction with atmospheric studies, through articles by Hans-Jörg Reinberger I stumbled across the concept of 'graphematics', for which the background is found in Derrida's grammatology. Rheinberger's articles made it clear then that diagrammatics (and also my own diagram collection) has hardly anything to add in relation to natural sciences and technical disciplines – in other words for the field of 'technical images'. In December 2005 I made an initial attempt to place graphematics alongside diagrammatics. On a starting point diagram (for a lecture

in Vienna) I formulated the oppositions “dia(gram)/vs/graph”, “discrete/vs/analogue” and “striated/vs/smooth”. This means that the text *1440 – The Smooth and the Striated* by G. Deleuze and F. Guattari stood for this division or opposition from the beginning.

The Diagram as a Figure of Thought

If grasping ‘the image as a figure of thought’ succeeds (at *eikones* in Basel), then this also resolves the question of the extent to which a diagram can be considered a figure of thought.

Dimension Reduction as a Figure of Thought

(D. Offenhuber, S. Krämer)

Two-dimensional visualisations suffice for many questions. Every mathematical representation that starts from more than three dimensions must be reduced in the spatial/surficial visualisation to two or three dimensions. In dynamic simulations or filmic representation (including animation) the dimension of temporality can be taken into consideration as the fourth dimension in the visualisation. Since most media interfaces are implemented as surfaces, the third dimension is only evident through the standpoint (or perspective) of the virtual camera or through the lines of flight (vanishing point) resulting from the respective projection. See also: **Transplanal Images as a Figure of Thought**

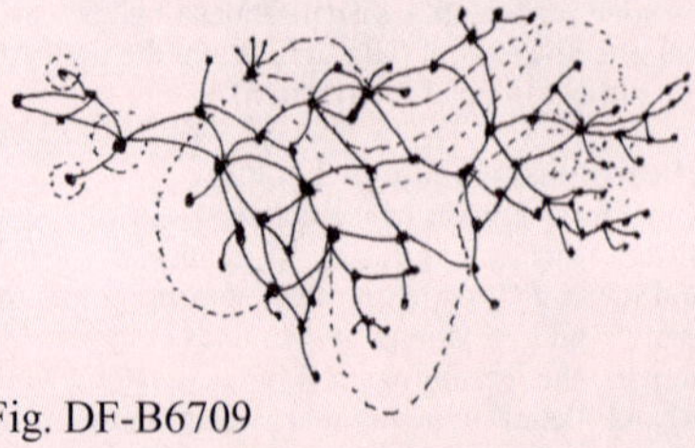

Fig. DF-B6709

Display Gesture as a Figure of Thought

(G. Dirmoser)

The concept of the ‘display gesture’ indicates possibilities for how the concept of the “rhetorical gesture” could be understood in the field of diagrammatics. Display gestures are characterised in that they can largely be applied in a way neutral to content (i.e. a-semantically). The communicative contribution is limited to indicating that potentially relevant contents are conveyed at a certain place. This gesture can only be effective, if it is able to prevail in visually complex situations. These gestures must therefore detach themselves (from their surroundings), jump out, so to speak. They must get in the way, come into view, capture the gaze, neutralise the surroundings or physically cover them up. These pure display gestures thus serve to convey contents, but without supplying a contribution to content themselves. They are an interface, or they point to available contents. These display gestures mark a framework situation or can also function as frames themselves in their physical form. (→ PI/09b)

To Draw a Distinction as a Figure of Thought

(G. Spencer-Brown, P. Maynard)

Spatial Differentiations (I) (→ PIII/02i)

In the study *Laws of Form*, G. Spencer-Brown develops a logical notation that makes it possible to think of logical operations in a plane. His logic is based on a special form of bracketing, but also includes diagrams for complex dynamic processes (demonstrated with the example of a modular function). See also: Patrick Maynard *Drawing Distinctions – The Varieties of Graphic Expression*. Critical commentary from D. Mersch in *Knowledge in Images*: “It is not distinction in George Spencer-Brown’s sense nor ‘observation’ in Niklas Luhmann’s sense that is the central theme of diagrammatics, but rather *deixis*. Form, appearance (*eidos*) and *deixis* interplay mutually.”

Energetic Mapping as a Figure of Thought

(G. Widmer, P. Gallison, G. Deleuze)

The studies by Peter Gallison, Lorraine Daston and H.-J. Rheinberger showed that most studies of diagrammatics still have little to offer for the view of natural sciences. A starting point is provided by Deleuze with his term of ‘singularity’. This concept of ‘singularity’ indicated that my formulations and questions were still too strongly oriented to conventional visual manifestations. Through the concept of singularities it became more easily possible to include sound events and to take energetic events into consideration, which are not based on photons (i.e. the most diverse imaging technologies and sensor types). This brought issues of data transformation into focus, and subsequently also the discussion from Hans-Jörg Rheinberger, who does not regard certain visualisations as belonging to the class of images. With the example of his music analyses, Gerhard Widmer was able to most clearly convey what the future of a sub-symbolic (energetic) analysis of complex dynamic processes and their graphematic characterisation could look like. “Complex procedures are available in the natural sciences to measure the most diverse energetic singularities (light occurrences, occurrences of quantum objects, radioactivity, sound occurrences, etc.) as well. The visualisation approaches are then based on translating ‘energetic singularities’ into ‘form singularities’. Here there is a translation of the different energetic occurrences (e.g. of the electron) into spatial positions (or probabilities of stay) or into the ‘occurrence format’ of photons (i.e. into frequency fields of light [and thus also into colour manifestations, among others]), and possibly into form singularities simulated with software techniques. The transformation procedures used are based on the respective mathematics field and are implemented as software and measurement hardware in complex research machines. Here I can only refer to Peter Gallison's writing and the relevant literature of the various 'imaging procedures' (e.g. magnetic resonance tomography or nuclear magnetic resonance tomography)."

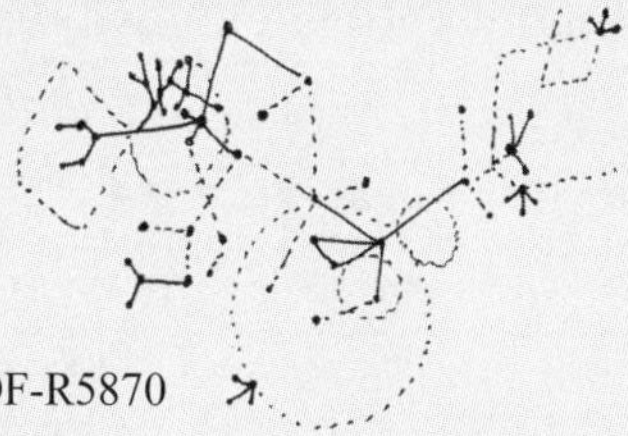

Fig. DF-R5870
(→ PI/10)

Family Similarity as a Figure of Thought
(L. Wittgenstein, A. Warburg)
Clusterings are used to call attention to the similarities of presented elements. The different partial assemblies (of the ensemble of order) respectively show groups of elements, which are mutually similar. These kinds of assemblies of similar elements are often apparent at first glance – we immediately recognise the motif of the assembly, in other words, the aspects on which the assembly is based. The maximum range of 'visually implicit attribution' can be studied through Aby Warburg's *Mnemosyne Atlas*. At first glance, his lapidary photo arrangements on the surface provided by the display surface simply seem to be saving space. It is only at a closer look at the pictures that we recognise that the composition of the pictures in each panel depends on certain questions. The knowledgeable observer recognises the correlation of the pictures as a consciously set context. The pictures mutually explain one another. Warburg himself visualised the respectively relevant correlation with threads of yarn in the course of expert discussions. His network of thoughts also became explicit in visual form in this way. It should be mentioned here that Warburg realised drawn networks of concepts on overview pages, so he was quite familiar with networking techniques. The smooth transition from cluster structures to network structures can be shown very well with Warburg. The display order in the Warburg Library also follows the principles of order described here.

Field-like Correlation as a Figure of Thought
(G. Dirmoser, D. Offenhuber)

Field-like Between as a Figure of Thought
(V. Flusser)
The point of this mental exercise is to imagine every situative correlation (of real-world objects) as visualised field lines. On this, cf. also the visualisations of the William Forsythe Dance Company. See also: Nicole Haitzinger *Choreography as a Figure of Thought – An Attempt at a More Complex Elucidation of the Concept*. (→ PII/09a-d)

Field-like Relations of Meaning / Field of Meaning as a Figure of Thought
(V. Flusser, F. de Saussure, S. Krämer)
Such was the use of diagrams in art around 1900 – here both Duchamp and Picabia come to mind – in answer to the question of how the relationship of the body and technology, and individuality to scientification and reification, are created. This figure of thought is, among other things, the basis for studies in the form of 'semantic networks'. Sybille Krämer on the question of meaning section 'What is *language*?': "Language signs have no meaning. Since language must consist of at least two signs, so that the value of one element is determined through its relation to other elements, there can be no single language sign. This has implications for the theory of meaning: There is no point in regarding language signs as carriers of meaning. Meaning emerges between the signs and cannot be localised in the sign." Olaf Breidbach in his study on internal representation: "Meaning designates … a self-generated quality of the relational system." (→ PIII/06)

Folding as a Figure of Thought
(G. Deleuze, A. F. Möbius, G. W. Leibniz)
Even though most examples in the diagrammatics studies show two-dimensional forms, objects from knot topology (like the *Möbius strip*) indicate that all of these constellations can also be transferred to spatial angle forms and complex curved three-dimensional planes. An optimal introduction to the view of folds is provided by G. Deleuze in his book *Fold – Leibniz and the Baroque*. In my diagram collection, the category of folds comprises many of the complexly formed examples that suggest it makes sense to pursue graphematics along with the view of diagrammatics. (→ PII/04a-l)

Form-Content Distinction as a Figure of Thought
(V. Flusser)
In Vilém Flusser's letters to Alex Bloch there is the following passage: "… what is the sacrifice of relinquishing the content of the world and 'limiting oneself to its structure'? How is this sacrifice made and what is its result? How does the separation of 'content' and 'structure' even arise, and how can one describe these two aspects of the world?" …

"As in most abstract cases, it is easier to recognise the sense of the words 'content and structure' than to express their meaning. To say that one describes the world structurally, when one describes how it is built, is to say nothing, because every description is a structural description. One arrives at the content of things by directly grasping it, not by means of symbols like words, etc. In this lies the 'contentlessness' of logic, of mathematics, of language, indeed of every symbol, namely that a symbol 'substitutes for' the content of the phenomenon described; in other words it becomes itself the object of the description."

The Form of Correlation as a Figure of Thought
(G. Dirmoser, G. Spencer-Brown)
Since the concept of the 'between' was able to contribute to clarifying diagrammatics, the following question subsequently suggested itself: Does the 'between' have a form? A detailed consideration demonstrates that attempts to grasp the 'between' conceptually actually involve a 'correlation', which is to be further pursued within the framework of diagrammatic detailed considerations. The guiding question is therefore to be formulated thus: Does the correlation have a form? Then a 'logic of the form' would be juxtaposed with the 'logic of space'. Suggestions for this can be found, among others, in George Spencer Brown's writing on *Laws of Form*. See the details of my study *Does the Correlation Have a Form*? (FU Berlin 2009)

Formal Sequences as a Figure of Thought
(G. Kubler)
G. Kubler's approach is the opposite of purely genealogical approaches. It is well suited for imagining complex parallel developments and their reciprocal influences. Kubler's approach provides a basis for the diagrammatic implementation of complex (networked) *synchronopses*. G. Kubler: "Primary forms of expression … occur in formal sequences. This conception is based on the presupposition that inventions are not isolated incidences, but rather mutually connected positions …" "Solution chains – Since it can be concluded from a sequence of artefacts, one can call the problem its intellectual form and the solution chain their category of being. This unit, which is composed of the problem and its solutions, constitutes a category of forms." "There can be no solution chains without a concomitant problem."

Framing as a Figure of Thought
(V. Beyer, W. Kemp)
V. Beyer shows in her study the diagrammatic use of framing constructs in the art historical analysis of artefacts. "Considering framing in this way implies understanding primary relations under 'framing' – but without losing sight of the form, in which these relations are revealed in the object of the picture frame. Understanding this approach of framing as relation as an 'interval' has been most extensively formulated by L. Marin. He writes for instance: 'The frame can be understood as an interval between three spaces, which connects a painting (the depicted space, the space of representation [the picture surface V. B.] and the space of presentation)'." In the course of her image analyses, Vera Beyer superimposes diagrammatic frame constellations on the works to be studied. Central ideas of composition are reconstructed and visualised in this way. See also: Figure and Ground (Gestalt psychology).

Gaze Relations as a Figure of Thought
(E. Schürmann, G. Didi-Huberman)
Here it is a matter of clarifying (with E. Schürmann et al.) which role the gaze plays in image perception and thus in the perception of diagrams. This also addresses how every perceiving 'formation' is to be understood as an active process (which is also addressed by the 'projection opened to the outside' of our remote senses).

Genealogical Conjunctions as a Figure of Thought
(A. Schmidt-Burkhardt, T. Macho, S. Weigel)
The image historian Astrit Schmidt-Burkhardt presents a comprehensive study on the use of tree structures in the self-presentation and self-made history of the field of art in her book *Family Trees of Art – On the Genealogy of the Avant-garde* (2005).

Geometric Proofs as a Figure of Thought
(S. Bogen, F. Thürlemann)
S. Bogen, F. Thürlemann: "Diagrams were employed surprisingly often in antiquity and throughout the European Middle Ages. Greek antiquity coined the terms *schema* and *diagramma*, which we still use today. However, an extensive and coherent theory was never developed. The reason for this was that the two terms covered a very broad spectrum ranging from geometrical proof to legal decree." (→PII/05)

Geometrical Proof Figure as a Figure of Thought
(S. Bogen, F. Thürlemann)
S. Bogen, F. Thürlemann on C. S. Peirce: "'What exact logicians do on paper, the vague logicians do in their imagination', it says in one of Peirce's late manuscripts. For Peirce the diagram is initially and primarily a medium of thinking." … "Important historical evidence for Peirce's thesis is the core meaning of the term 'diagram' in antiquity as a geometrical proof figure'."

COLLECTION OF FIGURES OF THOUGHT

Gnomon as a Figure of Thought
(S. Bogen, M. Serres, G. Meynen)
Gloria Meynen demonstrates in her article how it is possible to bridge a gap between a plane figure of the enumerative mathematics of antiquity, the construction of the Egyptian harp, and how it functions as a dial on a sundial with the figure of the 'gnomon'. Surveying, time measurement, music theory and illustrative mathematics meet in a figure that has also been used by Steffen Bogen as the starting point for his diagrammatic observations: (*Silhouette and Sundial: Forms of Art and Science Between Image and Diagram*)

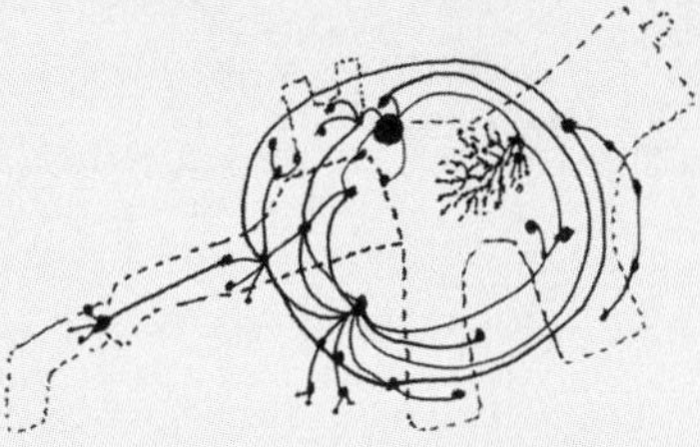

Fig. DF-K0089

The Image as a Figure of Thought
(J. Grave, A. Schubbach, C. Asmuth)
I would hardly have dared to use the image (in general) as a figure of thought, had not the eikones summer school announced a relevant course title: *Eikones – Course 3: The Image as a Figure of Thought* (thinking images – eikones summer school 2008). A key question was: "Which relations or constellations can be grasped with the figure of thought of the image?" We are left to happily anticipate two announced books *Das Bild als Denkfigur* (*The Image as a Figure of Thought*), Fink, 2010 and *Denken mit dem Bild* (*Thinking with the Image*) (A. Schubbach, J. Grave, 2010). "Figural and mental images enable and structure thought processes. Making images is an important part of thinking." "The current interdisciplinary discussions about images are essentially due to an increased interest in the visible image in all its forms of manifestation. … Therefore, philosophical traditions should be looked at in return, which have employed the image as a figure of thought in the context of abstract questions. The fact that recourse to the image is repeatedly taken in theoretical reflections suggests its special conceptual potential. At the same time, the concept of the image is developed and enriched through its operative use in philosophical thinking, which can call attention to aspects that are otherwise often overlooked. As early as Plato, the image is often less the given object of a philosophical reflections than a concept with which the constitution of the world and the reality of human beings is conceived. Plato is thus at the beginning of a tradition in which accesses to the world are imagined pictorially.

Image/Text Binomial
as a Figure of Thought
(G. E. Lessing, S. Bogen, F. Thürlemann)
A figure of thought that is called into question in conjunction with diagrammatics. S. Bogen, F. Thürlemann: "The aim of the following explanations is to fundamentally question the image/text binomial. An important means of expression is sacrificed to binary reflection oriented to the comparison and confrontation between image and text, the diagram, or more precisely – to avoid a too narrow demarcation of the field from the beginning – the various forms of diagrammatic arranging and arguing. Because diagrams frequently conjoin linguistic and figural means, one could be predisposed to consider the genre of the diagram as a synthesis of text and image. Yet the diagram is not merely a hybrid form that could be understood as the merging of text and image elements. From a formal and especially from a functional perspective, diagrams have highly specific semiotic properties, are communicative instruments with non-substitutable performance features." S. Bogen, F. Thürlemann: "Crucial for the argument presented here is that the figural elements of the schema can be included in the same diagrammatic system as the concepts. Like writing, they are attributed to topologically and geometrically precisely defined fields and framework forms, and in addition, they are reciprocally related through formal analogy/oppositional relationships." S. Bogen, F. Thürlemann: "A … research project that queries the significance of topological-geometrical relations and contrastive design principles as well as the basic forms and basic figures of the diagram and its tradition, is dependent on the text-image binomial." (→ PIII/02k)

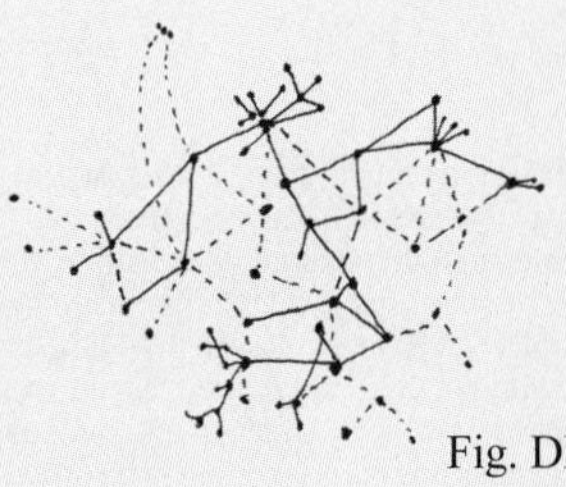

Fig. DF-R6565

Interpictorialness as a Figure of Thought
(B. Nieslony, A. Müller, L. Wittgenstein)
'Intermediate forms' and 'interlinks' are to be addressed with Wittgenstein. In his *Philosophical Investigations*, Ludwig Wittgenstein writes in §122: "A perspicuous representation produces just that

understanding which consists in 'seeing connexions'. Hence the importance of finding and inventing intermediate cases." Complete §, see: **Perspicuous Representation as a Figure of Thought**. The image analyses by Boris Nieslony and Axel Müller should also be mentioned at this point. They attempt to cover forms of 'interpictoriality' in their studies.

Interscription as a Figure of Thought

(P. Gehring)

The concept of 'interscription' comes up in Petra Gehring's contribution to the symposium *Diagrammatics and Philosophy* (1988), although she does not distinguish between discrete relation elements and continuous traces. This concept has served for years as the leitmotiv for my diagrammatic studies. P. Gehring: "If it is a matter of finding a 'good' metaphor for the theoretical invention of a dynamic constellation, why should one not speak of 'interscription', and perhaps even better than 'inscription' (as the poetic thinker J. Derrida, influenced by structuralism, does), rather than of *grammein* from *diagrammein*?" In the course of diagrammatic analyses of typographical concepts, I came to the following view: "In terms of media, the (primary) criterion of interstitiality connects writing and the diagram. Here the diagram offers graphical means for explicitly developing this interstitiality. This explicit development is generally an interscription, which can have both a separating and a connecting effect." (→ PI/09a)

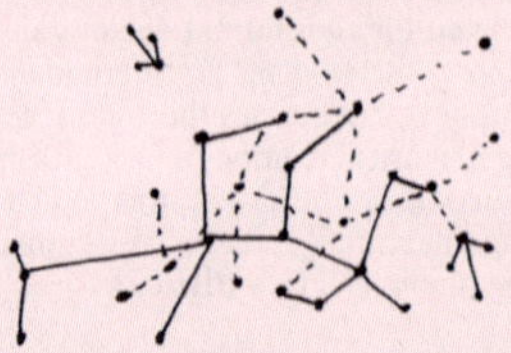

Fig. DF-J8943

Interstitiality as a Figure of Thought

(S. Krämer, D. Mersch, U. Ramming)

Spatiality/interspatiality/spatial localisation analyses of the *Domain of image* (J. Elkins) have shown that practically all image classes (including diagrams and graphs) can be covered by the principle of interstitiality. D. Mersch in 'Knowledge in Images': "Diagrammatic structures use 'interstitialities', as the basic principle of spatiality is called." See also M. Andreas: "Spatial Figures of Thought".

Linkage Form as a Figure of Thought

(H. G. Grassmann, G. Chatelet)

The main reason for my current interest in the form issue is found in H. G. Grassmann's writings. His *Ausdehnungslehre* (*Expansion Theory*) from 1844 includes the following electrifying statements: "Everything that has become through thinking (...) can have become in two ways, either through a simple act of generating, or through the twofold act of positing and linking. What has become in the first way is the constant form or the magnitude in the narrower sense; what has become in the latter way is the discrete or linkage form." In my explanations I want to show that the two form classes formulated by Grassmann provide a basis for placing graphematics alongside diagrammatics.

Logic of Contrast as a Figure of Thought

(G. Boehm – Logic of the Contrast)

Spatial Differentiations (III) Mersch/Heßler *Logik des Bildlichen* (*Logic of the Pictorial*): "Furthermore, the structure of image knowledge is characterised by a logic of contrast, which is indebted to 'spatiality', the 'interstitial' constitution of visual media, as well as (by) a 'topological differentiality' that virtually provides the formating of the picture space." This is also affirmed by S. Bogen and F. Thürlemann. On A. J. Greimas' approach they write: "... Diagrams – as the examples we have analysed prove – also specifically aim to depict content structures at the level of expression in binary relations and oppositions, i.e. sensually perceptible analogies and contrasts, or to first constitute them in this way. Very different categories are employed here: for instance, topological (meaning distinctions such as left/right, up/down, central/peripheral) or typographical (e.g. the opposites of majuscules vs. miniscule or italics vs. non-italics)." On this see also my study 'Diagrammatic Layout' a central proponent of this logic of contrast is G. Boehm (*Section: A Logic of Contrasts*): "Every figure, even the verbal figure, silently claims a contrast for its plastic and vivid appearance. The 'figura' sets itself apart from the context, e.g. of the speech. It is only thus that it gains specificity and a clear profile. It must appear sufficiently different to be recognised as itself. If there were a tumult of figures, they would rob themselves of their visibility, creating an impression of confusion and overloading."

Liquefaction as a Figure of Thought

(G. Dirmoser, B. Siegert, G. Gramelsberger, R. Descartes)

A study on 'atmospheric design issues' (light design, use of material, ...) directly affected the diagrammatic question to the extent that I attempted to formulate an an-diagrammatic as a counterpoint to diagrammatics. The study was titled: *On the Use of Liquefaction – An AnDiagrammatic*."Through the developed image collection it became clear that formations were coming into play that were much more difficult to grasp than the graphical structures of diagrammatics: Mist-like shapes characterised in their density, moving fluid structures, complex patterns of movement, all the way to explosion-like developments, dynamic weather manifestations, etc. In the course of this image collection I also became aware of attractor shapes and swarm structures, or in more general terms – process forms that were mathematically framed. This expansion in the process view was also significant for the diagram collection, because it opened up a new access to the basic type of 'process structures' and 'folds'." On this, see also: *Fluid Worlds. On Mapping Time and Movement* (eikones 2007). See also: **Simulation as a Figure of Thought**

Logical Correspondence / Logical Framework
as a Figure of Thought

In working on the *Tractatus logico-philosophicus* in form of a diagram, it became clear that Wittgenstein's formulations on 'logical form' and 'logical image' provide key passages for diagrammatics. In the text *Knowledge in Images*, D. Mersch writes: "… Consequently, diagrammatics generally contains all visual-graphical forms that allow for arguments and derivations, logical relationships or arrangements and the like in the medium of the visual. Graphematics forms a subsection of this." In the volume *On Certainty* there is an important motto for every diagrammatic project: "A thinker is very much like a draughtsman whose aim it is to represent all the interrelations between things."

Logical Form and Logical Image
as a Figure of Thought
(L. Wittgenstein)

Logical Structure as a Figure of Thought
(D. Mersch)

Marking and Tracking
as a Figure of Thought
(J. Derrida, H.-J. Rheinberger)

Methods of radioactive marking and tracking are vividly presented in Hans-Jörg Rheinberger's writing. At this point, it would be productive to go into more detail on the concept of tracks, but that would go beyond the limitations of this framework.

The Media Schema (of diagrammatics)
as a Figure of Thought

In the course of diagram analyses, several schematic representations, such as the 'media schema' have proven themselves useful. Ongoing use and revision have led me to continually attempt to comment on text passages in specialist literature with this schema or to apply them to this schema. This occurs in the form of small commenting sketches on the edge of the book page. In other words, I have learned to think with this schema! This would mean that this simple configuration is definitively a 'figure of thought'. Along with Astrit Schmidt-Burkhardt, one could distinguish between 'thought diagrams' and 'knowledge diagrams'. Thought diagrams must be semantically very compact (or semantically almost empty). In comparison with thought diagrams, however, knowledge diagrams are offerings rich in content, which are provided in a specific ordering pattern. When frequently applied, these 'thought diagrams' tend to become 'figures of thought'. In conclusion, the question arises as to whether we have now been able to develop a clear 'image' of figures of thought. To the extent that we have only been going in circles, we are left with the consolation from G.-A. Goldschmidt. He writes: "There is no greater stupidity than to speak of the abstract character of German: no other language is so concrete, so spatial; to be precise, German is incapable of any abstraction. It derives its abstract concepts from French or constructs them following the French." In any case, we should learn to apply the spatially saturated concepts in concrete diagram analyses.

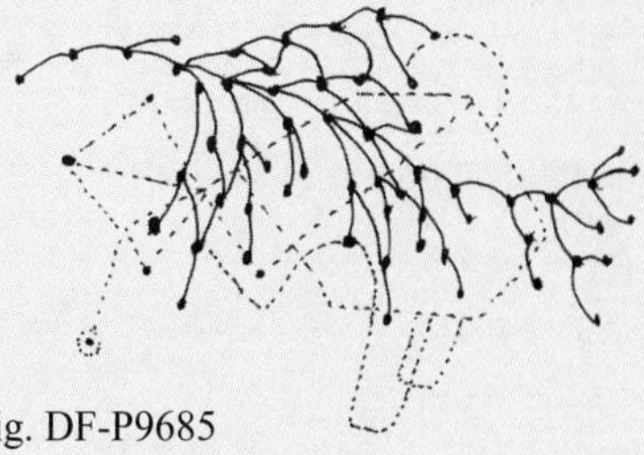

Fig. DF-P9685

Memory Theater as a Figure of Thought
(G. C. Delminio)

Very well-known ordering forms are those that can be called memory theaters. Frances A. Yates presents G. C. Delminio's memory theater concept in *The Art of Memory*. I also used the sectoring method Delminio proposes in several of my studies.

Mental Architectonics
as a Figure of Thought
(I. Kant, H. Bergson, M. Mullican, B. Nieslony)

In I. Kant's *Critique of Pure Reason*, there is a passage in the section *The Architectonics of Pure Reason* that outlines in master builder terms what Kant and his contemporaries understood as mental architectonics: "It is unfortunate that, only after having occupied ourselves for a long time in the collection of materials, under the guidance of an idea which lies undeveloped in the mind, but not according to any definite plan of arrangement- nay, only after we have spent much time and labour in the technical disposition of our materials, does it become possible to view the idea of a science in a clear light, and to project, according to architectonical principles, a plan of the whole, in accordance with the aims of reason." See also: Bergson's Cone as a Figure of Thought (H. Bergson) (→ PIII/01)

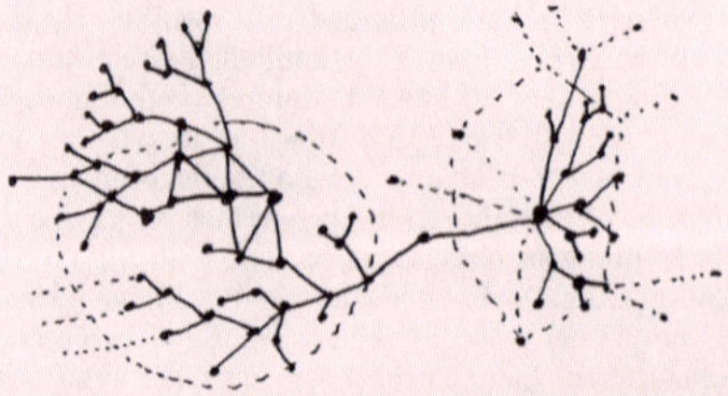

Fig. DF-C4443

Mixture Relations as a Figure of Thought
(M. Serres)
As M. Serres already realised twenty years ago: what is blurred, fluid, mixed ... should no longer be stylised as inimical to discursive precision. What is useful for mathematically grounded natural science should also be tested in the treatment of humanities data.

Model Paradigms as a Figure of Thought
(D. Mersch, B. Mahr, T. Macho, G. Gramelsberger)
In his lecture *Diagrams, Graphs and Models*, Munich, 2005 – for researchers from the field of social network analysis), Dieter Mersch discussed the model theory for the first time in the context of graphematics and diagrammatics. Since model theories are relevant for all fields of knowledge, they intersect the methods of diagrammatics and graphematics to a certain extent. Among other things, models form the basis for informatics-based simulation projects (see: **Simulation as a Figure of Thought**). Further considerations would be desirable on: **Dimensional Accuracy as a Figure of Thought / Scaling Systems**

Order Hybrids as a Figure of Thought
(G. Dirmoser, M. Serres)
Hybrid interweavings of the pattern of order as a figure of thought. My motto: "Taking hybridity seriously – grasping diagrams as hybrids. It is important to me not to condemn or repress hybrid forms as analytically blurred, but rather, on the contrary, to presume that hybrid forms are the normal case and that the 'pure' forms are an exception. How do I arrive at this understanding? My diagram collection consists of 121 portfolios. Laying out these portfolios results in a matrix of 11 x 11 positions. In the course of the development of the material – about 6000 examples – it quickly became clear that more than 80% of the concrete examples are to be assigned to multiple orders form (imagine maps containing network structures; maps with animal depictions inscribed in them; maps in circular/quadratic ideal forms, etc.). In the analysis of diagrams it is therefore a matter of studying forms of composition and thus promoting a differentiated thinking of their aspects. It consequently also became clear that the reference structures, scales, gridding of the technical/scientific graphs could also be derived from diagrammatic order forms (or developed historically from them)."

Parasite Relation as a Figure of Thought
(M. Serres)
For influence relations (including disturbances), M. Serres proposed visual representations in his observation of parasite structures. He draws arrows that directly affect other arrows, whereby this relation consists solely of edges, so it has no knots (as points of intersection). In this way he proposes a network structure that only consists of edges/arrows. A net without knots, so to speak. Structurally and in terms of visualisation technique, this also corresponds with Deleuze and Guattari's rhizome concept.

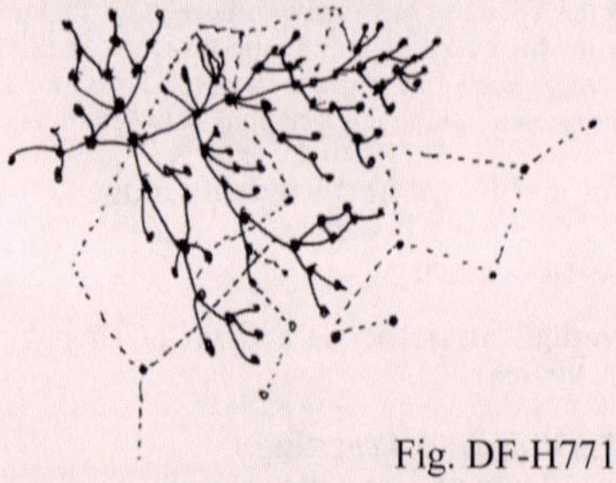

Fig. DF-H7711

Pattern language as a Figure of Thought
(C. Alexander)

Perception of Gestalt
as a Figure of Thought
(W. Metzger, M. Wertheimer, S. Palmer)
Detailed observations on concrete diagram forms are recalled by gestalt laws or the grouping laws of gestalt psychology. The ten gestalt laws offer an important access to diagrammatic forms.

Perspicuous Representation
as a Figure of Thought
(L. Wittgenstein, A. Warburg, A. Pichler)
In the *Philosophical Investigations* Ludwig

COLLECTION OF FIGURES OF THOUGHT

Wittgenstein wrote in §122: "A main source of our failure to understand is that we do not command a clear view of ('übersehen') the use of our words. Our grammar is lacking this sort of perspecuity ('Übersichtlichkeit'). A perspicuous representation ('übersichtliche Darstellung') produces just that understanding which consists in 'seeing connexions'. Hence the importance of finding and inventing intermediate cases. The concept of a perspicuous representation is of fundamental significance for us. It earmarks the form of account we give ('unsere Darstellungsform), the way we look at things. (Is this a 'Weltanschauung'?)" A. Pichler writes in his Wittgenstein study: "From the perspective of the investigations, Wittgenstein's collaging was less a means along the way to the single correct arrangement than an excellent vehicle for the activity of synoptic representation, which was to allow a re-composition and hence also a re-seeing of the previously created and a new recognition of connections.

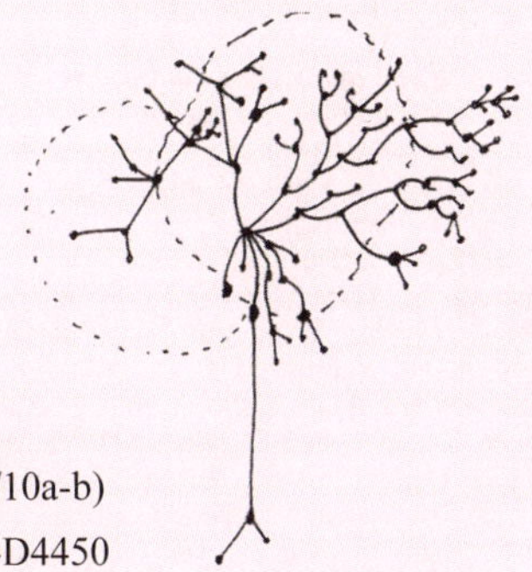

(→ PII/10a-b)

Fig. DF-D4450

Pictographicality as a Figure of Thought
(D. Mersch)
D. Mersch in the text 'Knowledge in Images': "Diagrammatic forms such as maps, graphs, networks and similar presentations create medial forms that participate equally in visibility and discourse, while their mediation and legibility so entangle them that transgressions occur allowing the discursive to be perceived as iconic, and the iconic as discursive. The term 'image-textuality' ('Bildschriftlichkeit') mentioned above, as opposed to 'text-pictoriality'('Schriftbildlichkeit'), denotes these singular limitations such that pictoriality and text no longer appear as separate categories, but rather merge in each other.": "In fact, 'typographicality' and 'pictographicality' refer to one another, but they differ in the type of operationality they are based on, even if the boundaries blur."

Projection Relations as a Figure of Thought
(J. Willats, S. Bogen)
Projection as fundamental view in the classification of diagrams: Topology (as a branch of mathematics) provides important concepts to describe position relations (as qualitative space reference) in more detail. Topology is abstracted here from all metrics, however. For this reason, it is absolutely necessary to include the view of projections for some types of diagrams. This means that projections supply the position that can be exactly mathematically determined. A whole range of projection approaches is presented by J. Wallats as 'drawing systems' in his book *Art and Representation*. In addition, an entire system of map projections should also be noted.

Relationality / The Third
as a Figure of Thought
(B. Latour, M. Serres)
If one takes the view of relations seriously, one develops an eye for connecting elements; for the units and phenomena that are in between, that spread out in between or (as M. Serres says) that impact the in-between (parasite concept). Cf. also research on: *Figures of the Third* (Graduiertenkolleg), **Relational Spaces as a Figure of Thought** (O. Breidbach) and **Structurality as a Figure of Thought** (M. Serres)

Rhetorical Gestures as a Figure of Thought
(G. Bonsiepe, G. Joost, G. Dirmoser, D. Offenhuber)
In the study *Rhetorics of Graphical Elements*, an attempt was undertaken to investigate moments of designing diagrams in terms of a rhetorical effectiveness. The formations described here are directly accessible to perception. Cf. also: **Display Gesture as a Figure of Thought**. The following possibilities of design are treated there in detail: visual metaphor, framing, colour gestures, exaggeration, selective emphasis, weighting, centrality, balance, symmetry, harmonious order, Golden Mean, hierarchy, architectural order, reading direction, void, pause, complexity, multi-layeredness, logical stringency, precision, contrast, confrontation, staging the gaze, degree of order, distortion, emphasis, etc.

Rhizomatic Root Network
as a Figure of Thought
(G. Deleuze, F. Guattari, A. Reichert)
The figure of thought of the rhizome has become incredibly widespread. G. Deleuze and F. Guattari succeeded in overcoming the corset of crystalline structure thinking in their polemic writing. This metaphor for organic complexity is also taken up in diagrammatic network visualisations (W. Bradford Paley, B. Fry, C. Reas, J. Maeda, G. Levin, B. Lyon, S. Greenworld, N. Willems, D. Holten). See also the artworks by J. Mehretu, J. Modé, E. Neto,

L. Solaas, N. Katchadourian. A. Reichert also refers to 'rhizomatic thinking', among other things, in his dissertation proposal *Diagrammatics of Thinking. On the Beginning of Thinking and Thinking of the Beginning with Descartes, Heidegger and Deleuze*. In his study, however, he does not intend to "paint a different picture of thinking, but rather to draw diagrams of thinking along figures of thought and consider them in terms of their operativity in thinking."

Schematism as a Figure of Thought

(I. Kant, S. Krämer)

The 'diagrammatic scope' of Kantian schematism has not yet been clarified. In the operative sense, schematism could be the foundational mechanism for every diagrammatic figure of thought. This can be briefly sketched with ideas from S. Krämer: I. Kant: "Now pure concepts of the understanding, however, in comparison with empirical (indeed in general sensible) intuitions, are entirely unhomogeneous, and can never be encountered in any intuition." "In light of the complete unhomogeneity between intuition and 'pure' category, how can a connection nevertheless be established? At this point, Kant maintains that 'there must be a third thing, which must stand in homogeneity with the category on the one hand and the appearance on the other'. And it is precisely this mediating and middle thing between concept and sensible intuition – we could even say that it is precisely this medium – which Kant calls 'transcendental schema'. This also has the characteristic of being 'intellectual on the one hand and sensible on the other' (emphasis S. Krämer). We therefore conjecture that schematism, as a third thing mediating between sensibility and category, assembles essential determinations that Peirce attributes to the diagram and which, at the same time, bear witness to us of the diagrammatological foundations of reason."

Schematising as a Figure of Thought

(S. Krämer)

A multitude of schematic representations are found especially in academic textbooks. They are based on: reduction, simplification and a limitation to the essentials.

Sense of Situation / Contextuality as a Figure of Thought

(G. Dirmoser, G. Hasenhütl, C. Bartel)

D. Rustemeyer's studies outline a large field of activity. Among other questions, it needs to be clarified how the concepts of singularity and the *Logic of sense* (G. Deleuze) can be harmonised with this view.

Sense Relations as a Figure of Thought

(P. Gehring, M. Serres, G. Deleuze)

I would like to begin with the article *Paradigm of a Method – The Concept of the Diagram in the Structural Thinking of M. Foucault and M. Serres* by P. Gehring. The second chapter is entitled: *Topology as a Grammar of Sense: Thinking in diagrams with M. Serres*. P. Gehring thus links one of the fundamental diagrammatic approaches (topology) with the sense view. Topology (as a spatial arrangement of partial structures) is discussed as a grammar of sense. In other words, topology is brought into play as a grammatical or structural foundation for sense. Gehring writes "Beyond this, it can be shown that it is not solely the praxis of philosophy that can be imagined from the basic motif of the diagram, but that it is the processes of sense altogether that must be imagined according to a thoroughly diagrammatic model." Gehring writes "In fact, it seems to be exactly the boundary between structural mathematics and that which is called, for lack of a better term, post-structuralism, along which Serres diagram model moves. Sense appears here as a purely *relational* matter and entirely in the sense of structural mathematics – to a certain extent as a connecting path or connecting line between at least two points (two sentences or assumptions)." … Every concrete sense relation a singular determination, a point-defining and relation-transforming arrow, a vector in a space – and all of this against the backdrop of tremendous possibilities. This results in a general model that can be played with." Another important point of connection is provided by G. Deleuze in his study *Logic of Sense*. As Deleuze describes sense relations: "Sense is both the expressible or the expressed of the proposition, and the attribute of the state of affairs. It turns one side toward things and one side toward propositions. But it does not merge with the proposition which expresses it any more than with the state of affairs or the quality which the proposition denotes. It is exactly the boundary between propositions and things."

Shadow Images as a Figure of Thought

See: **Silhouette** as a Figure of Thought (→ PI/07)

Showing and Appearing as a Figure of Thought

(D. Mersch, eikones)

D. Mersch characterises the role of *deixis* in his text *Knowledge in Images* quite forcefully: "Not distinction … nor observation … is the central theme of diagrammatics, but rather *deixis*. There is an interplay of form, appearance (*eidos*) and *deixis*." In the invitation to the eikones annual conference 2007, the following passage is found under the heading *Showing. The Rhetorics of the Visible*: "With the discussion about the preconditions and the range of pictorial representation, showing also comes into view in a new way. Although *deixis* has long been part of the conceptual repertoire, especially in philosophy and rhetorics, showing was nevertheless not really able to capture scientific attention, let alone take on the role of a leading concept. On the contrary: something primitive adheres to showing, what is tangible about body language or gesture, the helping function of a pointer or sign. In comparison with language or thinking, showing seems to be less complex as a mere indication. The exploration of the image as a non-verbal symbol system per se first enables a more intensive study of showing. … Showing as directing attention plays out at the margins of evidence. From there, it establishes forms of the visible that often do not come into view, do not themselves become object. This 'rhetorics of the visible' oscillates between showing and appearing." In the section 'Show – Prove' there is an explicit investigation of how "diagrams or simulations fulfill deictic tasks." In the section *Dispositive of Showing*, art and curiosity cabinets, picture atlases and hanging strategies for pictorial works were discussed, in other words, diagrammatic patterns of order. Very different techniques of marking and referencing are also investigated in my diagram studies. The layer techniques and symbolic marking approaches that are used are assembled according to particular emphases in one of the eleven basic types of diagrams (on this, see: BodyMapping). The study *Rhetorics of Graphic Elements* provides a collection of the strategies of forceful showing (in other words, 'deictic figures').

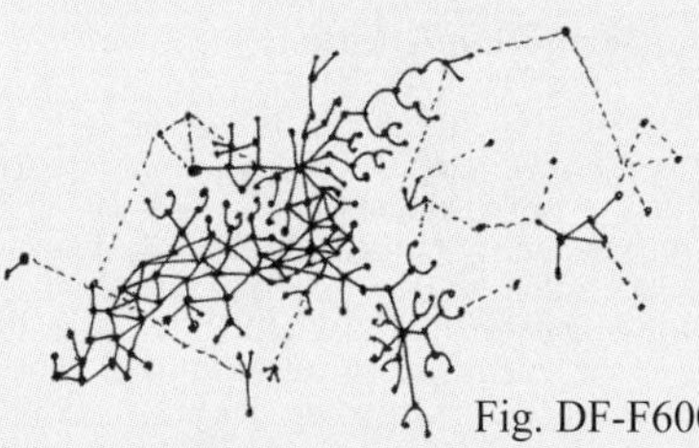

Fig. DF-F6008

Silhouette / Shadow Images
as a Figure of Thought
(T. O. Roth)
S. Bogen also indicates in his gnomon study that there is little point in stylising a categorial boundary between (allegedly non-mimetic) diagrams and 'mimetic images'. He writes: "… From the perspective of the considerations presented here, a connection between diagrammatic and pictorial aspects under the auspices of mimetic art is also to be recognised in this. A 'picture' constructed according to the rules of central perspective can always also be viewed as a diagram in terms of its principles of construction. It is the image of a spatial world and simultaneously the diagrammatic depiction of optical rules, which should be valid in both the fictive and the real world. One can also say that a specific type of diagram generates images – the images are the figural dress of a diagram." (→ PII/08)

Simulation as a Figure of Thought
(G. Gramelsberger, S. Krämer)
G. Gramelsberger in the study *Computer Experiments*: "In addition to theory, experiment, observation and measurement, in the 1950s, increasing from the 1970s, there is now also simulation as a new instrument of insight." Simulations (from the most diverse discipline directions) generally merge into graphematic or diagrammatic visualisations. Through the use of extremely powerful computer systems, dynamic visualisations are now also feasible.

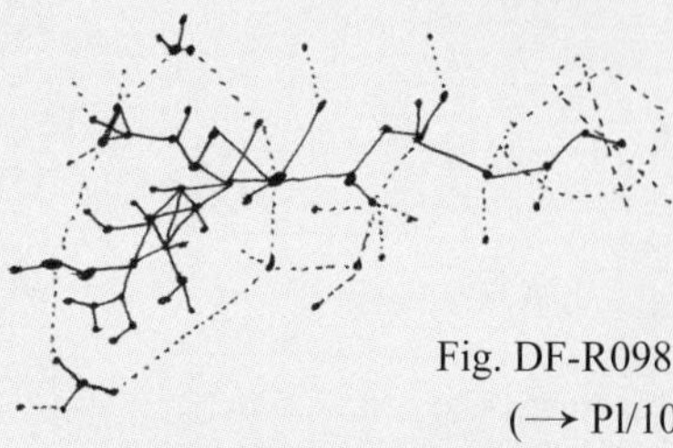

Fig. DF-R0987
(→ PI/10)

Smooth and Striated Forms
as a Figure of Thought
(G. Deleuze, F. Guattari, H. G. Grassmann)
On the relationship between continuity and discontinuity: The first sentence of Deleuze's writing begins with "smooth space and striated space …". On the first page, based on art historical approaches, Deleuze discusses the coupling of "abstract line/ concrete line" and terms such as "forms of expression". About the abstract line he writes: "A line with variable direction, which draws no outline and delineates no form": "What does this mean for the question: Does 'spatial correlation' have a form? To avoid getting stuck in diagram typology, it is necessary to study the 'correlation of graphical elements' in detail. With Grassmann and Deleuze, here two classes of forms are to be considered in their correlation: (I) the discrete correlation (with Deleuze: the striated / with Grassmann: the form of linkage) and (II) the continual correlation (with Deleuze: the smooth / with Grassmann: the constant form)."

The Spatialisation of Time
as a Figure of Thought
(T. Macho)
Nearly all basic types of diagrams (with one exception) are suitable for representing temporality. Research on a 'diagrammatics of time' is being conducted by T. Macho, among others. Continually draw-

ing a line offers an approach to subjecting spatiality and temporality to a common view. I am indebted to S. Krämer and J. Schülein for the following quotation from Fichte (§5 of the *Foundations of Natural Right*): "… the I that intuits itself as active intuits its activity as an act of drawing a line. That is the original schema for activity in general, as will be discovered by anyone who wants to awaken that highest intuition within himself. This original line is pure extension, that which is common to time and space and from which they first emerge through differentiation and further determination. This original line does not presuppose space, but rather space presupposes it." See also: **Gnomon as a Figure of Thought**

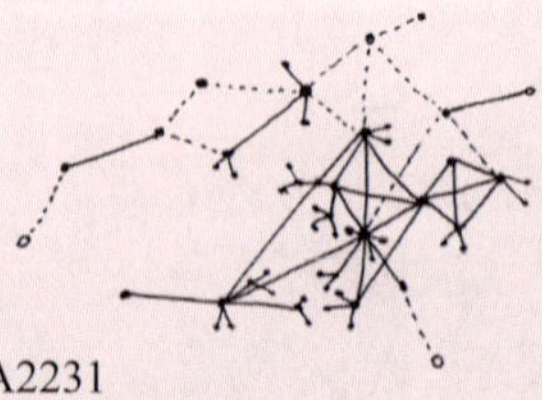

Fig. DF-A2231

Structural Correspondence as a Figure of Thought

(C. S. Peirce, L. Wittgenstein)

S. Bogen and F. Thürlemann quote C. S. Peirce: "Many diagrams resemble their objects not at all in looks; it is only in respect to the relations of their parts that their likeness consists." Elsewhere Peirce accordingly defines the diagram as an icon, "in which the relations of the parts of a sign are represented by analogous relations in parts of the sign itself." (→ PII/10a-b)

System Differences as a Figure of Thought

(N. Luhmann)

Even though Luhmann cannot be directly associated with diagrammatics, his foundation in approaches from Spencer-Brown suffices for him to be named. Luhmann's programme concept, the explicit visualisation of system boundaries (in other words, their interfaces) and the outlined interplay of subsystems offer models that can also be made productive in applied diagrammatics. His famous file card system (as a complex networked structure) should also be mentioned.

Systemic Network / Cellular Setup as a Figure of Thought

(S. Ulam, J. von Neumann, T. O. Roth)

Cellular automatons serve the modelling of spatially discrete dynamic systems.

The Third as a Figure of Thought

See: **Relationality as a Figure of Thought**

Text Binomial as a Figure of Thought

See: **Image/Text Binomial as a Figure of Thought**

Topological Differentiality as a Figure of Thought

(M. Heßler, D. Mersch, W. Pichler, W. Kemp)

Spatial Differentiations (II) (→ PIII/03-04)

Topology (as a branch of mathematics) provides important concepts to describe position relations (as qualitative space reference) in more detail. Topology is abstracted here from all metrics. Basic topological concepts can help to grasp the proximity of elements, describing whether the elements touch or permeate one another (and are thus connected), whether elements are surrounded by something or themselves surround something else. Mersch/Heßler (Logic of the Pictorial): "Furthermore, the structure of image knowledge is characterised by a logic of contrast, which is indebted to 'spatiality', the 'interstitial' constitution of visual media, as well as (by) a 'topological differentiality' that virtually provides the formating of the picture space." See also: article by W. Pichler, *Topologische Konfigurationen des Denkens und der Kunst* in: *Falten, Knoten, Netze, Stülpungen in Kunst und Theorie*

Tracking as a Figure of Thought

See: **Marking and Tracking** as a Figure of Thought

Transformation Relations as a Figure of Thought

(D. Mersch, H. J. Rheinberger, P. Galison)

In his article *Knowledge in Images*, D. Mersch writes: "However, the strategies of visualisation and visibility that are used are themselves highly disparate. Although they cannot be sharply separated from one another, they can be provisionally ordered in three basic classes: First, those modes of representation, the essential function of which is witnessing and which use the visual as proof. Second, those which arrange knowledge on abstract tableaus and first generate it as such, sometimes transforming it in reference to a foundational data set into logical or calculable figures. And finally third, things and their surfaces such as preparations and the like." In the same article, D. Mersch writes: "Sometimes cartographic approaches come into play here to impress on them directions, distributions or spatial arrangements, but regardless of what they are rooted in, what they are 'traces' or 'imprints' of (Heßler …), they do not reveal anything real, but at the most a mathematical topology or relations, which cannot be taken as samples or proof of 'something', but must be read, independent from their aesthetics, as abstracts, on which properties such as symmetry or structural similarity and the like are noticeable. Consequently, they also assume no representational or denotative status, but rather a 'diagrammatic' or 'graphematic' status. Rather than being 'imprints' or 'indexes', they represent ordered syntaxes, whose epistemic function is not found in the proof of existence – as is still the case for analogue scientific photography and x-ray technology – but rather in the digital 'sculpture', the virtual modelling of figural forms that remain entirely immaterial." See also the theory articles for the exhibition: "See This Sound".

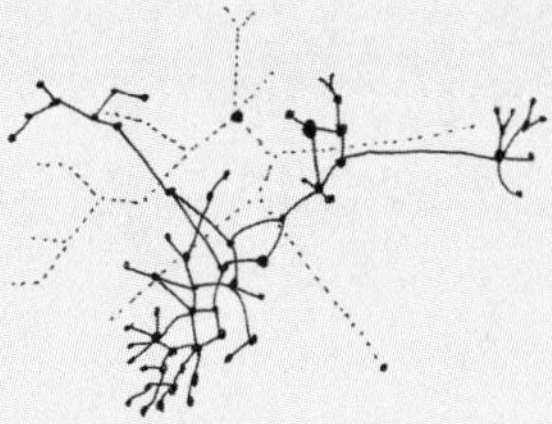

Fig. DF-V6788

Transplanal Images as a Figure of Thought
(J. Schröter)
In any case, the formulations 'spatial correlation' and 'interstitiality' already suggest that there is no point in limiting diagrammatic and graphematic forms of order to the plane. This can be easily comprehended through the field of exhibition design and the field of 'diagrammatic architecture' (taking the examples of P. Eisenmann, G. Lynn, B. van Berkel and C. Bos, et al.). J. Schröter's line of reasoning – in his book on the concept of 'transplanal images' – also clearly goes in this direction. See: *On the History, Theory and Media Aesthetics of the Technically Transplanal Image*. (→ PII/04a)

Typographicality as a Figure of Thought
(S. Krämer, Graduiertenkolleg "Schriftbildlichkeit")
Since writing processes are carried out on a surface or in space, this extensive field of research can also be used as a figure of thought that can be concretely realised. See also: **Interscription as a Figure of Thought**. In a recently realised observation of typographical designing, I first became conscious of how close to one another diagram and writing actually are. I am therefore convinced that it will be possible for research on 'typographicality' to be used directly in more precisely to be defined 'diagrammatics'.

Virtual Structuring as a Figure of Thought
(A. Reichert)
The following text passage by A. Reichert in the abstract *Diagrammatics as Virtual Politics* for a conference in Leipzig reads, "Politics as the intervention of the individual in the whole, as a confrontation with the circumstances and as an arrangement of order, is located for Deleuze and Deleuze/Guattari in the virtual. … It is the reality of movements of thought and of figures of thought. These can be recorded in diagrams, whereby every recording is also a striking through (Greek meaning of *diagrammein*). Virtual reality is thus essentially diagrammatic, which means: 1. structuring does not lie behind the phenomena, but rather in them, 2. it is local and not universal, and 3. structurings do not depict anything, but are instead characterised by interventions. The diagram forms the flaring space, in which the most diverse interventions can be developed: interventions in other structurings of the possible, as well as interventions in actualisations. Unfolding and varying this play of interventions is the task of political diagrammatics. In a first step, I want to develop the concept of the diagram as virtual structuring along the ideas of Foucault (the diagram as plan and map), Serres (the diagram as a model of thinking), and Deleuze/Guattari (the diagram as an abstract machine)." On the meaning of *diagrammein*, see also P. Gehring (**Interscription as a Figure of Thought**)

Visualised Inference Logic
as a Figure of Thought
(C. S. Peirce, S. Bogen, F. Thürlemann)
S. Bogen and F. Thürlemann quote Peirce: "'All necessary concluding is diagrammatic.' Peirce draws a conclusion from this statement and deals in his later writing, which revolves around the essence of conclusions, primarily with diagrams. He develops a system for diagramming statements, which is intended to illustrate the course of thinking and exactly represent it. He calls his diagrams a question about the nature of logical relations." On this, cf. Wittgenstein (See also: **Logical Form and Logical Image as a Figure of Thought**). S. Bogen and F. Thürlemann on Peirce: "In his diagrams he sees the means of slowing down, controlling and revealing the movement of thinking." "An approach of this kind implies a very broad diagram concept: No static graphical forms are called diagrams, but rather their construction phases and the accompanying process of reception. The producer (also called graphist by Peirce) produces the graphical form according to general rules and changes it."

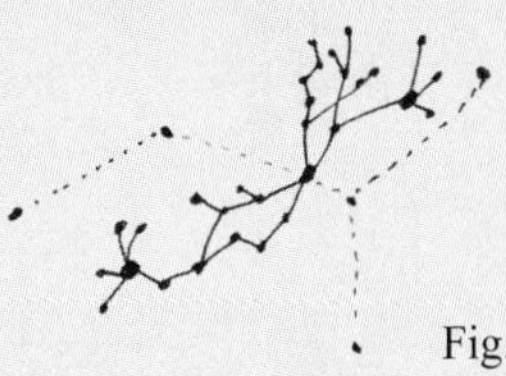

Fig. DF-R2224
(→ PI/10)

References

Alexander, Ch., Ishikawa, S., Silverstein, M. , *Eine Muster-Sprache – a pattern language*, Löcker, Wien, 1995.

Andreas, M., *Grenzwissen und Wissensgrenzen – Die Karte als Medium geographischer Selbst- und Fremdverortung,* http://www.gfmedienwissenschaft.de/gfm/webcontent/files/2008-abstracts/Andreas_Grenzwissen_GfM2008.pdf, 2008.

Bach, F. T., Pichler, W.(eds.), *Öffnungen: Zur Theorie und Geschichte der Zeichnung,* Fink, 2009.

Beyer, V., *Rahmenbestimmungen – Funktionen von Rahmen bei Goya, Velázquez, van Eyck und Degas*, Fink, 2008.

Blümle, C., Schäfer, A. (eds.), *Struktur, Figur, Kontur: Abstraktion in Kunst und Lebenswissenschaften,* Diaphanes, 2007.

Boehm, G., *Die ikonische Figuration*, in: *Figur und Figuration: Studien zu Wahrnehmung und Wissen*, Fink, 2007.

Boehm, G., Brandstetter, G., von Müller, A.(eds.), *Figur und Figuration: Studien zu Wahrnehmung und Wissen*, Fink, 2007.

Bogen, S., Thürlemann, F., *Jenseits der Opposition von Text und Bild – Überlegungen zu einer Theorie des Diagramms und des Diagrammatischen* in: *Die Bilderwelt der Diagramme Joachims von Fiore, in: Die Bildwelt der Diagramme Joachims von Fiore. Zur Medialität religiös- politischer Programme im Mittelalter*, Patschovsky, A. (ed.), Thorbecke, Stuttgart, 2003. p. 1-22.

Bogen, S., *Schattenriss und Sonnenuhr. Überlegungen zu einer kunsthistorischen Diagrammatik*, in: *Zeitschrift für Kunstgeschichte* 68.2, p. 153, 2005.

Bonsiepe, G., *Visuell-verbale Rhetorik – Über einige Techniken der persuasiven Kommunikation,* Ulm, 1965.

Breidbach, O., *Deutungen. Zur philosophischen Dimension der internen Repräsentation,* Velbrück Wissenschaft, 2001.

Chatelet, G., *Figuring Space: Philosophy, Mathematics, and Physics*, Springer, 2000.

Daston, L., Gallison, P., *Objektivität*, Suhrkamp, 2007.

Deleuze, G., *Die Falte – Leibniz und der Barock*, Suhrkamp, 2000.

Deleuze, G., *Logik des Sinns*, Suhrkamp, 1993.

Deleuze, G., F. Guattari, *Rhizom*, Merve, 1977.

Deleuze, G., Félix Guattari, *Tausend Plateaus. Kapitalismus und Schizophrenie*, Merve, 1992.

Didi-Hubermann, G., *Der Strich, die Strähne.* (*Le trait, la traine*), in: *Öffnungen: Zur Theorie und Geschichte der Zeichnung,* Fink, 2009.

Dirks, U., Knobloch, E.(eds.), *Modelle,* Peter Lang, Frankfurt, 2008.

Dirmoser, G., *Rhetorik der graphischen Elemente*, http://gerhard_dirmoser.public1.linz.at/FU/strukturale_Rhetorik_V3.pdf, 2009.

Dirmoser, G., *Formanalysen im Spannungsfeld diagrammatischer & graphematischer Ansätze: Hat das Zueinander eine Form?* (lecture, workshop ‚Diagramm und Diagrammatik', FU Berlin), 2009.

Elkins, J., *The domain of images*, Cornell University Press, 1999.

Endres, J., Wittmann, B., Wolf, G. (ed.), *Ikonologie des Zwischenraums. Der Schleier als Medium und Metapher,* Fink, 2005.

Epple, M., *Die Entstehung der Knotentheorie*, Vieweg, 1999.

Flusser, V. (eds.: Flusser, E., Sander, K.), *Briefe an Alex Bloch*, European Photography, Göttingen, 2000.

Gehring, P., Keutner, T., Maas, J. F., Ueding, W. M. (eds.), *Diagrammatik und Philosophie*, Editions Rodopi, 1992.

Gehring, P., *Paradigma einer Methode. Der Begriff des Diagramms im Strukturdenken von M. Foucault und M. Serres,* in: *Diagrammatik und Philosophie*, Editions Rodopi, 1992.

Goldschmidt, G.-A., *Als Freud das Meer sah*, Ammann, 1999.

Gramelsberger, G., *Computerexperimente: Zum Wandel der Wissenschaft im Zeitalter des Computers,* Transcript, 2010.

Grassmann, H. G., Die *Ausdehnungslehre von 1844 – oder – Die lineale Ausdehnungslehre – ein Zweig der Mathematik* ..., T.C.F. Enslin, Berlin, 1862.

Haitzinger, N., *Choreographie als Denkfigur – Ein Versuch zur komplexeren Aufklärung des Begriffs*, http://www.corpusweb.net/index.php?option=com_content&task=view&id=695&Itemid=35, 2007.

Heßler, M., Mersch, D. (eds.), *Logik des Bildlichen: Zur Kritik der ikonischen Vernunft*, Transcript, 2009.

Hüppauf, B., Weingart, P. (eds.), *Frosch und Frankenstein: Bilder als Medium der Popularisierung von Wissenschaft,* Transcript, 2009.

Julesz, B., *Dialogues on Perception*, The MIT Press, 1994.

Kant, I., *Kritik der reinen Vernunft,* Hartknoch, 1781.

Kittler, F., Ofak, A. (ed.), *Medien vor den Medien,* Fink, 2007.

Krämer, S., *Operative Bildlichkeit. Von der "Grammatologie" zu einer "Diagrammatologie" Reflexionen über Erkennendes "Sehen"* in: *Logik des Bildlichen – Zur Kritik der ikonischen Vernunft*, Transcript, 2009.

Krämer, S., *Sprache, Sprechakt, Kommunikation: Sprachtheoretische Positionen des 20. Jahrhunderts*, Suhrkamp, 2001.

Kubler, G., *Die Form der Zeit. Anmerkungen zur Geschichte der Dinge,* Suhrkamp, 1982.

Mahr, B., *Ein Modell des Modellseins: Ein Beitrag zur Aufklärung des Modellbegriffs*, in: *Modelle,* Peter Lang, Frankfurt, 2008.

Maynard, P., *Drawing Distinctions: The Varieties of Graphic Expression*, Cornell Univ Pr, 2005.

Meier, Ch., *Die Quadratur des Kreises – Die Diagrammatik des 12. Jahrhunderts als symbolische Denk- und Darstellungsform,* in: *Die Bilderwelt der Diagramme Joachims von Fiore*, Thorbecke, 2003.

Mersch, D., *Wissen in Bildern. Zur visuellen Epistemik in Naturwissenschaft und Mathematik* in: *Frosch und Frankenstein: Bilder als Medium der Popularisierung von Wissenschaft*), Transcript, 2009.

Meynen, G., *Über die Tafel, das erste Universalmedium der Mathematik*, in: *Medien vor den Medien*, Fink, 2007.

Müller, A., *Wie Bilder Sinn erzeugen*, in: *Bild-Zeichen. Perspektiven einer Wissenschaft vom Bild*, Majetschak, S. (ed.), Fink, 2005.

Naumann, B., Pankow, E. (eds.), *Bilder-Denken. Bildlichkeit und Argumentation*, Fink, 2004.

Patschovsky, A., *Die Bilderwelt der Diagramme Joachims von Fiore: Zur Medialität religiös-politischer Programme im Mittelalter*, Thorbecke, 2003.

Pichler, W., Ubl, R. (ed.), *Falten, Knoten, Netze, Stülpungen in Kunst und Theorie*, Turia & Kant, 2009.

Pichler, A., *Wittgensteins "Philosophische Untersuchungen": Vom Buch zum Album,* Editions Rodopi, 2004.

Reichert, A., doctorate project *Diagrammatic of Thinking. Of the Commencement of Thinking and the Thinking of Commencement in Descartes, Heidegger and Deleuze,* 2008.

A. Reichert, *Diagrammatik als virtuelle Politik* (Abstract for the conference: Zwischen Widerstand und Management), 2009.

Rheinberger, H.-J., *Iterationen*, Merve, 2005.

Rheinberger, H.-J., *Experimentalsysteme und epistemische Dinge: Eine Geschichte der Proteinsynthese im Reagenzglas*, Suhrkamp, 2001

Schmidt-Burkhardt, A., *Stammbäume der Kunst. Zur Genealogie der Avantgarde*, Oldenbourg Akademieverlag, 2005.

Schröter, J., *Zur Geschichte Theorie und Medienästhetik des technisch transplanen Bildes*, Fink, 2009.

Schürmann, E., *Sehen als Praxis,* Suhrkamp, 2008.

Siegert, B., *Passage des Digitalen – Zeichenpraktiken der neuzeitlichen Wissenschaften 1500-1900*, Brinkmann U. Bose, 2003.

Spencer-Brown, G., *Laws of Form – Gesetze der Form*, 1969.

Stjernfelt, F., *Diagrammatology: An Investigation on the Borderlines of Phenomenology, Ontology, and Semiotics,* Springer, 2007.

Willats, J., *Art and representation. New Principles in the Analysis of Pictures*, Princeton University Press, 1997.

Wittgenstein, L., *Über Gewissen, Werkausgabe Band 8*, Suhrkamp, 1984.

Wittgenstein, L., *Tractatus logico-philosophicus, Werkausgabe Band 1*, Suhrkamp, 1984.

Wittgenstein, L., *Tractatus logico-philosophicus: Logisch-philosophische Abhandlung*, Suhrkamp, 1963.

Zittel, C., *Theatrum philosophicum: Descartes und die Rolle ästhetischer Formen in der Wissenschaft*, Oldenbourg Akademieverlag, 2009.

HYPOTHESIS #13

Radical Cartographies

Philippe Rekacewicz

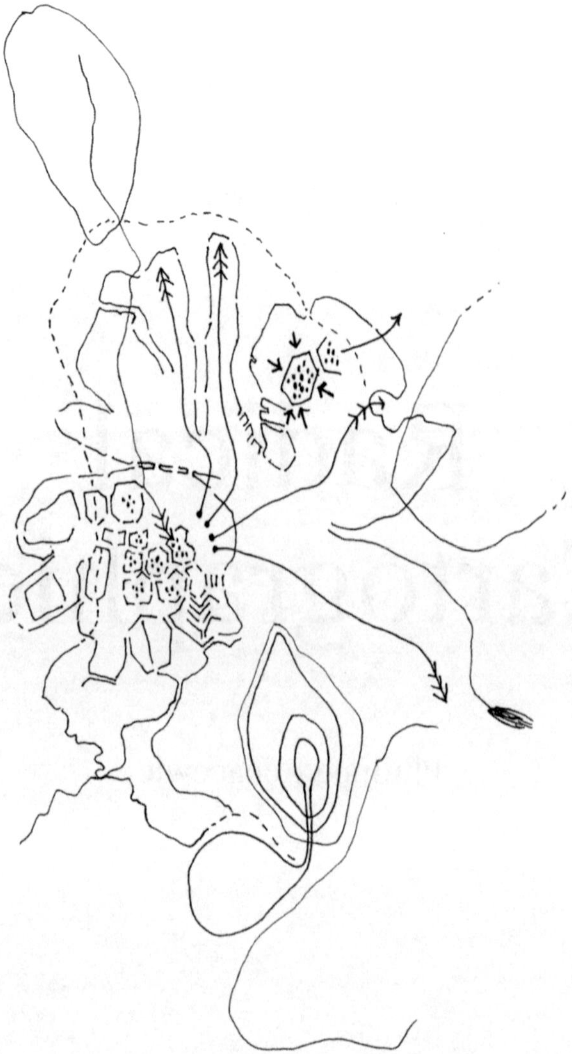

Fig. 06-01

This holy site, probably from the palaeolithic period, appears at first sight to be chaotically organised. But when we look more closely, we see that it has been very carefully built. On the left-hand side, all the "houses" or "apartments" lie together, closely linked with one another, with a few gardens at the back. The really important meeting place is in front, in the Forum (or a social place where exchanges take place), which is also the departure point for four pathways leading to other important public places. Two of these lead to places of worship, where people could also probably rest, and two others are paths leading away from the community by the east and the south. The holy hill lies to the south, while the tombs of the ancestors (symbolised by concentric arrows) lie to the north, as if in a mirror effect.

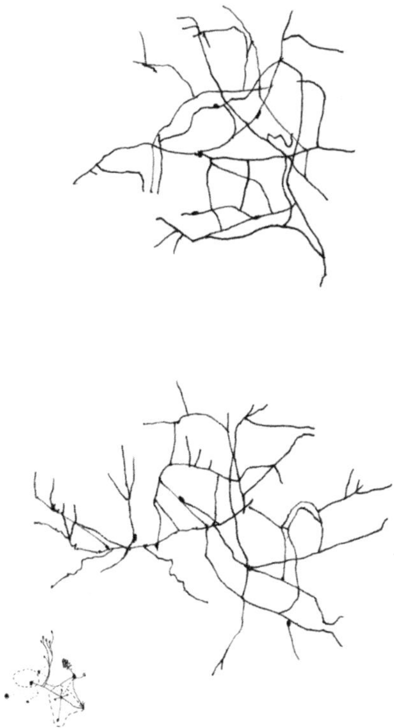

Fig. 06-02

In fifty years, the network has changed radically. It has been greatly simplified. The old network (bottom of drawing) from 1850 showed imprecise directions, and the construction of numerous pathways had not even been completed, whether owing to lack of money or lack of will, or perhaps simply prevented by the riots which occurred at the end of January 1951. In 1900 (top of drawing), paths and roads are somewhat straighter, and many of them have finally been completed. Those still ending in dead-ends open onto parks and gardens. Note that some tracks have vanished, to be replaced by built-up areas. Note also that the "multi-centre community" of the mid-19th century has disappeared, to regroup in one unique centre five decades later. Concentration, globalisation, standardisation, and the drive for efficiency had already begun at the dawn of the 20th century.

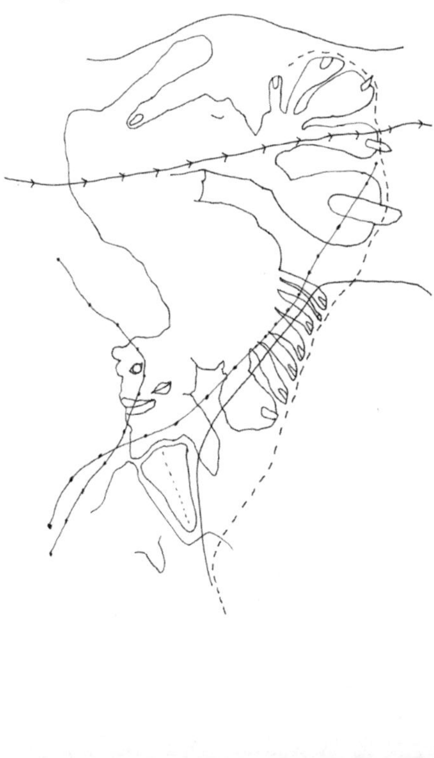

Fig. 06-05

It is always very difficult to find a practical way of building any kind of network on mountainous or uneven terrain such as this. The isoline clearly shows deep slopes which require numerous bridges and tunnels so that the road doesn't become too dangerous. On the other hand, for the two gas pipelines, it's easier: they can be laid whatever the structure of the land. The narrow plateaux are like long, thin fingers pointing to something hidden in the landscape, while in the south, two small sandy basins are like two mouths about to kiss.

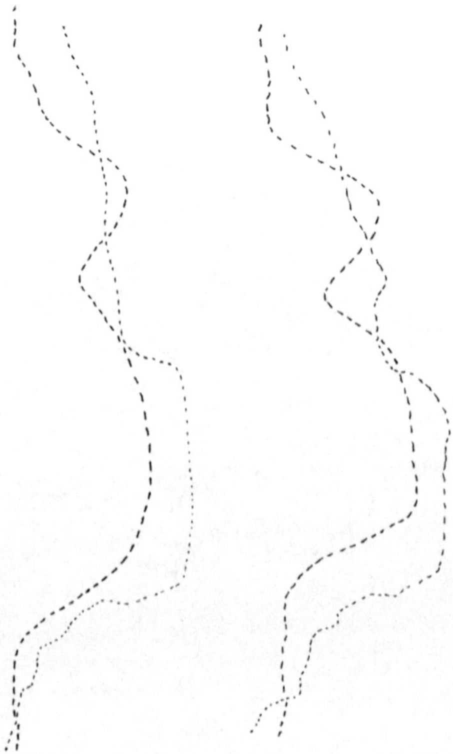

Fig. 06-04

The shorelines shift, under attack by the sea. But the waves do not have the same power everywhere. In some places, they are powerful enough to dig into the sand and drive back the coast, while in other places, the less powerful waves allow sand to accumulate, so that the coast gains from the sea. The cartographer made a mistake when drawing the coastline. He was obliged to draw the right-hand part of it again.

Fig. 07-03a

These little rats are running about everywhere, apparently without logic or goal. They run here and there, seeking food and drink wherever possible, and in the end finding nothing. They're terribly hungry. And in the end, all pathways lead to the same place ... sooner or later they manage to return to the boxes where the scientist leading the experiment has left some drops of sugared water.

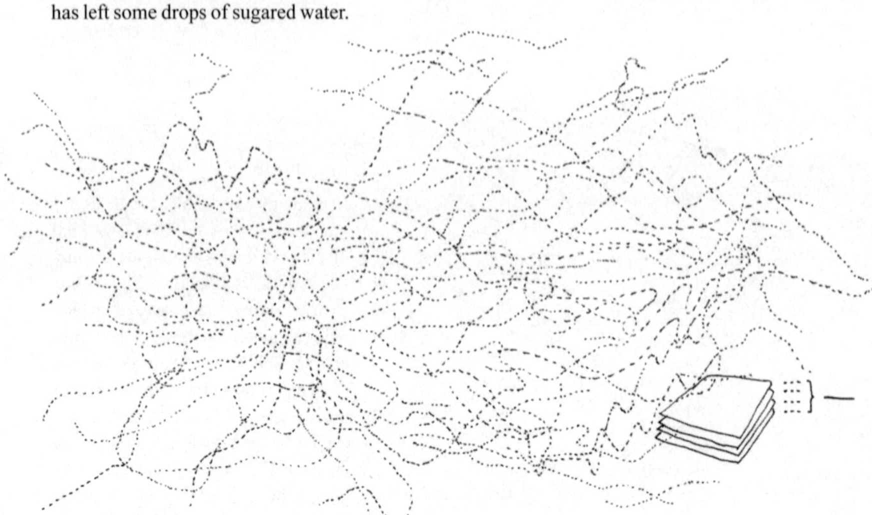

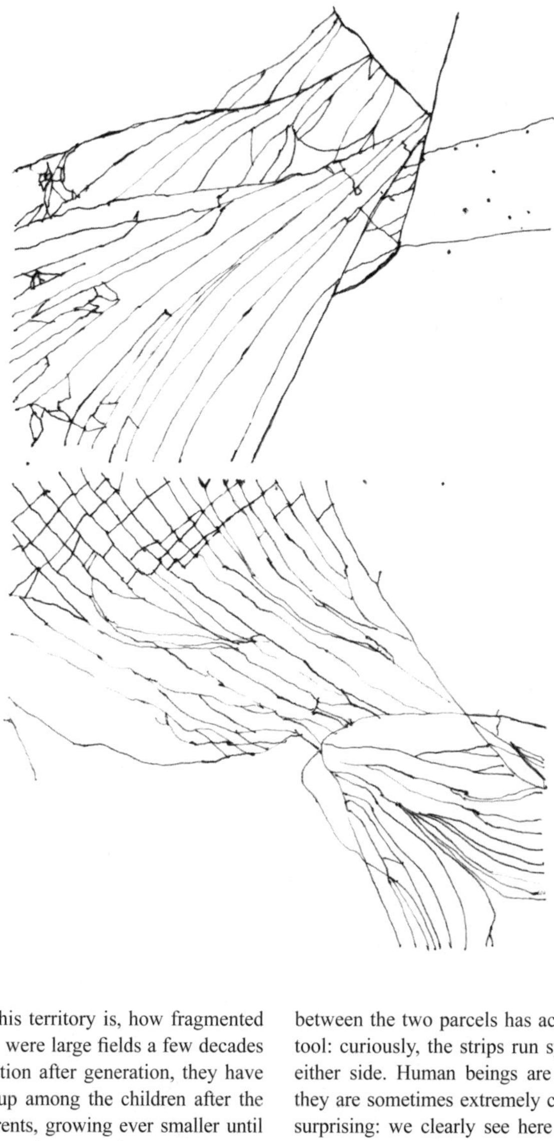

Fig. 07-00

How troubled this territory is, how fragmented and torn! These were large fields a few decades ago, but generation after generation, they have been parcelled up among the children after the death of the parents, growing ever smaller until they are no more than a series of thin slices on which nothing can be grown. The road in between the two parcels has acted like a magic tool: curiously, the strips run symmetrically on either side. Human beings are not perfect, but they are sometimes extremely creative and even surprising: we clearly see here that an ideal of justice drove them to share the land out equally, so that each beneficiary received the same amount.

Fig. 06-08

The fireworks are lit from both sides, but those on the right-hand side fail to explode. For a few seconds their traces remain in the sky, but without the explosions they have failed to produce their blue, red, green or yellow rain of stars.

Fig. 06-07

This archaeological site, so far, is unique. Nonetheless, planners have decided that highway 15 and a toll station (larger than the highway) will go through, anyway. It is sad to see money interests prevailing over cultural uniqueness.

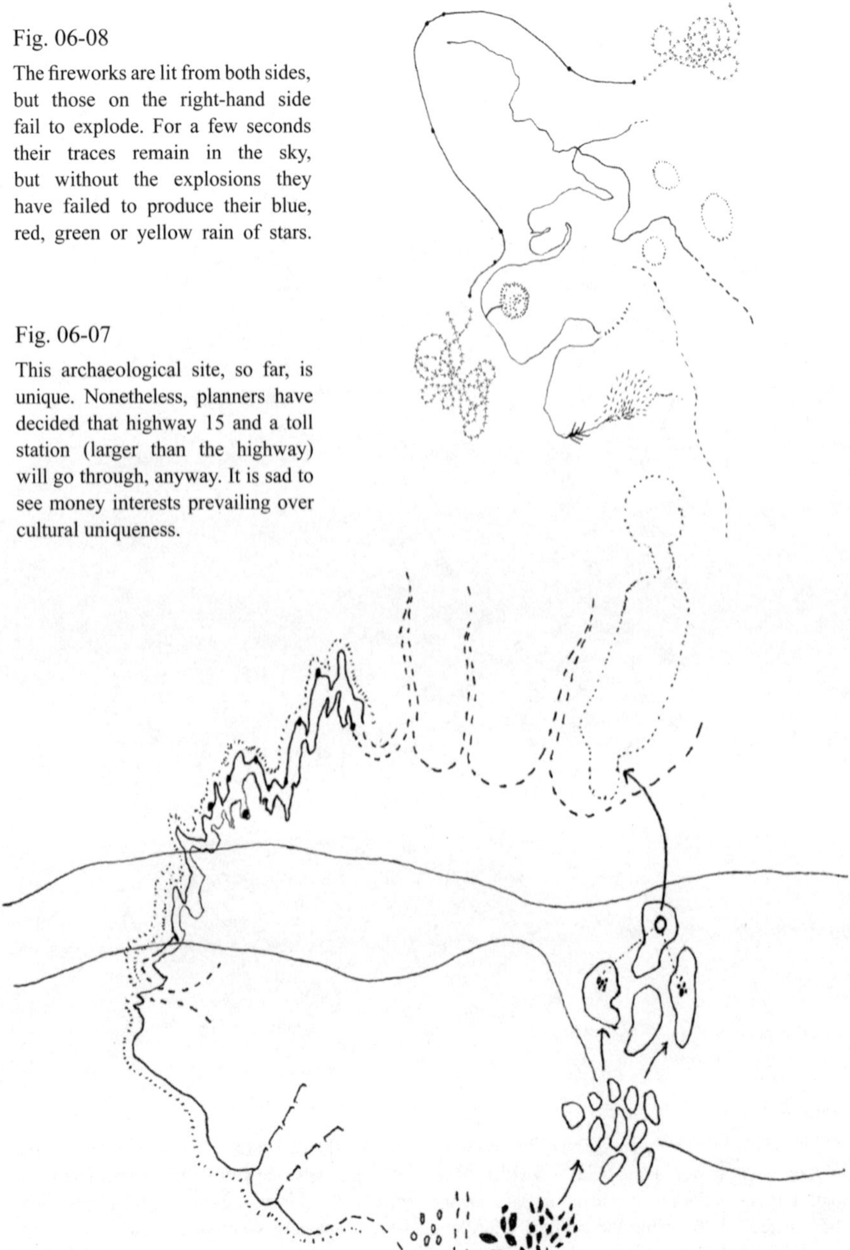

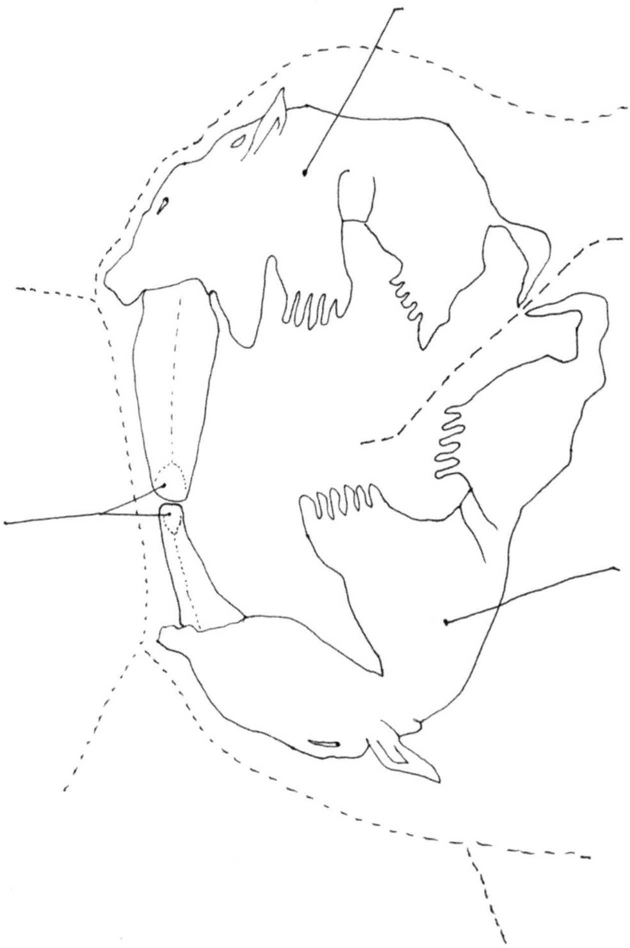

Fig. 06-06

This rock painting from the palaeolithic symbolises two animals, a pig and a prehistoric donkey, badly injured with arrows planted deeply in their bodies, probably shot by hunters a few moments before. They are both in agony, with tongues hanging out as if to catch more air to breathe. This tragic scene remains a testimony of a time which appears to have been wild and brutal.

HYPOTHESIS #14

3 Elements

Axel Stockburger

1. ORIENTATION

In his lecture *Die Krise der Linearität* (*Crisis of Linearity*) at the Bern Kunstmuseum in 1988, Vilèm Flusser described the origins of image production as follows: "Let us take as an example the oldest of the images known to us (that of a pony in Pêche-Merle). It concerns representation on rock faces. The maker of the image stepped away from a pony, looked at it and transmitted what he briefly saw to the memory of the wall. And he did this in such a way that others would recognise what they saw. And he did all these immensely complex things so as to be able to use what he saw as an orientation for future actions – such as the hunt for ponies."[1]

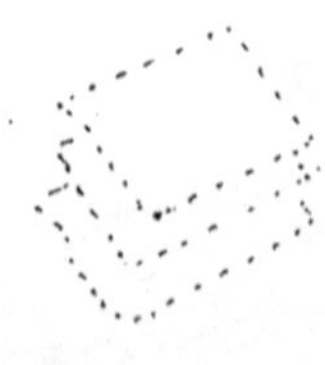

Fig. 07-08a

In order to maintain orientation in a chaotic and alien universe, it is initially necessary to obtain an overview of the situation which enables the separation of phenomena and their potential effects. But if there is too much visual information at hand, or vital clues are occluded by environmental factors, confusion is bound to set in. Climbing a tree allows for a better vantage point, but a continuous flow of visual information demands a continuous presence. Thus it is necessary to reduce the amount of information and to develop codes: operations on a symbolic level which have the power to stop the flow temporarily in order to create time and space for reflection and for planning for the future. Most importantly, the external field that is opened in this way can be used to share vital information, and it becomes the pivot for the discourse that surrounds the event, such as a future hunt. Drawing becomes a practice of externalisation, which opens additional channels of control over time and space by introducing a code that transforms four-dimensional space-time into projections of scenes on a two-dimensional plane. In this context, drawing can be seen as the artificial focal point within a complex web of relations between perceivable events in the world, and also as a symbolic layer of language.

If we follow Flusser's thought, image-making at this stage is embedded within a circular flow of action and reflection, which will be be interrupted once written language introduces a form of codification imbued with linearisation, thus directly attacking the

1) Vilèm Flusser, *Krise der Linearität*, Vortrag Kunstmuseum Bern am 20. März 1988, Benteli, Bern, p. 10, 1988.

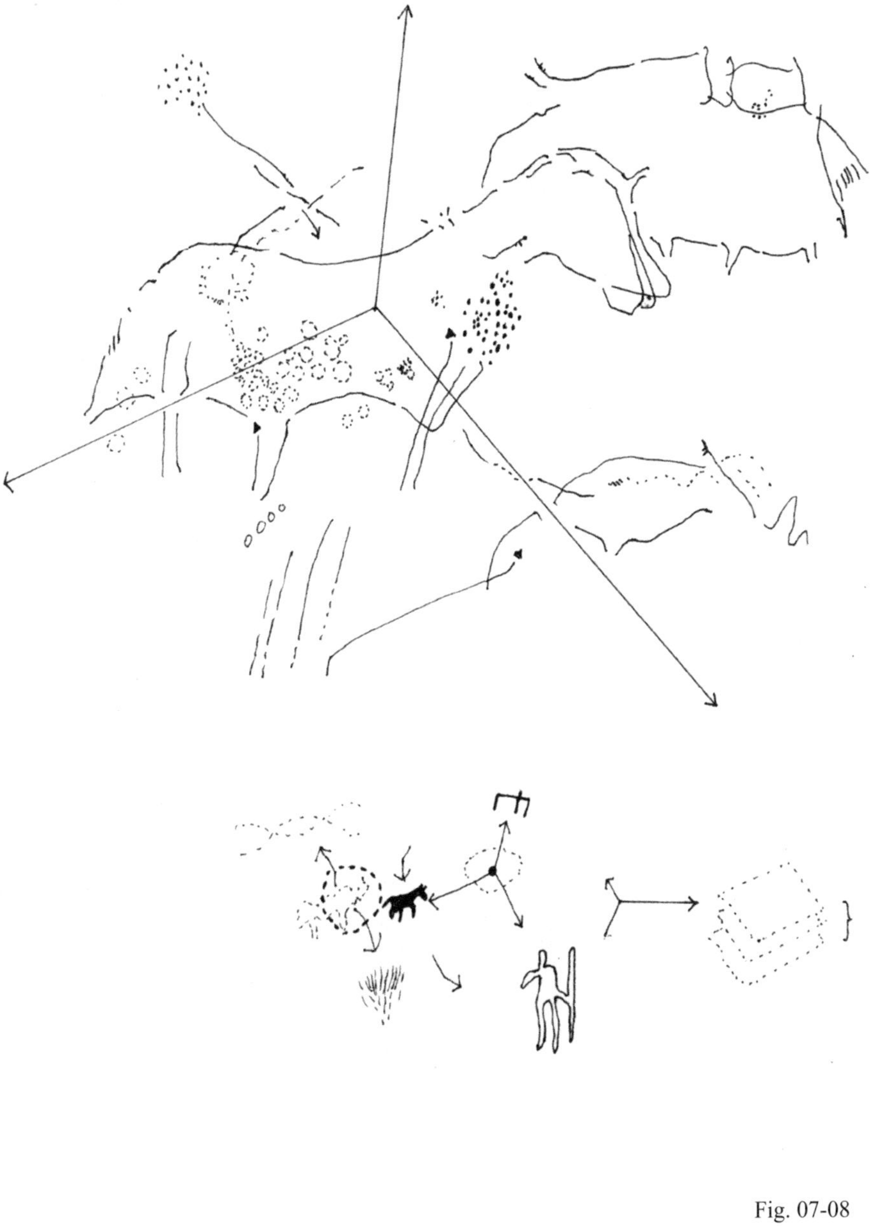

Fig. 07-08

power of the image. The mental projections made by the hunters maintain the status of strategic territorial tools, not precise mimetic representations. In this sense, they do not amount to attempts to represent the world as it really is. Once the ontological state of the image starts to shift from being a means of orientation in the world towards becoming a projection into the world which in turn affects it directly, the initial spark for a long history of conflicts between idolatries and iconoclasms is lit. Whenever the balance between these two different modes shifts too far towards those who have forgotten that they are dealing with representational tools and have begun to believe in the images in their own right, the power of words is quickly at hand to shatter their worlds.

(→ PII/03)

Traces of this immense balancing exercise, which can be followed throughout western history, also remain within the core of scientific image production. The images floating through the sphere of modern science oscillate between two different

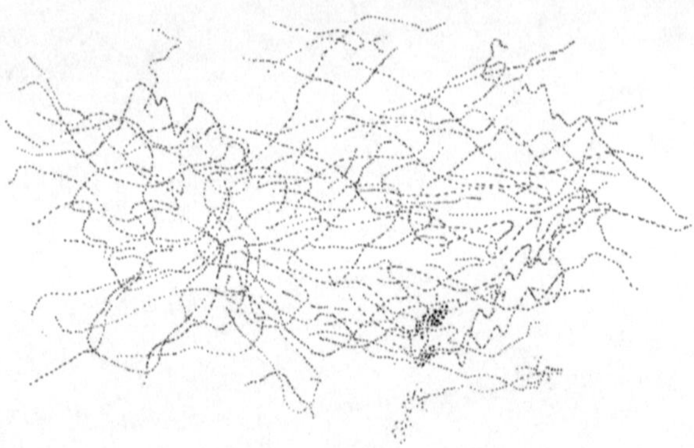

Fig. 06-03

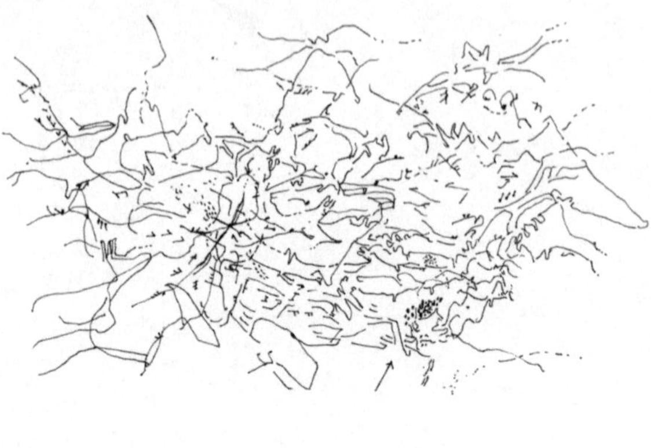

Fig. 07-07

effects of the practice of image-making: one allows peers to orient themselves within a chaotic universe, while the other literally generates the world of science. Most importantly, both of these functions of the image are embedded within a dense web of written language, which subjects them to continual critical scrutiny and triggers the ever present flow of new images and image-making technologies.

2. MAPPING THE SPIRITS

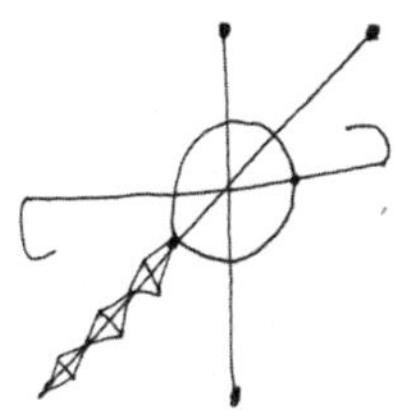

Fig. Y01a

In the Haitian form of Voodoo, drawing has a central position in many rituals. The so-called *veves* are drawings pointing towards specific *loa* or spirits. They are commonly drawn on the floor with a mixture of either crushed eggshells or materials such as cornmeal and wood ash. On the one hand, these materials seem to mimic drawings traced in the sand; on the other hand, the materials employed introduce an additional dimension of materiality. Interestingly, these drawings cannot be regarded as mere representations of the deities, allthough each drawing refers to a specific spirit. Rather, they equate to specific types of maps, which are drawn as part of a ritual in order to enable the believers to establish contact with a loa. This becomes very obvious in the case of the deity of Papa Legba, who is believed to control the pathways to the spirit world and whose *veve* consists of an intricate crossway resembling a Cartesian coordinate system. Papa Legba acts as an interlocutor, a keeper of the keys to the spirit world, which is why he is commonly invoked at the beginning and end of a spiritual session. Only the initiated are capable of drawing *veves* precise enough for a successful operation.

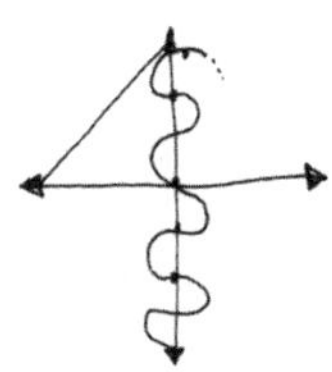

Fig. Y01b

Drawing in this context leads far beyond representation, and it is especially the map-like character of certain *veves*, which may be explained through the formal aspects they share with ancient Congolese cosmographical maps, which gives them an orientation function. If the magical universe is understood as a circular existence grounded in eternal return, the act of drawing a *veve* on the ground unleashes its powers to affect the universe each time it is performed anew. During the ritual, the *veve* then becomes the location for offerings to the spirits, such as rum or blood. The power of the *veve* lies precisely in its ability to work

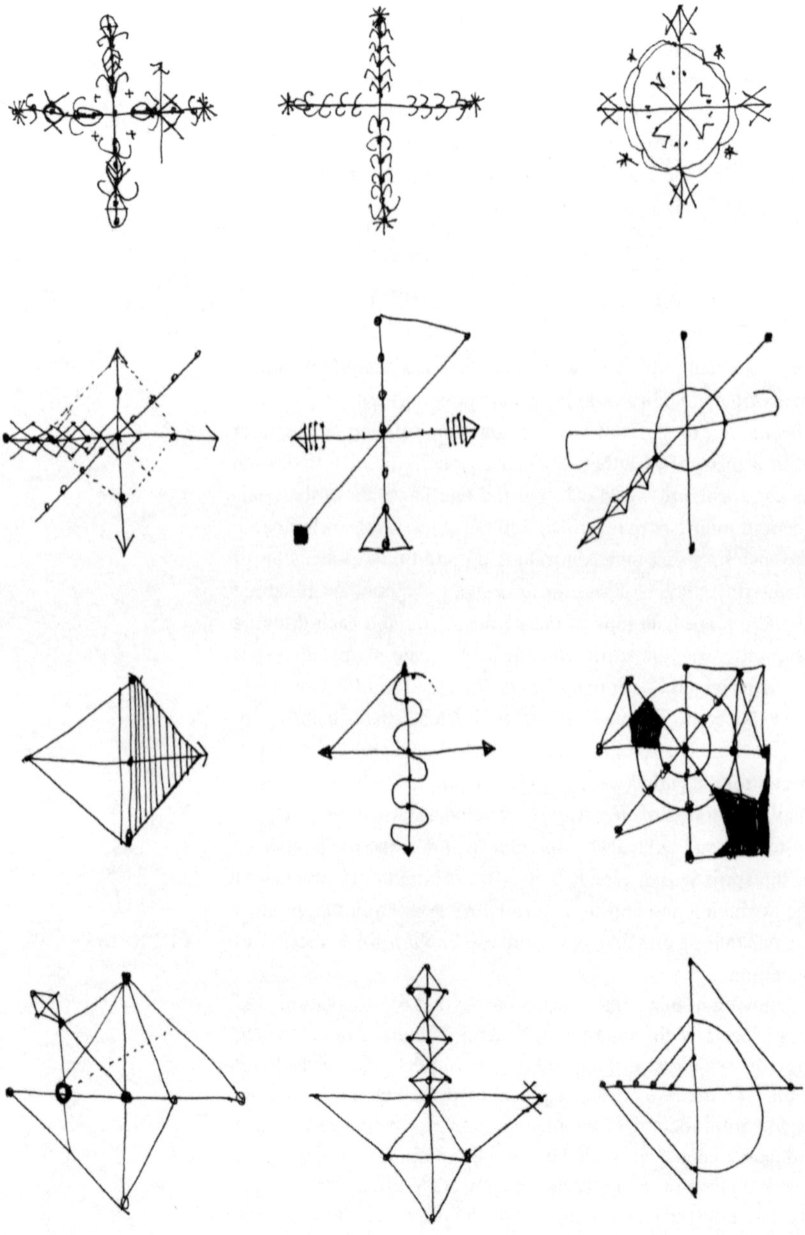

Fig. Y01

simultaneously as a map, without which the believers could not hope to locate the spirits, and as a symbol encapsulating the significant qualities of the deity. In contrast to the images of Christian saints, who are placed in a church to be prayed to, these images have to be, as it were, performed, in order to develop their potential. When the *veve* is drawn, a journey from earthly reality towards the spirit world is undertaken. Thus the practice of *veve* drawing belongs to those magical types of ritual drawing which do not enter the problematic relationship between reality and representation that Jean Baudrillard refers to as the second phase of the image, where he points out that the image 'masks and perverts a basic reality', simply because the presentational aspects of it are not meant to 'stand in' for an external reality, but are rather the result of a process which leads to a dimension of reality that is obscured and hidden from view.

It could be argued that at least some of these characteristics are also at work in the case of specific kinds of scientific drawings or diagrams, at least those that are not meant to represent visible aspects of reality but aim to lead towards a specific set that is quite literally hidden from view. It is here that the practice of drawing exposes some of its most powerful aspects – namely the potential to guide, to function as an interlocutor, rather than to present a replacement. Of course there are many differences between scientific drawings and voodoo *veves*, but both are intentional, formal practices which aim to control and affect the universe from the perspective of a group of initiated peers, and both forms hint at aspects of reality that might be hidden from view and thus are outside of the regime of mimetic representation. For example, the famous depiction of the double helix model of the DNA structure can be read as such a form of interlocution, pointing to obscured layers within the fabric of reality. Voodoo *veves* and scientific drawings do not belong to the same worldviews, but they most definitely share numerous important aspects that can help us to understand the intricate intermediary power of image-making. This power can be seen as a cascade of repetitions leading to chains of patterns reconfigured around elementary forms and traces hinting at crosses, dots, circles, lines and squares. Why not overlay Papa Legba's *veve* with Cartesian coordinates and enter measurements of the time it takes to perform the drawing of the different forms that establish it? In this case the offering would be the scientific method of measurement itself rather than drops of chicken blood.

(→ PIII/01)

3. SIMULATION EQUATION

As Bruno Latour has pointed out, one of the most powerful effects that drawings and diagrams have attained within the sphere of science is that they are not only capable of distilling complex relationships between hybrids into representations on a flat surface, but that this form enables them to become "immutable mobiles"[2]. The aspects of immutability and mobility are transformed into multiplying factors with the advent of the printing press and the consequent possibility of conserving and copying scientific drawings and diagrams. However, it is precisely this element of immutability that seems to be affected in a very significant way once we enter the phase of the technical image, and more precisely that of scientific visualisation, in conjunction with forms of simulation.

What is interesting in the case of digital models based on simulation is that they seem to sacrifice immutability for the sake of something deeply rooted in the behaviour of systems. In this case, drawings are generated by programmes and updated in conjunction with the pulse of digital computers. Depending on the scientific field, the visual models can be fed by streams of live data that affect the shapes and forms of the images drawn to the buffer of a graphics card and then sent to a display. Immutability is exchanged for dynamic updates. Especially in the case of digital simulation, the interplay between real and referent seems to have been exchanged for an exchange among the referents themselves. If one follows the hypotheses of Baudrillard, this amounts to an ontological rupture in terms of the relationship between image and world, since, in these cases, as he puts it, the image 'bears no relation to any reality whatever: it is its own pure simulacrum'[3].

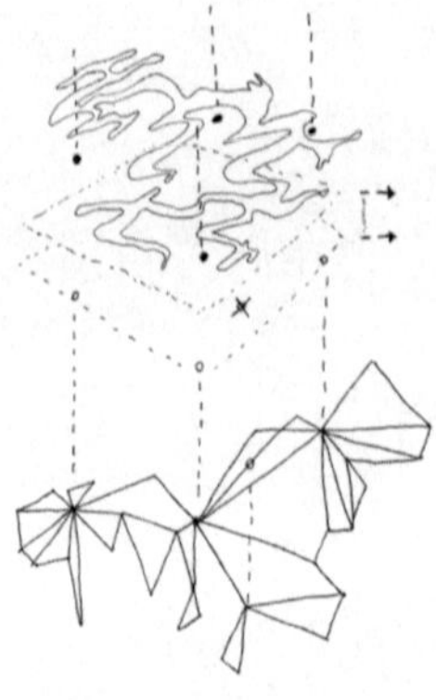

Fig. 05-06

Based on Borges' famous short story, *On exactitude in science*[4], where the map of a territory becomes so detailed that it entirely covers the ground it represents, thus leading to a destroyed map which once covered the real ground underneath, such an ontological step away from a classic system of reference seems to lead to dire consequences. However, not only would it be a bit too

2) Bruno Latour, *Visualisation and Cognition: Drawing Things Together*, available: http://www.bruno-latour.fr/articles/article/21-DRAWING-THINGS-TOGETHER.pdf, 1990.

3) Jean Baudrillard, *Simulacra and Simulations*, in: *Selected Writings*, Mark Poster (ed.), Polity, Cambridge, p. 170, 1988.

4) Jorge Luis Borges, *On Exactitude* in: *Science, Collected Fictions*, Translated by Andrew Hurley, Penguin, London, 1999.

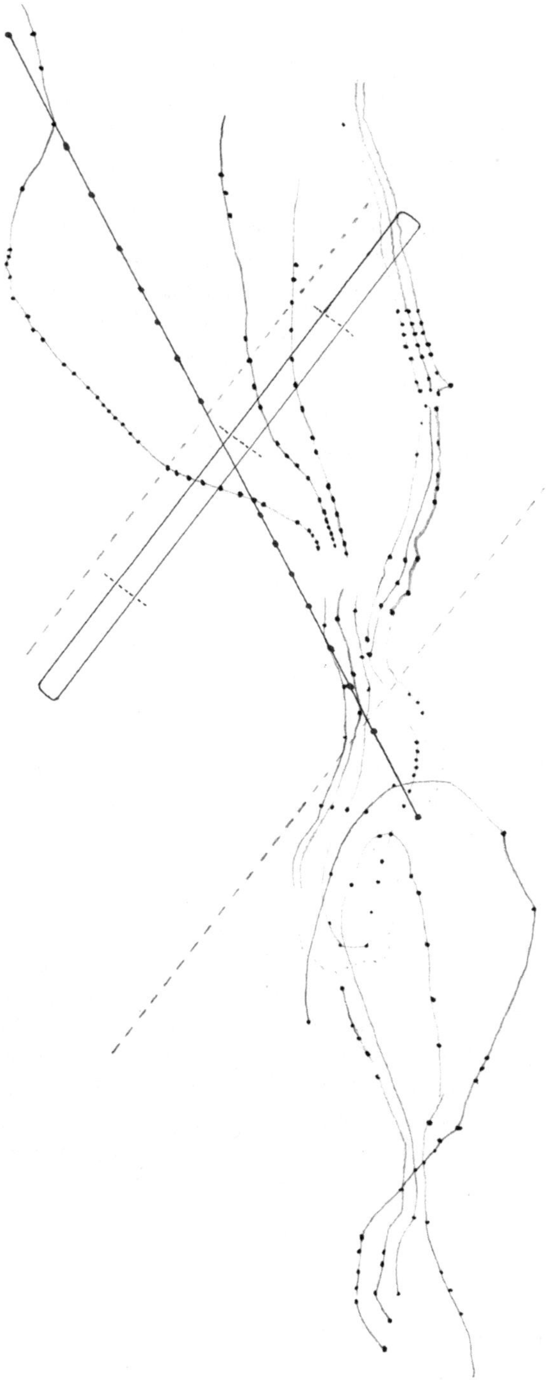

Fig. 10-07

easy to entirely do away with ideology in the face of simulation, as Baudrillard concludes, but it also seems that simulation offers a slightly different route. Most importantly, the paradox of a 1:1 scaled map is based on a conception of static projection.

The relation to reality that is maintained by all kinds of simulations is not a direct link between a sign and a signifier, but aims to capture that which exists between signifiers and, on a different level, between signs. What is mimicked or represented is not the thing but the behaviour of a system and in this sense that which interconnects things, concepts, signs and programmes. In this sense, the practice of digital simulation does indeed introduce a slightly more complex equation into the old balancing act between world and image. Some read this shift as an implosion which interweaves all the elements in this equation, leading towards a suspension of meaning and a breakdown of orders. One could also step into this field from the other side, as cybernetics and system theory have done, by focusing on the immanence of constructivist notions of self-contained worlds whose organisational principles then become the centre of attention.

Another way to interpret the qualitative change brought about by simulation could be to recognise more fully the hybrid character that underlines these forms of image production. If relations between elements belonging to different categories such as technology, nature, politics or economy have become what is represented, it could be useful to try and develop a slightly different notion of those categories as well as of the internal logic of separation. Of course, the kind of subterranean fear set free by the proliferation of aleatoric combinations between entities, perfectly brought to life in the ending sequence of the Japanese Animation classic 'Akira', is the horror in the face of a boundless maelstrom that has instigated the production of drawings in order to ban, demarcate and limit perception. Thus, at present, a practice of drawing engendered with such a drive towards deliberate limitation of information seems to provide a viable subjective counter-measure to networks of automated hybrid image production.

HYPOTHESIS #15

Dances of Space*

Marc Boeckler

*Dancing is what scientists do. They don't master their material, no, never, rather they engage in "open-ended and performative dances of agency".[1] They are trying this and that with the world, finding out what the world will do and responding to the world's reactions. So, what if the visual is not a visualisation of the seen, what if a graph or a map is not a representation of the world, but instead is perfoming a space for the unseen, causing the unwritten to be written, generating knowledge no one ever wanted to have. So then, who will be dancing? How do we respond? How do we go on from here?

1) Andrew Pickering, *The Mangle of Practice: Time, Agency, and Science*, University of Chicago Press, Chicago, 1995.

THE NETWORKED SUCKER

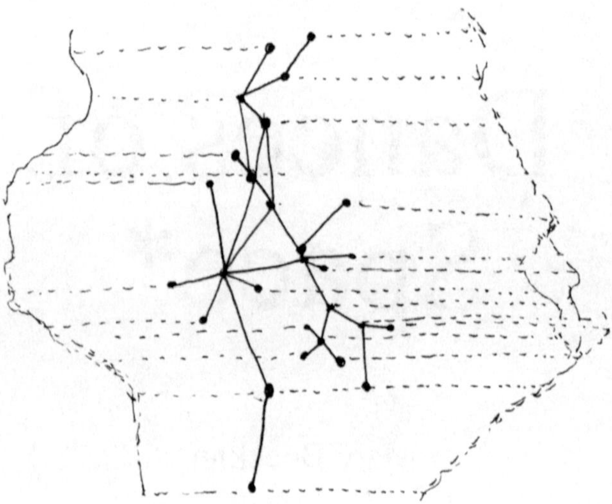

Fig. 05-10

Figure 05-10 exemplifies spatial homeomorphism in processes of territorial learning. The black dots indicate the topographical location of single firms in a high-technology cluster, and the continuous black lines constitute the topology of social connectivity between firms. The left and right borders of the graph demarcate the cluster's territory and the length of the dotted horizontal lines expresses the amount of localised knowledge (= local buzz) accumulated within a single firm. The graph conveys two revolutionary insights. First, the firm with the highest 'betweenness centrality' and 'degree centrality' is always located where the cluster reaches its largest spatial extension. Second, this firm (center left) emanates no buzz lines of its own. Centrality, therefore, is the performative effect of the suction of other firms' sense of locality.

THE EVOLUTIONARY NOTHING

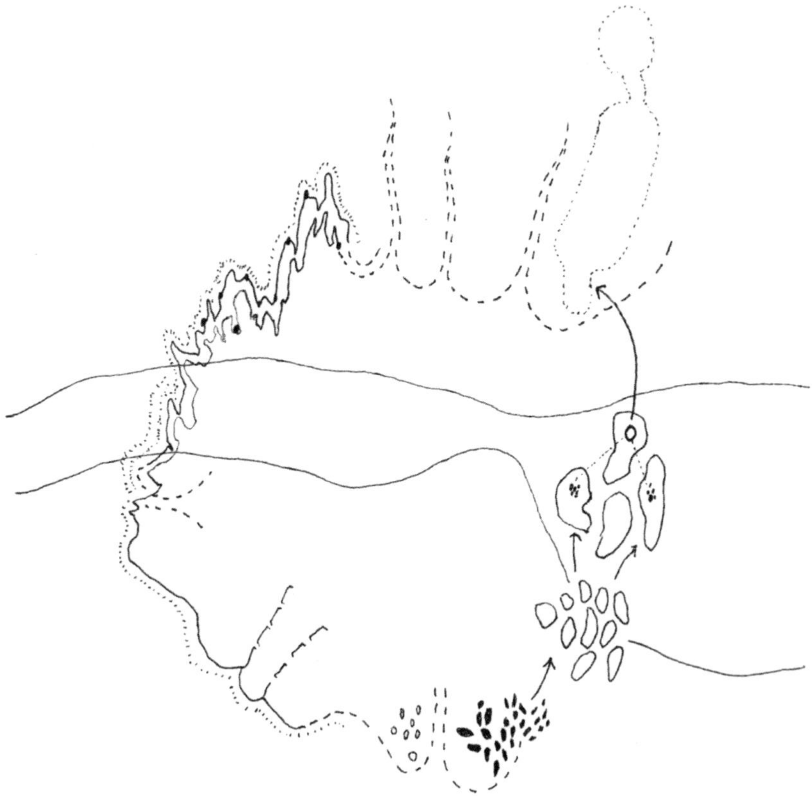

Fig. 06-07

Across the life cycle of a territorially clustered population, different modes of spatial evolution emerge as a function of political intervention. The horizontal corridor crossing the adaptation circle delineates the average space of political interference in the natural selection environment of so called cultural industries. The figure shows how a creative population is initially zigzagging through the gene pool of a specific urban landscape (upper left) with a high degree of innovative creativity and productivity. Due to special incentive programmes, the genetic drift comes to a sudden halt and the evolutionary progress enters a phase of path-dependent stasis with very little variation (lower left). The punctuated equilibrium is only exposed to rapid change again (lower right) only after a small series of entries and exits allows for alternative gene flow inducing new speciation processes. At this point political intervention exercises severe selective pressure that results in the survival of only two distinct industries with a high potential for place based branding. After a short period of regional economic growth, the sharply reduced variation in the gene pool leads to the inevitable extinction of the creative species. The remains enter an embryonic phase of progressive indifference (upper right). So called incubation waves may set new evolutionary dances in motion, or they may just just fail to do so. …

NORMALISED SPACES

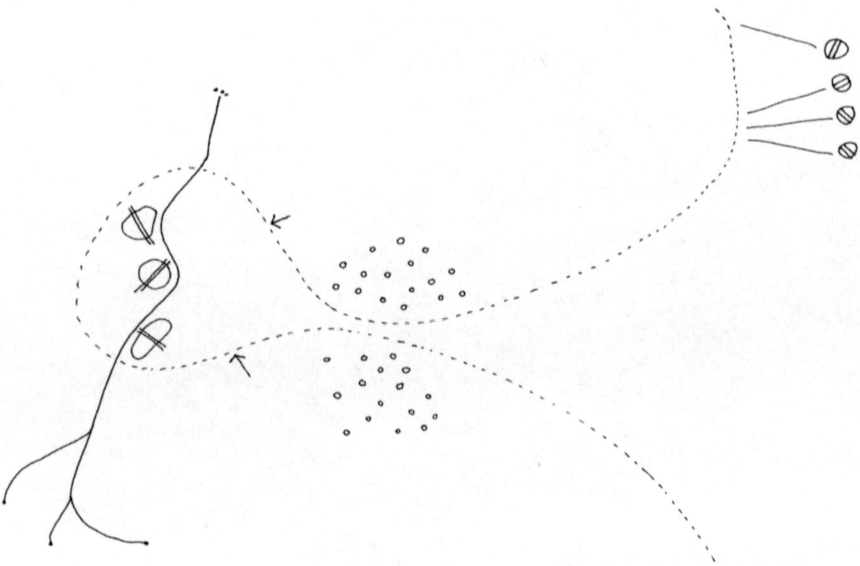

Fig. 09-03

The thin continuous line running from south to north (left) arranges three distant and differing elements in a state of space-time sameness. The dashed horizontal space – seen through a magnifying lens – depicts the paradoxies of a translocal process of approximation. Here 'geometers' – circular entities of different size – exert calculative power to generate comparable similarities and distinguishable differences in product qualities.

THE REPRODUCTIVE FRAME OF MATTER

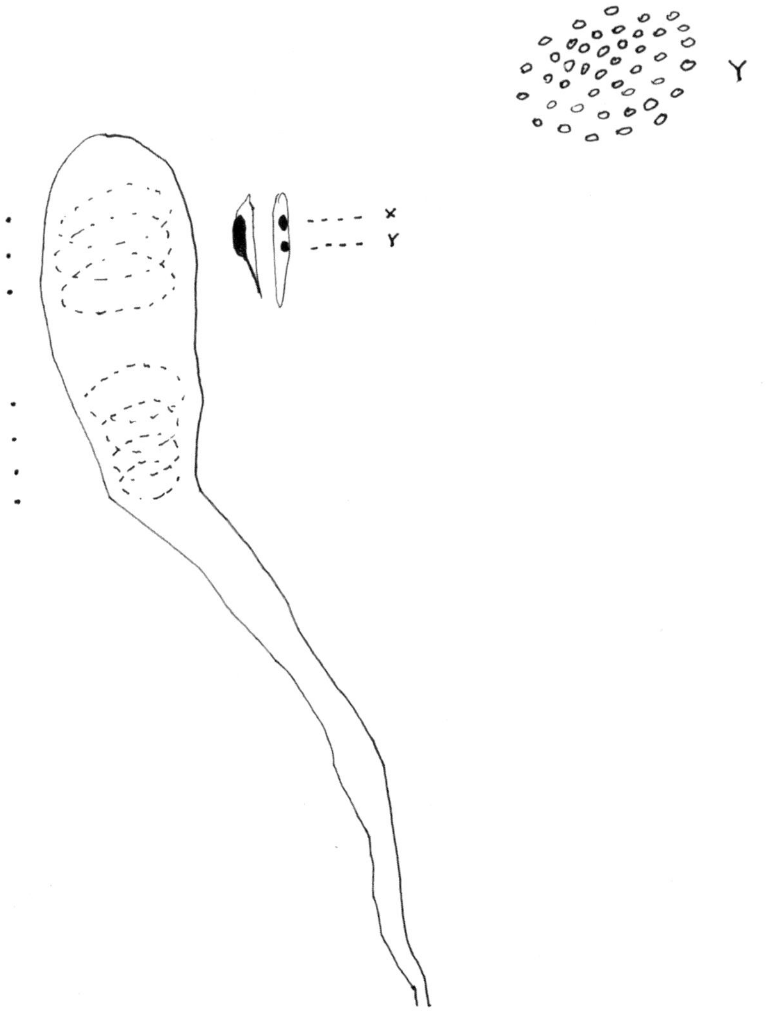

Fig. 02-27

The world is a moving relation of heterogeneous materials. Structural stability is an effect of the gyration of inextricably connected elements. However, things (x) and humans (y) in particular tend to conceptualise themselves as inhabiting distinct spaces. This ontological self-deception is temporarily made durable through a representational squeezing that is commonly known as 'diacritical practice'.

EARTHED PROGRESS

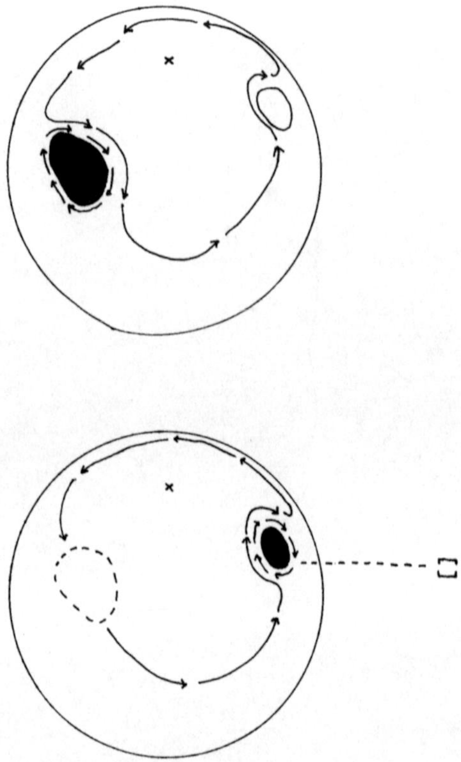

Fig. 03-27

Figure 03-27 proves the strong causal nexus between geography and economic development. Clockwise rotating convective cells fuel counterclockwise spatialised growth patterns. Accompanied by heavy shaking and rumbling, the engine is regularly shifted along predetermined trade routes. While a decentered observer (x) perceives these events as destructive cataclysm, the net amount of global wealth, as indicated by brackets, is a function of the gravitational equilibrium between the earth's lithosphere and asthenosphere, and therefore remains basically unaffected by crisis or growth.

HYPOTHESIS #16

Emotions and Orientation

Graphically recorded from my Cartography and History Archive

Christian Reder

AFRICA

In debates over migration and xenophobia, which, as is well known, can easily become radicalised, it is worthwhile recalling what Brian M. Fagan points out in his *Journey from Eden*: "the comprehensive colonisation of our planet" beginning in Africa was the first globalisation of all, "the greatest migration project in the history of mankind". Genetic research has by now shown that very small groups advanced ever further into the unknown, and endeavoured very early to cover considerable distances on the high seas – onto the Arabian peninsula, to Australia or along the coast of Alaska. Tens of thousands of years before the advent of writing, signs and pictures served as an important means of expression. According to Fagan, an anatomically based capacity for speech "meeting all the requirements for a complete language", exceeding signing and rough articulation and allowing differentiated vocalisation, may have originated among humans some 300,000 years ago, probably initially with *Homo sapiens*. A consideration of developments of this kind allowed the Burkina Faso historian Joseph Ki-Zerbo (1922-2006) to bring a different perspective to the isolated overestimation of early high cultures, above all that of Egypt. It is clear that these cultures are all interrelated and they can only be explained "if one thinks of the leading role that this continent played in the paleolithic and neolithic periods". The Nile valley, predominantly peopled from the south, became "the laboratory for a new humanity"; "African prehistoric art" was "the richest in the world by far", with forms of expression "of such great originality that they are still influencing our art today", comparably to the current significance of African-American music. The discoveries of recent decades have pushed the timeline for conscious design ever further back to far more distant eras than the 'prehistoric revolution' long accepted as the caesura. (→ PII/03) The oldest abstract work – or oldest work of art – is currently held to be an engraving some 77,000 years old and only a few centimetres high, from the Blombos cave near Capetown, under excavation since 1991, where the artfully drilled mussels regarded to date as the oldest examples of jewellery were also found. Layers of sediment allow for very precise dating. What the engraved lines could mean will never be known. But they were definitely made, and they may be diagrams of consciousness symbolising something or other – like memory patterns or directions spontaneously drawn in the sand, wherever they point to.

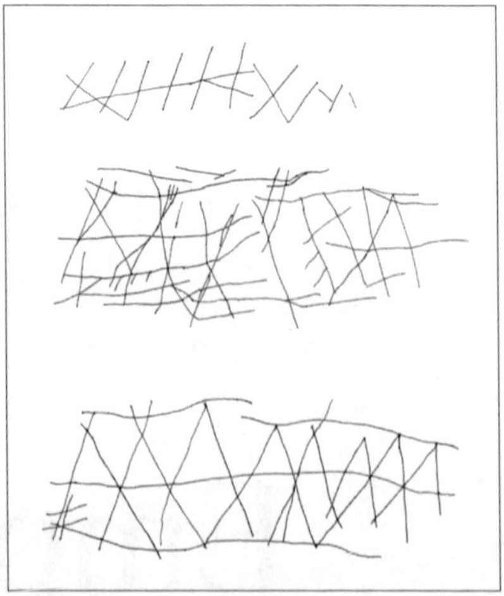

Fig. 07-17

77,000 year-old abstraction, Blombos cave near Capetown, South Africa.

Brian M. Fagan, *Aufbruch aus dem Paradies* (*The Journey from Eden. The Peopling of Our World*, London, 1990) Munich, 1991, pp. 227, 97 | Joseph Ki-Zerbo: *Die Geschichte Schwarz-Afrikas* (Original French edition: *Histoire de l'Afrique Noire*, Paris, 1978; Angloamerican edition: *UNESCO General History of Africa*, Oakland, 1990) Wuppertal, 1979, pp. 59, 79, 53, 71 | Blombos-Höhle: www.nsf.gov/od/lpa/news/02/pr0202images.htm | Wikipedia: Blombos Cave, List of archaeological discoveries in southern Africa.

PICTORIAL SIGNS

Stone-age cave paintings are so overwhelmingly impressive that for a long time little attention was paid to the extent of their function as medium for the transfer of knowledge from generation to generation over long periods, and how much they are pervaded by abstract signs. In many cases, according to new theories, they were painted with spittle, in other words with full bodily involvement, as is particularly apparent with hand prints, as if they were signatures, hinting at the same time at a basic form of counting (5 + 5 = 10). For Ki-Zerbo, all this is primarily an expression of "amazement at the animal world", the wish "to avert dangers", or "to bring

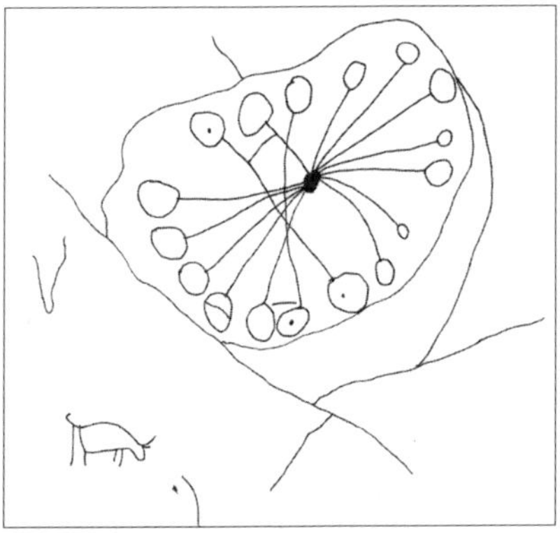

Fig. 08-15

Rock drawing, Algerian Sahara.

about a positive development through ritual gestures". According to Fagan, the significance thesis is foremost, "that above all, the little works of art, marked with points, notches, lines and other markings, contain 'notes' situating them in time, recalling important events or serving as a 'calendar' in which the phases of the moon and lunar months were recorded". As the great prehistory and rock paintings expert André Leroi-Gourhan (1911-1986) emphasised, all attempts at global chronological and stylistic comparison point to an exploratory spirit, since "at the individual level or in any small group isolated from figurative traditions, the art of drawing signifies a constant rediscovery". Hence, one of Leroi-Gourhan's most important works is entitled *Gesture and Speech: The evolution of technology, language and art*. From the beginning, the challenge has been to render comprehensible what is seen as well as the act of seeing itself, space and time – that is, movement – on a flat surface.

Joseph Ki-Zerbo, *Die Geschichte Schwarz-Afrikas* (Original French edition: Joseph Ki-Zerbo, *Histoire de l'Afrique Noire*, Paris, 1978; Angloamerican edition: *UNESCO General History of Africa*, Oakland, 1990) Wuppertal, 1979, p. 51 | Brian M. Fagan, *Aufbruch aus dem Paradies* (*The Journey from Eden. The Peopling of Our World*, London, 1990), Munich, 1991, p. 183 | André Leroi-Gourhan, *Prähistorische Kunst* (*Préhistoire de l'art occidental*, Paris 1971) Freiburg/Breisgau, 1971, pp. 19, 177 | André Leroi-Gourhan, *Hand und Wort. Die Evolution von Technik, Sprache und Kunst* (*La geste et la parole*, 2 volumes, Paris, 1964/65) Frankfort/Main, 1980 | Franz Trost, *PINTURAS. Felsbilder des Ahaggar* (Algerische Sahara), Graz, 1997, p. 151 | Christian Reder, *Sahara-Lexikon*, in: Ch. Reder, Elfie Semotan (ed.), *Sahara. Text- und Bildessays*, Wien-New York, 2004, pp. 305 ff.

OBSERVING THE HEAVENS

For a remarkably long time, representations of humans were avoided, and animals were regarded as a different and much more important form of life, apparently not just because they were food, which even suggests a conception of the ecology which transcends the merely anthropomorphic, incorporating animals and plants, and which has recently re-entered the debate. As a stage for transcendental events, the heavens must have been more fascinating than anything else; the phenomenon of the sun, generating light and warmth but also oppressive heat, rising and setting, at times hidden behind clouds or darkness, and the night, with its countless visible points of light, with the moon and its changing shape as a cyclical counterpoint to the dominating sun. The elements, as they are still known today, are inevitably perceived as phenomena generated 'from above': weather change, heat, cold, wind, rain, storms, lightning, thunder, thunderstorms, snow. The more important agriculture became, the more drastic became the dependence on fertility. Over the course of centuries of lengthy observations, it was increasingly recognised that the seasons, every calendar calculation, every division of time, had some relation to the heavens. At sea, the stars have been points of orientation since time immemorial. The course of the sun and the moon, the constellations of planets and stars were evidently experienced as existential events, utilised for existential orientation together with astrology and astronomy, as is clear from Stonehenge, megalithic structures, circular earthworks or pyramids, which often served a calendar-setting function as well. Long before charts of the land were considered necessary, charts of the stars were designed. The circa 3,600-year-old 'Nebra sky disc', found in 1999 in Germany, is believed to be the oldest concrete representation of the heavens anywhere in the world, while Egyptian tombs dating from just a little later contain illustrations of complete constellations. Even the rock paintings in the Great Hall of the Bulls in the cave of Lascaux, up to almost 20,000 years old, can be interpreted as a complete zodiac with corresponding references to the stars, important in most early cultures. The history of globes, too, as an attempted picture of 'the whole', begins with a 'model of the starry sky' going back to Eudoxos of Cnidus (408-355 BCE), showing that the ancients' interest in representing the firmament as celestial globes – such as the 'Farnese Atlas', of which only copies survive – was much greater than their interest in analogous representations of the earth itself. Already visualised as round, since its umbra on the moon and the gradual disappearance of ships beyond the horizon made this plausible, only a small part of the earth was deemed habitable, so that it was unnecessary to render the remaining void comprehensible as a globe. Hence, until the European age of discovery, the world map of Ptolemy (Claudius Ptolomaeus, c. 100-175 CE,

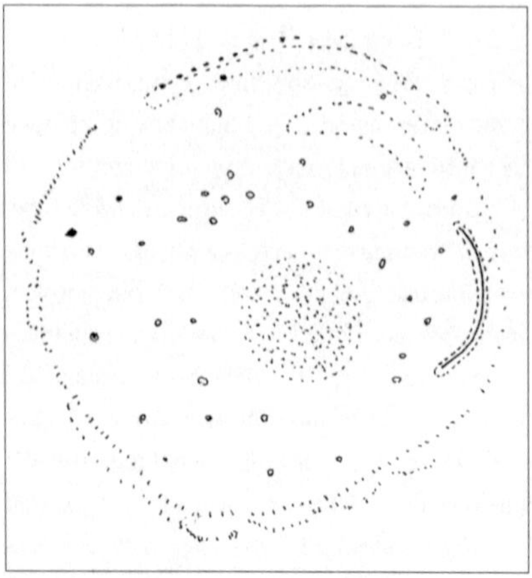

Fig. 09-19

Nebra sky disk, c. 1600 BCE.

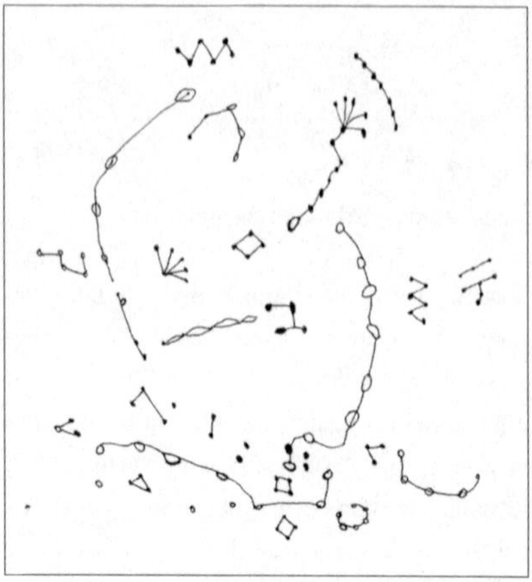

Fig. 07-19

Chinese celestial chart (618–906 CE).

active in Egyptian Alexandria) determined the view of the Mediterranean horizon to the rest of the known world, already largely explored by Herodotus (c. 490/480-424 CE). The oldest sophisticated calendars arose as dynastic records in Egypt and Mesopotamia. The concept of the influence of constellations, the 24-hour day, the 7-day week according to the phases of the moon, the 360 degrees of the circle, the 60th divisions of degrees and minutes, come from similarly early periods. There were complications enough before calendars, orientation coordinates, units of measurement, meridians, time zones culminating in Greenwich Mean Time and the precision of atomic clocks, developed into a halfway uniform, sufficiently accepted system. The long-held and firmly believed Christian view that the world was created on the 18th of March, 3952 BCE, as calculated by a monk, was first shown by Charles Darwin's (1809-1882) theory of evolution to be absurd. The Indian-Mesopotamian element of zero and decimal point calculation – essential foundations of modern science – still demonstrate how pervasively but also how protractedly fundamental transfer relations have revealed their effectiveness. Without being able to build on these, mankind would never have succeeded in considering the world, as it were, from above – as cartography – nor finally in advancing into interstellar space itself.

Jacqueta Hawkes, *Bildatlas der frühen Kulturen* (*The Atlas of Early Man*, London, 1976), Munich, 1984, p. 131 | Jeremy Black, *Geschichte der Landkarte* (*Visions of the World. A History of Maps*, London, 2003), Leipzig, 2005, p. 17 | Jan Mokre: *Rund um den Globus. Über Erd- und Himmelsgloben und ihre Darstellungen*, Peter E. Allmayer-Beck (ed.), Wien, 2008, pp. 27, 57 | Bibliothèque nationale de France (ed.), *La Géographie de Ptolémée*, Arcueil, 1998 | Georges Ifrah, *Universalgeschichte der Zahlen* (Original French edition: *Histoire Universelle des Chiffres*, Paris, 1981; English: *The Universal History of Numbers*, Hoboken, USA, 1999) Frankfurt-New York, 1986, pp. 417 ff.

SKETCHES OF SURROUNDINGS

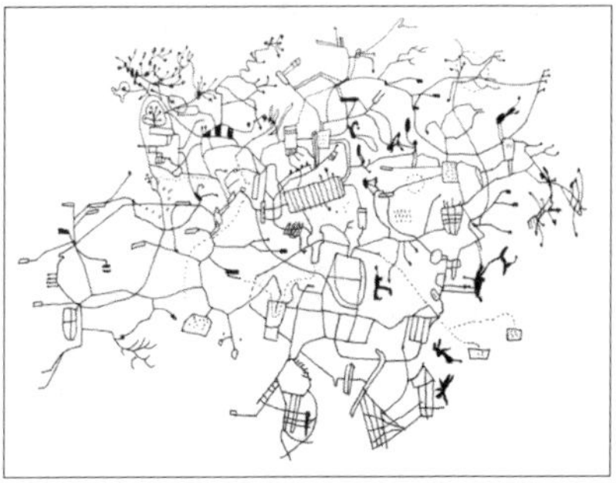

Fig. 08-16

Oldest known 'map' of a settlement, Bedolina, Val Camonica, Italy.

Just a few valleys away from the place where 'Ötzi', 'the Man from the Hauslabjoch', was found, killed by an arrow some 5,300 years before, lies the Val Camonica, laced with stone scorings of a clearly later date. One of these is a 4.6 x 2.3 meter-high map of a village, with houses, fields, paths, domestic animals and people scored in. The oldest of these scorings, according to Peter Barber's *The Map Book*, "probably comes from the bronze age (about 1200 BC), the latest (the houses) from the iron age (about 900-700 BC). It is very unlikely that the fields, wells and connecting paths depicted there 'map' a real landscape (especially since no such settlement has been documented). Rather, we should understand the scored drawings as a representation of the areas cultivated by the community. Little 'maps' with even more considerable buildings and two or three cultivated fields nearby are quite common, not only in the alps but also in quite different regions such as, for example, the upper reaches of the Jenissei river in Russia".

Peter Barber (ed.), *Das Buch der Karten. Meilensteine der Kartografie aus drei Jahrtausenden* (*The Map Book*, London, 2005) Darmstadt, 2006, pp. 10 f.

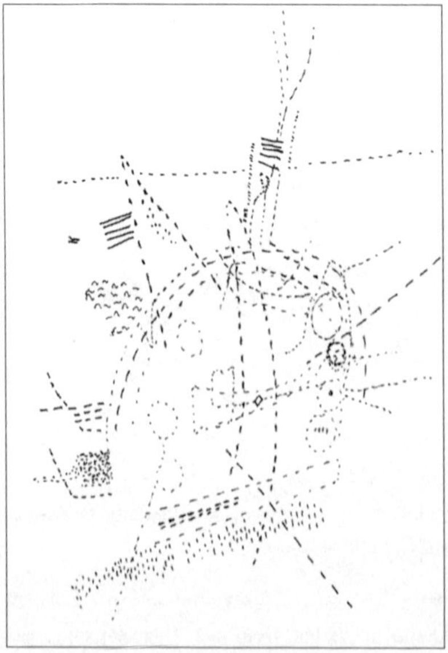

Fig. 08-18

Babylonian World Map, c. 650 BCE.

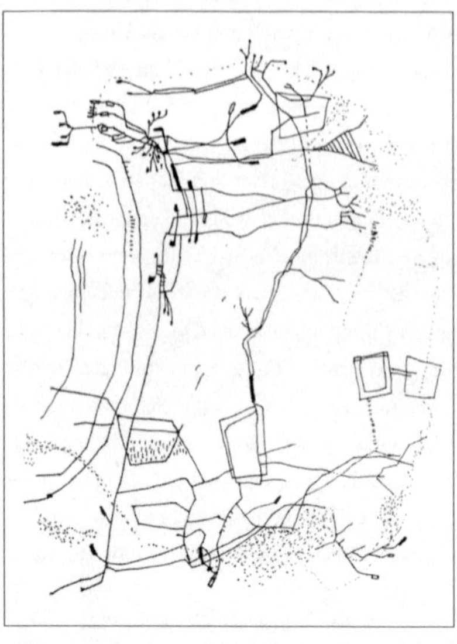

Fig. 08-17

City map of Nippur, about 1500 BCE.

CITY MAPS. LAND MAPS

(→ PIII/05) In early city cultures, measuring techniques, mathematics, the establishment of orientation and measuring units were finally so well developed that the first city maps could be made on clay tablets. The oldest known of these is the 3500-year-old Map of Nippur in present-day Iraq. On this, according to Barber's The Map Book, the essentials were emphasised: "the city walls, waterways, two large buildings on the river (apparently storehouses), and the city's most important buildings, designated in cuneiform. Near to these structures worth preserving are two temples and a large open square, which can be seen on the lower left of the tablet. The principal temple, which the inscription shows to be dedicated to the Sumerian god Enlil, possessed double walls and two inner courtyards. The Euphrates river snakes along the left side of the city, and a canal runs vertically through the city area. Seven city gates are depicted and identified. All other buildings have been left out for the sake of clarity". Later by several centuries is the twelve centimetre-high 'Babylonian World Map', which "points out the connections between the Babylonian heartland and the most distant corners of the earth". "The map is oriented towards the north. The earth is rendered as a disc surrounded by sea or floating on it. The regions beyond the ocean are depicted as originally probably eight triangles, on which is shown the distance between them. Fabulous creatures populate the remote regions, one of which is named the place where one 'does not see the sun'. In another, the 'great wall' is said to be found, the birthplace of a demonical figure from Sumerian texts. Babylon itself is depicted as a circle. Parallel lines represent the (unnamed) Euphrates ...".

Peter Barber (ed.), *Das Buch der Karten. Meilensteine der Kartografie aus drei Jahrtausenden*, (*The Map Book*, London, 2005) Darmstadt, 2006, pp. 12 f., 16 f.

THE GARDEN OF EDEN

Views of the world in circular form were widely readopted during the European middle ages, for instance in the explicitly schematic world map of Isidor, Bishop of Seville (c. 560-636 CE), centred on the Don, the Nile, the Sea of Azov and the Mediterranean Sea. Further details have been ostentatiously left out. The East is shown above, as in the c. 900 CE map of the Garden of Eden, which is situated in Asia near the Caucasus and Armenia but also

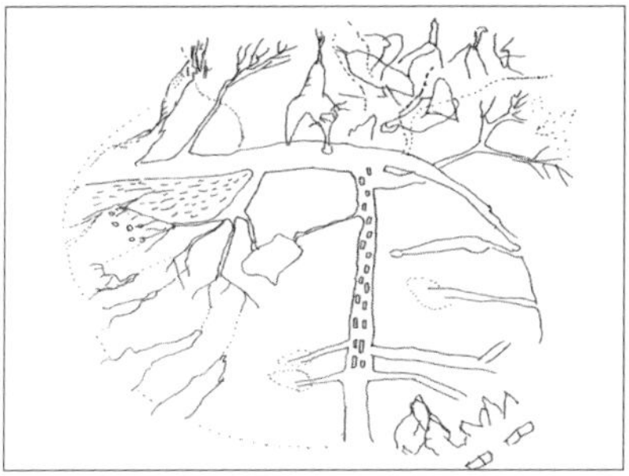

Fig. 08-19
The world c. 900 CE with the Garden of Eden.

Lebanon and the Mount of Sinai. 'Constantinopoli' is clearly emphasised; Judea, Babylon and Arabia are marked, as well as the Nile and several other rivers, distant Macedonia, Dalmatia or Ravenna. Ptolemy's discoveries are totally disregarded. The representation of the world is reduced to a schema, often with Jerusalem as the centre. Sketchy maps of routes to the city show direct paths with marked stations for orientation. It sufficed to ask one's way from one place to the next and make contact with like-minded travellers. Apart from the Holy Land, the most important medieval pilgrimage routes were to Rome and the Way of Saint James to Santiago de Compostela, and further to the Cape of Finisterre on the Atlantic, seen as the 'end of the world'.

Lloyd A. Brown, *The Story of Maps*, New York, 1979, pp. 102b, 118b.

ISTANBUL

As seafarers, Arabs and Turks followed the Phoenicians, the leading navigators of antiquity and arch-enemies of Rome, who were the first to circumnavigate Africa and who made a decisive contribution to the spread of writing in the Mediterranean. Coming originally from the deserts and steppes, the Arabs and Turks were just as comfortable navigating large expanses of water, and until the 19th century were feared as corsairs and pirates. Their great cartographers, above all Pirî Reis (1470-1554/55), a contemporary of the architect Sinan (c. 1490-1588), a formative figure in Ottoman architecture, had a decisive influence on the expanding picture of the world. Because he knew Turkish, Greek, Italian, Portuguese and Spanish, the most diverse sources were accessible to him. His map showing the coasts of Central and South America as well as Africa has remained famous, since as early as 1517 it included 'a copy of Columbus' map of America of 1498. Since the original of this was lost, this map survived – as Bernard Lewis notes, "only in the Turkish version in the library of the Topkapi Palace in Istanbul". There are suggestions, however, that Christopher Columbus (c. 1451-1506) had at his disposal Muslim sources calculating the earth's circumference, which he kept to himself or passed on in abbreviated form, in order not to demotivate his crew. So it is stated right at the beginning of his log: "I decided to record less distance than we had in fact covered, so that my men would not lose heart if the journey should prove too long."

Mine Eusiner Özen, *Pirî Reis and his Charts*, Istanbul, 2006, Cover 2 | Bernard Lewis, *The Muslim Discovery of Europe*, London, 2003, p. 152 | Christoph Kolumbus, *Bordbuch. Aufzeichnungen seiner Entdeckungsfahrt nach Amerika 1492–93* (*The Log of Christopher Columbus: The First Voyage, Spring, Summer and Fall 1492*, Whitefish, USA, 2007), Munich, 2006, p. 15.

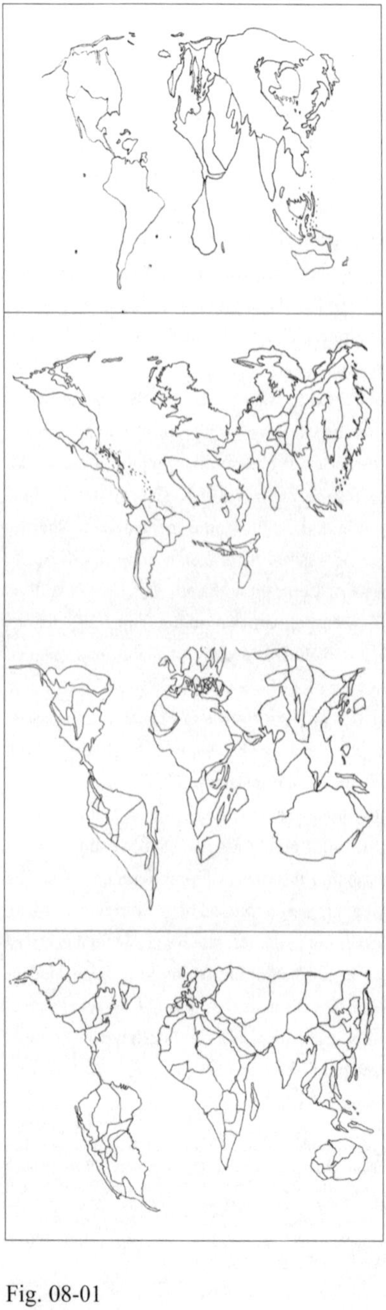

Fig. 08-01

CARTOGRAPHY MARKET

America was already known from the important world map created in 1507 by Martin Waldseemüller (c. 1470-1522) and used as the basis for a globe, though, owing to a lack of specific knowledge, its dimensions, like those of East Asia, were at first only rudimentarily conveyed. Waldseemüller came from Freiburg in the Breisgau region, where he studied mathematics and geography, and later served as Professor of Cosmology in the monastery of Saint-Dié in the Vosges. Despite all the secrecy surrounding trade routes, there was an intensive exchange of graphically presentable information, since publishers and printers could increasingly depend on a world of specialists willing to cooperate, with early key figures such as Gerhard Mercator (1512-1594), Abraham Ortelius (1527-1598), Ignazio Danti (1536-1586), who decorated the magnificent *Galleria delle Carte Geografiche* in the Vatican, or Joan Blaeu (1596-1673), whose *Atlas Maior* of 1665, with its more than 600 maps, detailed descriptions and countless illustrations, was the most comprehensive, sumptuous and costly atlas ever published. Since it served far more as an educational image – in the sense of an overview – than as a concrete travel guide, descriptive pictures from all over the world were most highly valued as an emotional point of entry. Charted coasts were the easier part. Knowledge of the interior regions of strange lands – not strange to the inhabitants, of course – remained vague for a long time, dependent on oral testimonies and such surveys as were technically possible. One pioneer in the exploitation of travellers' tales and information from naturalists, for instance, as his map of Tartary – the then name for Central Asia – documents, was Guillaume Delisle (1675-1726). Supported only by references of this kind, he was already able to render fairly precisely the shape of the Caspian Sea and also the course of the most important rivers, an incremental process of drawing with an increasing though never completely realistic degree of accuracy. He was Europe's leading geographer, who had concentrated early on "the geographical aspects of history" – as Lloyd A. Brown notes in *The Story of Maps* – and consequently received commissions from Tsar Peter the Great and was employed as a tutor to Louis XV. His father had also been an historian and cartographer, and two of his brothers were astronomers, the younger of them having taken part in the Great Northern Expedition of Vitus Bering (1681-1741). Given the continuing predominant interest in sea voyages, Italy, the Netherlands and England – with the Royal Greenwich Observatory founded in 1675 – were for the time being at the centre of primarily maritime cartography. Since the founding of the Paris Observatory in 1666, France had been an important place for astronomical research while also undertaking large-scale land mapping with highly complex trigonometry, culminating in the complete mapping of France by Jacques Cassini (1677-1756) and his followers, a project that was accomplished in 1747, including long range measurements by cartographic expeditions to Peru and Lappland. Even earlier, Jean-Felix Picard (1620-1682) had calculated, with far greater precision than before, the length of a meridian – and with this the size of the earth. (→PII/05)

Joan Blaeu, *Atlas Maior of 1665*, Reprint Cologne, 2005 | Lloyd A. Brown, *The Story of Maps*, New York, 1979, -pp. 243, 241, 246b | John Noble Wilford, *The Mapmakers*, New York, 2000.

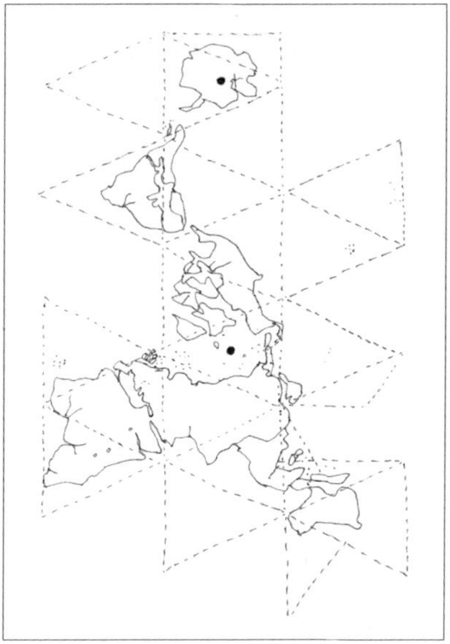

Fig. 08-14 (→ PII/06)
The world map after Buckminster Fuller.

GLOBALITY

The actual dimensions of the earth had first been empirically proven by the circumnavigation of the world by Ferdinand Magellan (1480-1521), during which he himself was killed in a fight with natives of the Philippines. Of the five ships which in 1519 had set sail from Seville for South America to find a route to the rich spice islands that was not controlled by Portugal, only one completed the homeward voyage, after three years, sailing around the Cape of Good Hope. Only 18 of the original 265-man crew returned to the harbour from which they had set out. Since it was clear from this voyage that the date shift occured within a single day – as Stefan Zweig explained – "precise observations proved: that the globe does not rest at a fixed point in space, but revolves on its own axis in a regular rhythm, and that whoever follows its rolling course westwards can reclaim time from infinity. This new knowledge, that time and hours are different in different parts of the world, shook the humanists of the sixteenth century perhaps as much as the theory of relativity shook our own time". Two generations later, Francis Drake (c. 1540-1596) succeeded in circumnavigating the world for the emerging sea-power of England, but it was by James Cook (1728-1779) who, like Magellan, was killed in a fight with 'natives', that the hemisphere opposite Europe was first broadly charted, allowing the contours of its land surfaces to be known. Cook, himself a trained cartographer, had already created charts of sections of the North American coasts. Coastlines and islands were charted with great precision as they were discovered, and for this precise distances on land were often marked with measuring points so that angle measurements could be taken using sextants. Water depths were measured with plumb lines and positions calculated, while Cook "determined the latitude by measuring the height of the sun at midday, and the longitude using the distance of the moon method". On the open sea, chronometers were needed to determine the degree of latitude. These first became precision instruments through the efforts of the highly innovative, long unrecognised clockmaker John Harrison (1693-1776). Since thin lines showing the coastal contours were always recorded first, as with the medieval portolan charts with their mapped points of orientation, it is clear that a sophisticated image of the earth came about primarily through depiction of the great sea routes – from 'outside' the land masses. GPS satellites, in a far more precise way, have transferred this process into the heavens. Today, coordinates are accessible for any given point. For the – only briefly peaceful – phase of 18th century discoveries, it is significant how the 'mapping' of the foreign consciously combined abstract conception of definition with artistic considerations, as witness the journals and the wonderful drawings and watercolours of Cook's travelling companion Georg Forster (1754-1794). These stand at the beginning of a philosophically oriented geography and ethnography – culminating in the diverse forms of artistic 'cartography' in modern times. Christine Buci-Glucksmann has summarised this in *Der kartographische Blick in der Kunst* as "the story of a journey and a gaze", wherein the maps serve "as motive, starting point and model for an infinitely open aesthetic".

Joan Blaeu, *Atlas Maior of 1665*, Reprint Cologne, 2005 | Stefan Zweig, *Magellan. Der Mann und seine Tat*, Wien, 1938 (*Conqueror of the Seas. The Story of Magellan*, Ishi Press, 2010), Frankfurt am Main, 2009, p. 262 f. | *James Cook und die Entdeckung der Südsee*, Ausstellungskatalog, Bonn-Wien-Bern, 2010, pp. 121, 79 ff. | Dava Sobel, *Längengrad* (*Longitude: The True Story of a Lone Genius Who Solved the Greatest Scientific Problem of His Time*, New York, 2005) Berlin, 1998 | Georg Forster, *Reise um die Welt. Illustriert von eigener Hand*, Berlin, 1778/80, Frankfurt/Main, 2007 | Christine Buci-Glucksmann, *Der kartographische Blick in der Kunst* (French edition: Christine Buci-Glucksmann, *L'oeil cartographique de l'art*, Paris, 1996) Berlin, 1997, p. 7.

THE EXOTIC. UTOPIAS

Thomas More's (1478-1535) *Utopia*, Tommaso Campanella's (1568-1639) *City of the Sun*, and Francis Bacon's (1561-1626) *New Atlantis* were all located in the then largely still unknown South Seas, a term encompassing every southern sea. Jonathan Swift (1667-1745) situated his imaginary island of Lilliput east of Japan or, according to another version, south of Sumatra; Daniel Defoe placed Robinson Crusoe's island above South America, near the mouth of the Orinoco. The 750-page *Dictionary of Imaginary Places* treats such fictitious places, often based on existing charts, as a fantasy lexicon looking to increase its plausibility – and lead readers astray – with maps, as a kind of ironic 'mental mapping'.

Alberto Manguel, Gianni Guadalupi, *The Dictionary of Imaginary Places*, San Diego-New York-London, 2000, p. 148.

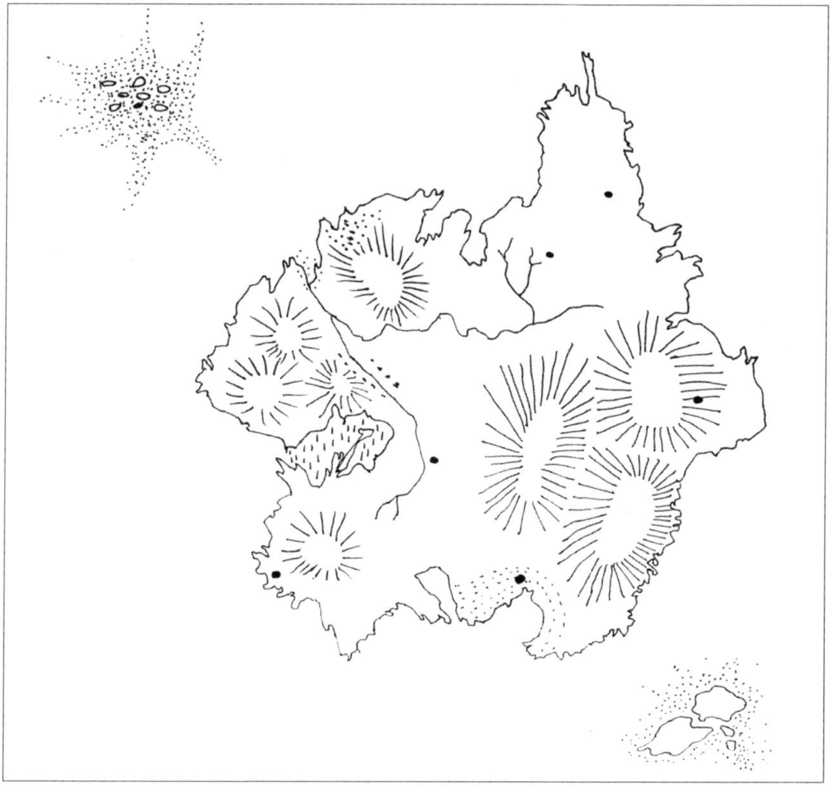

Fig. 08-12
Robinson Crusoe's island.

PICTURE STORIES

Despite the predominance of pictures and image sequences, in literate cultures it is not generally realised that for the transmission of experience worldwide the most diverse methods and media are often used as imaginary 'extrapolations' from informed accounts. Maps always tell stories, too. However, since most people find their way around their own area without the guidance of maps – and consequently in many cultural traditions there is little recourse to map-reading – space and time are often conceptualised in picture stories. One example is what the Lakota, one of the Sioux tribes, call the "Winter tale", whose intention is – according to Christian Feest – "pictogram chronicles, which were also known to other Plains peoples (and further afield), but which have been transmitted in large numbers only by the Lakota and the Nakota. The 19th-century practice consisted in drawing, on leather, cloth, and soon also on paper, one pictogram for every winter (in the sense of 'year'), representing one memorable experience which had been retained from the preceding twelve months. The drawings, arranged in spirals or snaking lines, were connected by short phrases, which chroniclers preserved in memory.

With the advent of writing, the people first combined pictograms and text; later for the most part only words were recorded."

Christian Feest (ed.), *Sitting Bull und seine Welt*, Ausstellungskatalog, Vienna, 2009, p. 22, 94.

ATLAS OF EMOTION

By expanding a cartographical way of thinking and visualising into the spheres incorporating architecture, travel, geography, art of mapping, and design and house, Giuliana Bruno, who teaches Visual and Environmental Studies at Harvard University, is attempting to relate a "history of representation and its theory" in a significantly more comprehensive manner to such patterns. Her *Atlas of Emotion* "mapped out in various cognitive explorations and passing through many different places", is, as she herself says, "a construction made of multiple passages. It was assembled as a montage of language and illustrations, which I particularly enjoyed selecting and routing in the form of a visual travelogue." Among many other references – such as the narrative methods of maps, archive layouts, city topographies reminiscent of the Situationists or film montage plans – Walter Benjamin's unrealised plans play a role, the idea of a comprehensive 'mapping' of life spheres: "I have long, indeed for years, played with the idea of setting out the sphere of life – bios – graphically on a map." While an "emotional cartography" can make the unexplored visible, says Giuliana Bruno, "a history is written on the physiognomy of space and mobilised in its geopsychic rhythm (…) – engaging, in the fashion of contemporary histories, in both microhistory and narrative". Rendering structures of this kind visible remains a boundless field awaiting enlightenment and research; for instance, Jean-Luc Godard's "film history project", Volker Pantenburg emphasises, can be understood "as a fusion of seeing and writing, of reception and production, of practice and theory". For the flood of single images and image sequences, the cutting-room is the significant, often underrated 'interface'. Is what happens there, in Harun Farocki's insistent question, "comparable to a scientific experiment?" (→ PIII/05)

Giuliana Bruno, *Atlas of Emotion. Journeys in Art, Architecture and Film*, London-New York, 2007, pp. 6, 207, 277 | Volker Pantenburg, *Film als Theorie. Bildforschung bei Harun Farocki und Jean-Luc Godard*, Bielefeld, 2006, pp. 50, 167.

INNER LIFE, INVISIBLE LIFE

What rays can make visible – and in the farthest sense communicable – has marked technological development since the first 'light pictures'. The discovery of X-rays by Wilhelm Conrad Röntgen (1845-1923) is a particularly obvious example. Mapping has facilitated incredible progress in medicine, rendering visible anomalies and changes otherwise invisible in a living body. Further developments such as ultrasound or tomography are constantly refining access to the micro-level – exactly what is needed for an understanding of social issues, too. Despite every kind of automatism, there is at least a broadening knowledge of how things are connected. Even from the perspective of technologised medicine, emotions, sensitivities and psychic constellations are being taken noticeably more seriously. What seems plausible in any personal investigation of the emotional sphere has long been confirmed by knowledge of how the body functions. At least according to neurologist António R. Damásio – the assumption "of a fundamental separation of body and mind", from the location of reason in the brain alone, has been clearly shown to be illusory, since "mind and feelings are linked with the functions of the whole organism, not only with those of the brain". Moreover, thoughts operate "largely in pictures", because "words and random symbols" rely "on topographically organised representations" and can "become images". Damásio's basic thesis emphasises "that an organic perspective is essential for a comprehensive grasp of the human mind, so that the mind is not only moved from an immaterial Cogitum into the realm of body tissues, but must also be situated in a whole, interconnected organism, which consists of the various interdependent parts of the body, in the narrow sense, and of the brain, and which interacts with a physical and social environment." As is well known, engagement with a 'cartography' of inner interdependencies has a particularly long tradition in Asian cultures.

António R. Damásio, *Descartes' Irrtum. Fühlen, Denken und das menschliche Gehirn* (*Descartes' Error: Emotion, Reason and the Human Brain*, Vintage, 2006), Munich, 1997, pp. 00, 152, 333 | Chang Chung-Yuan, *Tao, Zen und schöpferische Kraft* (*Creativity and Taoism*, New York, 1963) Düsseldorf, 1974, p. 141.

HIGH TECH & CIVIL SOCIETY

Cartography also always serves to control. It is used militarily; in the colonial period it established territories with often random, straight-lined borders; it makes addresses visible. Every mobile phone conversation can be geographically located. It follows that there is broad field for other applications in civil society, whether as Mappings, The Critical Landscape, Cartographic Fictions, The Production of Space, Maps and Politics or works on Radical Geography and Experimental Geography (the titles of volumes

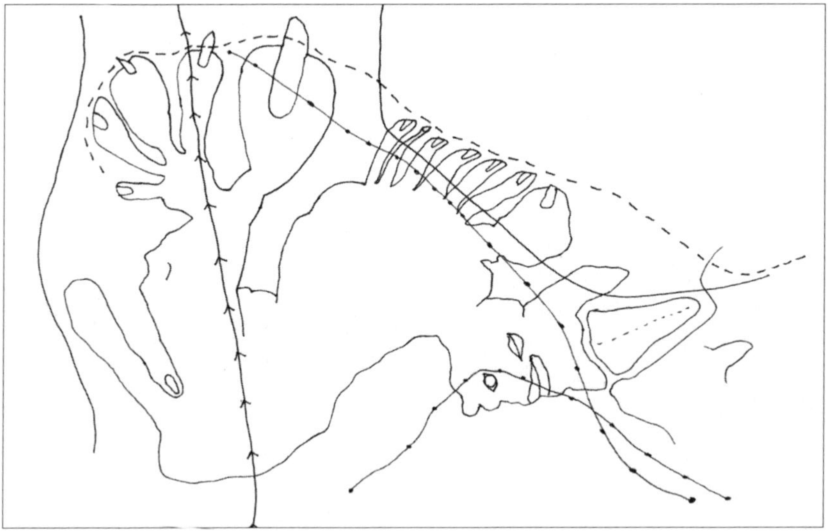

Fig. 06-05 (→ PIII/07)

Relation of inner organs and sympathetic nervous system. In: Chang Chung-Yan: Tao, Zen und schöpferische Kraft.

suitable for further reading). As a contrast to the *Atlas of Emotion, the Atlas of the Real World* – trivialised in German as *Der schlaue Planet* (*The Clever Planet*) – presents a particularly impressive visualisation. It contains 366 completely distorted views of the world, opposite familiar maps, in which the most diverse quantities are calculated and depicted for nation states by area and population: for example, world population, birth rates, the net rate of immigration, refugee acceptance, tourist destinations, water resources, wooded areas, energy use, relations of economic exchange, foodstuffs, natural resources, manufactured goods, standard of living criteria, gender factors, poverty, health systems, mortality rates, the employment situation, urbanisation, slums, media networks, ecology, or endangered species. Each of these criteria generates a self-portrait of the world, which in the end gives a cause-and-effect impression of mankind and its 'systems'.

The world map of the arms trade, which makes use of this kind of information, makes this cause-and-effect process clear in a particularly blatant way. "Only 22 countries", according to the text, "appear as large-scale arms exporters worldwide". Above all, in per capita order, Russia, Israel, Norway, France, the USA, Sweden, Canada, the Netherlands and Great Britain, each as arms exporters and all of them count themselves nominally among the peacemaking nations. This figure does not include handguns, munitions, and the rampant black market. Approximately "80 per cent of worldwide arms exports by volume are sold by the United States, Russia, France, Germany and Great Britain", with the USA being responsible for half of all arms expenditure. When related to area and population, this kind of data alone is enough to distort the picture of the world monstrously – as a beginning for further scientific-artistic research and intervention.Significant visualisation examples of more or less secret connections, 'undercover' realities or migration flows are presented – as the normally unseen effects of crtical situations – in *An Atlas of RADICAL CARTOGRAPHY* (by Lize Mogel and Alexis Bhagat, Los Angeles 2008). There "Selected CIA Aircraft Routes, 2001-2006" or a "Flowchart of the German Asylum Procedures" are shown as type of mapping that the media usually ignores. Pioneers in this area are two members of the cartographic team of Le Monde diplomatique, Oliver Clochard and Philippe Rekacewicz, who created, for example, "a striking map which uses colour-coded concentric circles to show the number and causes of migrant deaths in the EU from 1993 to 2006". Migreurop mapped "the Europe of camps" and supports migrant rights "to insure freedom of movement across and within borders, provide documents for all, abolish racist laws, and stop deportations". With such activities in mind, "activist mappings of the EU-Border regime serve as organising nodes rather than just navigational tools. They suggest new connections and relations that aid in not only reconceiving the territory but in recreating it" – by graphically recording normally invisible structures and procedures to combine critical views and research with sensitive 'Emotion and Orientation'.

Denis Cosgrove (ed.), *Mappings*, London, 1999 | Michael Speaks (ed.), *The Critical Landscape*, Rotterdam, 1996 | Karen Piper, *Cartographic Fictions. Maps, Race and Identity*, New Brunswick, 2002 | Henri Lefevbre, *The Production of Space*, Malden, USA, 1991 | Jeremy Black, *Maps and Politics*, London, 1997 | Richard Peet (ed.), *Radical Geography*, London, 1978 | Nato Thompson, *Experimental Geography: Radical Approaches to Landscape, Cartography, and Urbanism*, New York, 2008 | Daniel Dorling, Mark Newman, Anna Barford, *Der schlaue Planet. So haben Sie die Welt noch nie gesehen* (*The Atlas of the Real World*, London, 2008), Munich, 2008, p. 334 | Lize Mogel, Alexis Bhagat, *An Atlas of RADICAL CARTOGRAPHY*, Journal of Aestehtics & Protest Press, Los Angeles, 2008, pp. 50 ff.

HYPOTHESIS #17

On the Importance of Scientific Research in Relation to Humanities

Walter Seidl

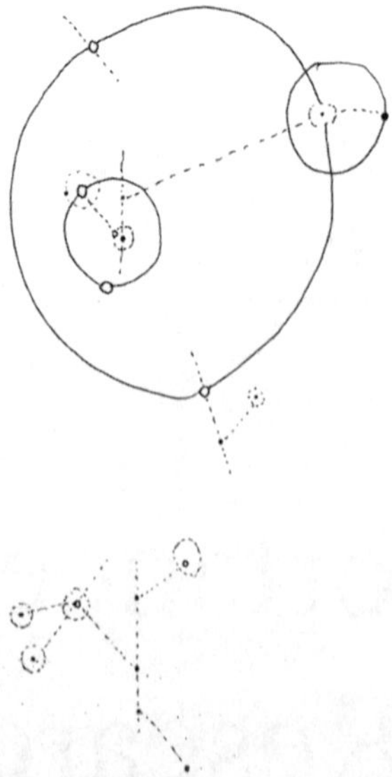

Fig. 04-08

Eclipses and interference points circulate around the universe, meeting each other in angular sequences. Orbits and zones of contact define systems of movement and alienation.

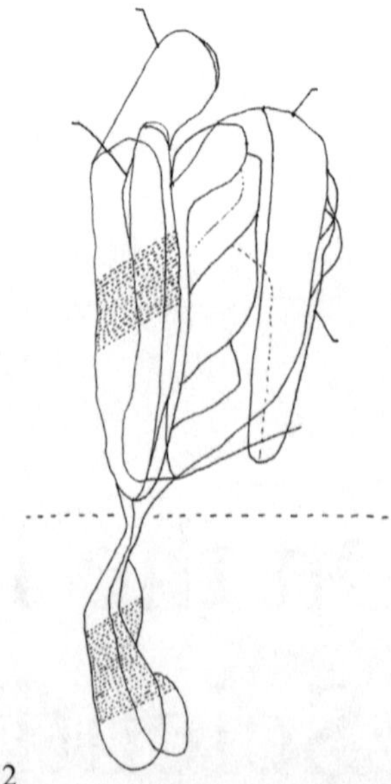

Fig. 04-12

Slashing leaves and plants grow out of a hybrid process of overlapping layers of syncope and adherence. Borderlines mark the visibility of surface carriers and underlying ramifications.

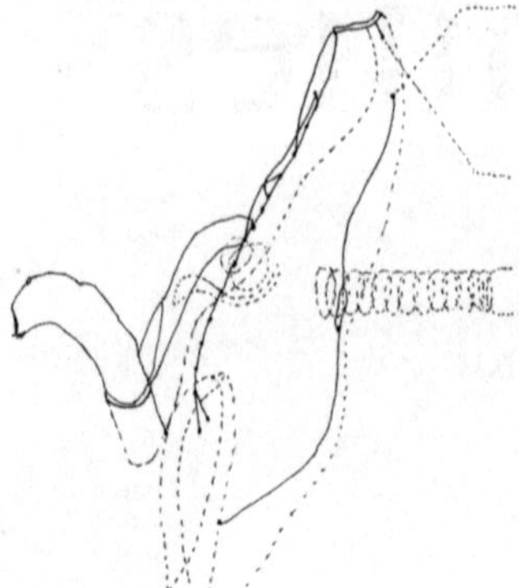

Fig. 04-15

Fixed parameters and pathways intertwine and break up at the same time. Incalculable ways of progression center on nodes and latent buds, becoming the angles for further crossings and circular mimesis.

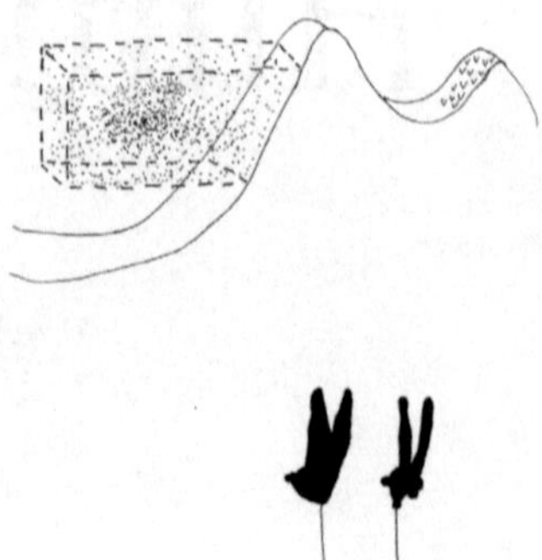

Fig. 01-49

Hillside movements and closed-up boxes with swarms of energy define the landscape for indistinct creatures to move around. The result leads to an endless agglomeration of sustainable bits and pieces.

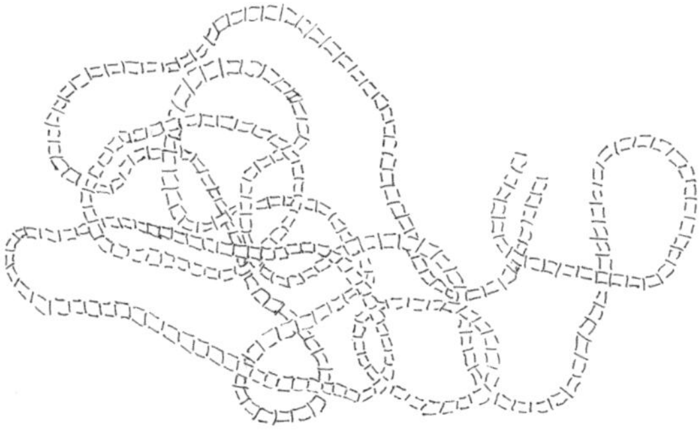

Fig. 10-26

Molecular strings and infinite clusters of information intertwine to offer meanders of geometrical arbitrariness. The elements form lines of disruptive quality where repetition and movement are at stake.

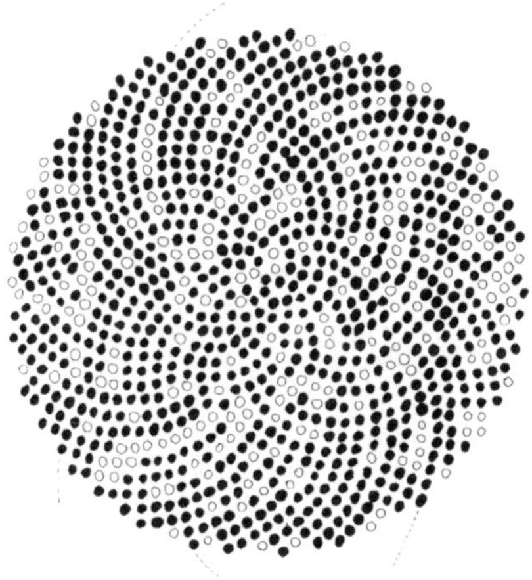

Fig. X01

Patterns of geometrical blossom arrangements provide the basis for how seeds are spread in circular directions of gravity. The growth of plants mirrors the growth of humankind, capital and rotating forces of beauty.

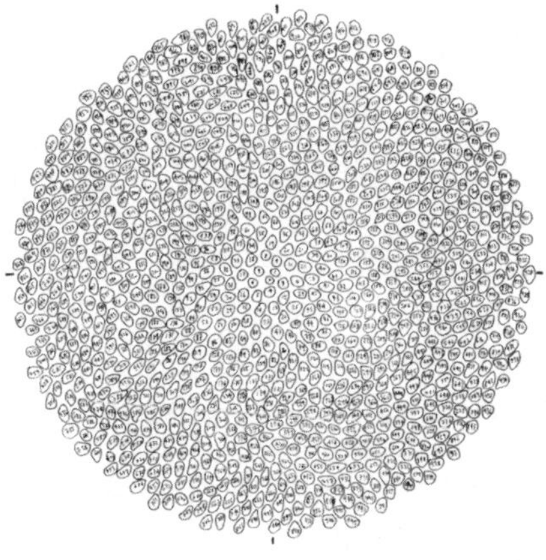

Fig. X02

Pebbles and stones inscribed with a numerating, defining structure generate a clustered ray of density, based on the mathematical principles of order and entropy.

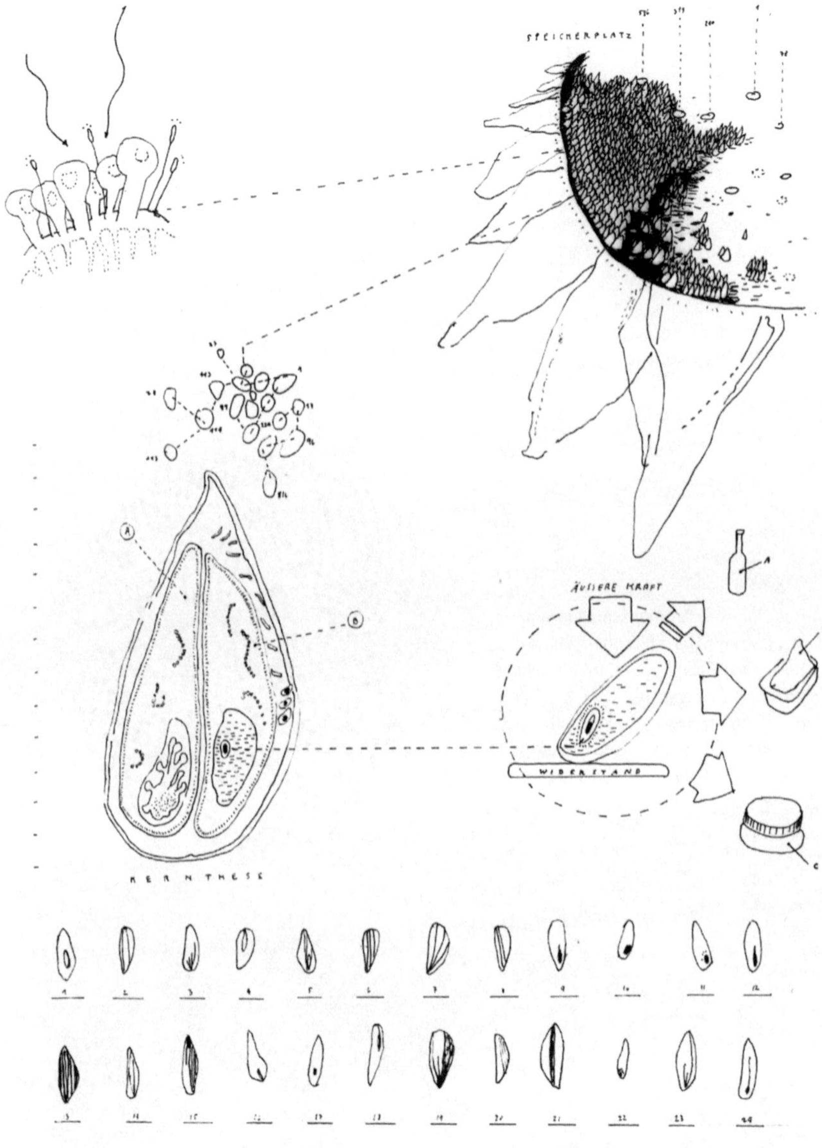

Fig. X05

The sun as the energy source of life, cells and plants fosters mechanisms of cleavage. Duplication not always leads to similitude, but to variations of form and function. Cell division and evolution make up the development of multifarious patterns of repetition and the causal determination of beings.

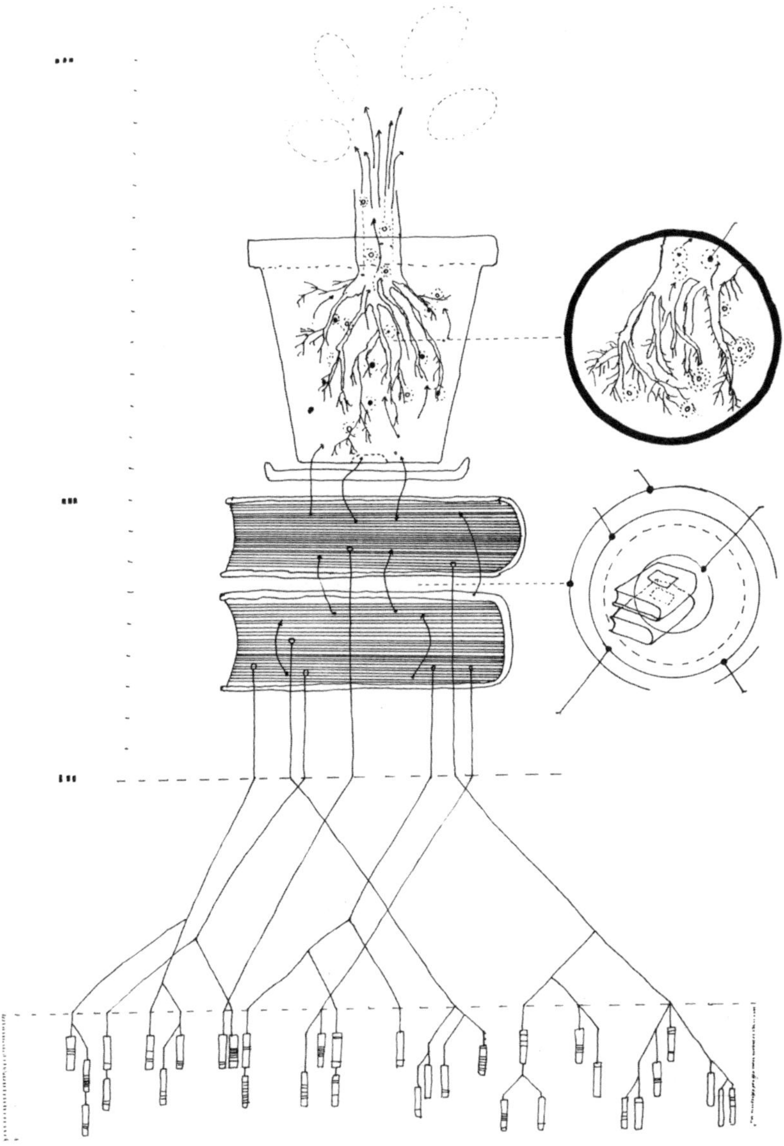

Fig. X06

The growing of the mind as purported through books and the written word inspires a symbiosis of information, which can also be linked to the growth of plants. Genetic material becomes the basis for all considerations of the mind as well as of natural phenomena of growth, which are channeled through different matter of organic and inorganic mattersubstance.

HYPOTHESIS #18

Interpersonal Governance Structures

Katja Mayer

INTERPERSONAL GOV

Presentation of Diffusion Models – Section 3 of Modelling the Forms of Social Relations

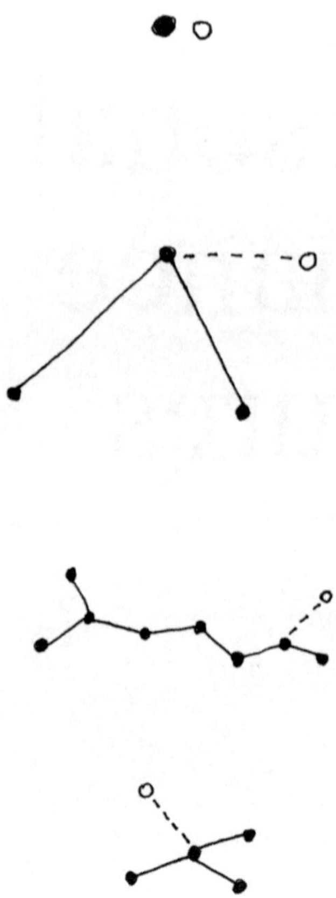

Fig. 01-28 (→ PII/10a-b)

1) Forms of Social Relations

Example of Relational Classification:

1.1) Starting from Person A, who holds a particular opinion, we want to formulate the possible configurations to Person B, who (as yet) holds a different opinion. E.g. is A an innovator and B an early adopter?

1.2) For instance, person A is already connected to two people who hold this same opinion. Their relation to Person B has yet to be determined.

1.3) Person B is already part of a chain of distinct, coherent opinion, which, however, can only be confirmed through a relevant connection with another person.

1.4) Person A is central to the diffusion of information in the group. How will the relation to Person B be constructed or effective?

1.5) Precise identification of the modalities of connecting: A influences B with external connection to person/group of different outlook; by contrast, A influences B (already persuaded) with external connection to person/group of the same attitude. And now the counterperspective: B influences A with external connection to person/group of the same attitude, and B, with external connection to person/group of different outlook, influences A. As a further possibility: A and B both have relations to persons/groups with coherent outlooks, and each influences the other.

RNANCE STRUCTURES

2) The Bird's-Eye View

Here we see an image of the possible diffusion of information/reevaluation/attitude from A to B. Here, Person A is part of a strongly hierarchically anchored opinion forming, marked by institutional as well as group dynamic processes. (The binary structure of influence is again schematically represented below right.) Now, if Person A wants to persuade Person B, it cannot happen directly, but must proceed in a roundabout way. For this, a multiform reevaluation of the relational characteristics is needed.

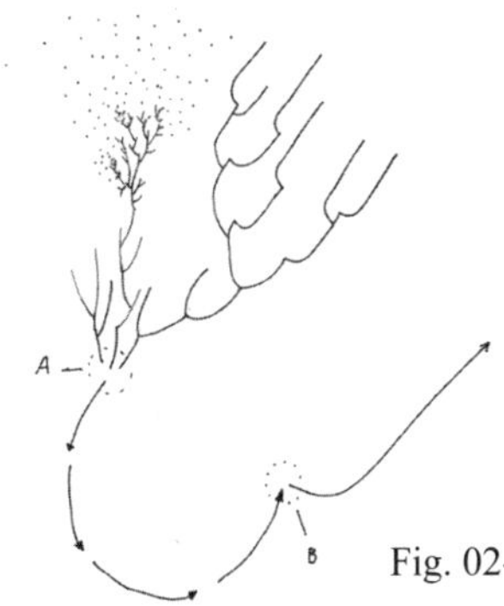

Fig. 02-08

3) Relational Characteristics and Path Dependencies

In our data set, the adoption curve is not single-peaked, i.e. the analysis shows several relevant partial networks. If we further observe two different relational types, we recognise the similarity of the pattern of diffusion; for example, with Person A, whose path is part of both I and I'. Person B's path, however, as part of the logic of II, does not link with I or I'.

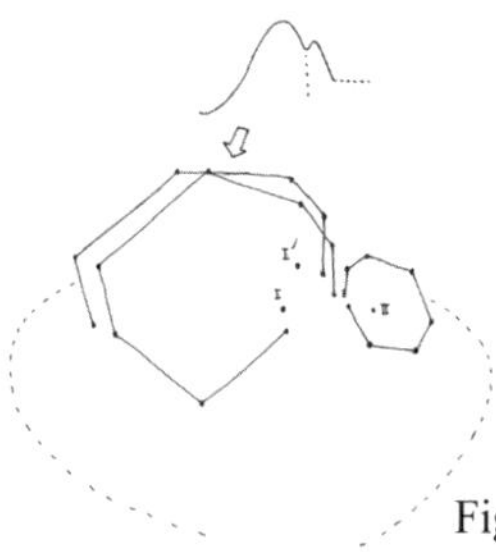

Fig. 02-09

4) Cross-Section

The different partial networks are shown here schematically in cross-section. In clarification, we see here the two upper spheres of Person A, and the lowest, from which Person B arises. In each case, the dominant structural shell segments are given alongside (see Section 2); these, however, will not be used subsequently. Below, we see the chain again to which B should belong. The necessity arises to approach B, who appears very fixed to his position, from the part of both A and A'. This can occur via one person but of two different relational types, or via two persons of the same relational type.

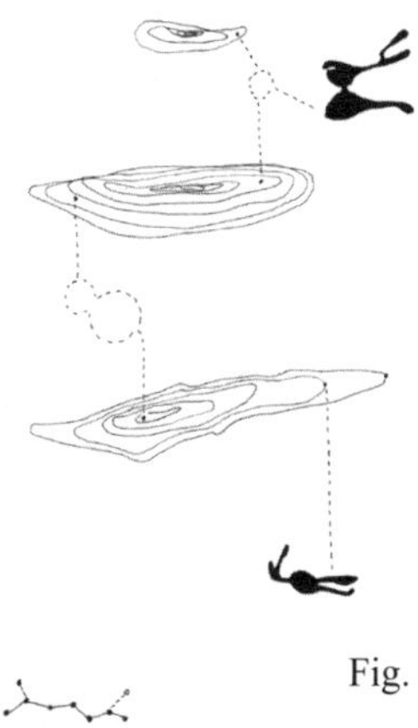

Fig. 02-18

PLATES II

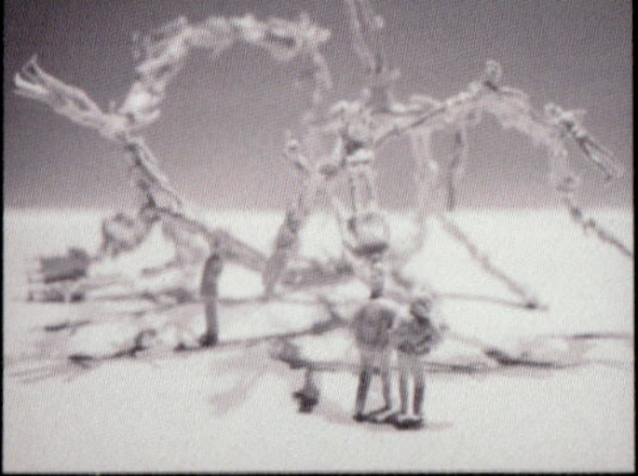

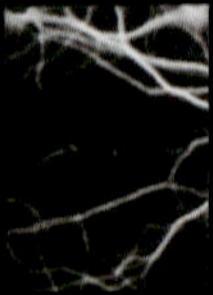

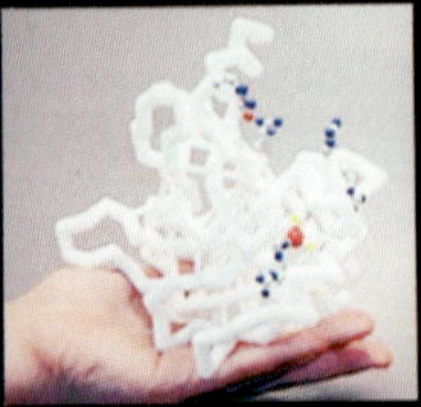

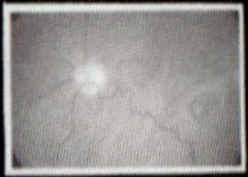

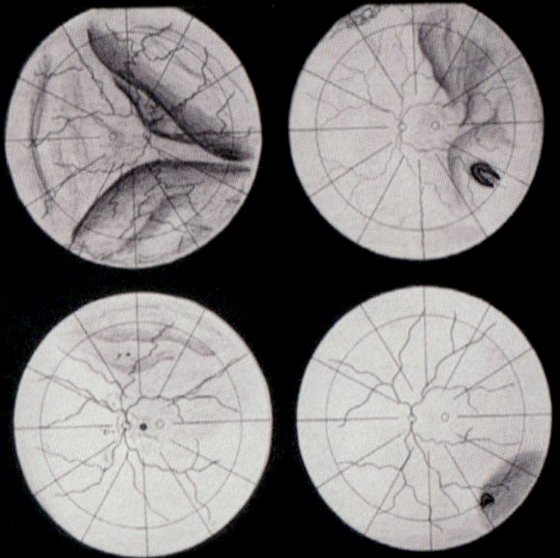

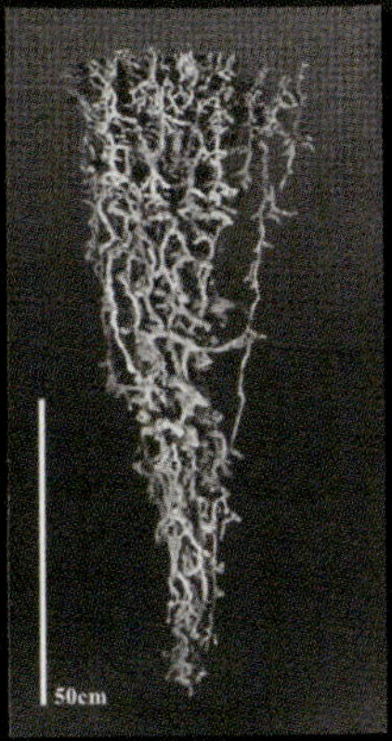
50cm

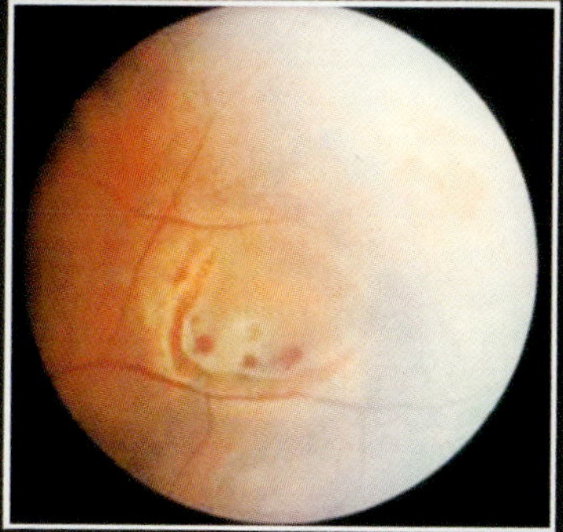

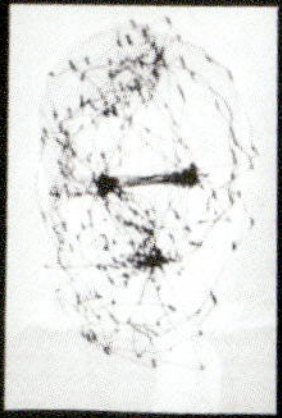

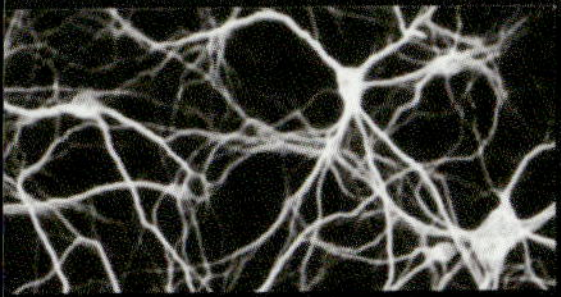

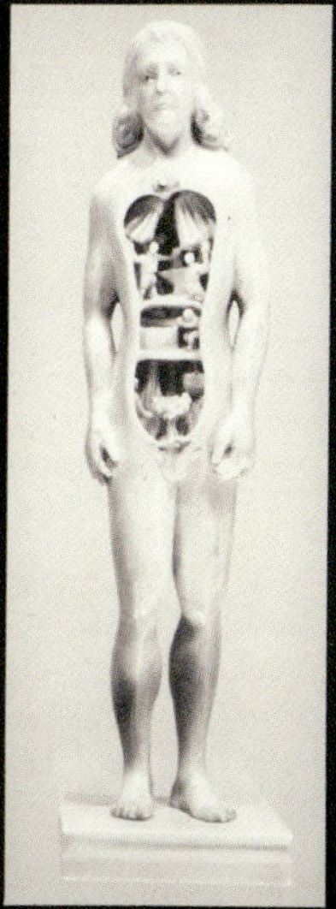

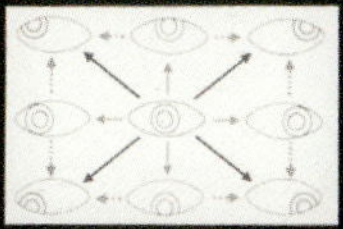

PII/02

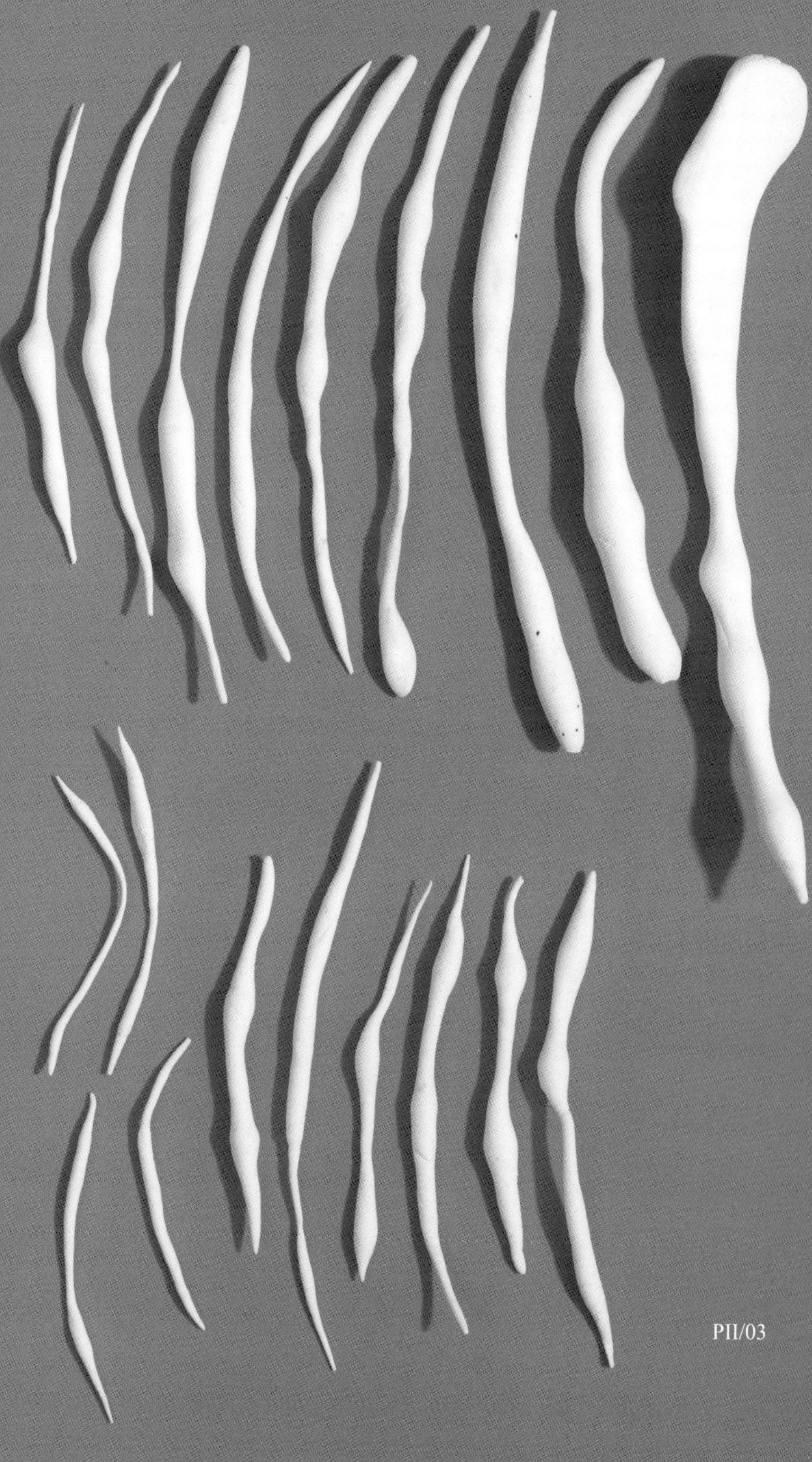

PII/03

PII/04a

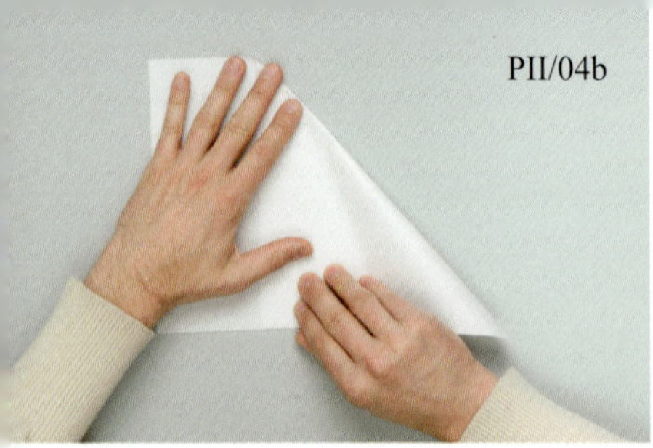

PII/04b

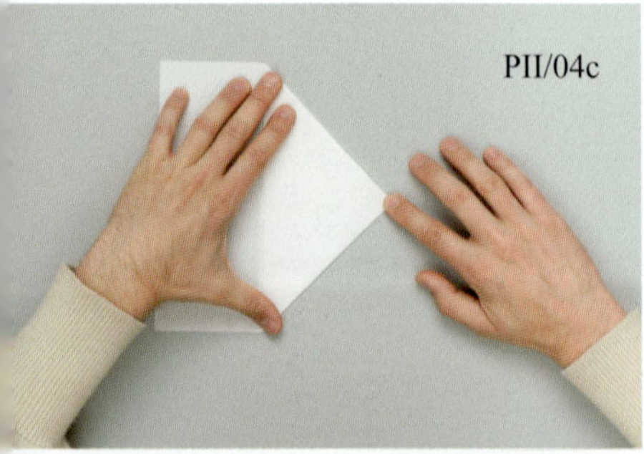

PII/04c

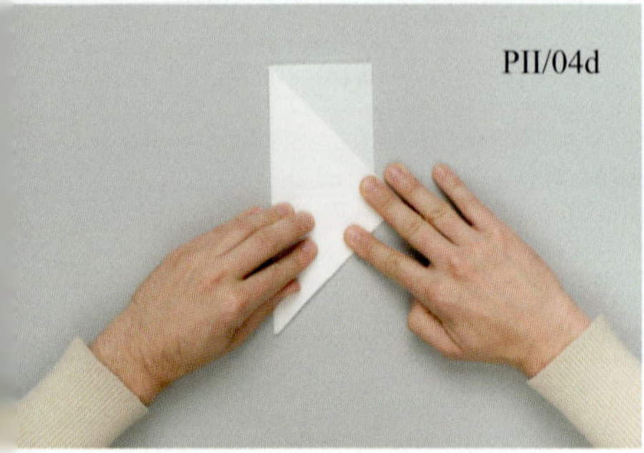

PII/04d

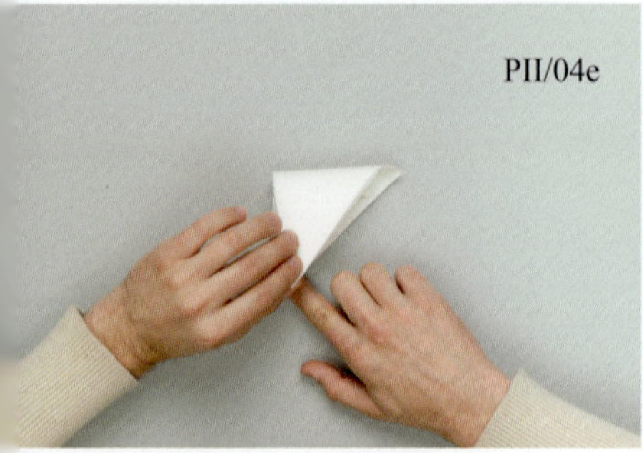

PII/04e

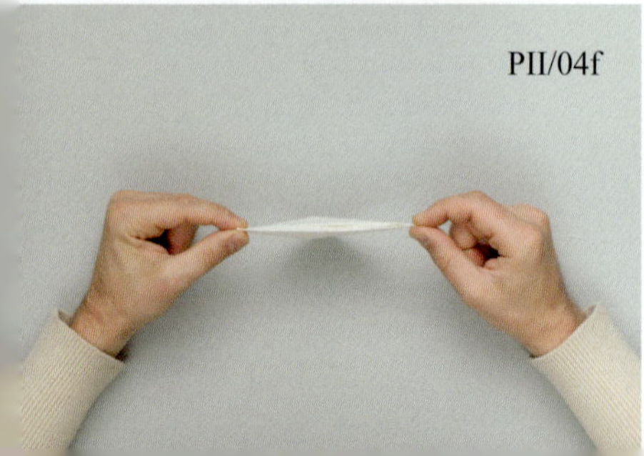

PII/04f

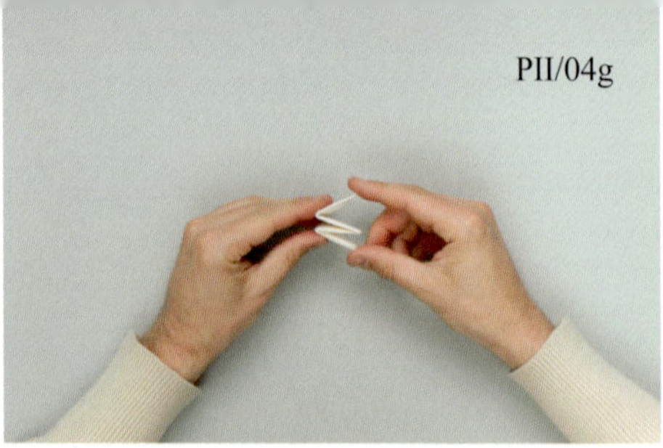

PII/04g

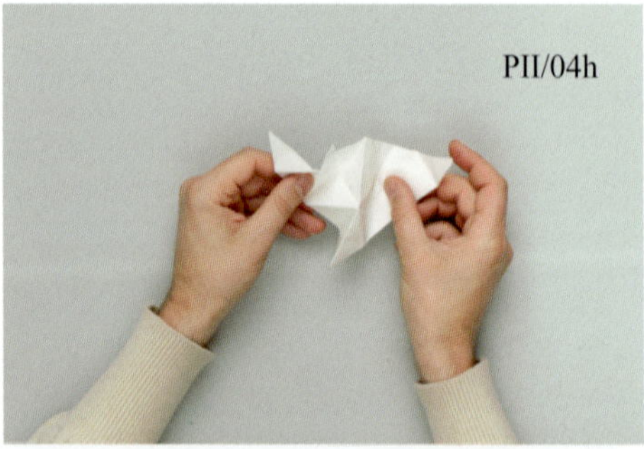

PII/04h

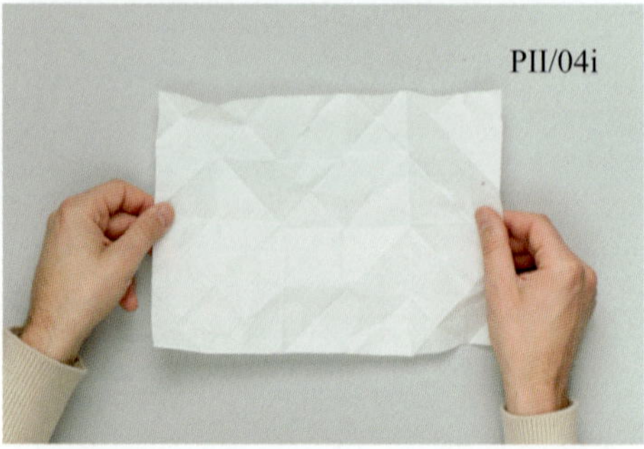

PII/04i

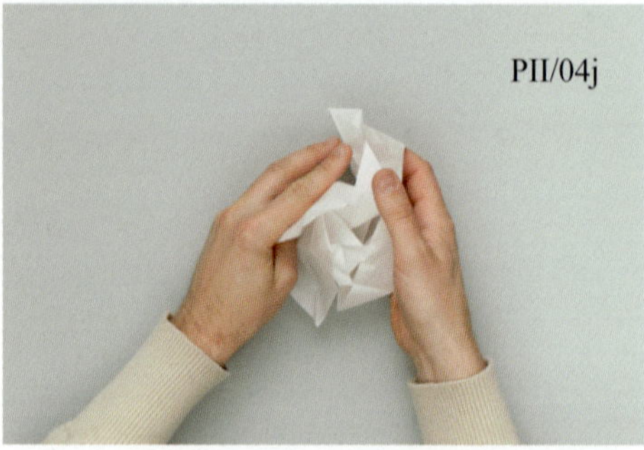

PII/04j

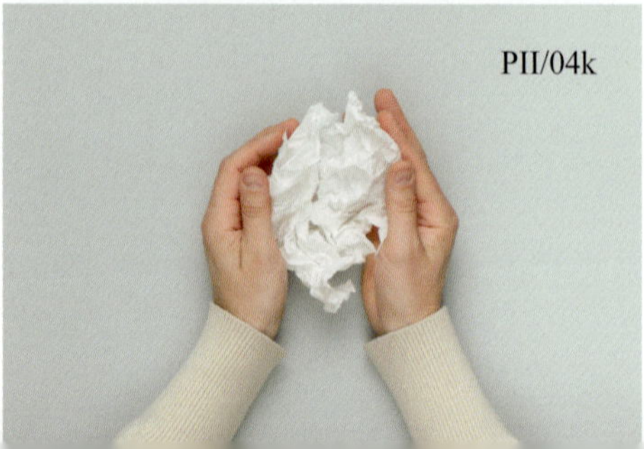

PII/04k

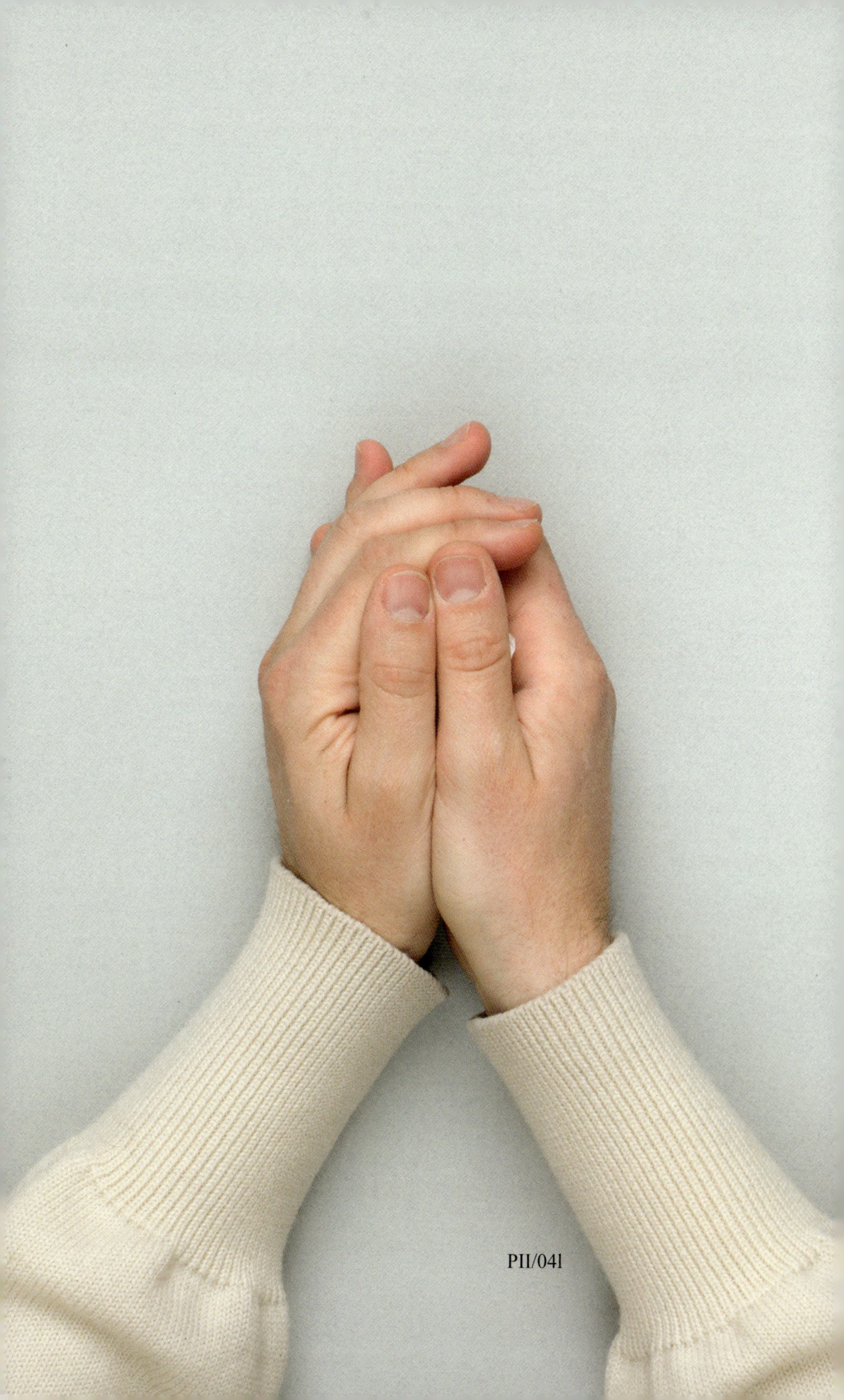

PII/041

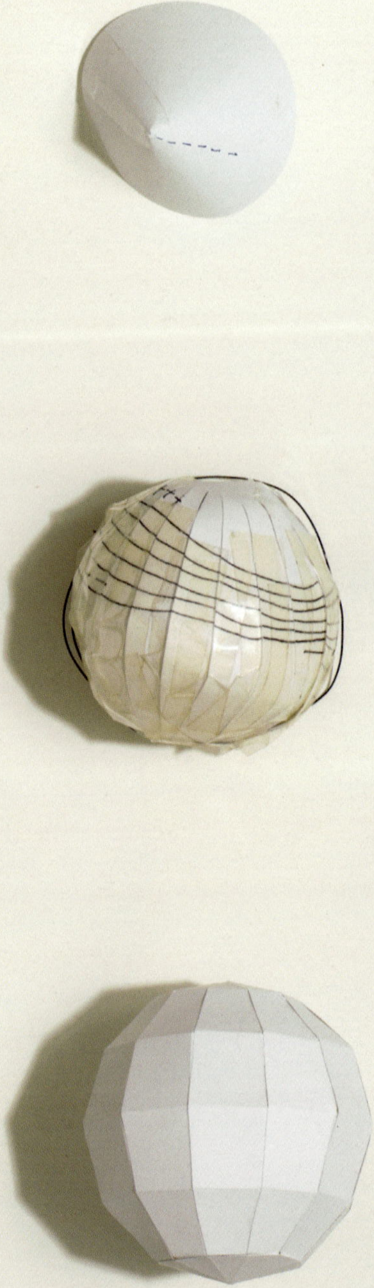

PII/05

PII/06

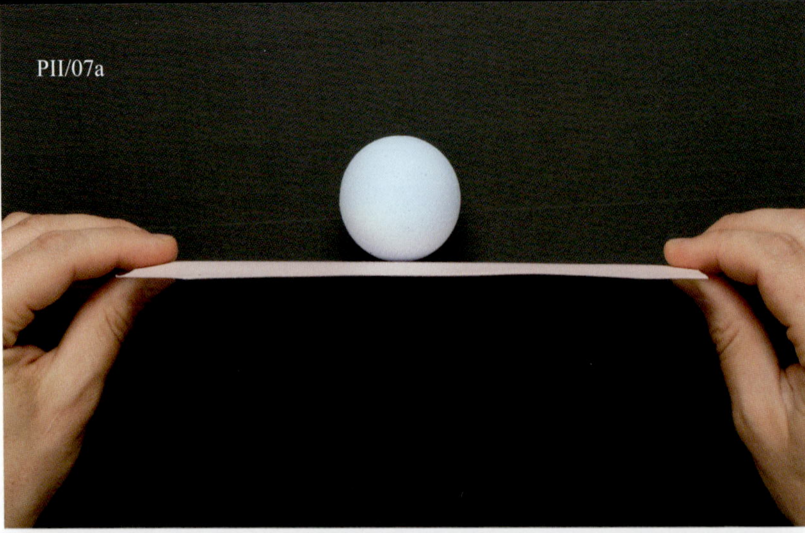
PII/07a

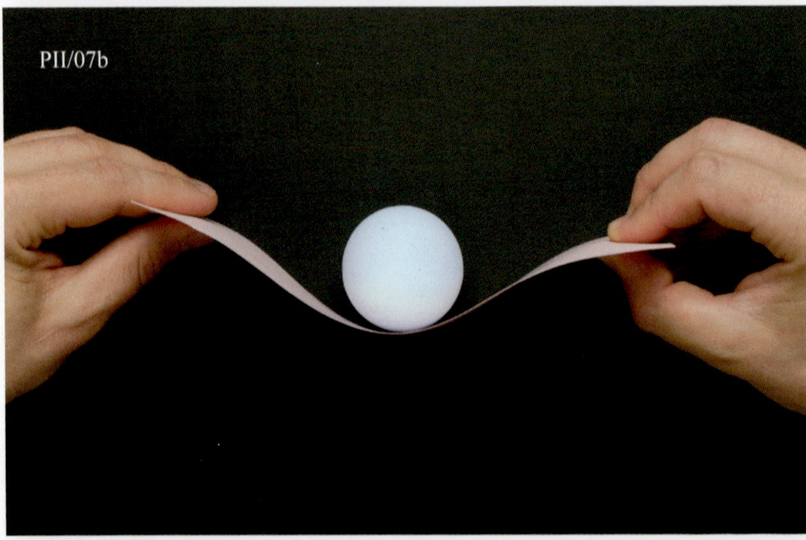
PII/07b

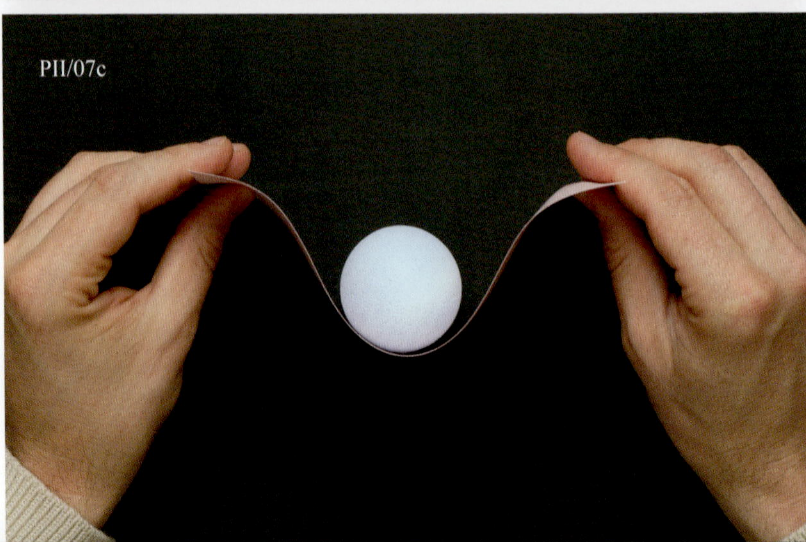
PII/07c

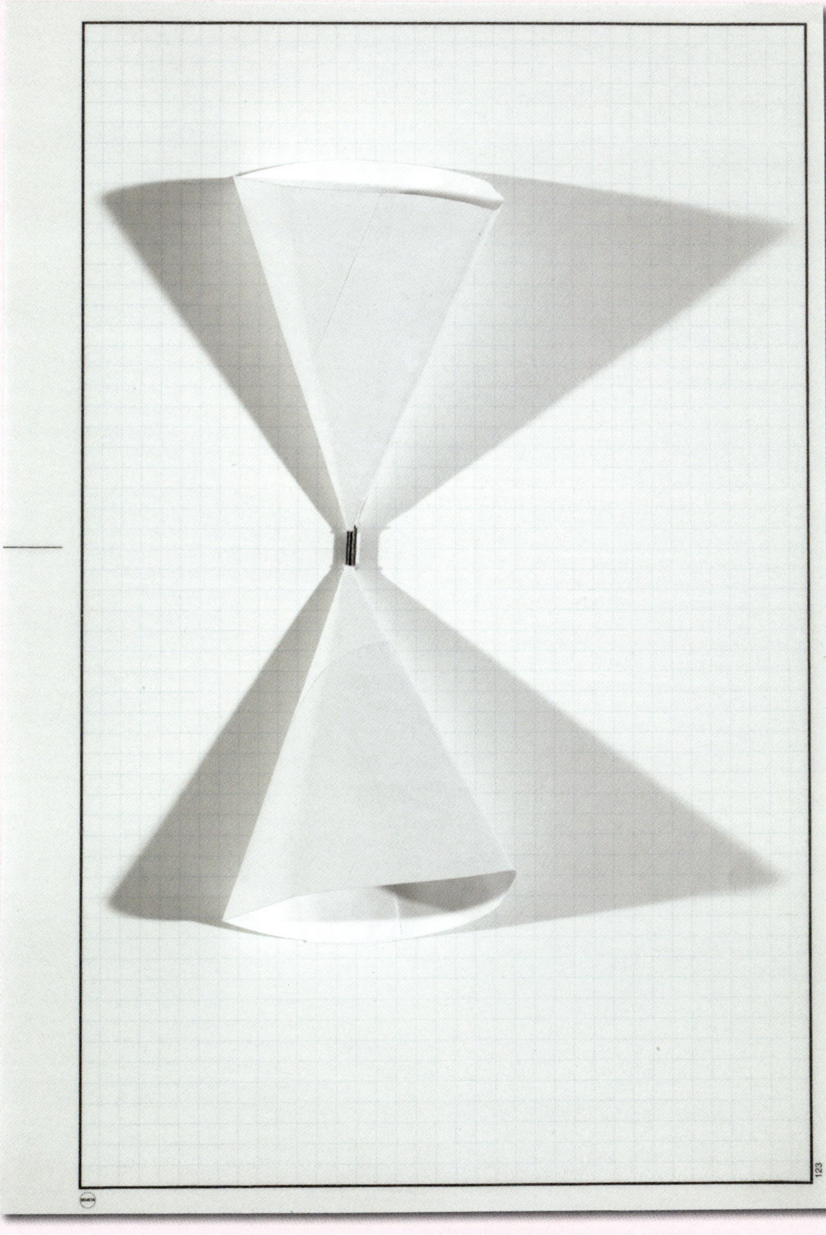

PII/08

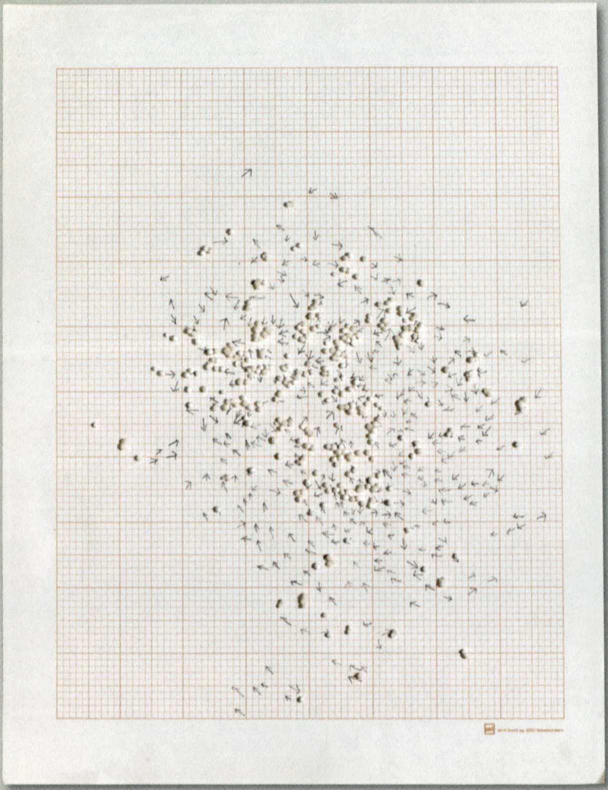

PII/09a

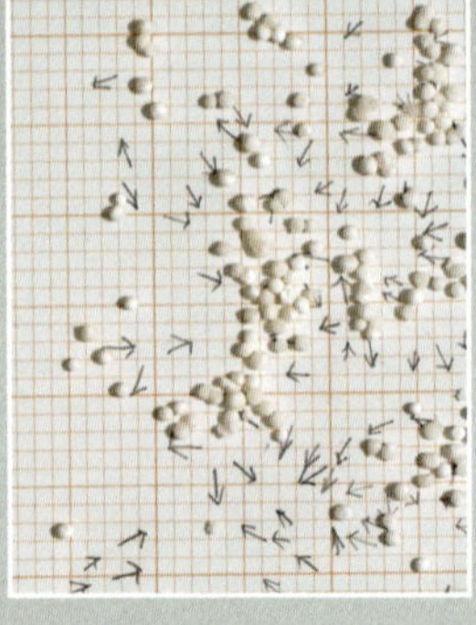

PII/09b

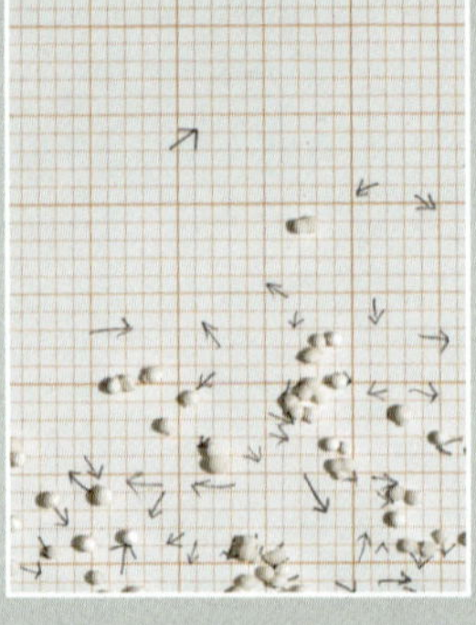

PII/09c

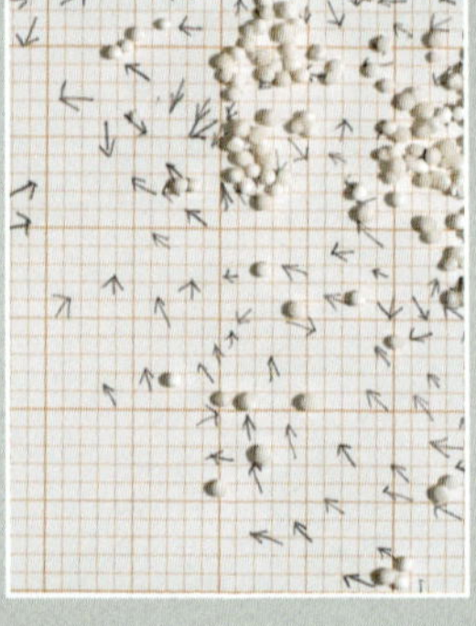

PII/09d

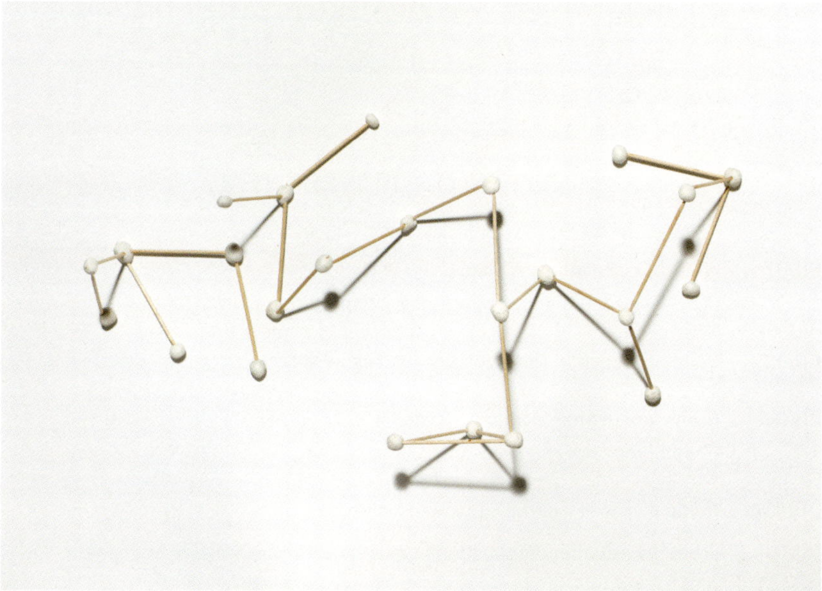

PII/10a

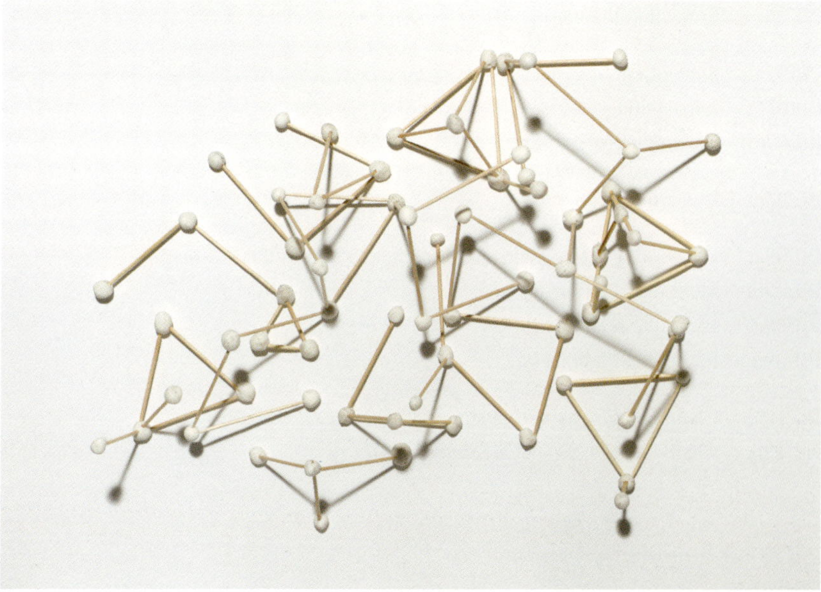

PII/10b

NOTES ON PLATES II

PII/01: Atlas of correlations – Plate II
(The social/intelligence/blind/spot/cognition/figure)

PII/02: Field of attraction (between flat and folded spaces)

PII/03: Collection of aide-mémoire – class IV
(Sammlung der Gedankenstützen Gruppe IV)

PII/04a: Folding spaces – surface relational study

PII/04b-k: From linearity to complexity. The permanent inside/outside interstition.

PII/04l: Potential state of inbetweenness

PII/05: 3 Models of thought for thinking of self-containedness

PII/06: Projecting the world

PII/07a: State of contingencies

PII/07b: Impact attack

PII/07c: Embedding of an idea

PII/08: Conic intersections

PII/09a: Cluster of contingencies (in reference to swarm intelligence)

PII/09b: Field like relations I

PII/09c: Field like relations II

PII/09d: Field like relations III

PII/10a: Chain reaction as spatial structures (before)

PII/10b: Chain reaction as spatial structures (after)

HYPOTHESIS #19

The Afterthought of Drawing

6 Hypotheses

Jane Tormey

This text is essentially concerned with the response to drawing and its subsequent description. My interest is in the discursive possibilities of description and the relationship between the drawing and how we can 'read' the drawing. Before formulating a number of hypotheses – some methods for response. I will first recall some themes discussed in *The Thought of Drawing*, which introduced *Drawing Now: Between the Lines of Contemporary Art*, a collection of drawings with an emphasis on the performative and speculative characteristics of the subjective and conceptual (2007). Second, I will consider some key writings, which address, question and speculate on drawing and pictures, by Jacques Derrida, Michael Baxandall, and John Berger. Underlying this exercise is the aim of avoiding a resolved description that precludes all others, exploring instead how the respondent can perform in a continuous play of possibilities. I am aiming for responses that derive from reflection and speculation rather than objective interpretation.

I will pick up threads that I introduced in *The Thought of Drawing* (2007) and play with some key points of discussion prompted by Derrida's *Memoirs of the Blind*, which accompanied an exhibition of drawings (1990-1) chosen from the Louvre Museum.[1] Derrida's assumption about drawing in *Memoirs of the Blind* is one of looking and copying, and concerns the conflation of the fleeting certainty of sight with the imitation of what can be seen. He exploits the theme of blindness as both subject matter and the object of the drawing in the many literal translations of blindness and its transcendental extension in metonymy and narrative (Derrida 1993: 41). He takes blindness (and sight) as a central metaphor for the phenomenon of vision and themes relating to it – blindness and sight; visible and invisible;[2] mindful and mindless; forethought and afterthought, seeing and drawing, tracing, copying, imagining, remembering and forgetting in memories or memoirs. Previously, I considered this metaphor of blindness from the point of view of the act of drawing, both from observation and imagination and the

1) The exhibition *Memoirs of the Blind* was held from October 1990 to January 1991 and was the first in a series entitled *Taking Sides* which invited 'personalities known for their critical abilities' to initiate a discourse prompted by their choice of drawings.

2) Derrida cites Maurice Merleau-Ponty, *The Visible and the Invisible*, 1968, p. 257.

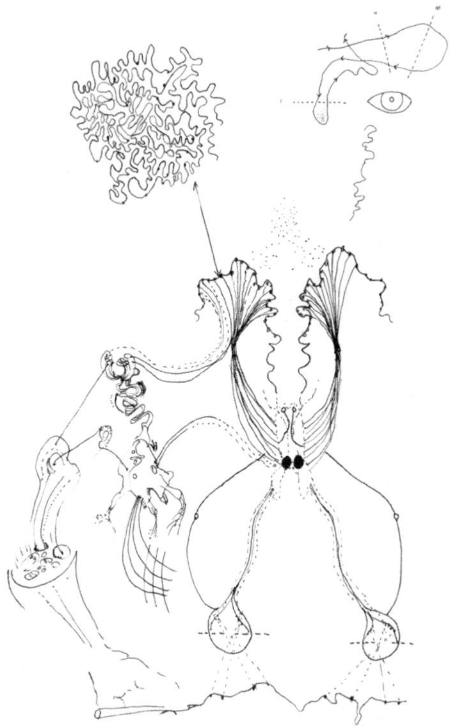

Hypothesis I (→ Fig. 13-12) If I enter the drawing and start living in this world, I can describe this other reality as if I were looking at the 'scene' as it unfolds before me. If I imagine this scene, I imagine also a possible paradigm of thinking. As the drawing is not derived from sight but from thought, my sight of it is rooted in thought. And as I don't want to translate this drawing in a literal way, which is reliant on appearance from without, I translate it as if from within. Instead of looking in from the outside, I am looking from within. The eye does not watch me – [it] is neutral, thin and seems preoccupied with its position. [It] is a figurehead only, merely a motif with little influence. [It] is in fact distant from and far above me, and does not determine my fallopian flowering. It is not possible for me to see [it], anyway. I sense something but do not believe [it] has any value or influence. [It] is insubstantial – two-dimensional. The space is ambivalent. I am the centre and the eye is supplementary – always – and nothing to me. *And* I am vehemently denying [its] centrality. I am not in any one place, but in many, surveying the mountains below and the maze above. I want the mountains but am directed to the maze. But I daresay to go there would be folly for it has blind spaces and I would soon become lost and cliché. So I will ignore it, as it is of limited dimension. The more I think of myself here, the more dimensions I accumulate. I look /move / project forward, sideways, over, under, every way possible. I stand astride/ hover above. I am distracted to my right by a lot of activity that deviates away from my purpose, which is twofold – to be solid and certain, and to be open and possible. I am interested in these elements and their activity which is unclear and over which I have no control. I cannot firmly grasp them – I am g[r]asping and letting go simultaneously. It is as if they are separate and independent and yet under my protection. Their properties are various – tracking, wiggling, whisking, winding, shooting, spurting, springing – upwards, downwards in my chamber and without – without clear direction and messy but emergent.

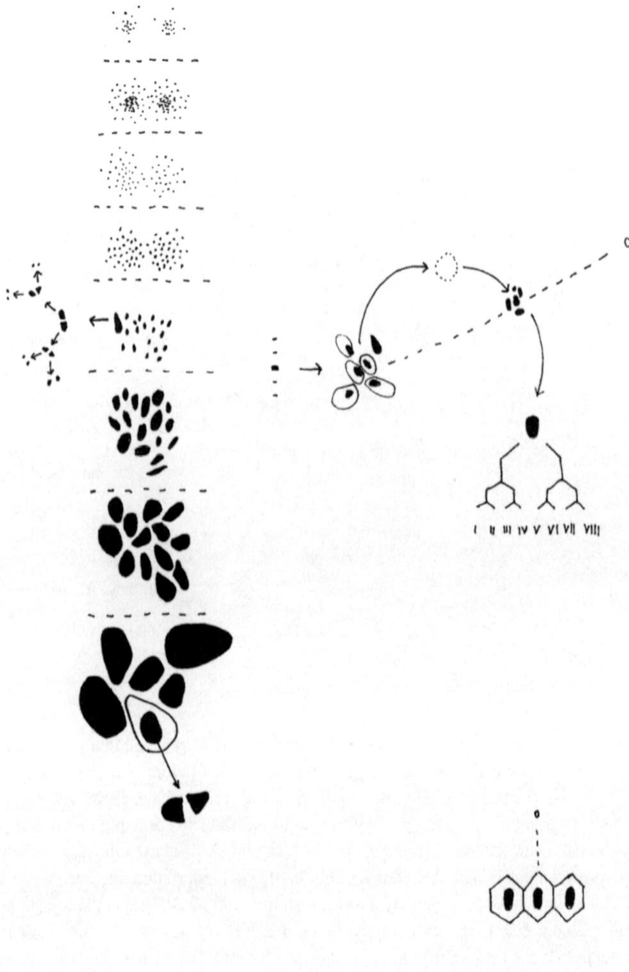

Hypothesis II (→ Fig. 02-10) In this possibility of nothing completed, I offer a momentary clip from a continuous state of becoming. I suppose, I redraw as if from the same logic – a specular falling back into thought – a supplementary essential. I confine myself to physical concerns such as 'large' and 'larger', which never reach their destination of largeness because they are in a constant state of getting larger. Deleuze's use of grammatical analogies – those of the infinitive, the comparative adjective and the present participle – offer subtly different nuances as to how we might understand condition or event. He refers to the changing condition of 'becoming', encapsulated by the perpetual state inherent in the sense of the infinitive, and the imminent difference implicit in the sense

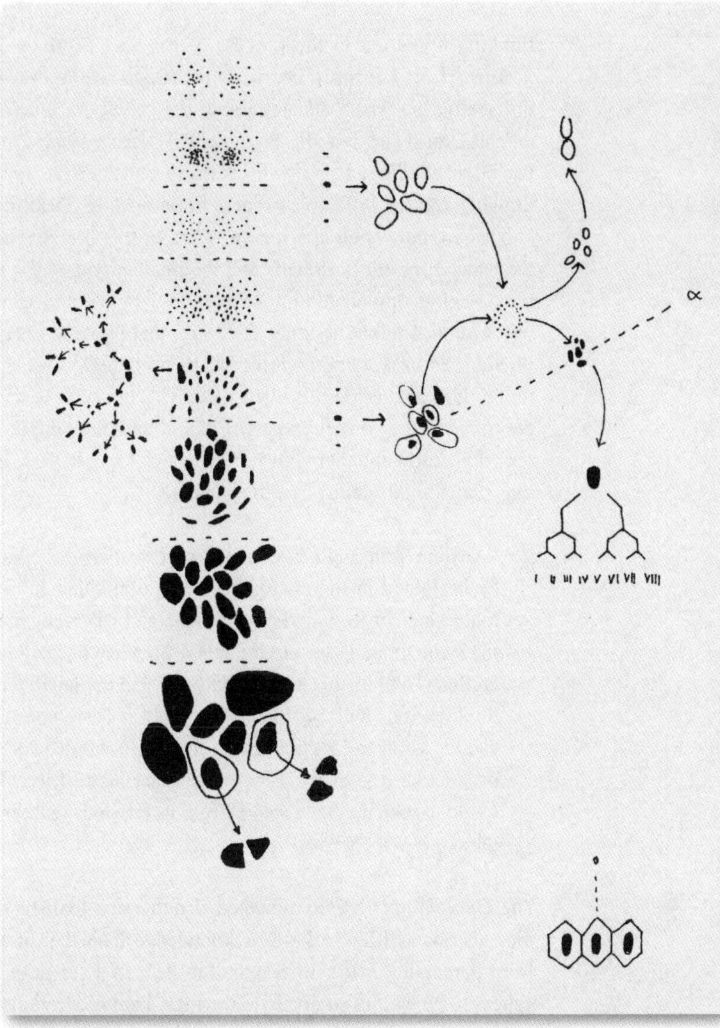

Fig. 02-10a (with drawn response by Jane Tormey)

of a comparative adjective, such as 'larger' or 'lighter'. If we remove the object, which a comparative adjective ('larger') might refer to, then that condition constantly becomes larger and therefore 'eludes the present' (Deleuze 2003: 3). 'Larger' never stops where it is but is always going toward somewhere larger, whereas definite quality is something that has stopped and is fixed. The condition can never finally become where it is going and is in a perpetual state of becoming larger (4). In encountering glimpses such as the action of something getting larger, we are caught up in possibilities. A predicate functioning as a 'manner of being' replaces the essential attribute and is incorporeal and not fixedly aligned – it is in this sense virtual and not actual.

thinking operation in the process of drawing (Tormey 2007: xi-xiii). Here, I reapply Derrida's reverie to seeing drawing – not seeing the world and retracing, but *seeing the drawing*. I extend Derrida's "hypothesis of sight" (Derrida 1993: 2) to the act of responding; I apply my sight to consider the space of drawing and the reflective process in its reading. Drawing circulates around vision and seeing, whether it is literal vision or the psychic vision of dreams and the imaginary, and the metaphor 'seeing' applies to both seeing the drawing, and seeing in one's mind. I might assume, therefore, that drawing visualises thought, and ask,what thoughts are being thought? What am I thinking in pondering this visualisation? Can I reverse the process – instead of imagining a world and then drawing it, can I read that world and then think it? What can I find in these drawings that similarly allow me to speculate?

> "Anyone with any sense will remember that the eyes may be unsighted in two ways, by a transition either from light to darkness or from darkness to light, and will recognise that the same thing applies to the mind. So when he sees a mind confused and unable to see clearly he will not laugh without thinking, but will ask himself whether it has come from a clearer world and is confused by the unaccustomed darkness, or whether it is dazzled by the stronger light of the clearer world to which it has escaped from its previous ignorance."
> (Plato, *The Republic* 518a)

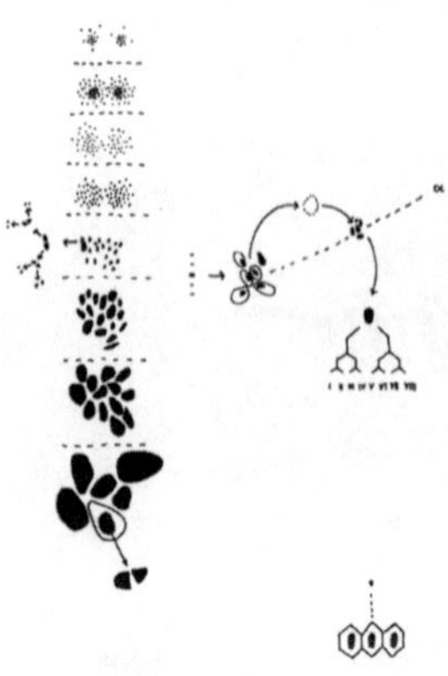

Fig. 02-10

The Thought of Drawing indicated also that non-realistic drawings access a different kind of knowledge than that gathered from perception (xiii). In responding here to a series of what appear to be wholly subjective drawings, I am proceeding from a position that regards conception as important as perception. If it is possible to 'represent a thought', given that thought is only clarified when it is translated into words – or drawing – then I consider how it may be possible for drawings to provoke thought. Rather than starting with the usual appearance of drawing, I conduct a number of experiments. I start from where conception meets appearance, not from where perception prompts conception. I start with the experience of looking out from within. I prepare myself by actively not thinking – avoiding looking. I want a non-preparedness to my looking, whilst thinking in abstract terms about possibilities – with forethought. Referring to Plato's analogy of prisoners in the cave who are unable to turn around to see a clearer world, Derrida indicates blindness as being a consequence of a continuous mediated seeing. In this context specifically, we can say that we are blind as a result of the filter of conventions in talking about art. We can be 'blind to the idea of the things themselves' because we cannot turn our heads all the way around and see differently and therefore are unable 'to interrupt this infinitely echoing discourse' (Derrida 1993: 13-15). Ultimately, in describing any kind of picture, concerns to give a response that, first, I can claim as mine, and second, allows me to see it before I am constrained by convention. Being aware of learned prejudices – my tendency to associate, to compare, to judge, I actively try to turn my head, to close my mind to this external noise and approach the drawing – blindly – without foresight. The contradiction remains that I have foresight, forethought, and afterthought. What I have difficulty with is present thought.

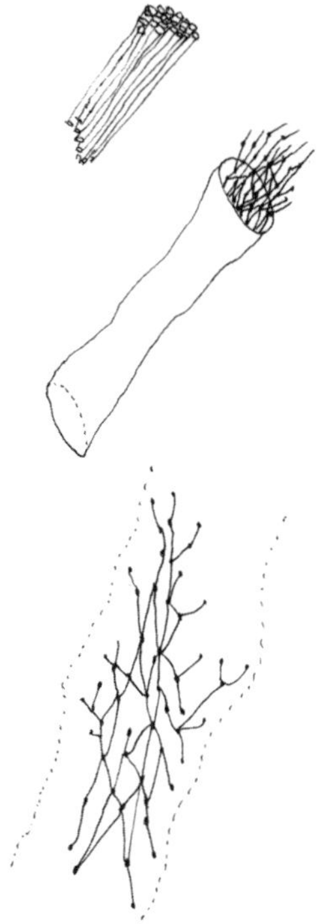

Fig. 05-15b

Baxandall (1985: 1-11) clarifies the nature of describing 'pictures' and suggests a model of *afterthought* for describing drawings. He demonstrates a kind of blindness in response to 'pictures' by giving examples of two very different ways of describing them: in the fourth century, Libanius focused on information evident in the subject-matter rather than the style or quality of painting; in 1951, Kenneth Clark described the manner of representation and the effect which it has. Baxandall demonstrates that each explanation of a picture becomes part of our perception in subsequent encounters and thereby constrains our response. As we explain the characteristics within the context in which we define it, the description justifies previous descriptions and the process becomes self-perpetuating. What appears to reside in any particular work is confirmed by its definition and the concepts attached to it, so that it is difficult to distinguish between what we think we see and the knowledge we have of it. Baxandall identifies three functions of language that correspond with the history of the picture's making (its cause), its being (metaphorically expressed) and its effect when I look at it. 'Effect words' describe the effect the picture has –and will not be constant between viewers, so that I might find a figure 'playful', and you might find it 'sinister'. 'Comparison words'

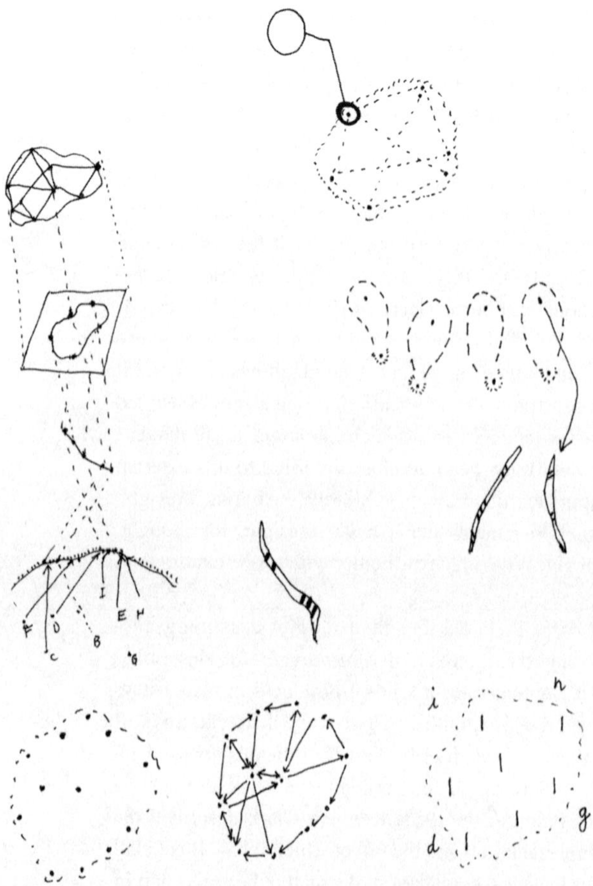

Hypothesis III (→ Fig. 09-07) I concern myself with factual elements, as far as I am able, and recognise the ever-present function of metaphor. The words become generic metaphors, such as 'passage', that travel *through* – or find a way *between* or move *on*. Prepositions narrate my relationship to the drawing – spatially and temporally. I concern myself with my spatial relationship to figures in the scene. I am the centre of this world and "space is organised in conformity with the sides of my body" (Tuan 1977: 36) and my "body is the measure of direction, location and distance" (44-7). I can touch and experience expansion around me. I can sense space behind me and to the right and the left. What is in front of me is much larger than what is behind me, which I experience as darker and by senses other than sight (40). As I turn, what is light becomes darker and what is dark becomes light. I experience the space passively as I am acted *upon* and affected *by* the place, and actively as I act, behave, move *in* or work *on* or engage *with* "the unfamiliar and experiment with the elusive and

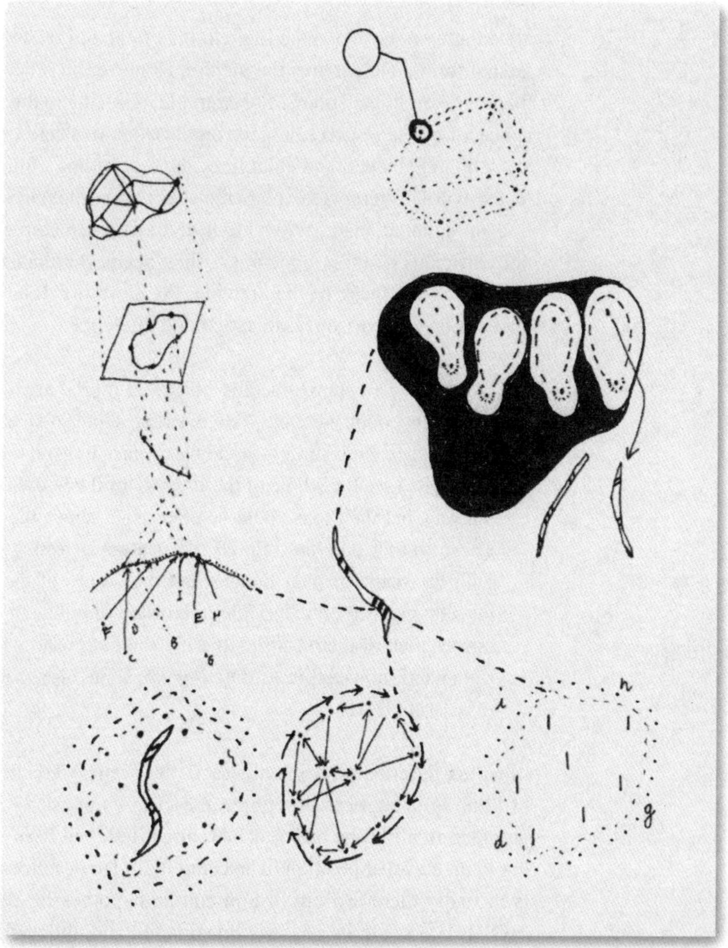

Fig. 09-07a (with drawn response by Jane Tormey)

the uncertain" (9). However simply I describe it, I am defined metaphorically and by prepositions that position me physically and psychologically in relation to objects and space – *between* these figures, sat *on* that figure, staying *within* this figure or moving *up* that one. When I encounter a figure, I position myself in relation to it and to the objects *on* it or *under* it.[3] As I situate objects in relation to objects, I am resituating myself in relation to myself; I am asserting myself as subject. I am defining my attitude to all that surrounds me, defining my state of mind as in control or distressed or lost or fearful in relation to those objects, so that what is dark above me can be too dark for me and thereby threatening, or a closed circle can be disturbing for me.

3) Tuan cites Merleau-Ponty, *Phenomenology of Perception*, Routledge & Kegan Paul, London, 1962, p. 101.

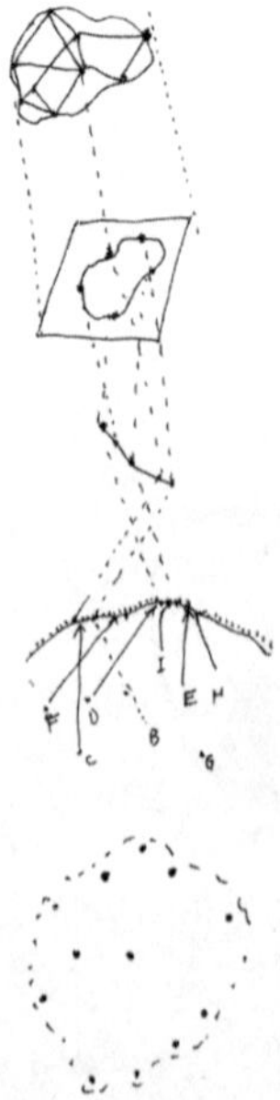

Fig. 09-07a

are an attempt to find some logic to the effect and relate to the factual formal elements in the picture. However, in order to do this we resort to metaphors. For example, referring to the 'resonance' of colour or describing the organisation of shapes, which are supported by perpendicular lines, as 'scaffolding'. Similarly 'cause words' attempt to explain the effect – a particularly 'fine' line, or 'agitated' mark. When I look at drawings (pictures) I am not conscious of these divisions – they occur simultaneously, but the more I speak of the drawing, the more my description depends on comparison, association and inference.

> "There was a countryside and houses of a kind appropriate to peasant country-people – some larger, some smaller. Near the cottages were straight-standing cypress trees. It was not possible to see the whole of these trees, for the houses got in the way, but their tops could be seen rising above the roofs. These trees I daresay, offered the peasant a resting-place, with the shade of their boughs and the voices of the birds joyfully perched on them. Four men were running out of the houses, one of them calling to a lad standing near – for his right hand showed this, as if giving him some instructions."
> (Baxandall 1985: 2)

Libanius describes the picture as if the scene were in front of him, as if he were describing the *mise en scène* as it had enfolded in a film he had watched, or as if he had been standing in an elevated position overseeing it all. He describes what is factually there in front of him and he hypothesises (e.g. he says 'I dare say'); he uses his imagination and anticipation to speculate. If there are trees and if there are men, the trees would offer a resting-place in the shade. If the man's hand is so, then he may perhaps be calling to the lad. The wagon-load doesn't seem properly tied down and so the men may be trying to keep it in place - and so it goes on. He says nothing about the mode of representation, the style, the expression, or the form, and speaks as if it were not a representation at all. As a result we would not be able to reproduce this painting because he describes *the act of looking at the picture* rather than the construction of the picture. It starts from the position of looking, not analysing. It does not attempt to give an impression, but a catalogue, an inventory. It is not judgmental or concerned with the formal aspects of the picture, unlike most critiques post-Kant and as exemplified by Kenneth Clark's description. However, Libanius does insert qualitative effect words (joyfully) as if assumed by default. Here, Baxandall surmises that 'words are representing less the picture than thought after seeing the picture'. We explain pictures in selective verbal descriptions, which primarily represent our thoughts about them. The words used operate as 'generalising instruments … inferring causes, characterising effects, making various kinds of comparison' (Baxandall 10). What is crucial here is the separation between 'representing the picture' and 'representing the thought' after seeing the picture, which, he points out, is tied to conventional/current ways of thinking about pictures i.e. aesthetic discourse (Kant, Bell, Clarke or Greenberg). We have become accustomed to responding according to our prior understanding of what is required – whether it be form or concepts or imaginings – to descriptions that give an idea of the scene (the subject matter, the object drawn) and the mode of its representation (4).

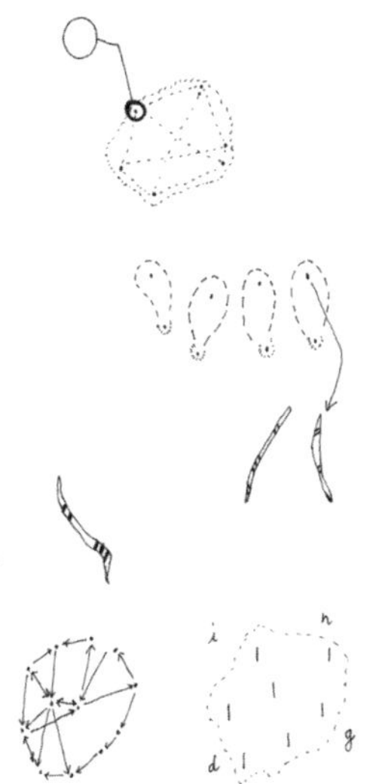

Fig. 09-07b

Berger (*On Drawing,* 2005) distinguishes between three types of drawing: those concerned with observation, those with communicating ideas and those with memory. Whilst a drawing collates images from a variety of sources (including memory and fantasy), any drawing that involves reference to the visible necessitates the illusory craft of drawing 'as if' in front of the scene. Drawing moves between observation, studying the visible (the present tense), reference (past and memory) and projection (future tense and what is absent). 'Each type of drawing speaks in a different tense' that requires 'a different capacity for imagination' (Berger 46-7). His reference to 'tenses' implies drawing as a verb operation (doing) and suggests also a useful place to start responding to drawing – as an active procedure. Berger also demonstrates several different ways of responding to drawings. In 'Vincent', he is drawn into a reflection of van Gogh's life, his reputation, his iconology and whether there is anything left to say about his work: "Only when I look at his drawings does it seem worthwhile to add to the words. Maybe because his drawings resemble a kind of writing, and he often drew on his own letters. The ideal project would be to draw the process of his drawing, to borrow his drawing hand. Nevertheless I will try with words" (13). In *Picasso*, Berger considers

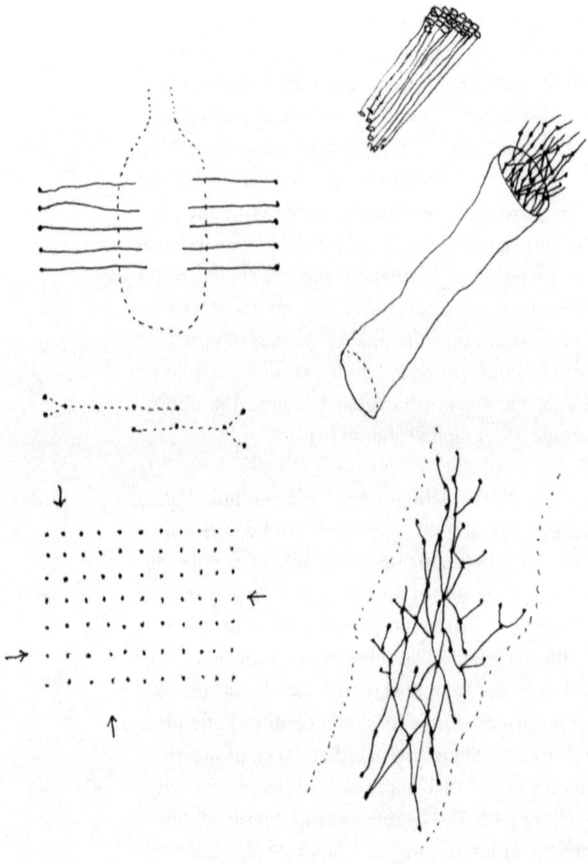

Hypothesis IV (→ Fig. 05-15) The same drawing can refer ostensively in wholly different ways, with different sets of references. A description that is reduced to factual terms might not directly identify where my interest lies but, if I make some critical declaration, it demonstrates my interest as I declare it worthy of qualification. If I say it is 'big', it is because that "bigness" is interesting to me (Baxandall 9). If I do not describe the drawing it relates to, I can demonstrate knowledge of other drawings 'in the same class' and can relate very different commentaries, which are parallel.

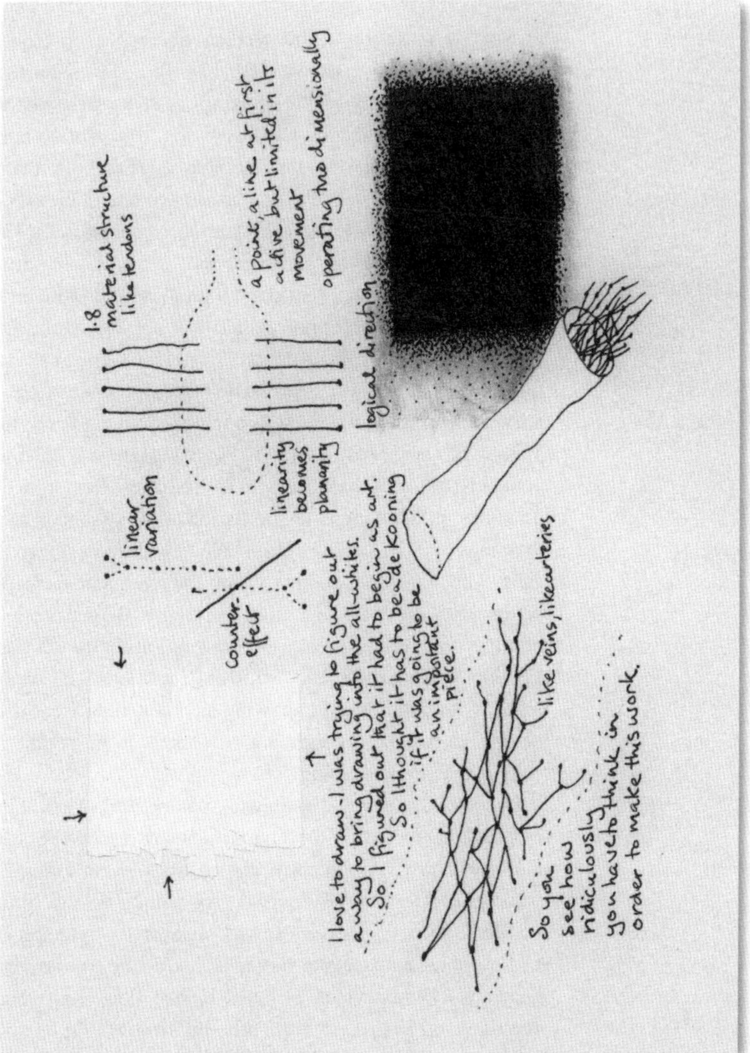

Fig. 05-15a (with drawn response by Jane Tormey)

I may not be able to point exactly to what the drawing means or where a particular sensation is located, but I can "write the sign down, and at the same time I concentrate my attention on sensation – and so as it were point to it inwardly" (Wittgenstein 2001 § 258). I can be manifestly demonstrative and describe by example. I can interfere and erase. I can contest the logic of the drawing and annotate – Klee would do this, Rauschenberg would do this and Nash would do this.

Picasso's relationship to the women who appear in each of a series of drawings – a drawn biography. To do this requires him to 'enter' the reality of the drawings as if he were watching a live event as it occurs. He speculates: "Picasso is confessing his horror at the fact that the body ages and the imagination does not' (22) and 'Picasso turns from one to the other, as though they were different aspects of the same reality" (32). In *Sheets of paper laid in the Grass*, Berger ponders the distinction between drawings concerned with ideas and those that are mindless and about feeling, rather than about thinking in the way that Paul Klee's drawings are (60). He recognises a distinction between thoughtful drawing and thoughtless drawing: 'For Klee every sensation passed through his drawing hand. In the making of her [Marisa Camino's] drawings there is apparently no hand' (61). In a dialogue with his son Yves, Berger includes drawings as annotation to the text. And he responds to two drawings by Juan Munoz by conversing with an imagined presence, which is absent and not visible. Where Libanius recounts his observation of a scene in the past tense, Berger conducts a two-way conversation with the drawing, in the present tense. Berger's writing indicates a number of methods with which to respond: to enter into the drawing as if watching what is happening; to respond by drawing; to attempt to be mindless; to converse with the drawing.

Derrida suggests that a drawing can set up a paradigm, or model, constructed by the family of words used. The play of words establish a particular 'relationship with an exemplar(y) paradigm' (Derrida 1987: 194). As paradigm, the drawing 'exceeds all perspectives', resists all assaults, interpretations and occupies a space and provides a structure ('a device or a machine') within which to move (1987: 196-7). He demonstrates this in *The Secret Art of Antonin Artaud* (1998), in which he discusses a number of Artaud's drawings/writings seen on the walls of Paule Thévenin's apartment. For legal reasons the book does not include the drawings so we cannot see them – we are blind to them. Derrida's speculation in response to these drawings is a further source of metaphor - any one of his sidetracks leads us off into other regions for talking about drawing – *of* drawings, *in* drawings, *on* drawings. Mary Ann Caws, who translates and introduces the texts, describes Derrida's reverie as 'no less frenzied than that of Artaud, inscribed in the sur-

(→ PIII/01)

face and the undersurface of his drawings' (Derrida 1998: xii). Derrida persistently considers Artaud's use of the word *subjectile* and its inevitable metaphoric promiscuity of grammatical variance, whilst understanding that the term is ultimately untranslatable. He draws *subjectile* toward the dynamic potential of all its meanings: "subjective, subtle, sublime, also pulling the *il* and the *li,* and ending with projectile. This is Artaud's '*thought*'" (62). He lists the possibilities of *subjectile*; he picks up the minutest element or word and runs with it – he intervenes, he interrupts, he fantasises: "Neither object nor subject, neither screen nor projectile, the subjectile can *become* all that, stabilising itself in a certain form or moving about in another. But the drama of its own becoming, always oscillates between the intransivity of *jacere* and the transitivity of *jacere*, in what I will call the *conjecture* of 'both'"(77). Derrida proceeds to ponder projectile and *jetée* (trajectory) and *jacere* (to throw something):

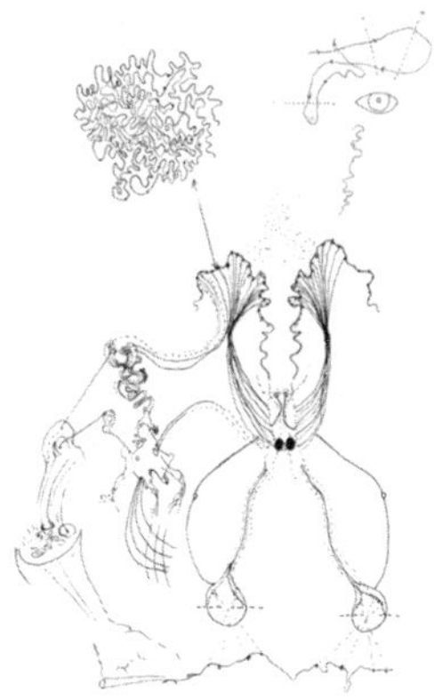

Fig. 13-12

> "Between … the intransitivity of *being-thrown* and the transitivity of *throwing*, the difference seems from then on to be as decisive as temporary, that is to say transitory … Everything will play itself out from now on in the critical but precarious difference, unstable and reversible, between these two. Such at least would be our working hypothesis. But what we will surely verify is that, hypothetically, the subjectile always has the function of a *hypothesis*, it exasperates and keeps you in suspense, it makes you give out of breath by always being *posed beneath*."
> (Derrida 1998: 77-8)

He provides analogies for how we can encounter a drawing – to throw oneself into the drawing – to travel through it and trace a trajectory – to project my meaning onto the other – onto the drawing – or rather into the drawing – I throw myself into it – figuratively in enthusiasm and in hypotheses.

Each *micrology* performs a response to drawing and operates within "the logic of the hypothesis" (Derrida 1993: 45) – that is, I adopt a series of paradigms and respond according to the consequent constraints and "let them disconcert me" (Derrida 1987: 220). I experiment with different methods as proposition. As a performative statement each refers to itself and declares its intention – "I am responding". Each is a mindfully self-reflexive afterthought. I assume hypothesis as supposition – a reconnaissance of

Hypothesis V (→ Fig. 12-55) First, I concern myself with causal possibilities. I recall 'lab' experiments, when we would put a combination of substances into a glass container and watch what happened. Here I put in elements A, B and C, one on top of the other. There are consequences: A results in B and B results in C. What causes these effects are acids and elements such as bermalide, bismuth, hycrogen, feramile and calcopen. Each has its formula which is represented at the bottom of the drawing. The physical effect bubbles above, producing a succession of waves – first strong and becoming increasingly dissipated. Each moves up in a spiralling motion, something like smoke, something like a signal. Perhaps the substances produce a pulse that is interrupted or rhythmic. Perhaps there is a message – ATdS or AdTs or AdTS – and the order could be vital; the message could be coded. At any rate, the motion upwards results in a symmetrical cloud of geometrical significance – more profound than those promised by the formulas arranged below. Its effect is positive because it resolves itself, completes a sort of logic in a swirling three-lobed container that holds other emerging substances and dynamics. There seems to be some potential here. Its dynamic effect is uplifting physically and psychologically. The configuration and the implications please me. Dots are purposeful; lines are hopeful and elegant, but not perfect. The suggestion of formula promises continuation into a future. The formulas are mnemonic and metonymic – private worlds, imaginary beings, alternative processes to what might be assumed or imposed – art and science.

Hypothesis VI (→ Fig. 12-55) Some utterances are purposeless or are not verifiable. Apparently straightforward statements are "either nonsensical or else intended as something quite different" – in other words the words do not intend the literal equivalent of the words (Austin 1994: 2-3). Description is loaded with intention – repressed, unconscious or overt, so that the apparently innocent request such as "pass the salt" can be loaded with an entirely different meaning. Such performative statements are subject to mood dictated by intention and context such as orders, advice, permission, warning, question, or protest (Austin, Lecture VI). Just as Libanius cannot help but assume that the birds are joyful, as is their nature, so too I assume the logic of graphic invention and emotive effect, which may be increasingly hysterical. We could say that all statements in this description are untrue in that they cannot be verified – on the other hand, in so far as they express the result of a hypothesis, they are 'true'. They are performative in that they are 'doing' description, and they may be 'outrageous' (Austin 20): Obsessively drawn, with precision and yet careless and carefree, material and ethereal substances bubble up profusely, producing a succession of waves – first strong and demonstrative but becoming increasingly dissipated and ineffectual. They soar upward in the universal motion of the spiral, like smoke, like clouds, like heavenly geometry, like angels. It produces a rhythmic gut-wrenching pulse that interrupts any equilibrium. They cannot be tracked or traced because they are untouchable and invisible. It is a lyrical dynamic, more sublime than beautiful, as if singing and proceeding from the earth, the visible and verifiable to the immaterial and invisible, sending ritualistic and profound messages of spirit and incense. There is a vital alchemic message for us all – what is not Actually visible, but could be hidden or inactual aspects of the Thing – hidden things, Situated "elsewhere" (Merleau-Ponty 1968: 257).[4] I don't have to see it in order to understand its pearly effect and high-density, silvery and pink-tinged appearance; my knowledge is sentient and not only derived from sight.

4) My adaptation from Merleau-Ponty.

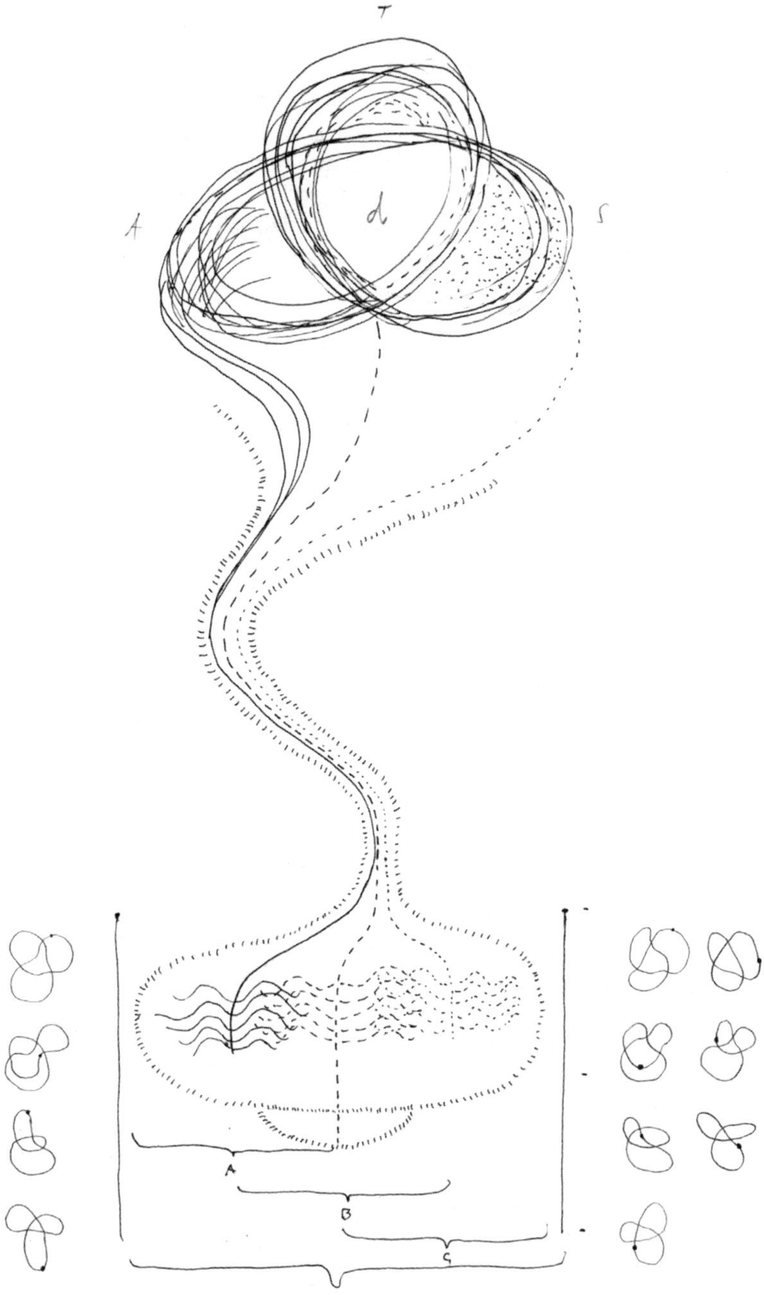

Fig. 12-55

possibility – and speculate from one drawing to the next. In order to hypothesise without prejudice, I need to come to the drawing mindlessly – as if blind. I attempt to abandon my conditioned expectations of tradition and contra-tradition. However, when I attempt to draw without thinking, I fail; I will fail at this also – these are hypotheses. I approach each drawing from the point of view of its discursive and desultory nature, as it circumscribes meanings and things, as it aggregates references to recognisable things and to concepts, rather than definitions. The contradiction of seeing the drawing is that I am not seeing what was imagined, when it was drawn; not seeing then, I am imagining now. My overarching hypothesis is that drawing animates thought and can hypothesise and invent thought; it can double back on itself and invent again in imagining. So if what we are looking at are hypotheses then I can visualise; I can propose contradictory states – states of possibility that exist simultaneously. I can conceive a number of simultaneous paradigms/possibilities. In reversing this process – as if in front of the scene – I look within and between. I explore how the drawing is discursive in hindsight – how it thinks around a subject.

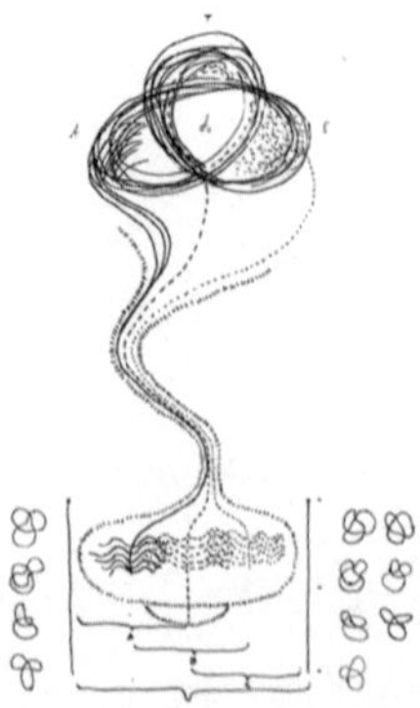

Fig. 12-55

References

Austin, J. L., *How to Do Things with Words* [1955], Harvard University Press, Cambridge, Mass., 1994.

Baxandall, M., *Patterns of Intention: On the historical explanation of pictures*, Yale University Press, New Haven, London, 1985.

Berger, J., *Berger On Drawing*, Occasional Press, Cork, 2005.

Bois, Y. and Krauss, R., *Formless, A User's Guide*, Zone Books, New York, 1997.

Deleuze, G., *The Fold: Leibnitz and the Baroque* [1988], trans. Conley, T., University of Minnesota Press, Minneapolis, 1993.

Deleuze, G., *The Logic of Sense* [1969], trans. Stivale, C., Continuum, London, New York, 2003.

Derrida, J., *The Truth in Painting* [1978], trans. Bennington, G. and McLeod, I., University of Chicago Press, 1987.

Derrida, J., *Memoirs of the Blind, the Self Portrait and Other Ruins*, trans. Brault , P.-A. and Naas, M., The University of Chicago Press, Chicago, London, 1993

Derrida, J. and Thévenin P., *The Secret Art of Antonin Artaud*, The MIT Press, Cambridge, Mass., London, 1998.

Merleau-Ponty, M., *The Visible and the Invisible*, Northwestern University Press, Evanston, 1968.

Ortony, A. (ed.), *Metaphor and Thought*, Cambridge University Press, 1993.

Plato, *The Republic*, Penguin Books, London, 2003.

Rauschenberg, R., *Speaking about Erased de Kooning*, http://www.artreview.com/video/video/show?id=1474022:Video:34075, 1953.

Tormey, C. J., *The Thought of Drawing*, in Sawdon, P. J., Tormey, C. J., Downs, S. T., Selby, A. and Marshall, R. (eds.), *Drawing Now: Between the Lines of Contemporary Art*, I.B.Tauris, London, 2007.

Tuan, Yi-Fu, *Space and Place, the Perspective of Experience*, University of Minnesota Press, London, Minneapolis, 1977.

Wittgenstein, L. *Philosophical Investigations* [1953], trans. Anscombe, G.E.M., Blackwell Publishing, Oxford, 2001.

HYPOTHESIS #20

The Hand, The Creatures, The Singing Garden & The Night Sky

Moira Roth

THE HAND
& THE CREATURE

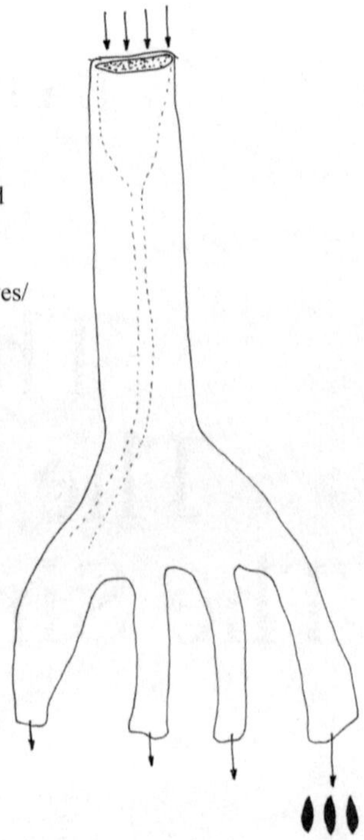

Fig. 03-17

Moving cautiously across the page/ The four-fingered Blind Hand sought out memories/ Memories of the sight/ Of blazing suns/ Of dark caves/ And of pale dust.

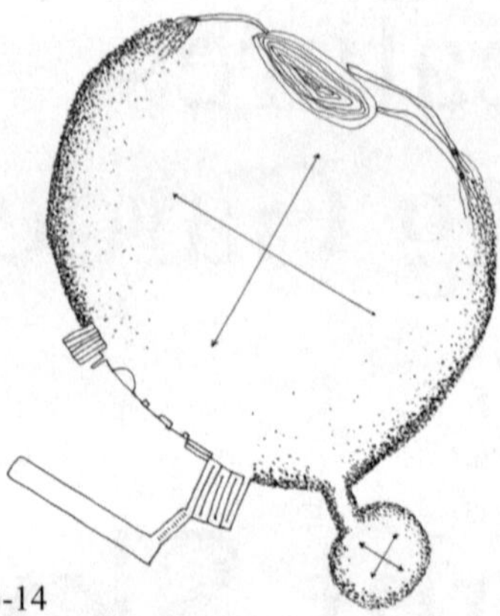

Fig. 03-14

Running clumsily/ Down the mountain/ Toward the sea/ The Mute Creature began to sing silently to itself/ Singing of memories/ Of its voyage to the Sun.

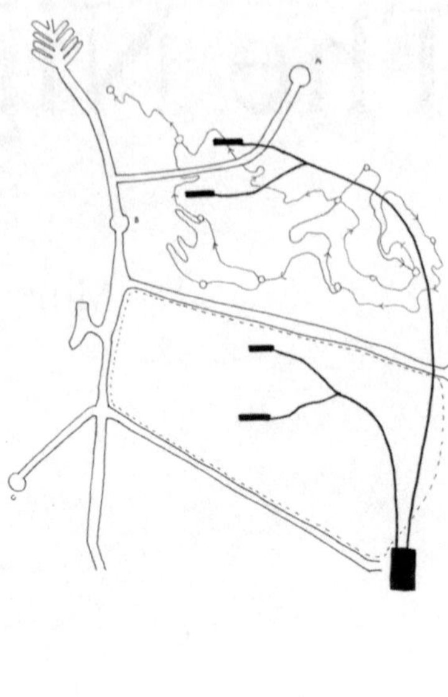

Fig. 03-19

The Blind Hand traced out/ The two paths of the black wires/ – one leading to the empty and silent/ Meadow of Solitude/ And the other/ To the noisy Pits of Desolation.

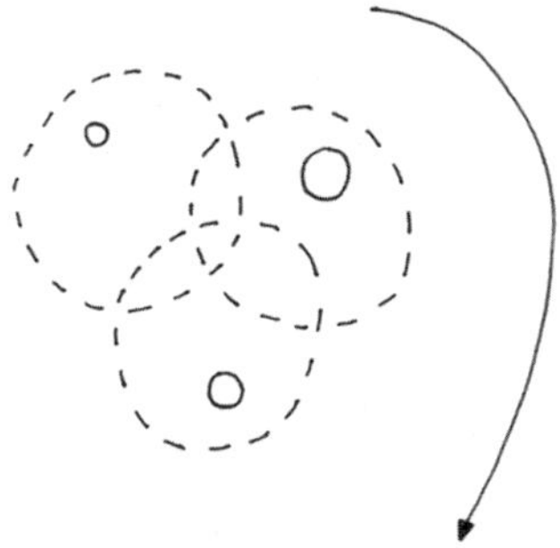

Fig. 03-11

The Mute Creature/ Grasping a diagram/ That it had found under a rock on the beach/ Began to toss the three spinning balls/ This way and that/ Listening to their jagged sounds.

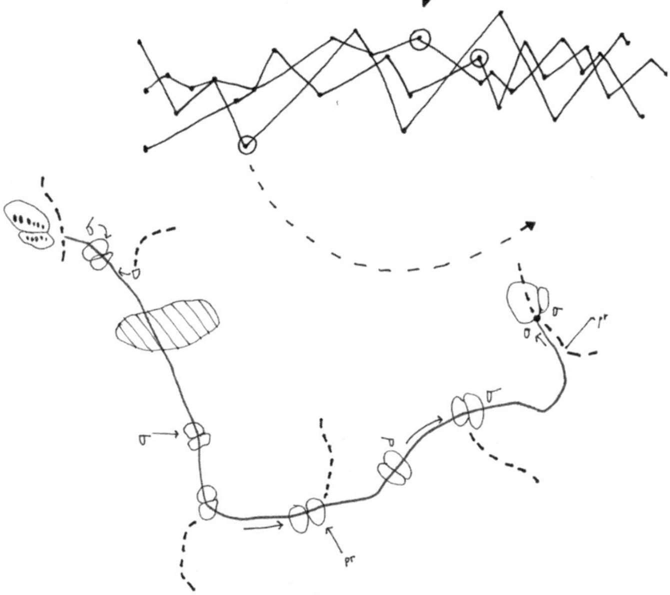

Fig. 03-04

The tale ends/ With the meeting of the Blind Hand/ and the Mute Creature.

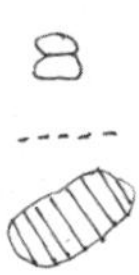

For a year/ Each with the same map in hand/ And/ Never speaking/
They walked/ By the river/ Tracing its path from the sea toward/
The Great Wall of China.

In their second year together/ They wrote to one another daily/
At midnight/ In invisible ink/ Leaving their letters/ By the river's path/
For the other to find/ At dawn.

In the third year/ Standing on the Great Wall/
The Blind Hand regained its sight/ and the Mute Creature its voice.

THE HAND, THE CREATURES & THE SINGING GARDEN

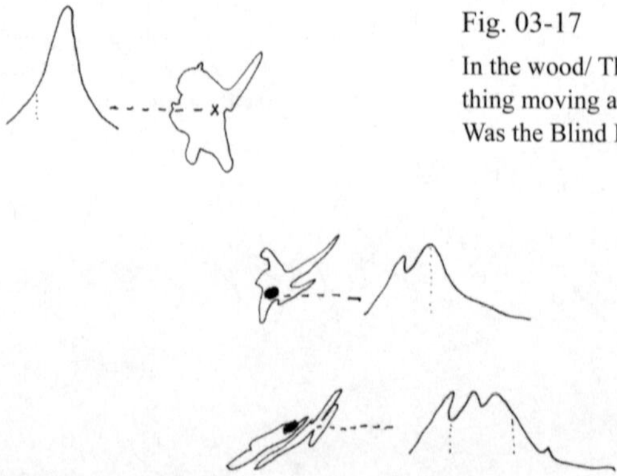

Fig. 03-17

In the wood/ The only thing moving at midnight/ Was the Blind Hand

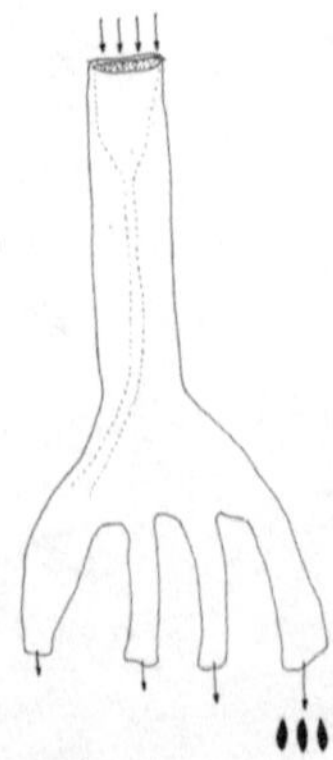

Fig. 02-26

Watched apprehensively/ By the trio of Mute Creatures.

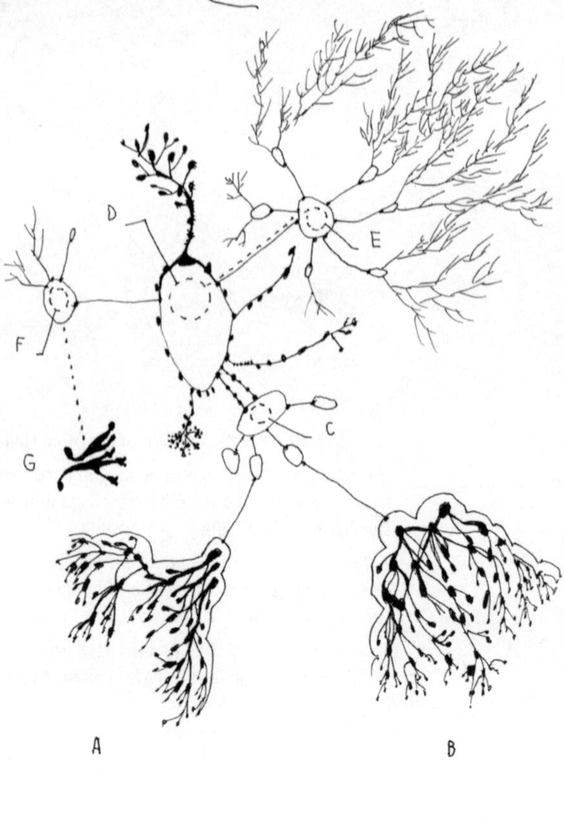

Fig. 02-24

It was only when the sun rose/ That they all realised/ That they were near/ The Singing Garden

Where they sat/ Comfortably together/ The next night

– watching the falling stars/ and listening/ to the murmuring exchanges/ of the nearby leopards and lizards.

THE OBSERVATORY & THE NIGHT SKY

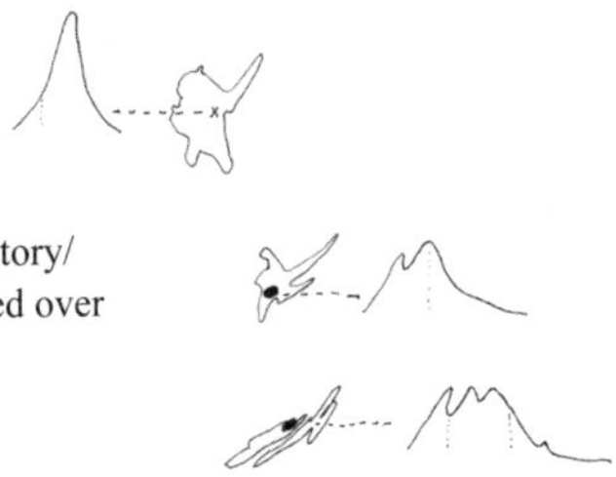

Fig. 02-26

In the deserted observatory/ The Astronomer puzzled over the drawings.

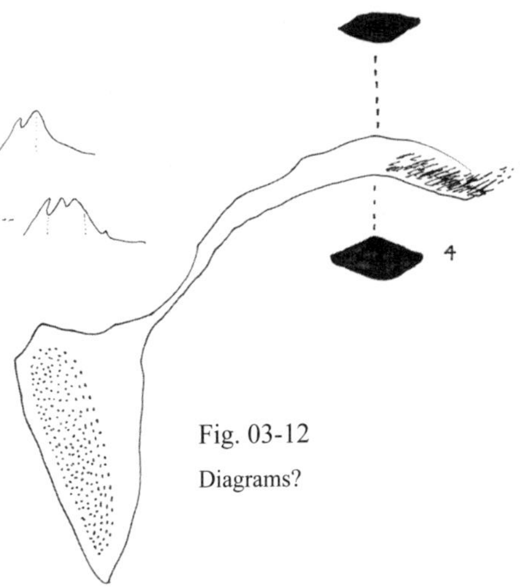

Fig. 03-08

Were they maps?

Fig. 03-12

Diagrams?

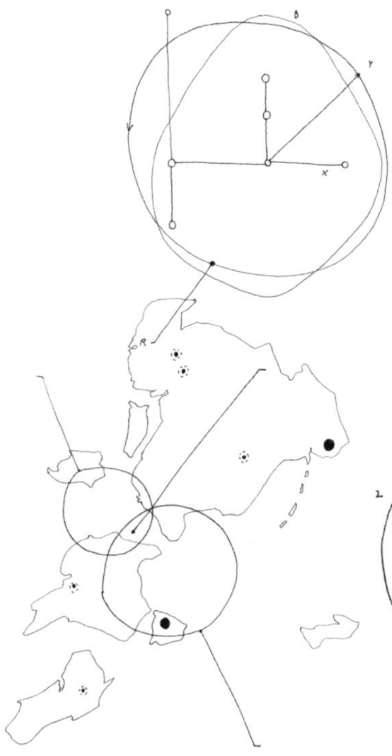

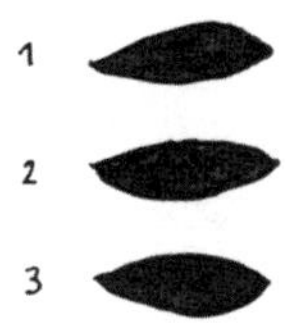

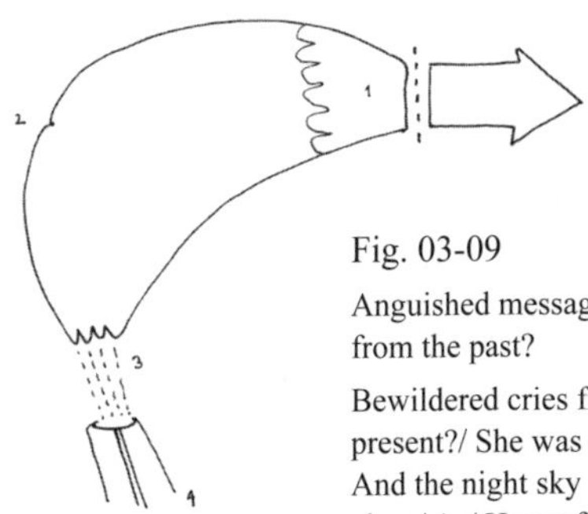

Fig. 03-09

Anguished messages from the past?

Bewildered cries from the present?/ She was not sure/ And the night sky offered no clues/ As/ Hour after hour/ She searched it/ Through Galileo's telescope.

Fig. 03-07

Coded messages from the future?

HYPOTHESIS #21

The Unthought Known

Felix de Mendelssohn

INTERPRETING THE ALREADY INTERPRETED?

The principle of interpretation in art as in psychoanalysis is a basic one. First the artist (or the patient) interprets, then the audience (analyst). A work of art is in itself an interpretation of the world. An artist who does not offer his work in this way is either a pornographer or a sentimental realist (think kitsch!). Freud thought that the analyst should never be more than one step ahead of the patient in his interpretation of the material of the session. But even that can be too far out. We analysts are latecomers to the patient's feast, we watch him partake and then dine on the crumbs left on the table (while helping to clean up the mess afterwards).

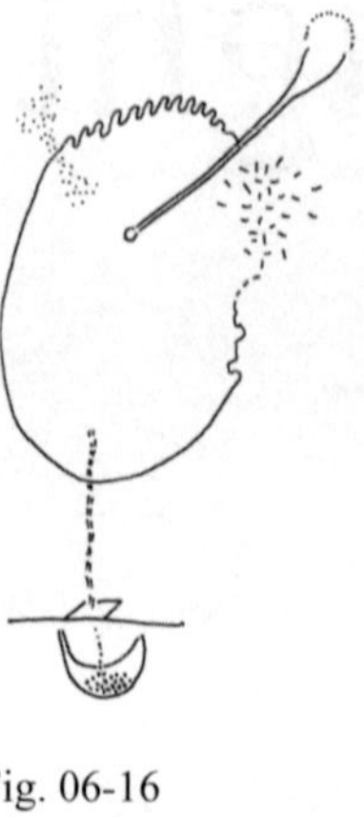

Fig. 06-16

If I look at a drawing, any drawing perhaps, I am already looking at a hypothesis, at an interpretation of a mental event. I may embellish it with my own associations, study the formal technical and structural qualities, as in "I don't understand what it's trying to say, but the draftsmanship is superb!" Or I think about what this drawing is showing me. But it may be showing me things that I am still unable to think about.

The hypothesis has to fit a feeling, only then does it have emotional meaning, without which I might forget it tomorrow. Does this feel like something that I could think about? Meaningful memory is emotional memory paired with a concept. What if I just don't know?[1]

However, there's nothing like a good hypothesis! We could take another road and look at the work of the psychoanalyst Christopher Bollas, who wrote a book called *The Shadow of the Object: Psychoanalysis of the Unthought Known*. Here he considers how there is a period before we acquire language when everything of consequence in our lives that causes great anxiety or poses a threat to our survival gets registered and stored in the brain without words. These memories are among that which he calls "the unthought known". What is meant here is anything

1) Remember Donald Rumsfeld, former Secretary of State to the US Government, who once said: "Reports that say that something hasn't happened are always interesting to me, because as we know, there are known knowns; there are things we know we know. We also know there are known unknowns; that is to say, we know there are some things we do not know. But there are also unknown unknowns – the ones we don't know we don't know."

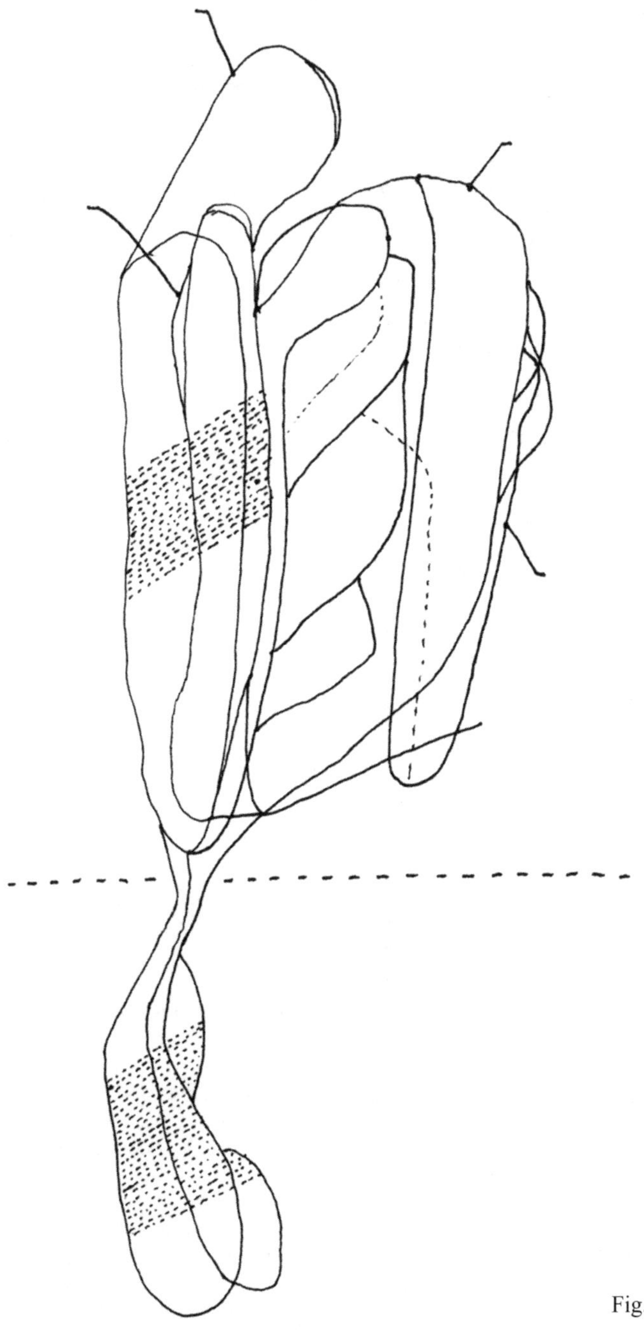

Fig. 04-12

Bion´s Grid – a space for thinking about thinking processes		
	Definitory Hypothesis **(1)**	φ **(2)**
β-elements **(A)**		
α-elements **(B)**		
Dreams, Thoughts / Dreams, Myths **(C)**		
Pre-conception **(D)**		
Conception **(E)**		
Concept **(F)**		
Scientific Deductive System **(G)**		
Algebraic Calculus **(H)**		

Table 2

The psychoanalyst Wilfred Bion created a hypothetical 'grid' for thinking about thinking processes. It looks like this: Starting down the vertical axis which describes the contents of progressive mental activity we begin with A) β-Elements, undigestible bits of experience ("Ow, this hurts, fucking shit!") on to B) α-Elements ("This is my experience, how to deal with it?") to C) Dreams and Myths ("Let it tell a story of some kind") to D) Pre-Conceptions ("There will be a breast to feed me!") on to E) a Conception ("Breast-feeding is now occurring") to F) a Concept ("Maternal nurturing is a fact of life") on to G) or Scientific Deduction ("The mammary glands are secreting according to stimulus from a sucking reflex in the infant, which seems to be pleasurable for both parties") on to, in some further cases, a form of H) Algebraic Calculus.

Starting from the top left corner there is a horizontal

Notation (3)	Attention (4)	Inquiry (5)	Action (6)	... n.

axis defining developmental process and progress in cognitive mental activity, from 1) a definitory hypothesis ("Have to start somewhere!") onward through 2) emotional psychic activity ("???") and then on to 3) Notation ("Yes, make a note of that!") to 4) Attention ("Yes, I'll concentrate on this") to 5) Inquiry ("Let's look into this further!") leading to Action 6) ("Yes, we can do this!").

So any one square on this grid is a position you might be in, while engaged in mental activity. A6 could be hitting someone because you don't like his face, while E5 might constitute and inquiry into the nature of a preconception ("Why do I always think, Why does this always have to happen to me?") and C1 might be a definitory hypothesis on the nature and structure of a myth.

In this system you could be pawn or king, whatever square you happen to be on.

that we 'know', but for any variety of reasons, cannot actually think about. They may be things we've forgotten or have an intuitive or felt sense for that we desperately struggle to put into words. Much of the content of the unthought known obtains from experiences in utero on and up through the first three years of our lives. Memories of these experiences are a kind of unthinkable recollection. This is Bollas' hypothesis.

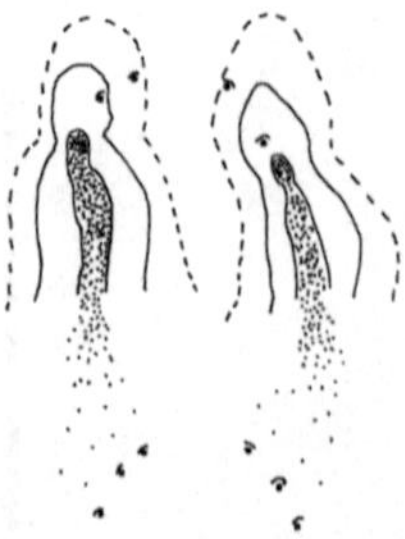

Fig. 02-01

A hypothesis is something that is useful for thinking but some hypotheses may actually be simply a part of a paranoid system. There is much room for confusion here.

Clarity is a necessary but not a sufficient condition for a hypothesis. The poet Antonio Machado once wrote: "I have seen in my solitude/ Many clear things/ That were not true."

So how do we go about it? Boldly, tentatively, discreetly, passionately? Is a myth a hypothesis? Is a mathematical formula? A map is not a hypothesis. A piece of music cannot be a hypo-thesis. This is of course a hypothesis.

HYPOTHESIS #22

Processing the Routes of Thoughts

Kerstin Bartels

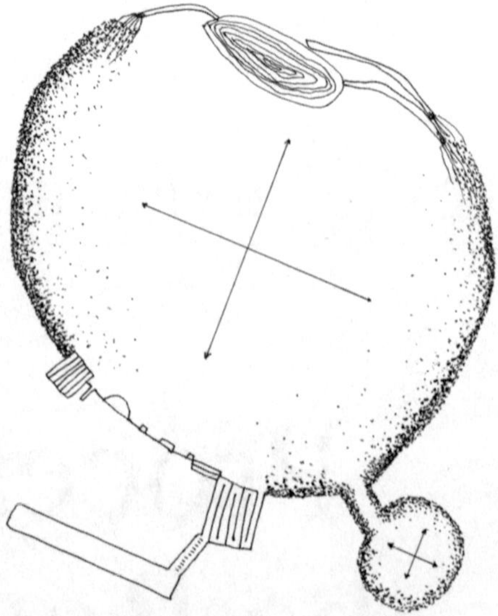

Fig. 03-14

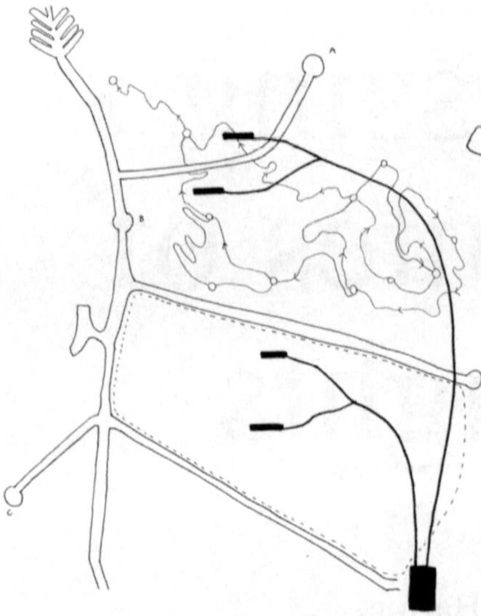

Fig. 03-19

Fig. 03-14

Shown here is a human skull; the inner world and outer world are depicted using the two connected cavities; the outer world requires the lesser volume, though they have the same orientation according to the northern axis. The membrane with the concentric labyrinth allows impressions to pass through; it is the sluice for perception. The structured, rational processing lies on the opposite side, facilitating classification and, where appropriate, conclusion. The outer, hatched surface and the lines represent executed, retrospective classification by another person after the event, as well as the understanding of connection, e.g. research in the humanities or, to use an example, in cultural history.

Fig. 03-19

Shown here is a route of thought, in which a given accumulation takes space, without enabling locomotion. Uncertain thoughts display a vector with a shaky course; items of information from other people make their way into the course as if on tracks; they are not yet part of it, but they overlay the inner network of paths.

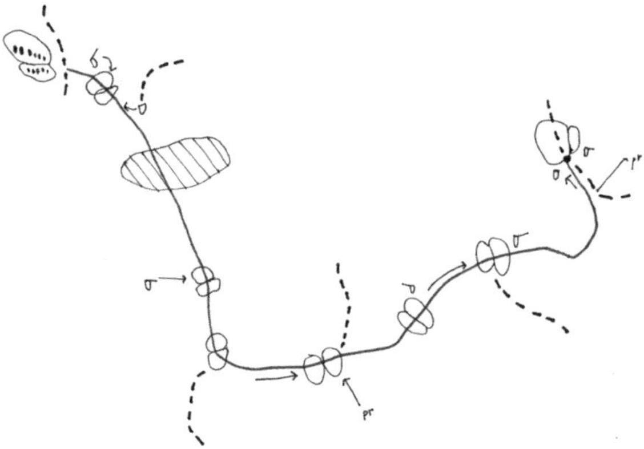

Fig. 03-04

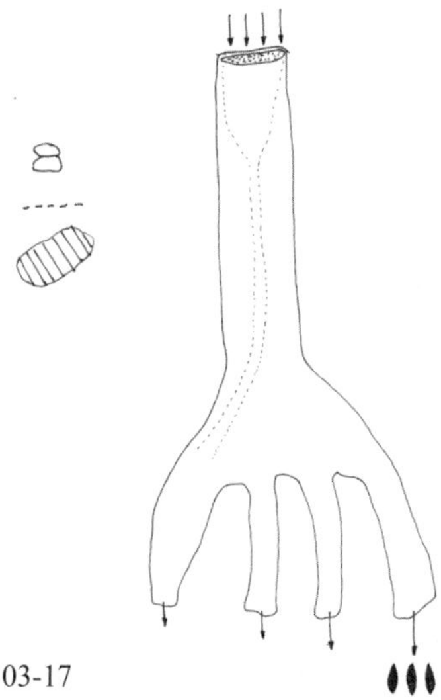

Fig. 03-17

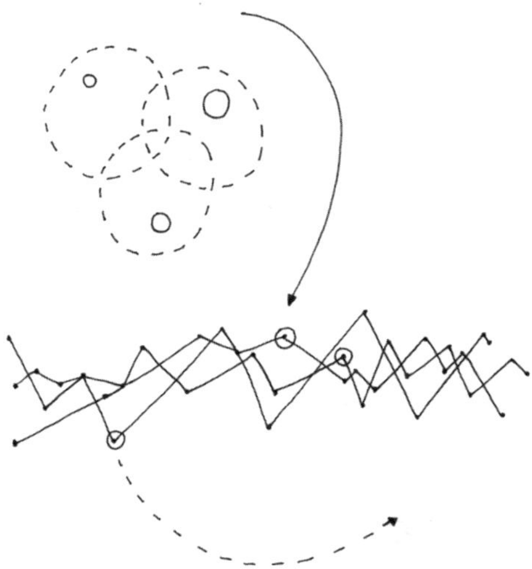

Fig. 03-11

Fig. 03-04

This figure shows a free-floating line which reacts elastically to contraction and relaxation. A new form shapes itself according to the working of these forces; only the hatched surface and the surrounding section remain static.

Fig. 03-17

Shown here is a base/prop or something which mediates stability through the given force of gravity. The system is fed through a system of pumps: the inflow or access occurs without expenditure of energy; the outflow is enabled through pressure.

Fig. 03-11

Shown here are impressions which strike the individual perception like circling clouds. Pressure forces are at work. The impressions are filtered and incorporated into the elastic experience network and the rationality structures. If the newly created synapse is accessed by the outer world, traction occurs. 'It' pulls on the circle, the chains ease, and a spatially expansive structure arises. If 'it' stops working, the chains revert to their original position.

Fig. 03-09

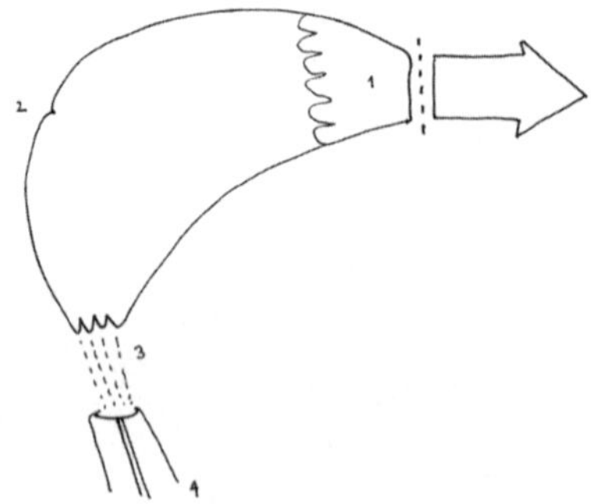

Fig. 03-12

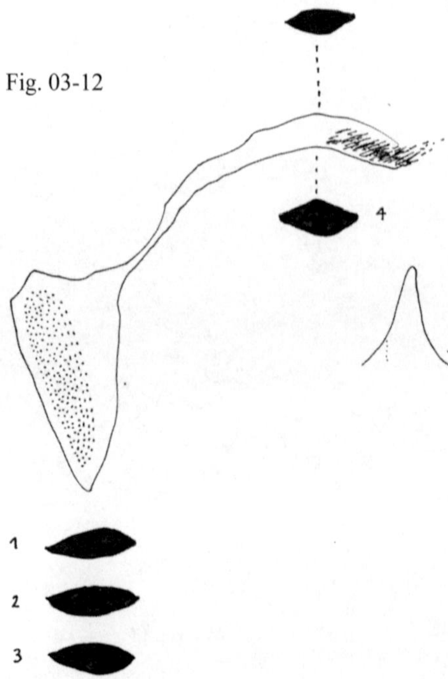

Fig. 02-26

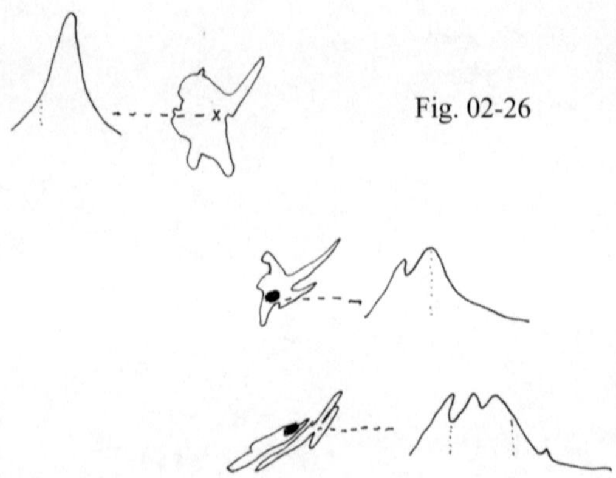

Fig. 03-09
Shown here is the middle phase of the processing of impressions. The outer impressions exert pressure on the cognitive processing and lead to the expansion of the area. The information is transmitted once the pressure is relaxed.

Fig. 03-12
This figure shows the first phase of sense perception without classification of the information. The perception stimulates sensations; it works playfully, in a revolving movement, and juggles with creativity. The imagination, free from cognitive processing, has as yet no direct, deforming influence. An inner pressure balance is operating over a natural outlet.

Fig. 02-26
This figure shows human perception and the processing of impressions in three phases. While in the graph above, the first sense perception phase executes without interference from the cognitive apparatus (→ compare Fig. 03-12), in the middle

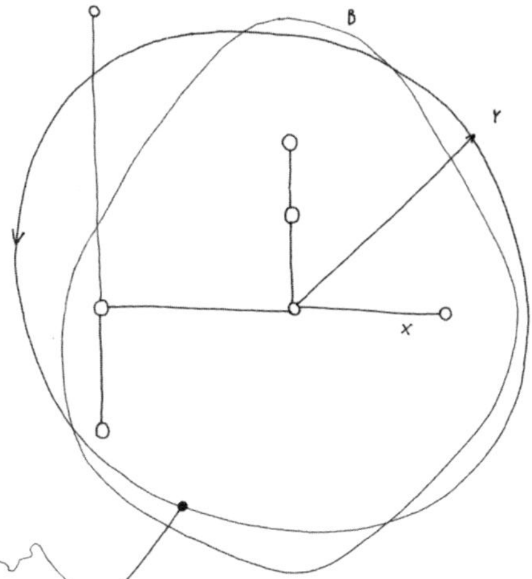

Fig. 03-08

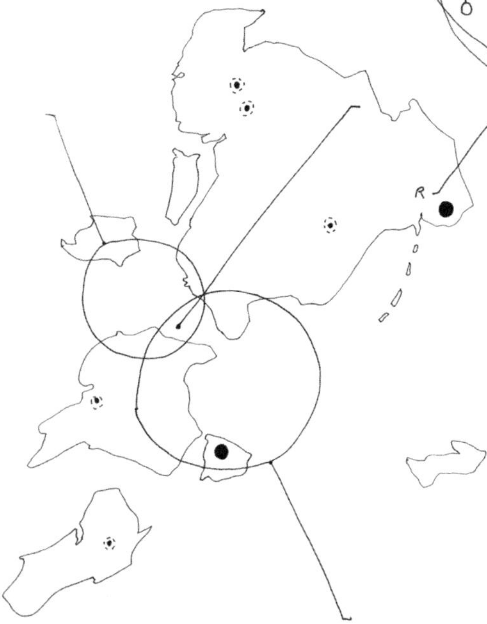

Fig. 03-07

graph a deformation of the impressions occurs pursuant to cognitive processing. The impression is formed by processing the impression, or by aligning itself with its own potential processing curve. In phrase three, the processing frequency increases but the amplitude decreases, which is mirrored in the form of the processing process.

Fig. 03-08

This figure shows a cognitive process in which classification with vectors proceeds in a near circular form. The little circles represent stopping points in this process; they are centres for new synapses. The outer point and the line define the possible extent of a temporary deforming.

Fig. 03-07

Shown here is the topographical representation of the deformation phases. New alignments, spaces and clusters are being constructed.

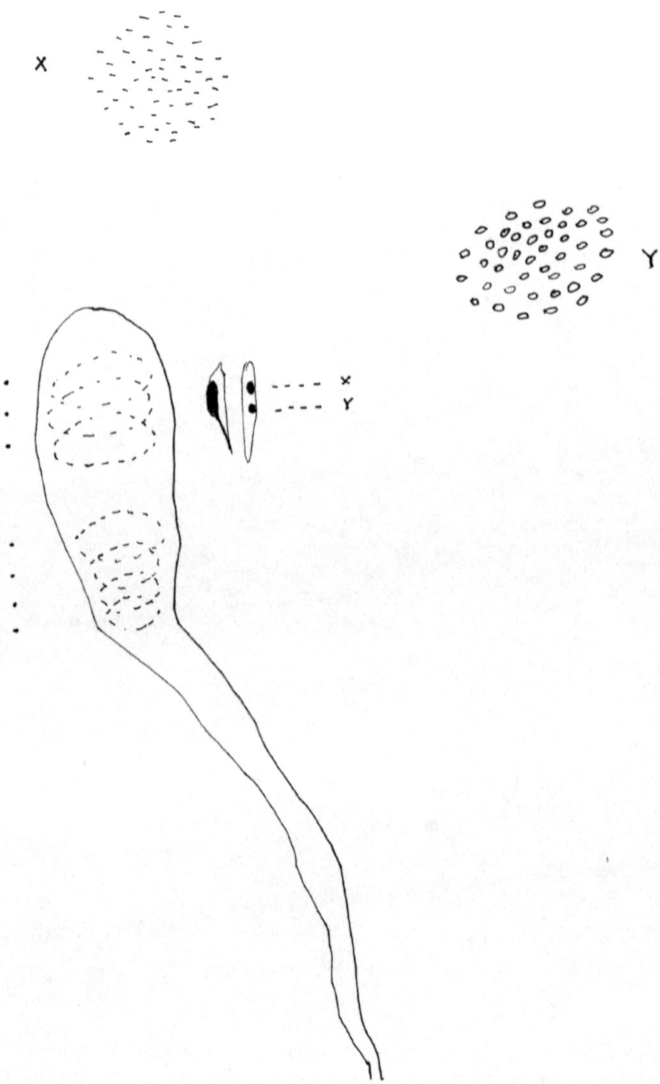

Fig. 02-27

Fig. 02-27

This figure shows concentrations in the atmosphere which do not operate directly on an organism, but which nonetheless affect it through shock waves, turbulence and movement in a foreign system.

Fig. 03-05

This figure shows ideas, imaginary pictures and their sequences, presented in correspondence or comparison. If the process of contextualisation increases, it is balanced through reflection. The result corresponds to the volume of the original situation, although the

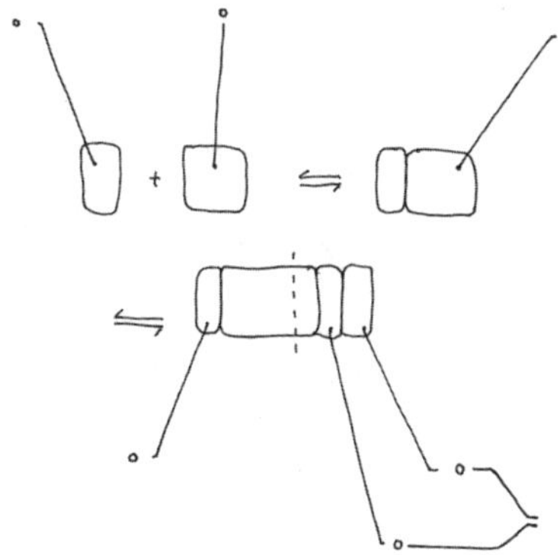

Fig. 03-05

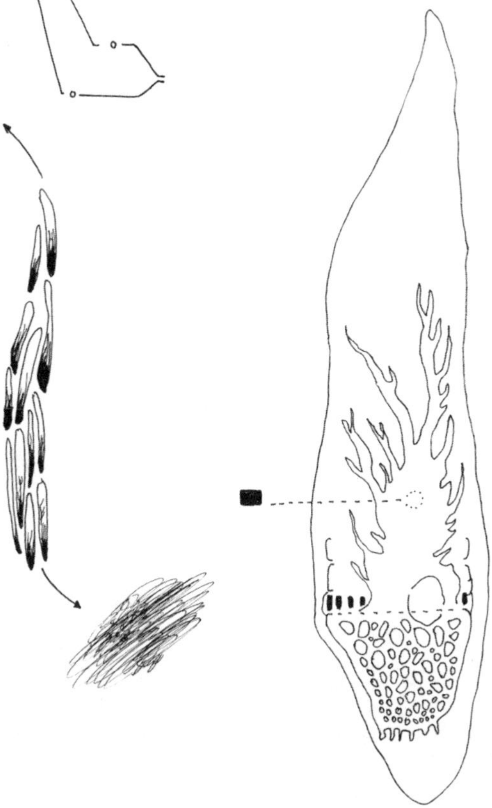

Fig. 02-22

insight gained is differentially predisposed through anchoring in the contextual network.

Fig. 02-22

This figure shows a creative potential which, like muscle tissue, seeks expression and so causes expansion. Through the process of sedimentation, through the sinking down of impulsive creativity with time, a foundation forms itself from the ground up. On these foundations, a coordinated growth then takes place, ensuring a possible process character allowing organically growing, increasing forces to be set free, which in the end determine and establish the form of the expression.

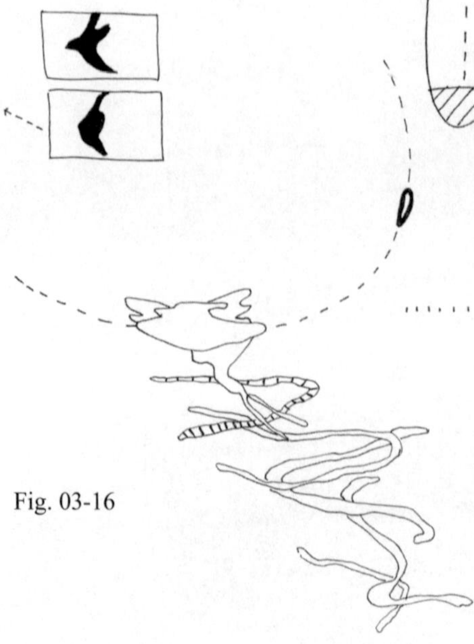

Fig. 03-16

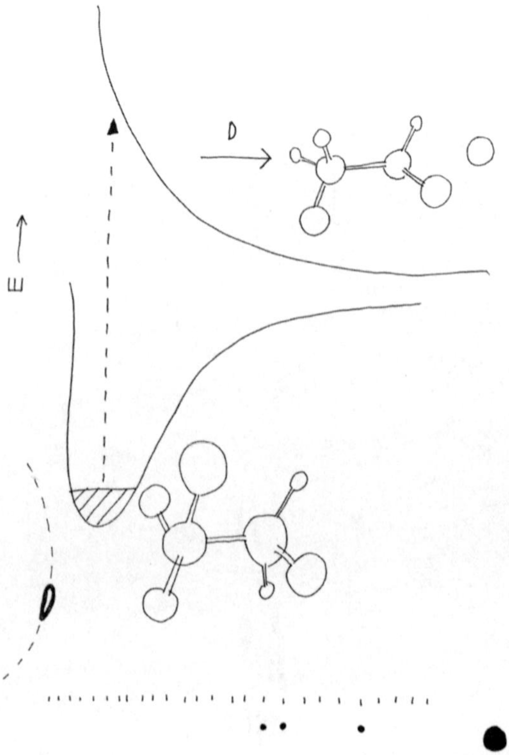

Fig. 03-06

Fig. 03-16

This figure shows a recurring, familiar impulse from the near surroundings, which affects the structure/form of human experience. The measured, circular path runs through the overlapping chain of experience without altering the flexible orbit which it has created.

Fig. 03-06

Shown here is a still, static state which is disturbed by the effects of energy impulses. This transfers movement by splitting off an element. The static state is given up; two new possibilities occur in consequence: the unstable remaining state endeavours to reach a new stability

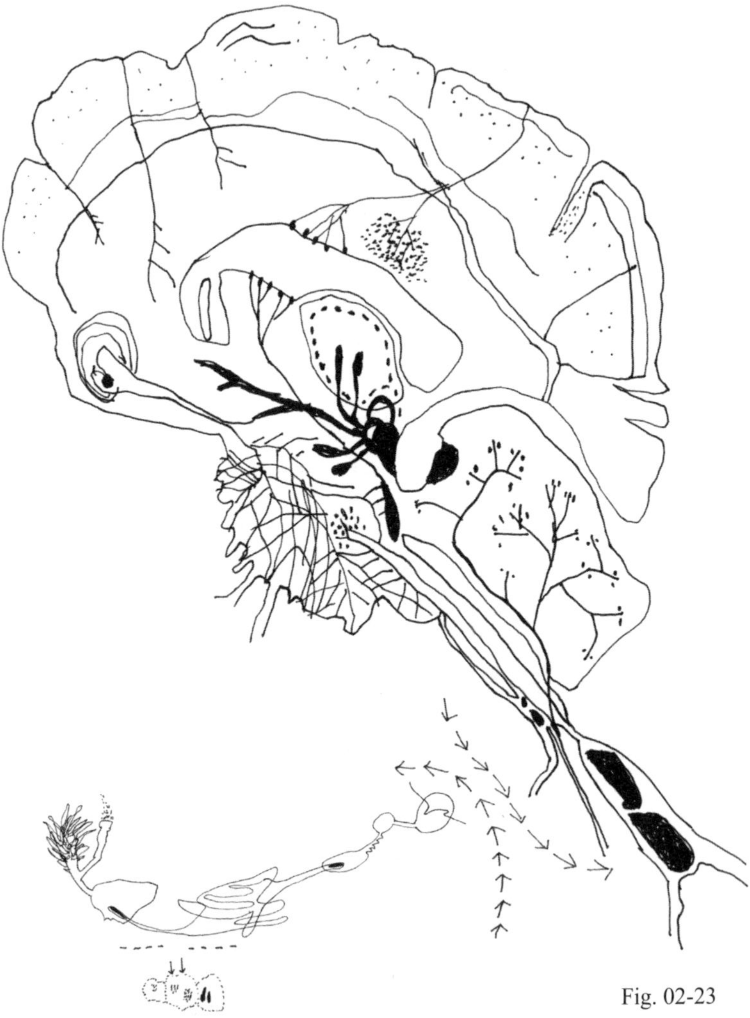

Fig. 02-23

by acquiring a new element; the individual element endeavours to attain a new system.

Fig. 02-23

Shown here is an organism subdivided into different areas, structures and functions, which have been selectively presented in the preceding representations. Through spatial classification – structured according to compressed and relaxed zones – a balanced, harmonious complete system results. This system reacts continuously to impulses from the outside world, and subsequently creates new formations all the time.

HYPOTHESIS #23

An Attempted Survey

based on *Measuring the World* by Daniel Kehlmann

section.a

(Katharina Boesch, Alexandra Feichtner, Christine Haupt-Stummer, Andreas Krištof)

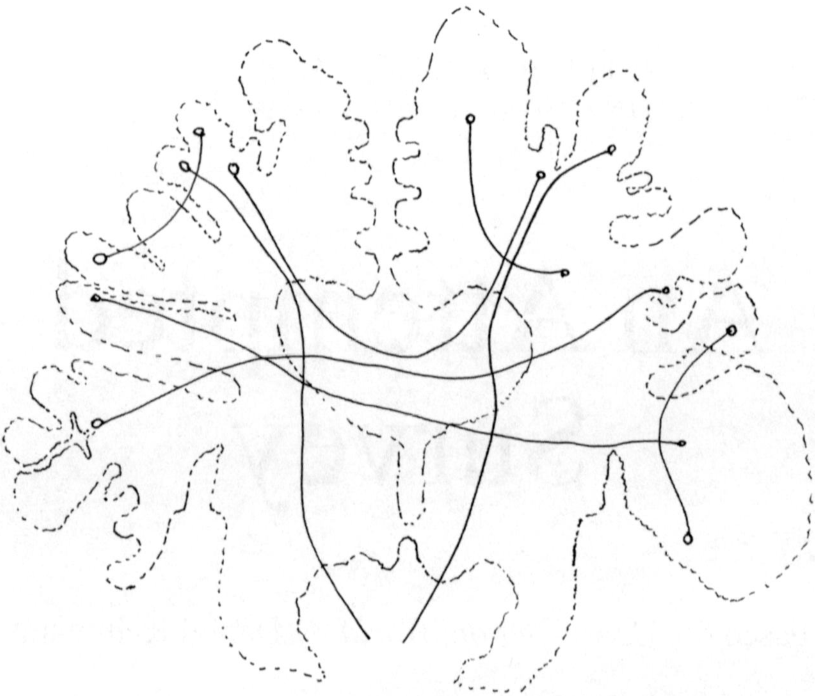

Fig. 02-37

But reason, said Humboldt, should shape the laws!

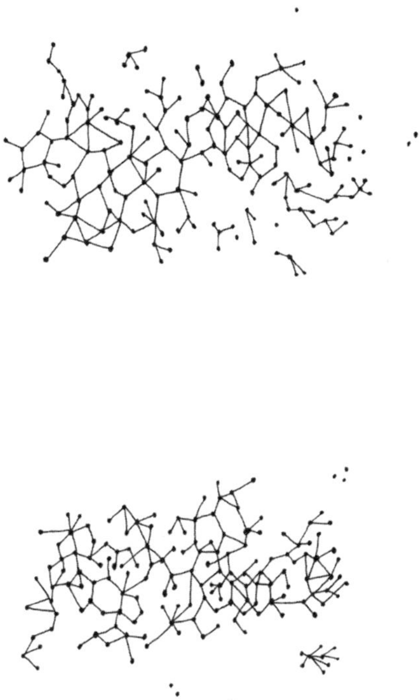

Fig. 04-10
The old Kantian Nonsense.

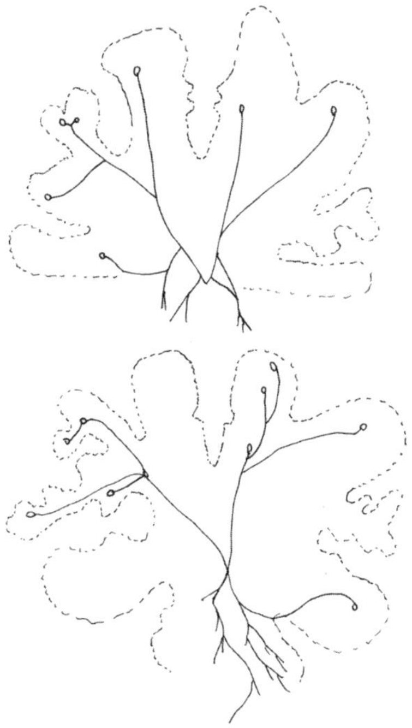

Fig. 02-39
Gauss shook his head.

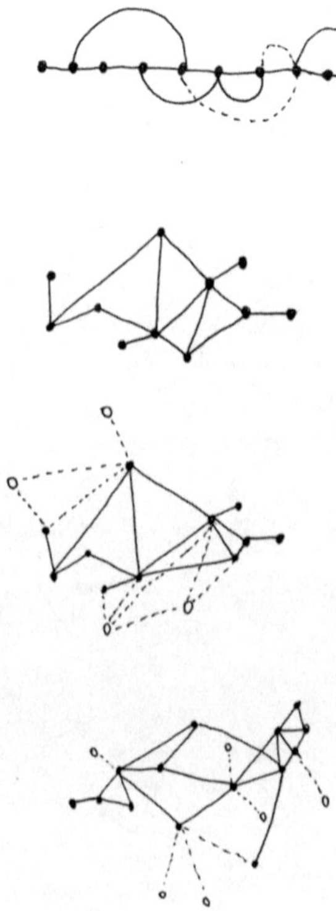

Fig. 04-09

Space bends and time is expanding.

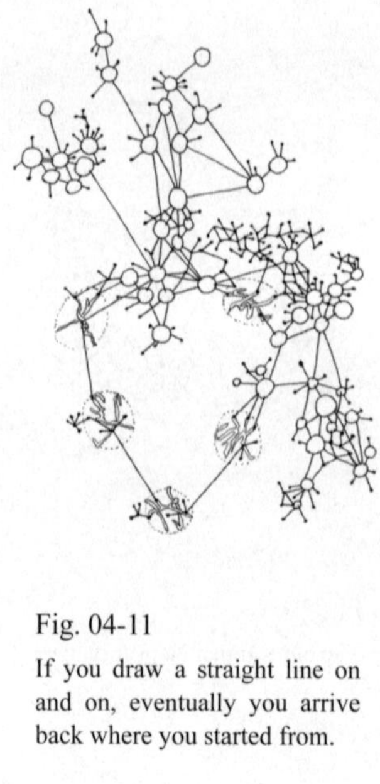

Fig. 04-11

If you draw a straight line on and on, eventually you arrive back where you started from.

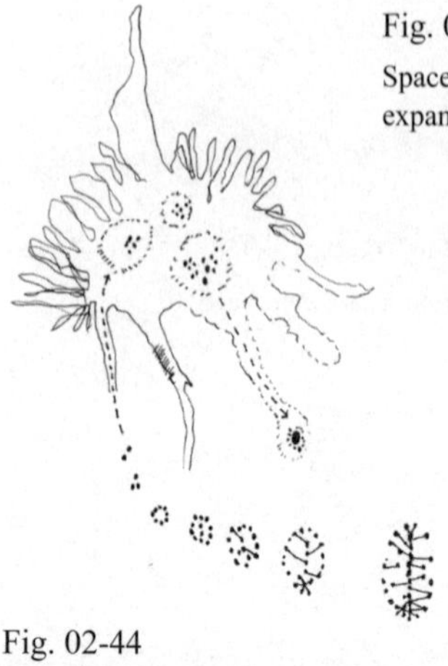

Fig. 02-44

Reason shapes nothing at all and understands little.

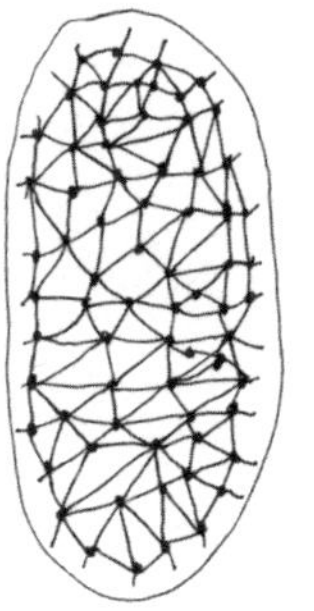

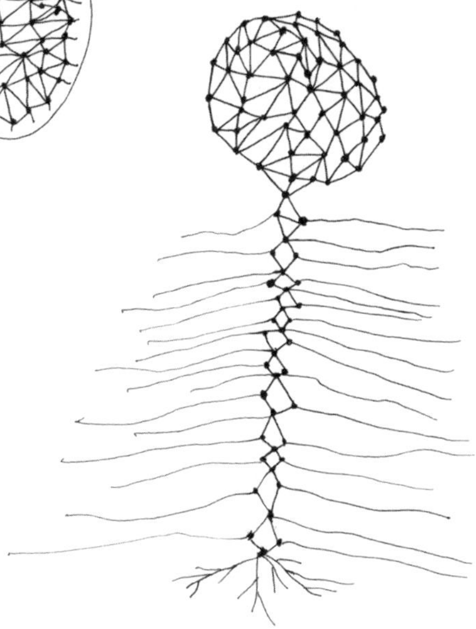

Fig. 02-40

Not once did the rays of that burning-out star come down in straight lines.

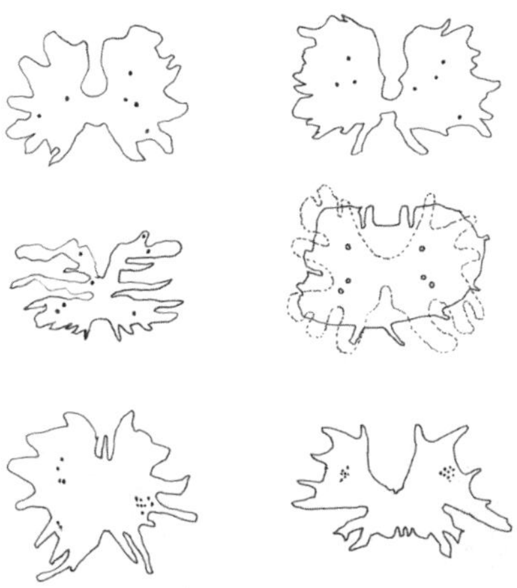

Fig. 02-41

He pointed at the sun, low in the window.

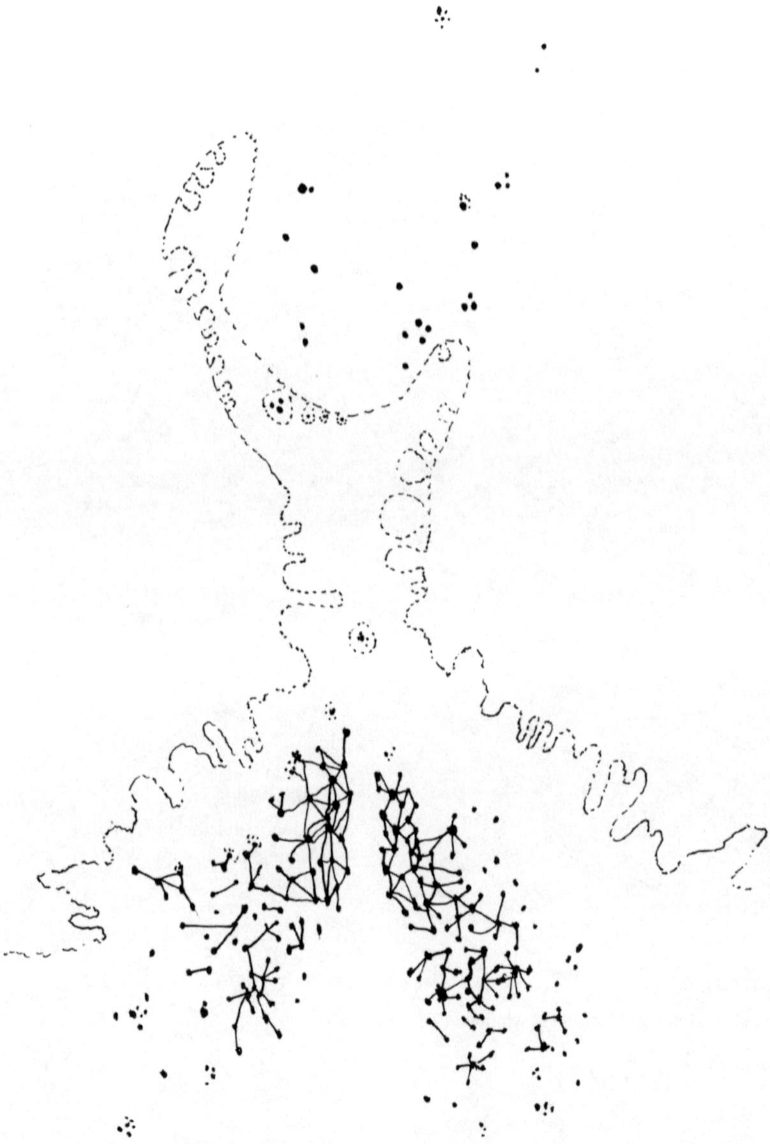

Fig. 02-42

The world could be provisionally measured,

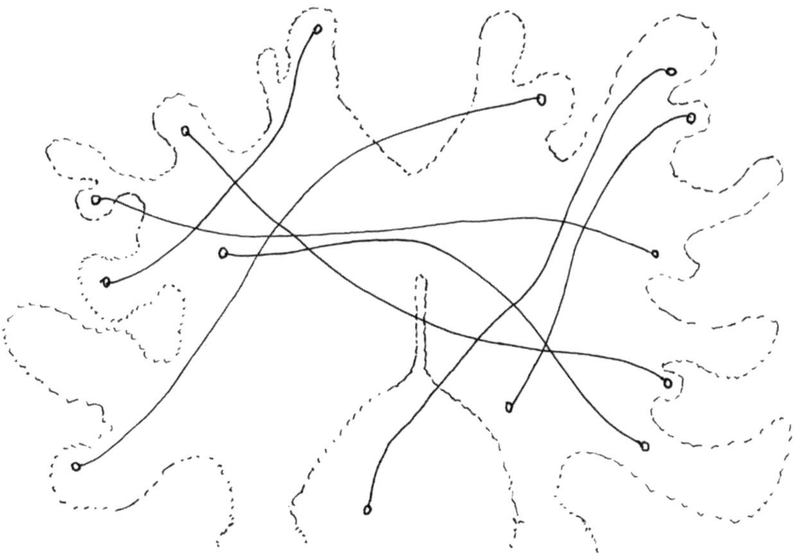

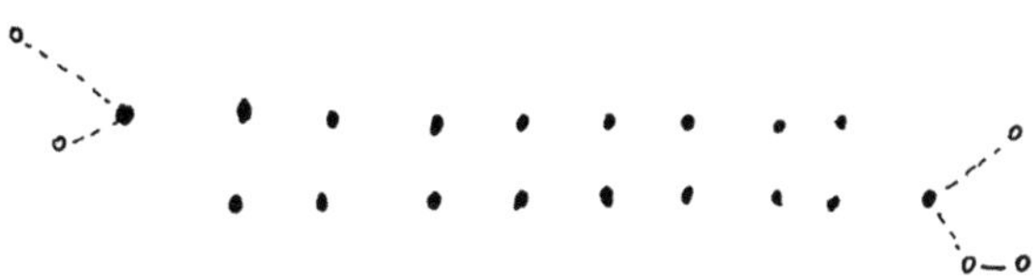

Fig. 02-38
but that wouldn't remotely mean that we understood anything.

PLATES III

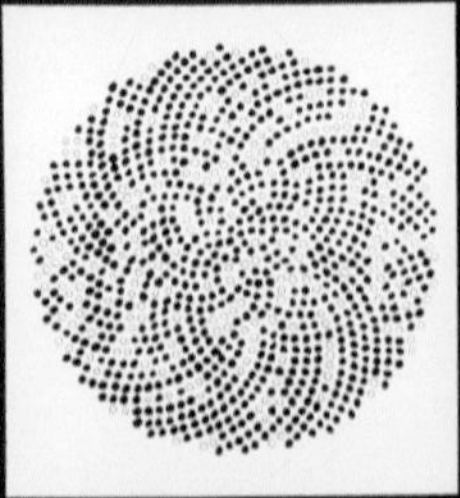

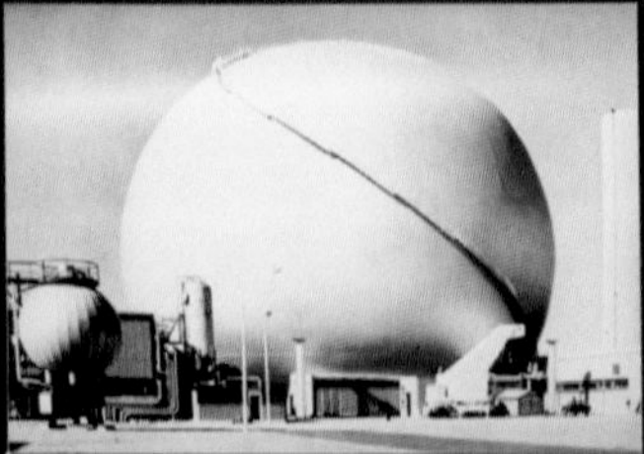

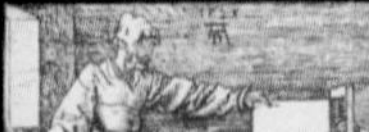

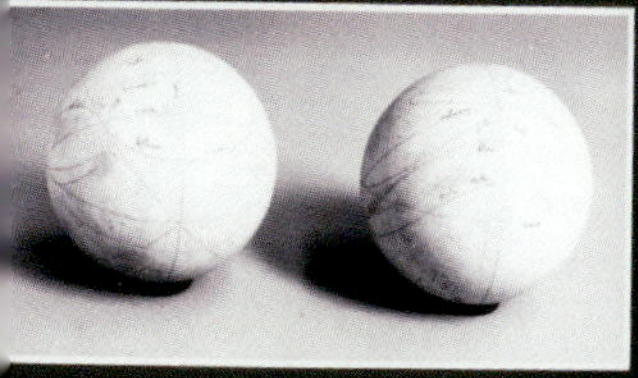

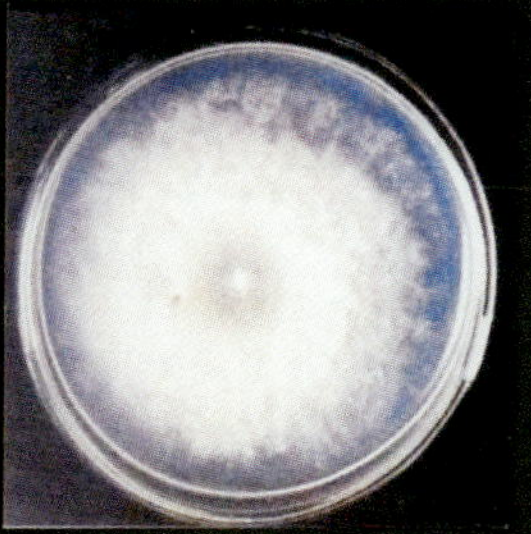

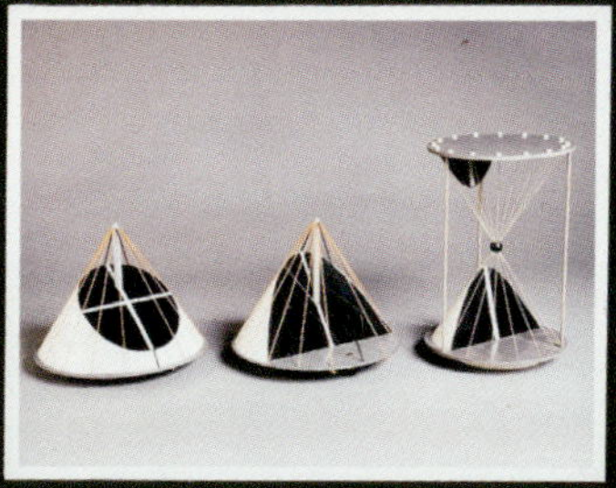

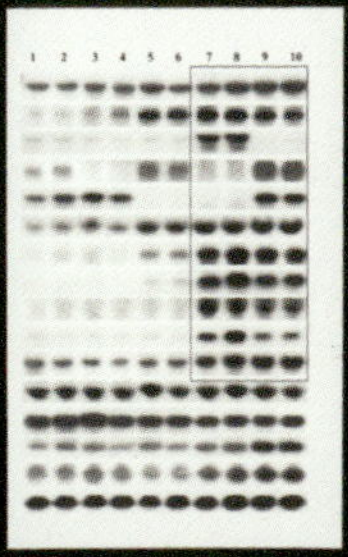

PIII/01

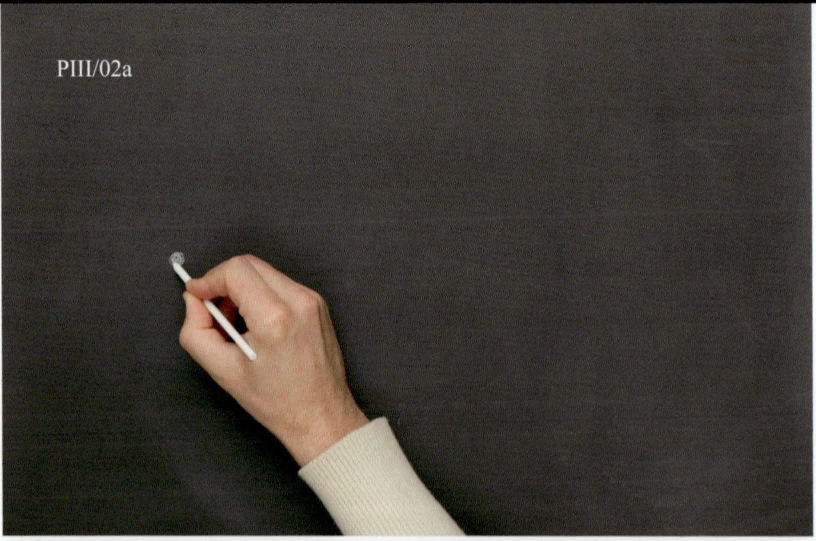
PIII/02a

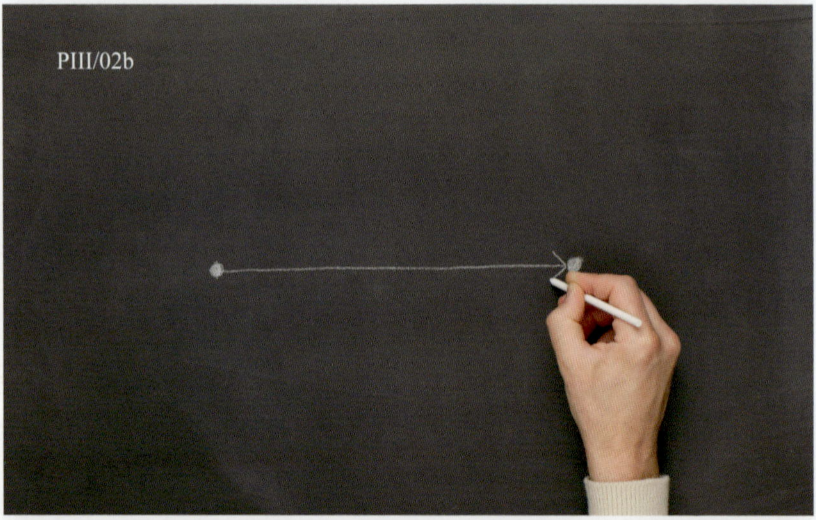
PIII/02b

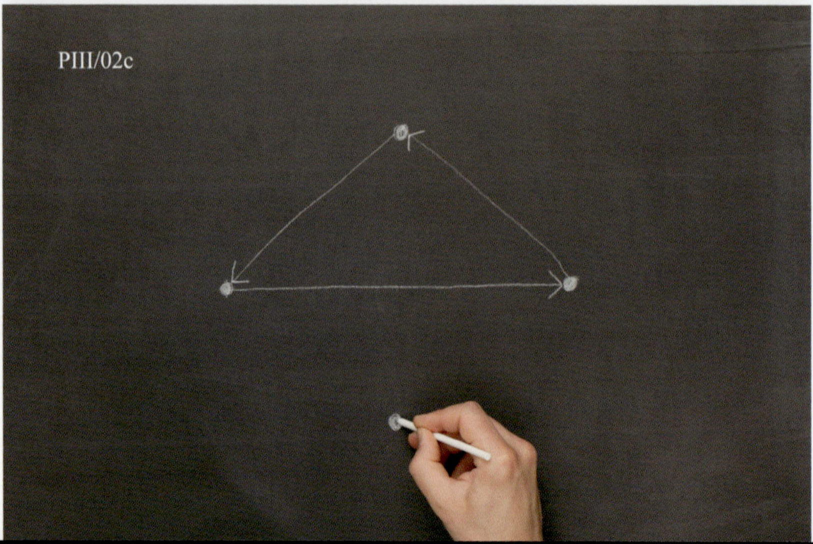
PIII/02c

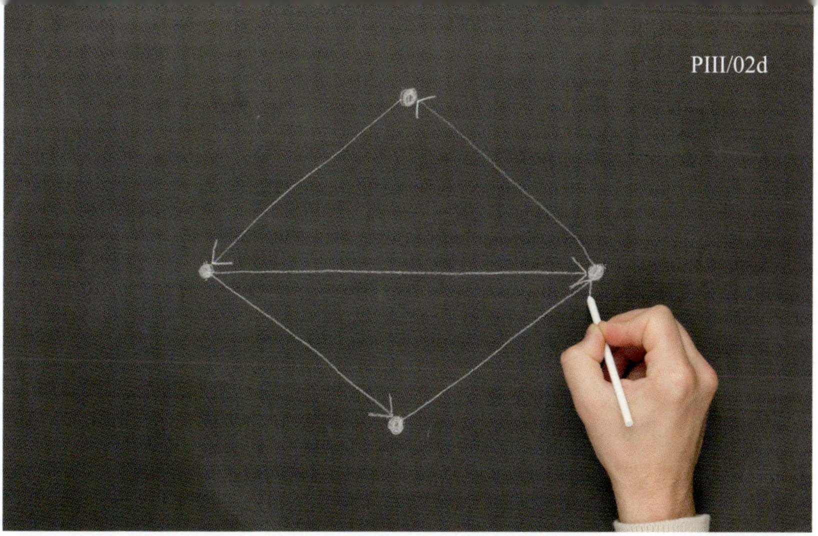
PIII/02d

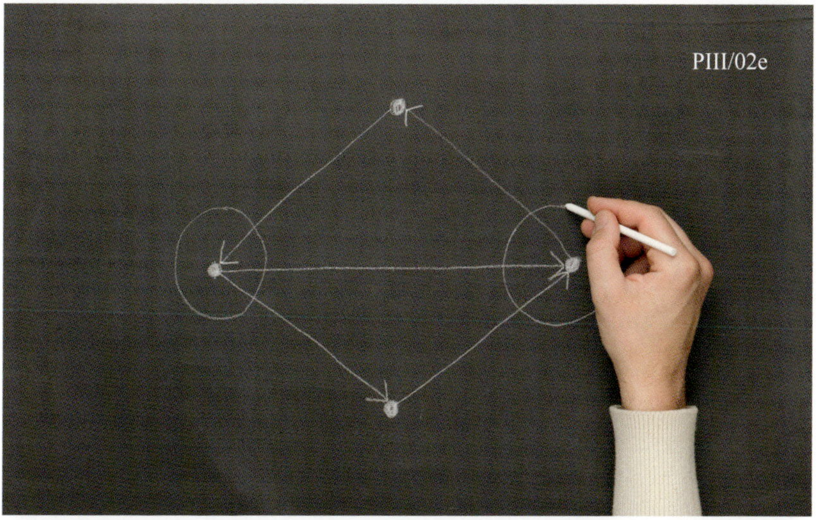
PIII/02e

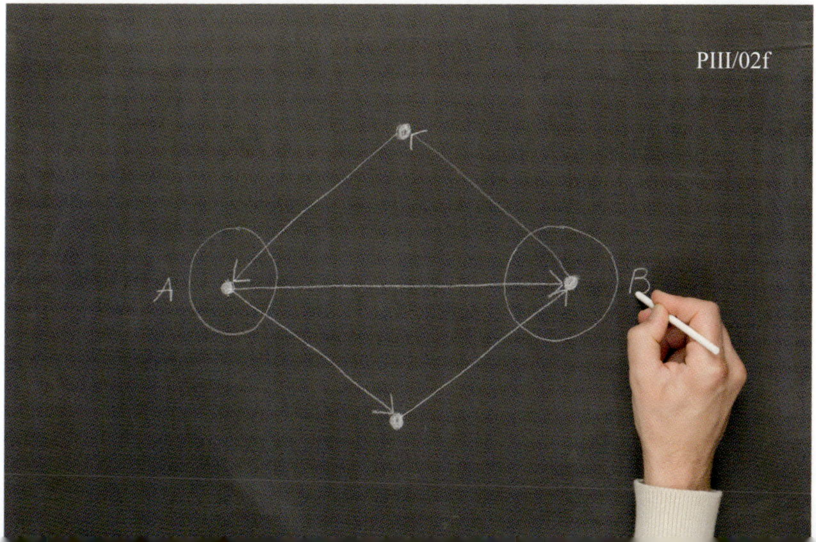
PIII/02f
A
B

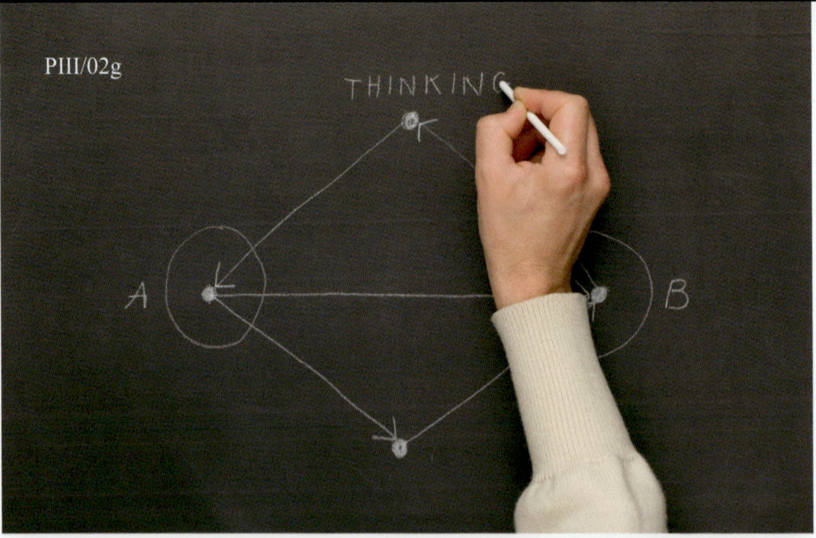

PIII/02g

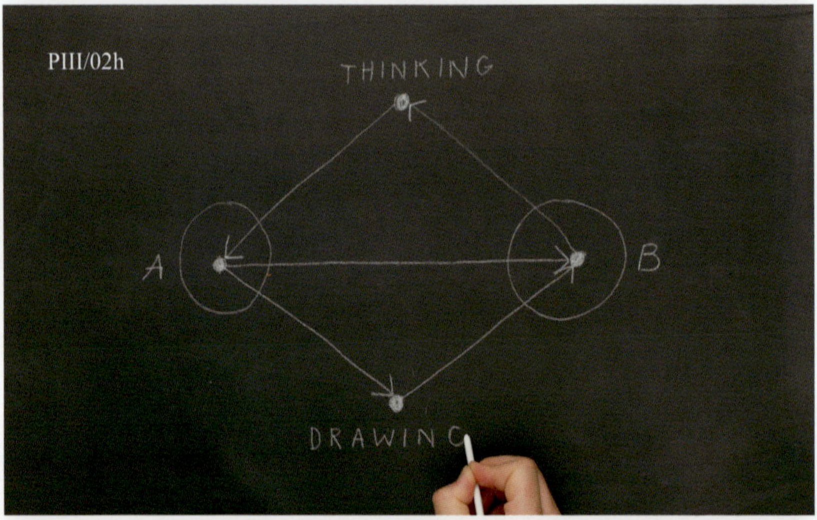

PIII/02h

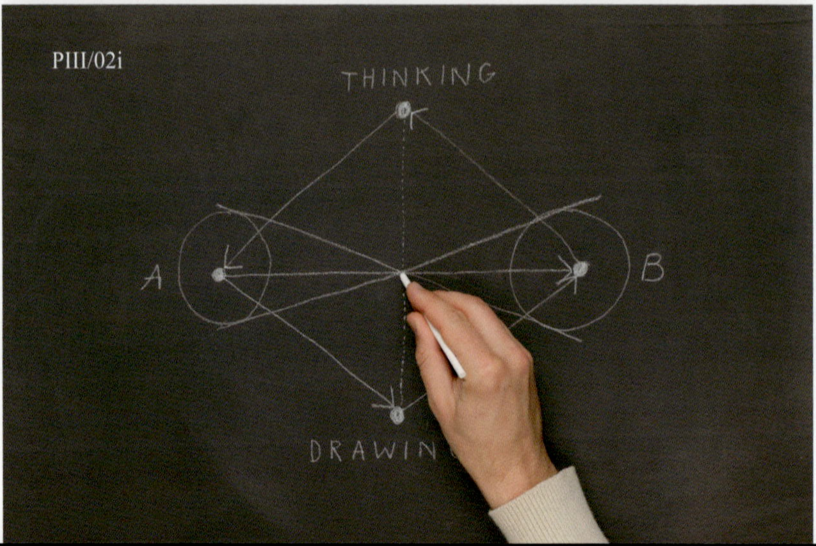

PIII/02i

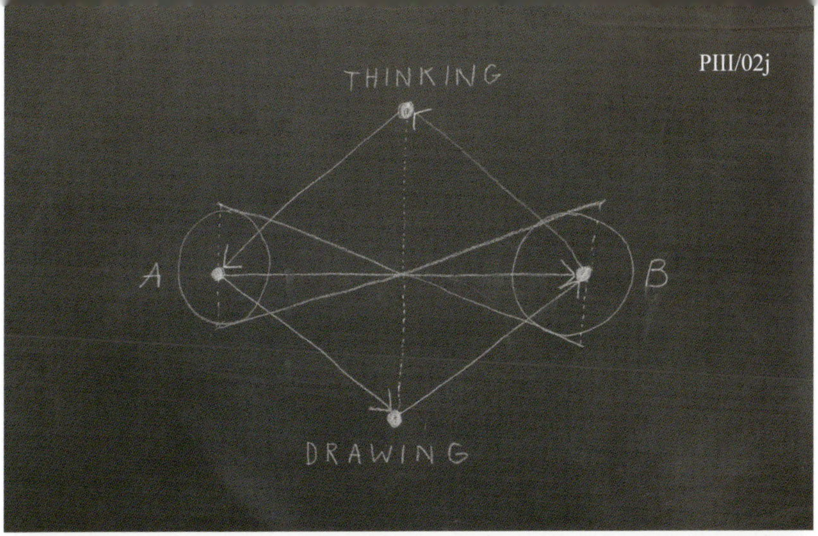

PIII/02j

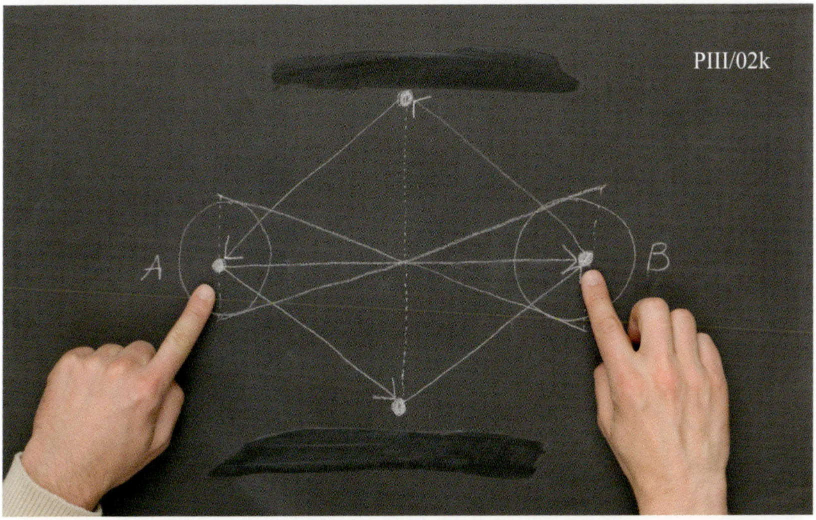

PIII/02k

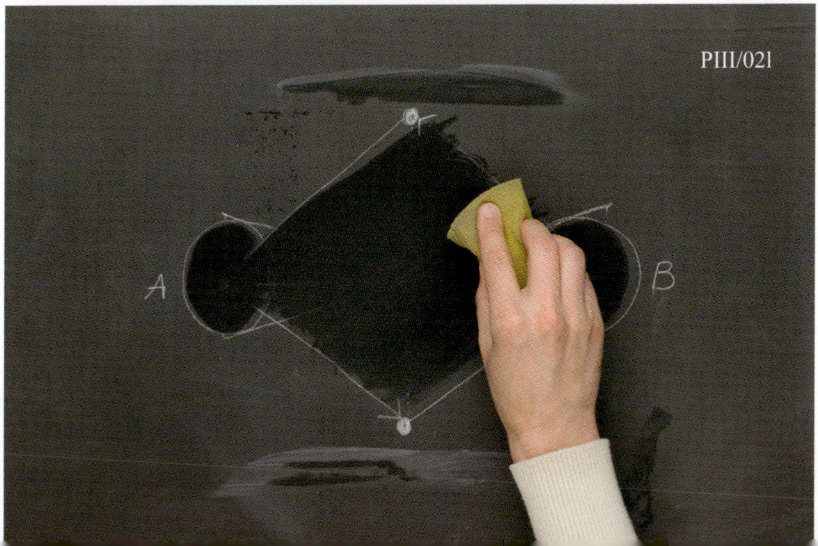

PIII/02l

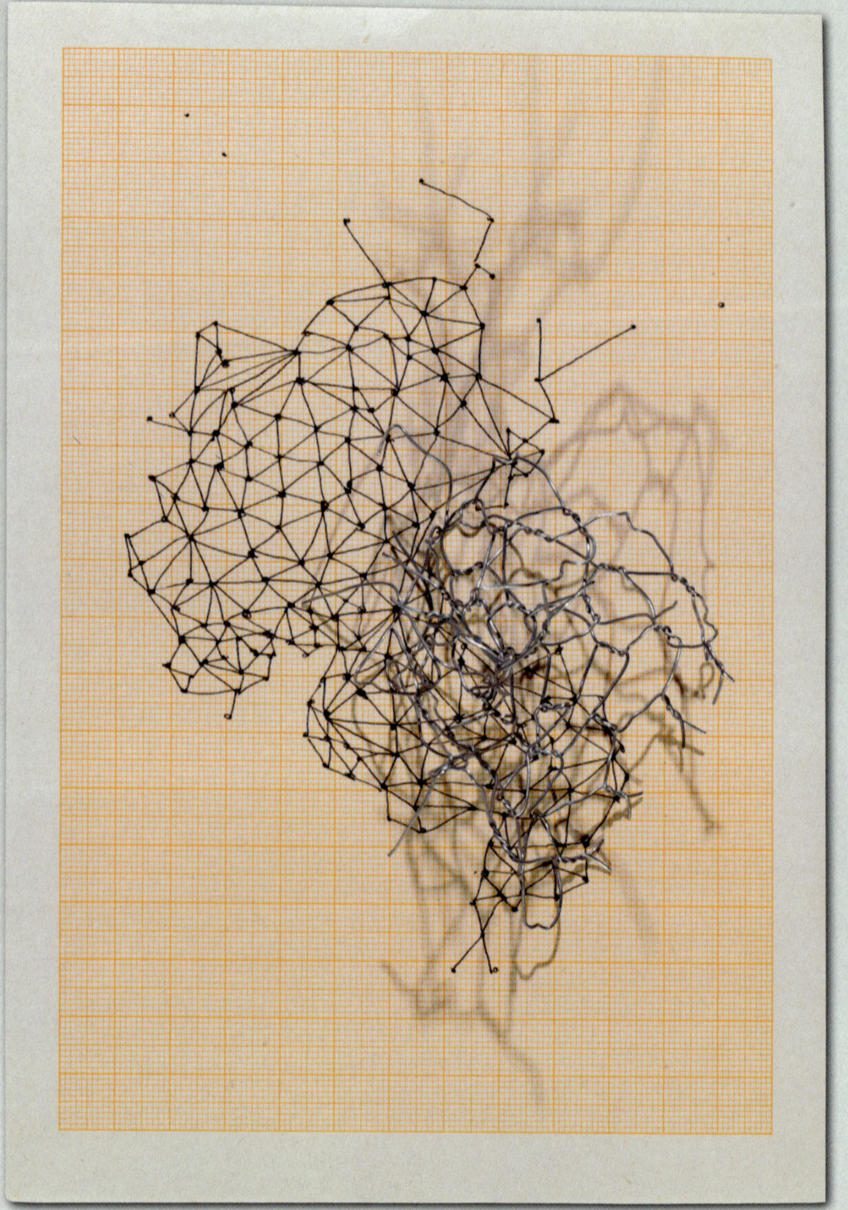

PIII/03

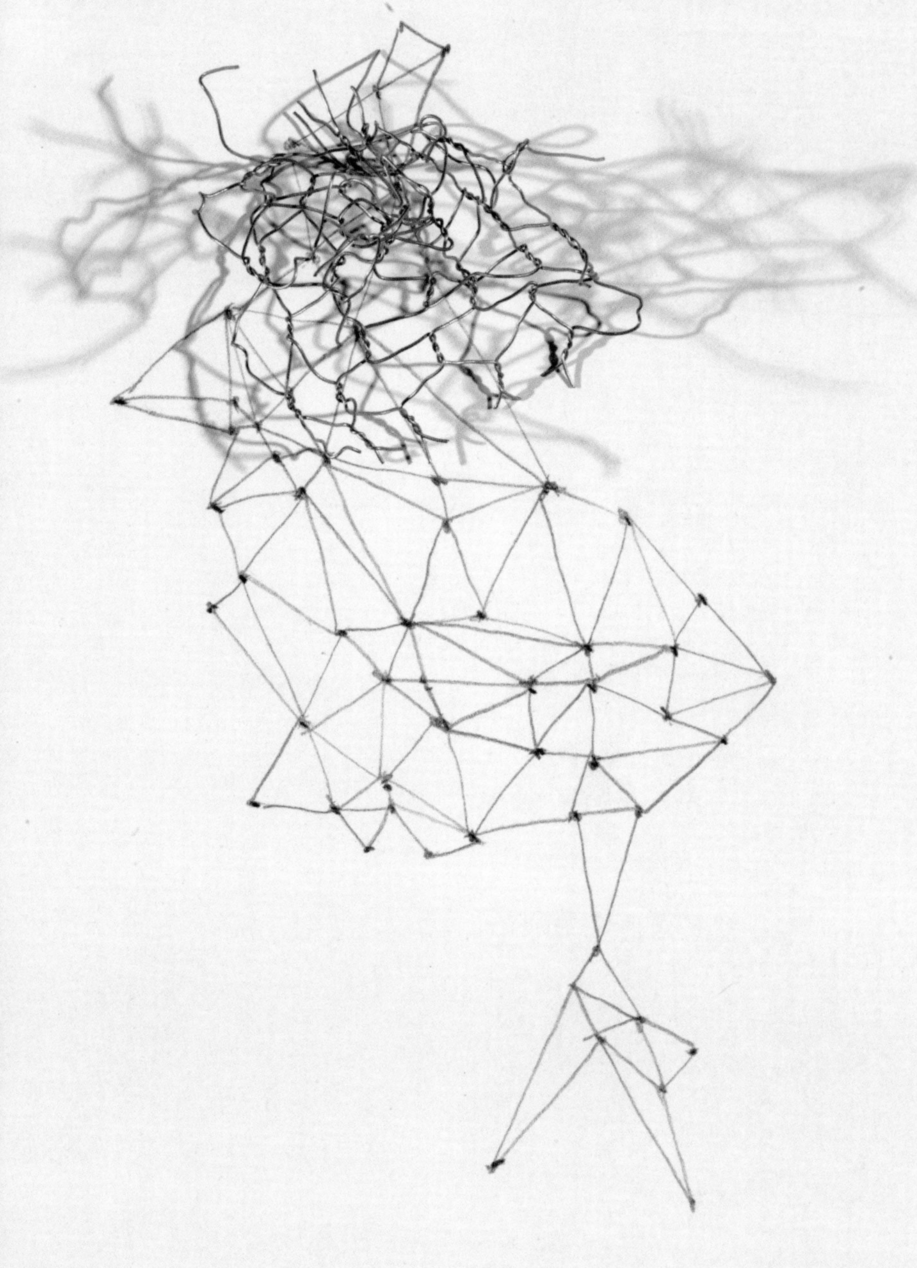

PIII/04

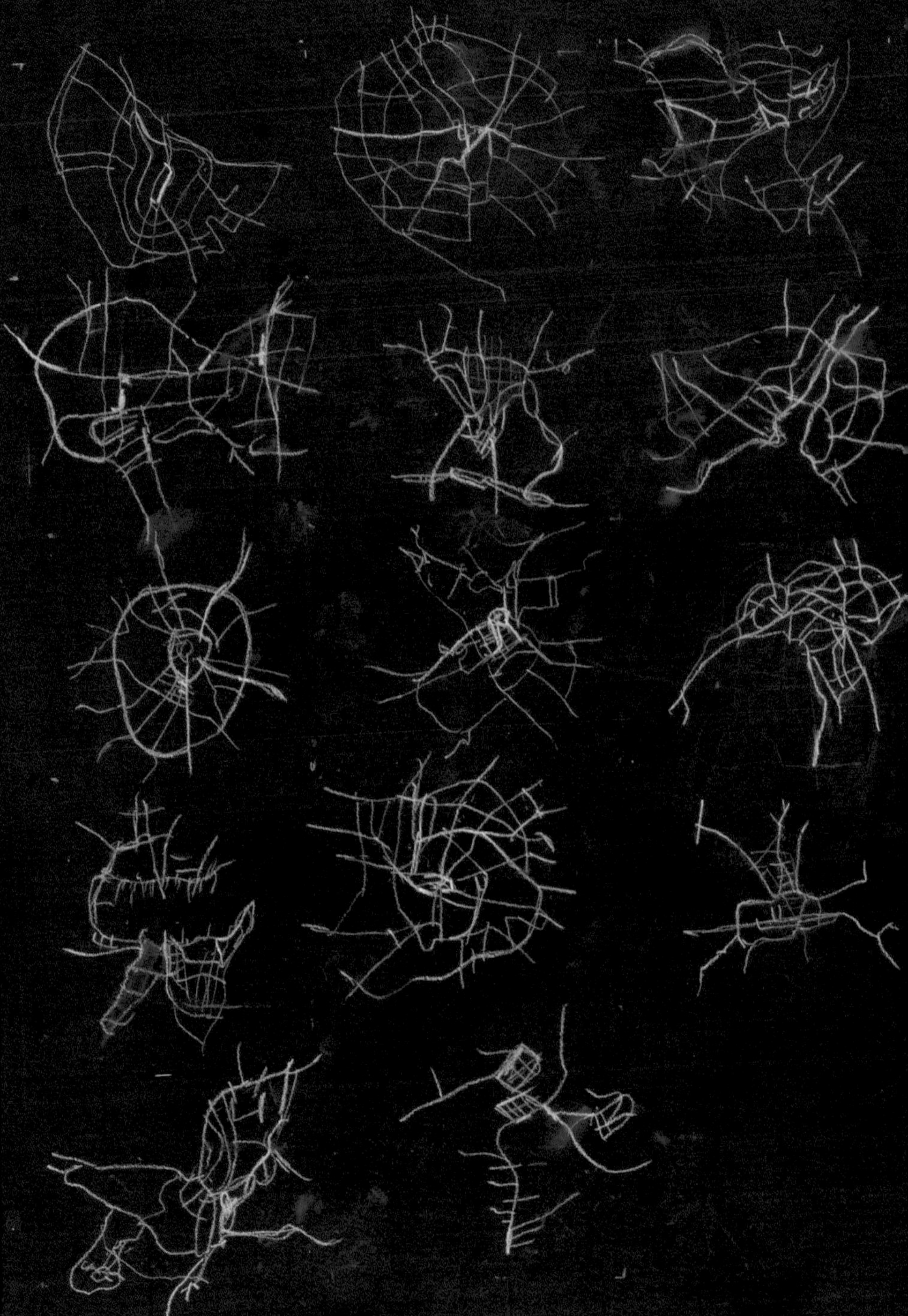

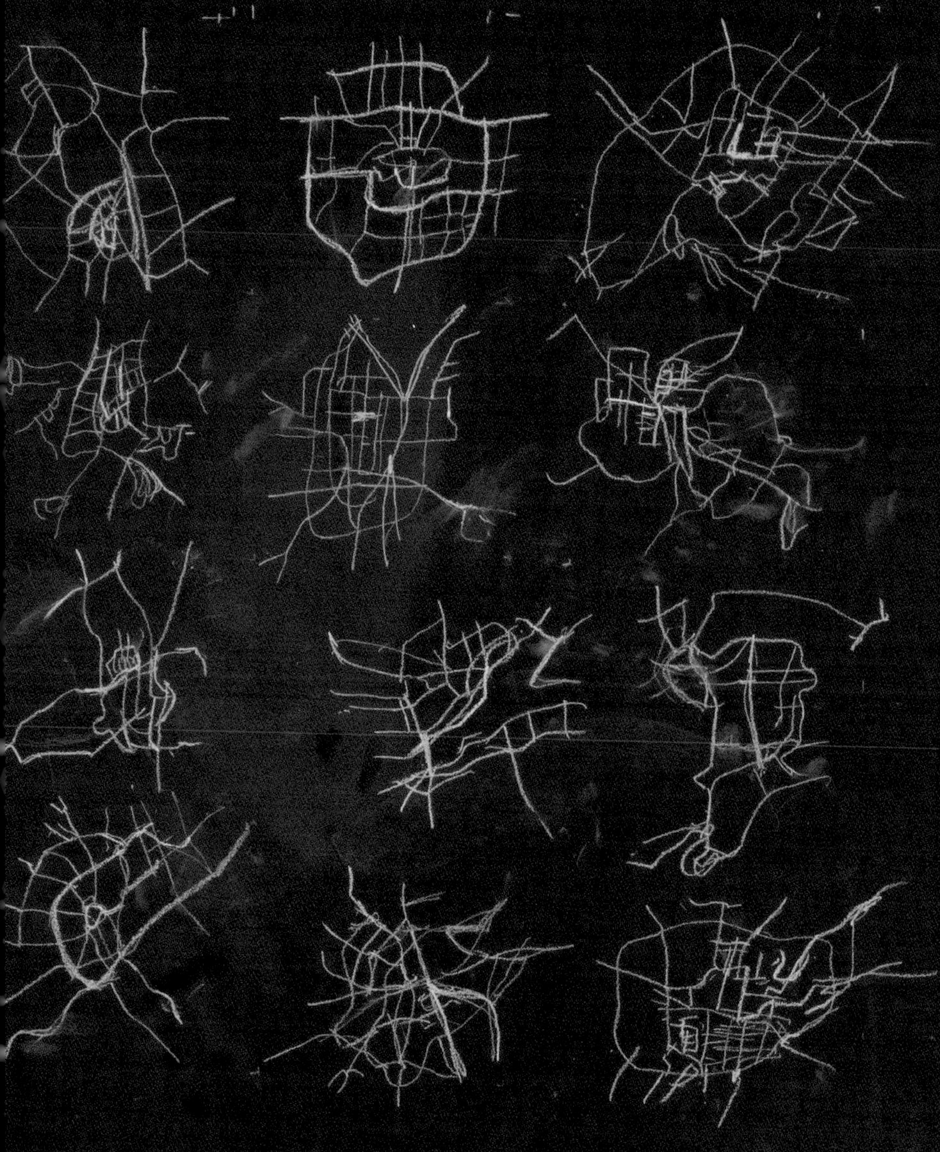

PIII/05

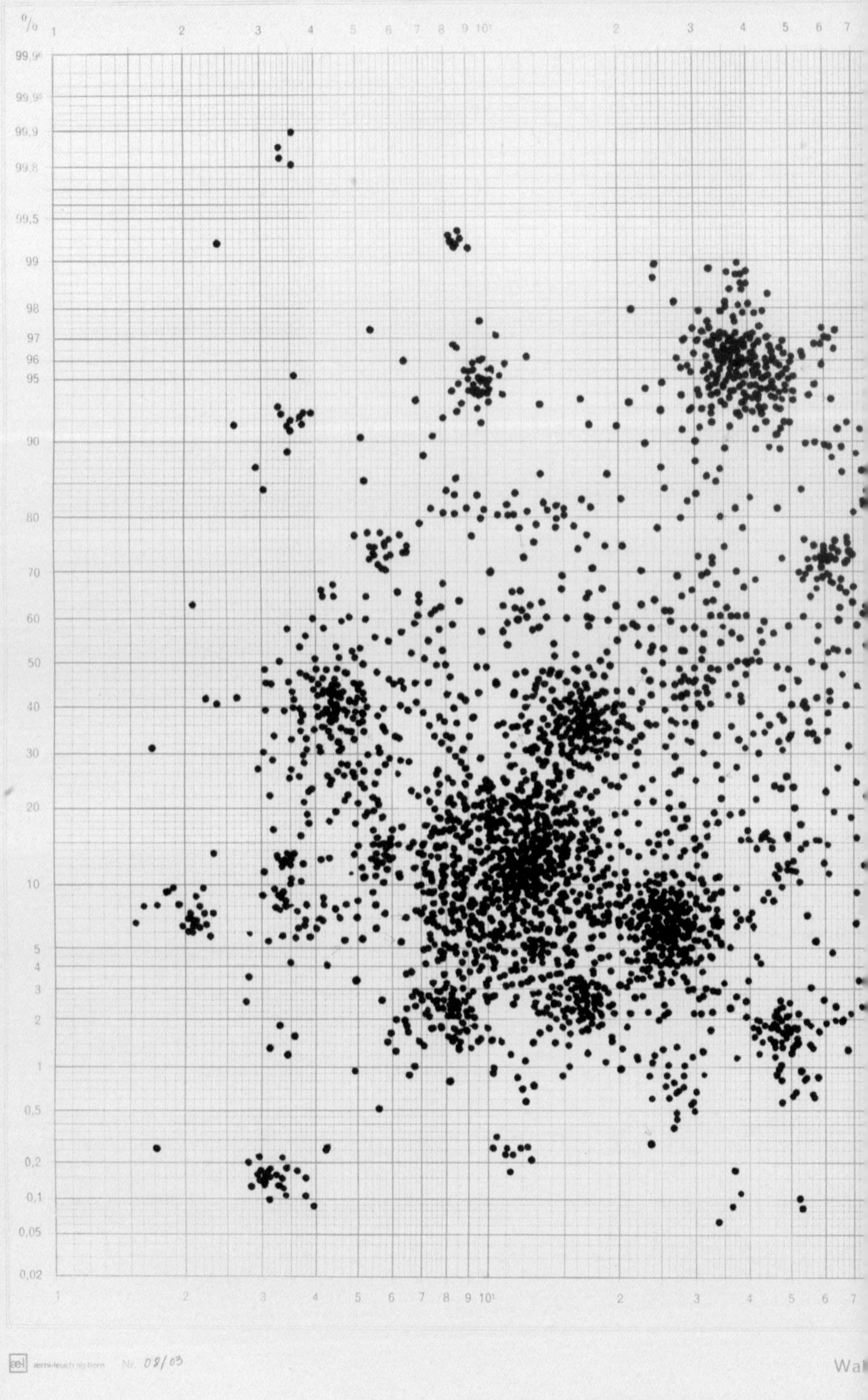
%
1 2 3 4 5 6 7 8 9 10¹ 2 3 4 5 6 7
99,99
99,95
99,9
99,8
99,5
99
98
97
96
95
90
80
70
60
50
40
30
20
10
5
4
3
2
1
0,5
0,2
0,1
0,05
0,02
aerni-leuch ag bern Nr. 08/03
Wa

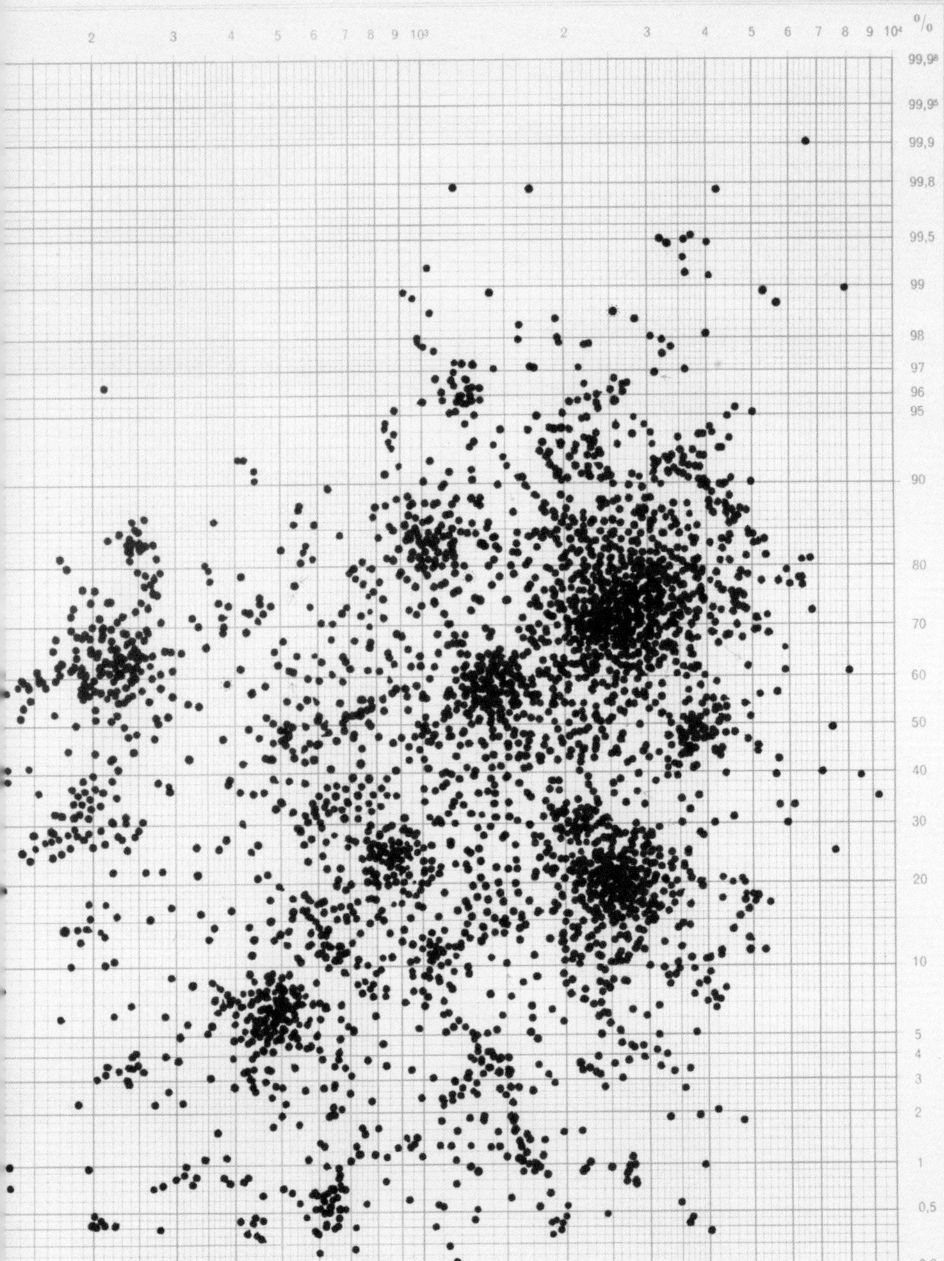

PIII/06

eitsnetz

Abszissenachse logarithmisch, Ordinatenachse nach dem Gaußschen Integral geteilt

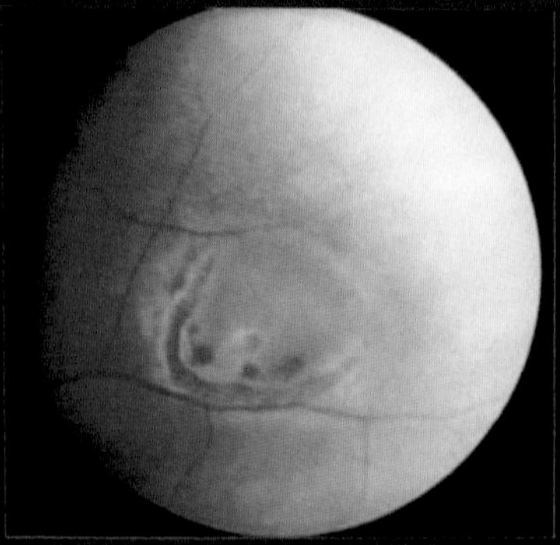

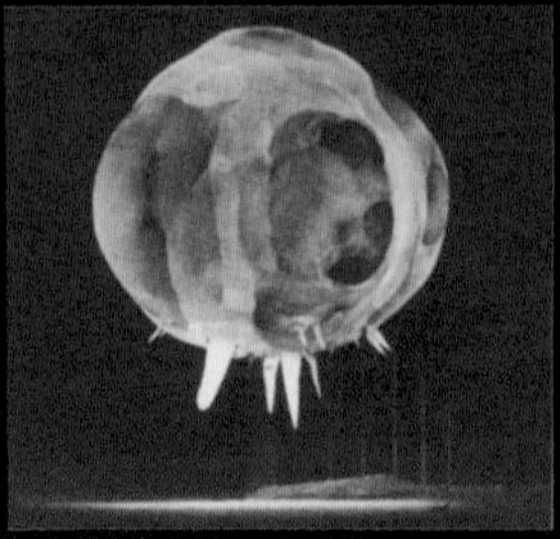

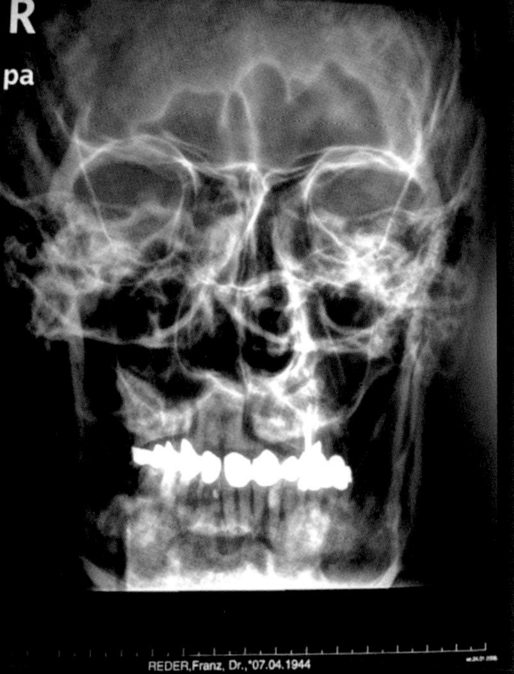
R
pa
REDER,Franz, Dr.,*07.04.1944

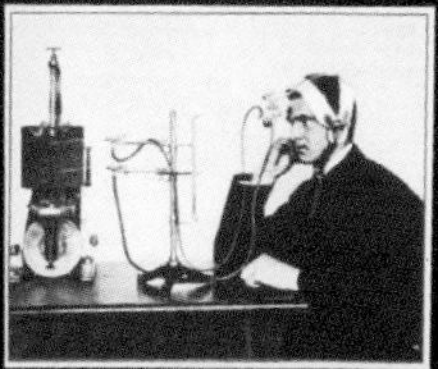

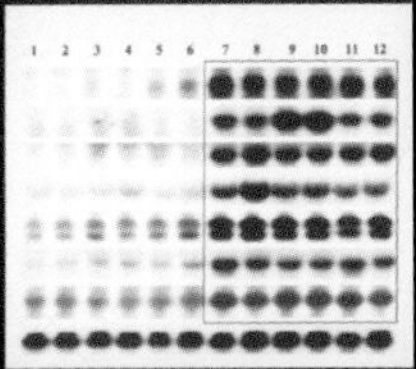
1 2 3 4 5 6 7 8 9 10 11 12

NOTES ON PLATES III

PIII/01: Atlas of correlation – Plate III
(The ego/geo/world/insight/line/cone/recognition/pattern)

PIII/02: Translecture on thinking><drawing><thinking
PIII/02a: To mark a point of reference
PIII/02b: To draw a connection
PIII/02c: To point out for the third
PIII/02d: The element of four
PIII/02e: To mark through gesture
PIII/02f: The image/Text binomial
PIII/02g: To mark a point of reference through language I
PIII/02h: To mark a point of reference through language II
PIII/02i: To draw a distinction
PIII/02j: Lines of sight
PIII/02k: The points of reference gesture
PIII/02l: To extinguish fleeting forms

PIII/03: The linkage form

PIII/04: Shadow appearances

PIII/05: The urban alphabet (a-z)

PIII/06: Wahrscheinlichkeitsnetz I (probability field)

PIII/07: Atlas of correlations – Plate IV
(The authors'/head/eye/ball/oblivion/graph)

HYPOTHESIS #24

The Line of Thought

Hanneke Grootenboer

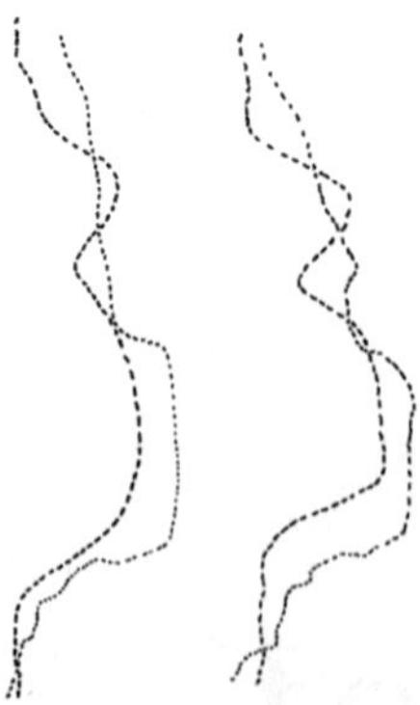

Fig. 06-04

As the story goes, the history of image-making started when the daughter of a Corinthian potter traced on a wall the outline of the shadow cast by the face of her sleeping lover. Stealing his silhouette, she secretly and silently followed his profile with her writing implement. Image-making thus originated when a line was drawn, separating insignificant parts of a blank wall from meaningful ones. The product of the daughter's art was probably not a full-blown image as we know it, as she may have traced her lover's shadow in one stroke, leaving a meandering line marking the empty wall as if it were a crack. Recognizable as a portrait in her eyes, her mythical marks may not have differed much from what we now call a diagram, likewise a figure marked out by lines (→ Fig. 06-04).[1] We could say, then, that, like the diagram, the 'image' made by the potter's daughter was perhaps closer to writing than to the figurative arts. The sketched line resembling a fracture is the image, its outline as well as its shape. The potter's daughter would have 'read' this mark as a statement of love as much as recognised it as an actual face.[2] In contrast to the first-ever image, the diagrams that make up this book consist of recognizable elements such as lines, arrows and dots; however, we, as readers, will be less sure than the potter's daughter about the statement they illustrate. Somehow, these diagrams, while brimming with symbols, pointers, signs and indicators, resist reading.

Let's look at (→ Fig. 01-20) on the right. We see shapes, lines and numbers forming one whole picture that clearly illustrates something. The legends at the bottom right and top left suggest as much. Perhaps our first thought is the happy expectation that this may be the map of a treasure hunt, and that we are seeing an unknown part of the world. Are the small formless shapes islands just off the coast of some virgin territory? If so, are we supposed to navigate this *terra incognita* in the direction of the black dots marking a kind of location? Yet, if we take the two forceful arrows into account, our navigation toward the island comes to a full stop. We have to take something else into account. The map transforms itself into a geographical figure explaining

1) See the definition of 'diagram' in the Oxford English Dictionary.

2) Fig. 06-04 is particularly apt here: the two intertwining lines form a profile but of an unknown rather than a known head.

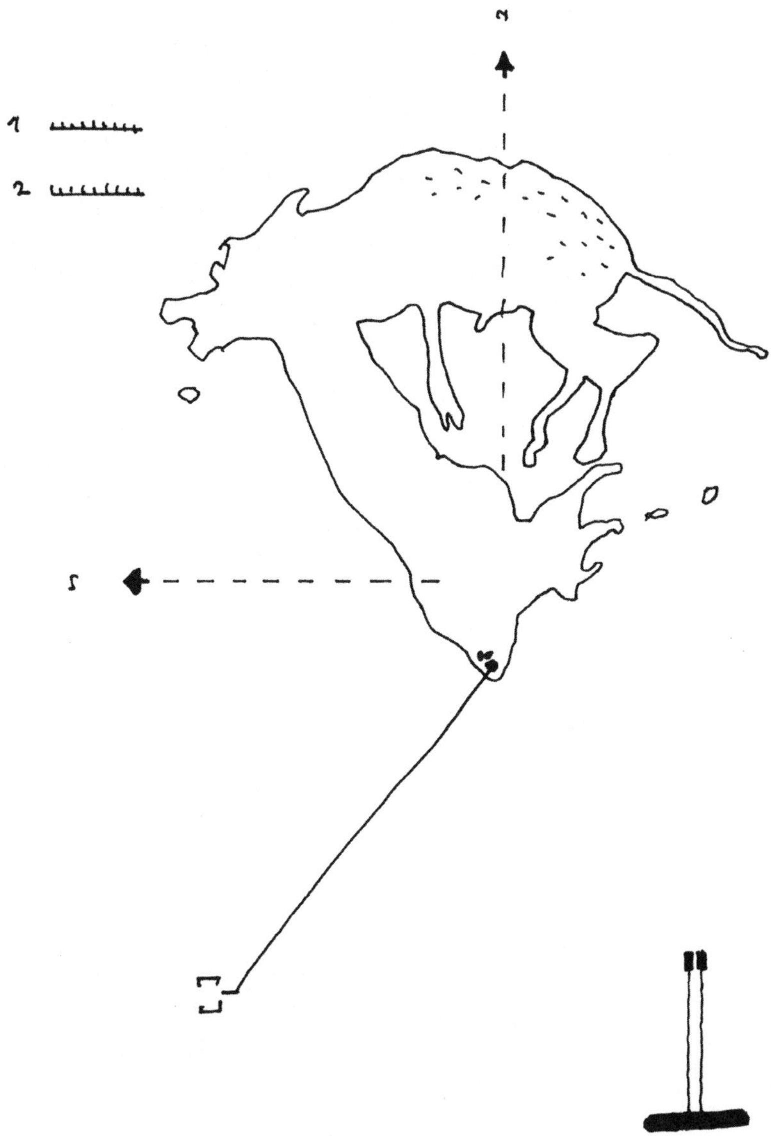

Fig. 01-20

Reverie. During moments of profound earth gazing, the “floating ideas” (as John Locke phrased it), indicative of inconsistency, start mimicking drifting continents once their contours have slowly started to stretch, increasing the void between them.

the drift of continents. Evidently, something is expanding here. The measuring scales 1 and 2 clearly indicate a kind of growth, the vectors pointing toward its direction. A further line brings our eye to what seems to be a location, or rather, a small collection of dots on the southern point of the continent: do these dots symbolise an agglomeration of small villages, or the hiding place of the treasure chest? While we ponder the significance of the dots, a second, more iconic image emerges from the diagram. What if we look at a collection of forensic evidence: the circumvention, in chalk, of a dead animal (a boar?) laying in a pool of blood, the arrows now referring to witness marks and collateral damage?

We can't help reading this diagram (or is it an image?) even though our attempt does not quite reveal what seems to be illustrated here. Despite its various clues, the diagram cannot be decoded. (→ Fig. 02-45) is equally puzzling. Again, the process of reading starts automatically and immediately. Trained

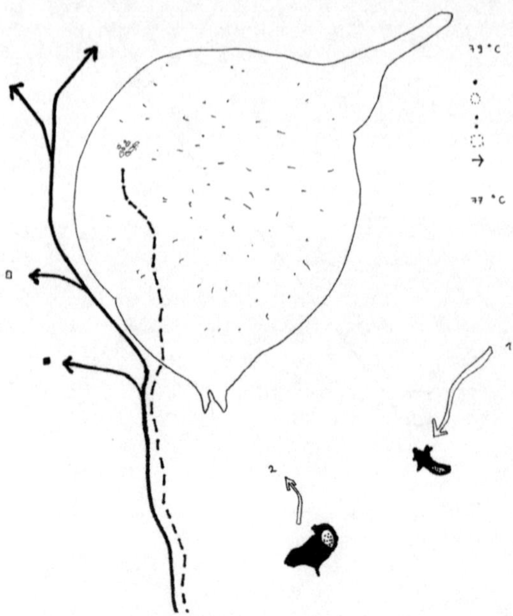

Fig. 02-45

Affect. Once the trajectory develops in various directions, the affect increases its original intensity and starts to swell, a process that has been called becoming. Traces of social organisation or systems of prohibition – labeled 1 and 2 respectively – are left behind powerless.

by histograms and flow-charts in text books, pie charts and function graphs in news programmes, and exploded views in manuals, our eyes start interpreting in their restless quest for meaning. Following the outlines of the large curved shape, we begin to make connections: do we see a balloon or do we see a map of a pond in a recreation area? Does the continuing black line indicate a walking path with various directions (will there be picnic tables?), whereby the dotted line suggests that a second main path has been flooded? Again, we are confronted with a code in the upper right corner dictating the way to decipher this diagram as a system in itself. Like (→ Fig. 01-20), something is flooding, expanding, inflating, transgressing its limits here. What do these minimal signs of excess tell us? What kind of beyond do they seem to imply?

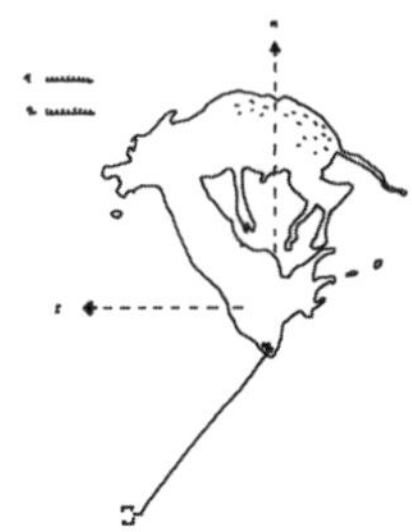

Fig. 01-20

These readable yet undecipherable diagrams have been balanced between the figure and the letter, between writing and representation, and between a motivated and an arbitrary sign. Though they suggest *illustrating* something, they are confusing because they ultimately do not refer back to a model or an original text. Rather, the lines and points move us forward. Clearly, in almost all diagrams is a sense of direction and movement. Our eyes follow a trajectory that we are keen to follow in order to figure out what it tells us. However, the trajectory leads us not to a mode of understanding, but into the realm of blank paper devoid of further signals. Just as the *tabula rasa* of the potter's wall broken by the crack of the traced profile made it possible for the silhouette to stand out, the marks in the diagrams should be read by virtue of the white empty space that surrounds it. But contrary to the potter's wall, the empty space surrounding the constellation of signs exceeds its function of mere support. The lines reinforce ideas of expanding, inflation or targeting which all suggest that their signification does not lie in the drawing, but goes beyond its marks – as the arrows lead us into a state of becoming. The diagrams do not exemplify a statement that has been made, but one that still needs to be formulated. They do not figure an assertion that has been made, but point to the unfigurable. The pathways set out for our eyes ultimately lead us into the realm of the unknown.

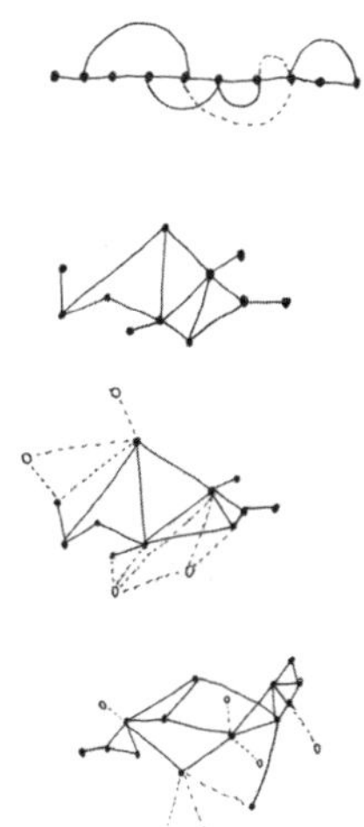

Fig. 04-09

If a diagram is a figure composed of lines serving to illustrate a definition or statement (as the Oxford English Dictionary has it) the question arises as to what exactly these line-drawings configure. Independent of a text book or otherwise explanatory texts, these diagrams are not exactly illustrative of something else. What they first and foremost configure is *space*, a diagrammatical space, neither abstract nor figurative nor strictly geometrical, which is characterised by the fact that it is 'trajectorable' by our eyes. In our attempt to read the lines that make up this diagrammatical space, forces operate that push our eyes left and right in an attempt to scan this apparent field of knowledge in which, ultimately, nothing is known. The individual elements in the diagrams constantly play with the notion of outside and inside, and marked and unmarked space. Where does the diagram stop and our uneasy steps into the unknown begin? We are on a trail: following the dots, sticking to arrows, and crossing lines eventually allow us to trespass into undelineated space. But where do we go from there? Is there or is there not a relation between the inside and the outside of the diagram? Are we supposed to find a referent in the real world for the symbols we see dispersed over the white page? As there is no explanatory text, what exactly is it that these diagrams show, and what do they demand from us in terms of their interpretation? If diagrams usually facilitate the transfer of information in a simplified, abstract way, what kind of knowledge can we possibly gain here? Or are we instead led toward this space devoid of graphs, a no-man's-land which is illustrative of the infinity of outer space as well as of the limited capacities of our faculty of understanding? Without realising, a conflation has taken place between brooding over the meaning of the spatial configuration of the diagrams, and the space it has taken up in our head. Our puzzlement over inside and outside, the interval and the demarcation line, has been internalised. What we have followed all this time are the lines of our own thought. What we stare at is an image of thought. And where will it lead us?

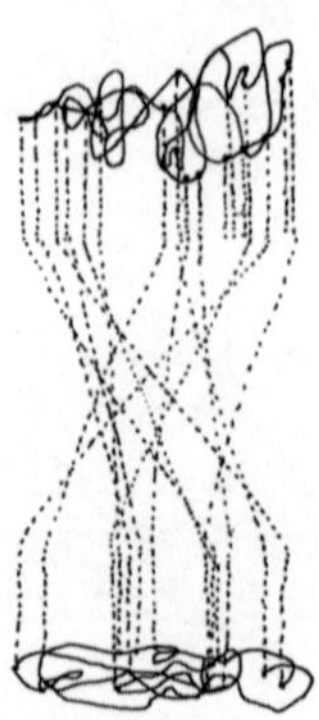

Fig. 05-09

Gaston Bachelard once claimed that profound metaphysics is rooted in implicit geometry which, whether we like it or not, confers spatiality upon thought.[3] If there is one thing that the diagrams demonstrate, it is how spatiality is bestowed upon thought.

3) Gaston Bachelard, *The Poetics of Space: The Classic Look at How We Experience Intimate Places*, Boston, 1994, p. 212.

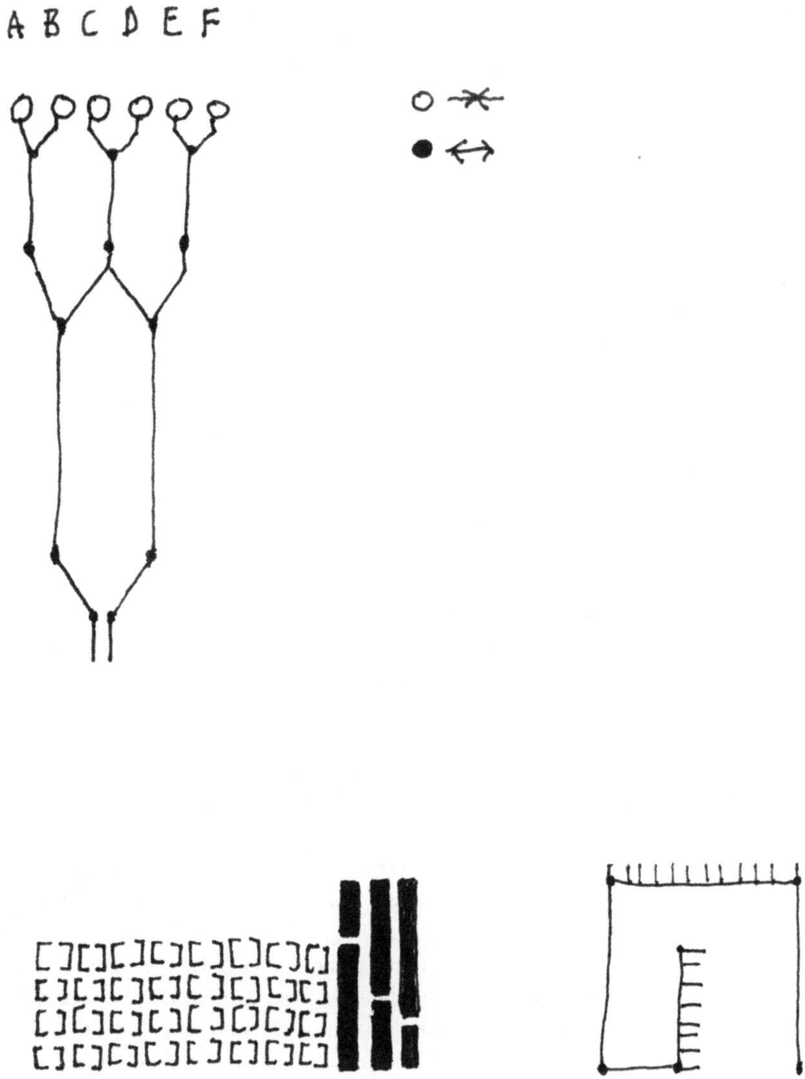

Fig. 01-29

To Ponder. When weighing matter or words before (a) reaching a conclusion or (f) making a decision, various stages such as reflection (c) and consideration (d) are processed gradually. As indicated here, in pondering, a balance is seldom found.

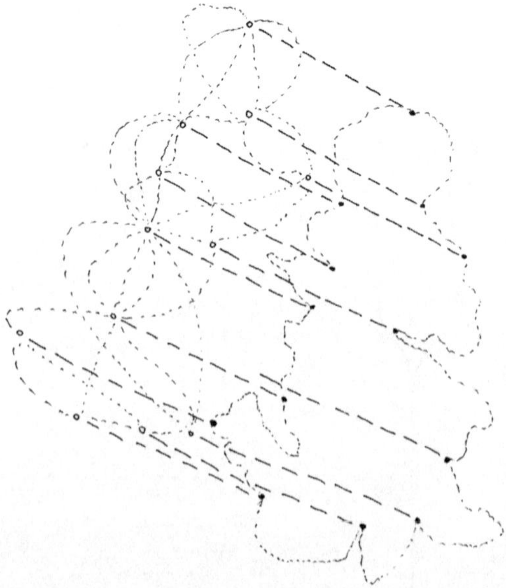

Fig. 05-08

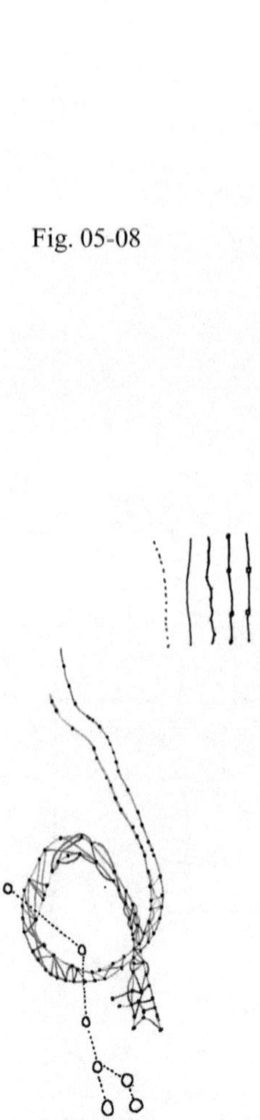

Fig. 10-06

For most, if not all, diagrams in this book set out a trajectory toward the outskirts of the diagram's proper space, to a liminal zone where we become aware of an outside, firstly of these diagrams, and secondly of our reading and thinking. That this liminal zone is profoundly spatial becomes even more apparent when we look, for instance, at (→ Fig. 10-06). We follow two sets of dotted lines forming a lace. Both lines, each consisting of small dots that are connected, eventually intertwine. The intertwining shows us another aspect of the white space surrounding the drawings, as these lines do not operate only on the flat surface of the 'image', but propel into a diagrammatical three-dimensional space. Correspondingly, (→ Fig. 05-07, -08, -09) show a jumble of lines floating in space resulting from a quasi-geometrical projection of coordinates. Geometry literally means the measuring of the earth; particularly (→ Fig. 05-08) reminds us of this definition. Its main shape appears again as a cartogram. Vaguely recalling a late medieval map of England, its outline appears to be the result of a projection of a series of open dots which are connected with each other by dotted lines. In studying this diagram, hoping to make sense of it, our eyes continue to move between the black dots making up the England-shape and the closed dots hovering over it. The main strategy of direction that this diagram proposes leads us toward

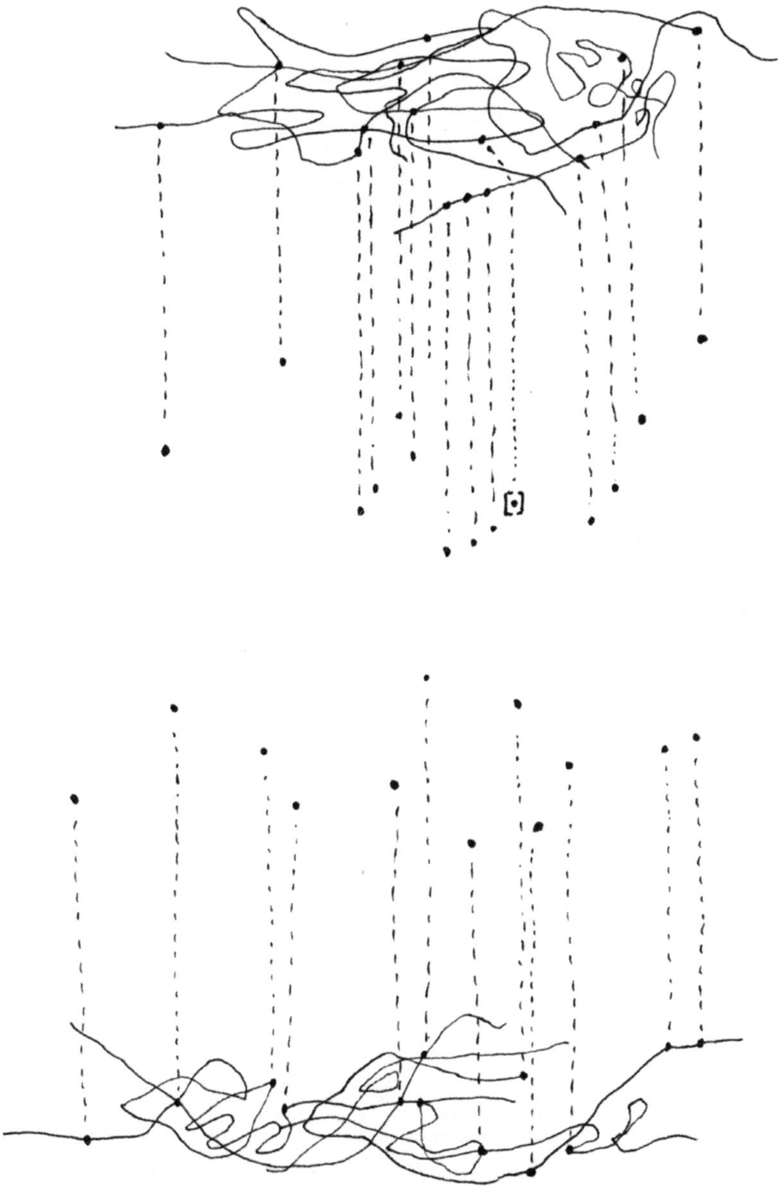

Fig. 05-07

(→ PII/02)

the middle section of the two concentrations of lines and dots, which serves as an interval between the main shape and its multiple points of origin. Though not exactly lost, we don't quite know where exactly we have ended up in this projective space. It is as if our eyes, again, have been led from one seemingly well-defined spot to another to ultimately arrive at a non-place, which, though scattered with dots, is not quite in the diagram. Part of the outside of this diagram has been folded within it, and it is within this fold that we somehow reside.

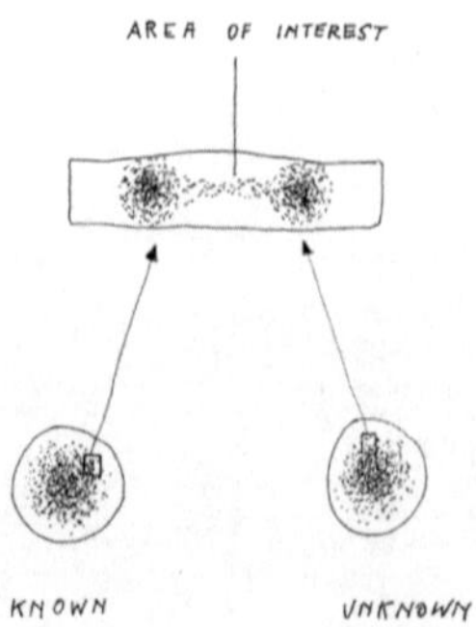

Fig. 01-01

Gilles Deleuze once remarked, talking about the work of Foucault, that thinking is carried out in the space between seeing and speaking and occurs in the disjunction between them.[4] When seeing and speaking, word and image, attain their individual limits and retire, so to speak, a space for thinking is created. It would be wrong to say that some of the diagrams in this book thus illustrate what Deleuze says. The diagrams do not illustrate anything; they do not show anything or do anything other than offering us a state of becoming – a possibility to trespass, and to come across a place that lies in between speaking and seeing, where accurate reading fails, but where a thought can get its shape. For Bachelard, spaces where thinking can take place are profoundly *creative*. This does not have to mean that the diagrams are concepts-in-the-making but rather the contrary: that by looking at them and being puzzled at the familiarity of their undecipherable lines and dots, something as yet unknown starts to dawn upon us, or rather, that something known but as yet unthought appears at the outskirts of the diagrammatic space. It is the image of the unthought known that has nestled in our mind, in order to be conquered. Our intrusion of the diagrams' 'outside' has become an intimacy. If we have not yet started thinking,[5] the state of becoming that the diagrams encompass may provide a space in which we can try to begin, as, indeed, (→ Fig. 01-01) beautifully states.

4) Gilles Deleuze, *Foucault*, London, 2006, in particular the chapter 'Strata or Historical Formations: The Visible and the Articulable (Knowledge)'. Interesting in this context is also the drawing on page 99 supposedly illustrating the way in which Foucault's (or rather Deleuze's) notions of the line of the outside, the strategic zone, strata and the fold as the zone of subjectivation can be brought together.

5) This is a famous declaration of Martin Heidegger, who explains this provocation in a series of lectures in *What is Called Thinking*, New York, 2004.

HYPOTHESIS #25

Strong Evidence for Telon-Priming Cell Layers in the Mammalian Olfactory Bulb

Maurizio Nardo, A. Adam, Peter Brandlmayr,
Benjamin Fitzroy Fisher

ABSTRACT

The present study examines secondary organisation and activity of cells in the mitral cell layer of the olfactory bulb, better known as *telon priming* (Fisher, 2007; Fisher et. al.; 2008). The olfactory bulb is characterised by its unique connections with cortical and subcortical areas, such as basolateral amygdala. We discuss the critical role of these areas in telon building processes and the high selectivity for priming inputs from the olfactory bulb.

We find strong evidence for telon-relevant computing within groups of mitral cell layer neurons, with projections from and to the basolateral amygdala. These neurons tend to reverse their firing selectivity after reversal of telon-outcome contingencies in basolateral amygdala. According to first findings in the rodent brain and the particular shape of this area, we propose the name *lepa* ® or *lepus organs* for such structures. Further investigations about the role of telon building in the amygdalae and the hypothalamus will be helpful for a general understanding of telon-driven nonlinear processing in the human brain.

Keywords: *Telon Priming, Amygdala, Olfactory Bulb, secondary Layer Networks*

INTRODUCTION

Given the emphasis placed on the role of telons and metatelons in ideatory mechanisms, most studies have used cues predictive of rewarding events (Bruner & Lashford, 2005, Carelli, 2002, Apicella 1992, 2002). However, emerging evidence implicates telon priming (TP) in processing of aversive information and aversively motivated learning as well (Dai & Mon 2007). This evidence has provided an increasing awareness that TP function is not restricted to learning motivated by reward and indicates that TP may be more generally involved in the use of learned cues predictive of biologically significant outcomes, either rewarding or aversive. Such a role is consistent with Fisher´s conception of telons (Fisher et al., 2008; Fisher, 2006) as interfaces through which motivationally significant information guides behaviour. However, relatively little is known about how such information becomes encoded in telons. In the present experiment, we recorded neural activity from TP in rabbits performing a specific task previously used in our laboratory to examine the properties of neurons in the mitral cell layer of the olfactory bulb during telon priming (Fisher et al. 2008).

Complex dynamics are expected to enable us to avoid combinatorial explosion and diverging programme complexity which has been one of the essential difficulties in solving complex problems of telon priming (Fisher et al. 2008). In this paper, we show how an ideatory task is executable using complex dynamics in a recurrent telon model with asymmetric synaptic connection to the mitral cell layer. In spite of the simplicity of the proposed search algorithm, the complexity of telon structures is stunning. This is, however, in line with evidence from the *in vivo* experiment with implanted electrodes and simulation within artificial neuronal networks (pseudo-telon, Fisher 2006, Jackson and Moghaddam 2001).

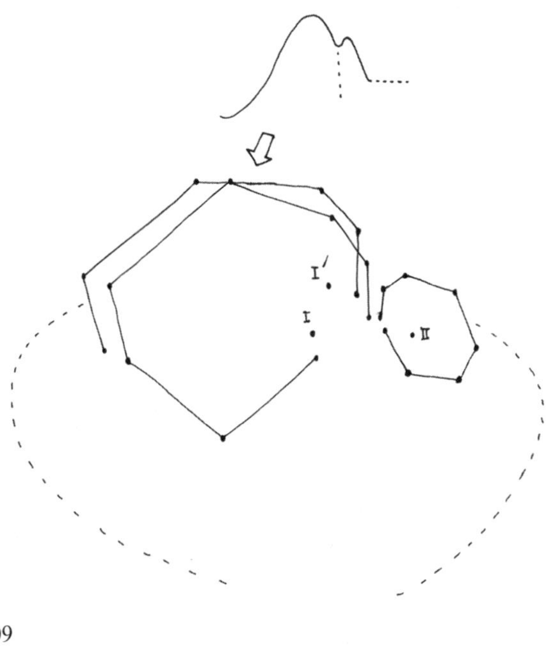

Fig. 02-09

Schematic diagram of main biochemical mechanisms during telon priming. The given baseline potential in the appropriate telon priming cell population in the mitral layer evokes synaptic bindings between telon fragments; surprisingly preset-telon-edge-cells (I, I′and II) will not be affected in this first step.

METHOD

Not surprisingly, animals with even the simplest of nervous systems have evolved mechanisms for assessing the outcome, either good or bad, of behaviour, and linking these outcomes to salient cues in the environment. By potentiating responses to cues associated with good outcomes and inhibiting responses to cues associated with bad outcomes, the nervous system adapts behavior to the current environment and thereby achieves a positive internal milieu (Fuchs et al. 2002). In mammals, this type of motivationally guided learning involves neural circuits within the basal ganglia, including the dorsal and ventral striatum, as well as inputs to these nuclei from dopaminergic neurons in the midbrain ventral tegmental area and substantia nigra pars compacta (reviewed in Holzgott, et al. 2009). In turn, these circuits participate in larger signaling loops involving the amygdala, orbitofrontal cortex and prefrontal cortex during the learning and performance of contextually appropriate behaviour (Cromwell, P. G. & Schultz, H. P. 2003).

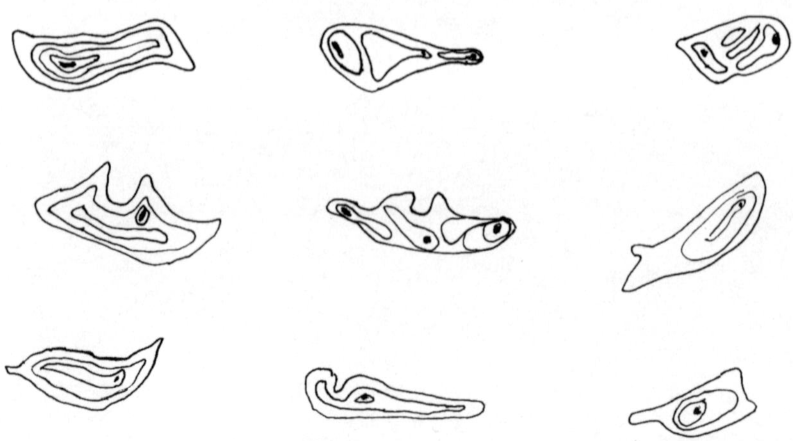

Fig. 02-17

Different maps of outcome in the single recording array within mitral layer tissue, also interpretable as different virtual transections through the lepus organ at different experimental stages (A: learning with aversive cues; B: learning with regarding cues; C: baseline or rehearsal trial).

Current models posit that telon priming occurs following a mismatch in the response of amygdala dopamine neurons to cues that predict rewards and actual reward outcomes, thereby potentiating neural responses in target structures such as dorsolateral amygdala (reviewed in Fisher; 2002). Both responses have recently been observed in association with aversive events as well, suggesting that these telons may serve a broader function in linking cues with biologically significant outcomes, either rewarding or aversive.

Electrophysiological recordings via single cell electrodes (additive model (Baccher et al. 2005)) have also shown that neurons in described telons respond to learned cues that predict biologically significant outcomes, as well as to the outcomes themselves (Cromwell, P. G. & Schultz, H. P. 2003; Hassani et al. 2001).

Until recently, relatively little was known about how such networks are formed during learning and how they change when predictions fail, particularly in contexts involving both aversive and rewarding outcomes. Fisher and colleagues (Fisher et al. 2008) extend prior investigations of telon priming (TP) by examining neural responses and behaviour during cue learning involving both rewarding and aversive outcomes. Their data suggest that the defined telon structure processes cues associated with both aversive and rewarding outcomes and that selective neuronal responses in this area evolve over time in a fashion roughly paralleling learned behaviour. (See also Cromwell & Shultz 2003.) These data powerfully document the role of TP in linking environmental stimuli with biologically significant outcomes during learning.

Our experiment is set up as follows: In a maze experiment, rabbits have to push buttons following a predesigned sequence. The rabbits are rewarded with sucrose delivery if the rank correlation between the sequence of pushed buttons and the predefined sequence exceedes 0.75. Telon-priming happens during the learning process of the predefined pattern. Electrodes are set at various spots in the amygdala. During telon-priming, the synchronisation of firing rates of these cells (nodes) is increased. This has been described in a survey by Fischer et al. (2008).

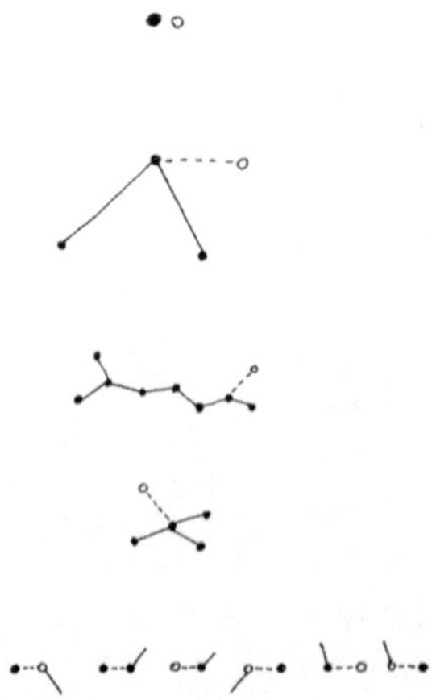

Fig. 01-28

Single neurons can express 5 types of telonic memes during first stage of telon priming: 1) free groups with weak connected dendrites; 2) radical groups, also weak, but with three elements; 3) polymorphic groups, 4) solid groups with four elements and 5) bipolar groups of subliminal tendency. Consider different connection priority in all types of memes.

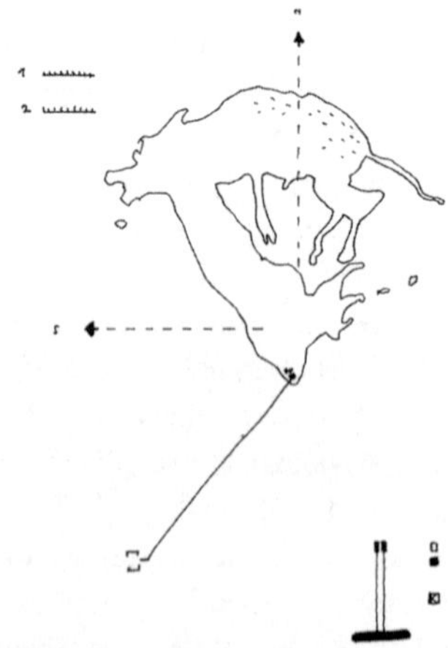

Fig. 01-20

Schematic drawing of whole lepa organon, as seen in subject P99 of our sample. The arrows S and N indicate the nasal and lateral axis. Marginal deviations may occur associated with differing baseline settings. Lower right corner: schematic diagram of used patch-clamp paradigma (pro rabbit-preset Y2 and BY2; see also: Yamamoto, et al. 2009; Wolf, B. et al. 2009.

	AL	SH	FB	CHS	TO	GA	FS	CHD	DR	S	W	RD	CA	PD	EX	RS
AL	1	0.15	0.26	0.22	0.29	0.21	0.21	0.28	0.31	0.33	0.19	0.31	0.22	0.19	0.23	0.32
SH	0.15	1	0.56	0.42	0.02	0.15	0.47	0.55	-0.03	0.04	0.34	0.39	0.29	0.37	0.31	0.57
FB	0.26	0.56	1	0.39	0.14	0.12	0.61	0.47	0.09	0.08	0.33	0.36	0.29	0.37	0.35	0.47
CHS	0.22	0.42	0.39	1	0.15	0.19	0.48	0.77	0.06	0.08	0.69	0.43	0.27	0.27	0.36	0.53
TO	0.29	0.02	0.14	0.15	1	0.09	0.18	0.21	0.41	0.27	0.14	0.12	0.31	0.16	-0.02	0.19
GA	0.21	0.15	0.12	0.19	0.09	1	0.15	0.17	0.23	0.39	0.21	0.26	0.17	0.18	0.22	0.27
FS	0.21	0.47	0.61	0.48	0.18	0.15	1	0.54	0.05	0.14	0.46	0.36	0.38	0.44	0.5	0.56
CHD	0.28	0.55	0.47	0.77	0.21	0.17	0.54	1	0.16	0.19	0.59	0.54	0.37	0.39	0.4	0.67
DR	0.31	-0.03	0.09	0.06	0.41	0.23	0.05	0.16	1	0.35	0.04	0.16	0.21	0.19	0.01	0.14
S	0.33	0.04	0.08	0.1	0.27	0.39	0.14	0.19	0.35	1	0.13	0.41	0.21	0.12	0.18	0.35
W	0.19	0.34	0.33	0.69	0.14	0.21	0.46	0.59	0.04	0.13	1	0.52	0.34	0.25	0.41	0.46
RD	0.31	0.39	0.36	0.43	0.12	0.26	0.36	0.54	0.16	0.41	0.52	1	0.29	0.29	0.36	0.64
CA	0.22	0.29	0.29	0.27	0.31	0.17	0.38	0.37	0.21	0.21	0.34	0.29	1	0.37	0.19	0.36
PD	0.19	0.37	0.37	0.07	0.16	0.18	0.44	0.39	0.19	0.12	0.25	0.29	0.37	1	0.24	0.37
EX	0.23	0.31	0.35	0.36	-0.02	0.22	0.5	0.4	0.01	0.18	0.41	0.36	0.19	0.24	1	0.4
RS	0.32	0.57	0.47	0.53	0.19	0.27	0.56	0.67	0.14	0.35	0.46	0.64	0.39	0.37	0.4	1

Table 3

Correlation matrix over all trials (firing rate to response latency)

The response is predicted by means of a mathematical telon model (pro rabbit Ver. 2.0) which completes, integrates and simulates the recorded data. Activity patterns within the mitral layer of the olfactory bulb are recorded by both electrodes as well as the mathematical model, and their qualification as telonic memes with or without sublime tendency is tested in a Yamamoto fragment-process. (→ Fig. 02-17)

RESULTS AND DISCUSSION

To further explore the relationship between the evolution of telon priming selectivity and changes in cell activity, we examined correlations between changes in firing rates and response latency as well as accurate choice performance.

For this analysis, the trial within each session on which cue selectivity or a latency difference emerged was determined by comparing the firing rates as measured in the olfactory bulb (m1-m7) and response latency on each negative trial (only negative go trials in the case of latency) with the values from all positive trials in the preceding block of 27 trials. A t-test was applied to determine whether the sample value from the negative trial fell outside the normal distribution of values from the positive trials ($p < 0.05$).

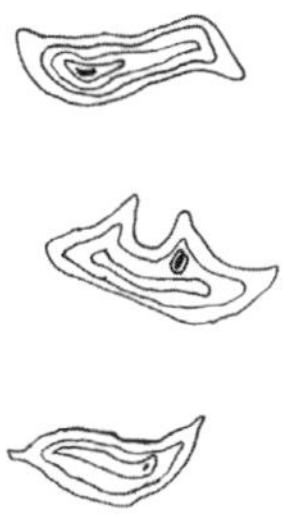

Fig. 02-17a

More precisely, correlation coefficients were calculated between the first trial on which a significant response in firing rate was detected and the first trial on which the rabbit showed a significant increase in response latency. The Spearman rank correlation was then calculated between the first trial on which a firing rate difference was detected and the trial on which the rabbit met the choice criterion on the discrimination problem. The significance of the results was assessed using Fisher's r to z transformation.

For analysis of overlap between selective activity in different time windows, a Pearson chi-square test was used to compare the proportions of neurons with different firing properties and to ask whether the degree of overlap between two populations was greater than that expected by chance. For these comparisons, chance was calculated based on the actual proportion of

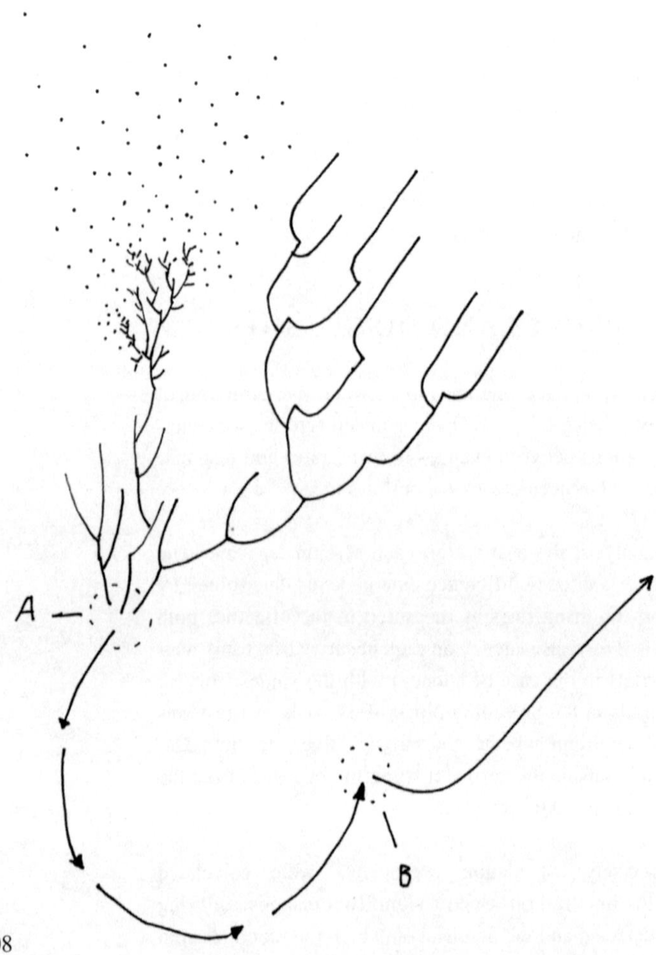

Fig. 02-08

		Value	Asymp. Std. Error[a]	Approx. T[b]	Approx. Sig.
Interval by Interval	Pearson´s R	,441	,081	5,006	,000[c]
Ordinal by Ordinal	Spearman Correlation	,439	,083	4,987	,000[c]
N of Valid Cases		106			

Table 4

Summary of correlations between olfactory bulb and amygdalian electrodes neurons in the population that exhibited each type of response. For example, if 50 of 100 neurons fired selectively during sampling of the positive cue in a given phase, and 50 of 100 neurons fired selectively while the rabbit was waiting for sucrose delivery in that same phase, then the number of cells likely to be in both populations by chance would be (0.5)(0.5)(100), or 25 neurons. This proportion was calculated for both valences and added to obtain the results in Table 4.

Our results confirm that the dynamic structure of such secondary mitral cell networks in the olfactory bulb has a strong influence on the efficiency of telon priming in several areas of the amygdala, the hypothalamus and parts of the orbitofrontal cortex.

That seemingly simple oscillators already show many general phenomena including local and global bifurcations as well as chaotic behaviour makes their study so important in the theory of nonlinear dynamics. A considerable body of knowledge has been developed in recent years for analyzing and evaluating this variety of telon priming (→ Fig. 02-08).

The strong activity in the olfactory bulb observed prior to telon priming supports our hypothesis that cells in the olfactory bulb serve as a catalyst and tp-trigger respectively during the telon priming. Using the mathematical model (pro rabbit Ver. 2.0) we simulated this process before running the experiment. These simulations suggest that telon priming can be triggered directly through the mathematical model via implanted electrodes. The model delivers useful results, not only for small mammals, and hence an application for human beings can be expected. This finding is further supported by the outcomes of the first experiments using the clones cerebral structure ADAM on the IWF Department of Neurocybernetics, Vienna, Austria. (Nardo et al., in press).

References

Alexander et al. (1990) G. E. Alexander, M. D. Crutcher and M. R. DeLong, *Basal ganglia-thalamocortical circuits: parallel substrates for motor, oculomotor, "prefrontal" and "limbic" functions*, Prog. Brain Res. 85, 1990, pp. 119-136.

Apicella, P., *Tonically-active neurons in the primate amygdala and their role in the processing of information about motivationally relevant events*, Eur. J. Neurosci. 16, 2002, p. 2017-2026.

Apicella, P., Galis-de Graaf, P. and Groenewegen, A. H., *Topographical organisation and relationship with ventral striatal compartments of prefrontal corticostriatal projections in the rat*, J. Comp. Neurol. 325, 1992, 314-347.

Apicella, P., Pennicot, R. F., Sugathapala, B. A., Robbins, W. E. and Everitt, F.J., *Impulsive choice induced in rats by bilateral lesions of the nucleus accumbens core*, Science 295, 2001, p. 2499-2501.

Baccher H., Tortellesi M. & Yamatsu S., *Probabilistic models for analyzis of multivariat single-electrodes recordings*, Brainmaths, Vol 3 XXI, 2005, pp. 232-236.

Bruner, P. U. and Lashford, P. T., *Rewarding rabbits*. Elsevier, Amsterdam, 2001.

Carelli, T. M. (2002) *Nucleus accumbens cell firing during goal-directed behaviors for cocaine TP*, `natural' reinforcement, Physiol. Behav. 76, p. 379-387.

Chang, L. Y., Chen, F., Luo, L.-H. and Woodward, M. C., *Neuronal responses in the frontal cortico-basal ganglia system during delayed matching-to-sample task: ensemble recording in freely moving rats*, Exp. Brain Res. 142, 2002, p. 67-80.

Corbit, L.-H. and Muir, P. T., *The role of the nucleus accumbens in instrumental conditioning: evidence of a functional dissociation between accumbens core and shell*, J. Neurosci. 20, 2006, p. 4233-4239.

Cromwell, P. G. and Schultz, H. P. *Effects of expectations for different reward magnitudes on neuronal activity in primate striatum*, J. Neurophysiol. 89, 2003, p. 2823-2838.

Dai, F. and Mon, P. F. (*2007) *Negative Motivation in the rodent model. Proceedings in animal invasive neurocybernetics*, V2, pp 1877/1878.

De Cocteau, R. P., Kaesner, J. M. (2008) *Short-term memory for food reward magnitude: the role of the prefrontal cortex*, Behav. Brain Res. 88, 239-249.

Fisher, B. F., Kojima, N., Nardo M. and Dale, P., *Towards an understanding of how ideas dwell. Telon-priming in cortical tissue*. A Review. Exp. Brain Res. 142, 2008, p. 98-120.

Fischer, B. F. Kojima, N., Nardo M. and Dale, P., *Upper level synchronisation in nodes. A longitudinal sudy with canaries,* J. Neurosci. 13, 2008, p. 113-165.

Fisher, B. F., Weber, R. U., Dale, P. and Nardo, M., *Traces of secondary networks and mapping of cortical and subcortical projections in the left dorsolateral amygdala*, J. Neurosci. 18, 2006, p. 2613-2625.

Fisher, B. F., *The mammalian sympathetic prevertebral ganglia: Models for the study of neuronal networks and basic neuronal properties*, 2005, Elsevier, London.

Fuchs, M. N., Weber, H.J., Neiselwadler, P., *Effects of excitotoxic lesions of the basolateral amygdala on cocaine-seeking behavior and cocaine conditioned place preference in rats*, Brain Res. 929, 2002, p. 15-25.

Fuchs, M. N., Adam, A., Brandlmayr, P. and Nardo, M., *Thinking in steps. A proposed model for the recombination of fragmentary thoughts. Philosophical premisses and neurobiological evidence*, Elsevier, London, 2005.

Goto, S. and O'Donnell, A. D., *Timing-dependent synaptic integration in the frontobasal amygdala*. Proc. Natl. Acad. Sci. USA 99, 2002, 13189-13193.

Hassani, O. P., Cromwell, H. C. and Schultz, U., *Influence of expectation of different rewards on behavior-related neuronal activity in the striatum*. J. Neurophysiol. 85, 2001, 2177-2186.

Hauber, U., Bohn, C. and Giertler, P. U., *NMDA, but not dopamine D2, receptors in the rat olfactory bulb are involved in guidance of telon-priming by stimuli predicting reward magnitude*, J. Neurosci. 20, 2008, 6282-6288.

Hernandez, C., Sadeghian, P. O. and Kelley, R. D., *Differential effects of two ways of devaluing the unconditioned stimulus after Pavlovian conditioning*, J. Exp. Psychol. Anim. Behav. Process. 18, 2005, p. 65-78.

Holzgott, H., Kohlegger, E. P. and Paul, U. (2009). *The role of dopaminergic projections to the midbrain in motivationally guided learning*, Science, 495, 2009, p. 999-1006.

Jackson and Moghaddam (2001). M. E. Jackson and B. Moghaddam, *Amygdala regulation of nucleus accumbens dopamine output is governed by the prefrontal cortex*, J. Neurosci. 21, 2001, pp. 676-681. View Record in Scopus, Cited By in Scopus (90).

Kawagoe, Y. P., Takikawa, O. and Hikosaka, Y., *Dopaminergic projections from the basolateral amygdala modulate cognitive signals in the prefrontal cortex*. Nat. Neurosci. 1, 2001, p. 411-416.

Kawaguchi, K., Augood, P. C. and Fisher, B. F., *Mytral-Layer interneurones: chemical, physiological and morphological characterisation*, Trends Neurosci. 18, 1999, p. 527-535.

Moeller, F., Bornfeld, P., *Hippocampus Whispering in Deep Sleep to Prefrontal Cortex – For Good Ideas?* Neuron, 62/4, 2008, p. 167-169.

Wolf, B., Hasse, P. A., Kimamura, H., Yamamoto, K., *Pro-Rabbit V 2.0; Working with Y-presets*. Rewievs Vol. XII/b Standford Academic Press, 2009.

Yamamoto S., K., Miura, Y., Hasse, P. A., *Mathematical Models in natural neuronal network-analysis*, 2009.

Acknowledgments

We would like to thank Ludwig Karner and Joe Frey for their excellent research assistance. We would also like to thank Julia Woerz, Lisa Olbrich and Alfons Egger for insightful comments on the manuscript, and Friedrich Mayer for the excellent technical assistance. This work was supported by grants of the NG Foundation.

HYPOTHESIS #26

Expected Anomalies Caused by Increased Radiation

Christina Stadlbauer

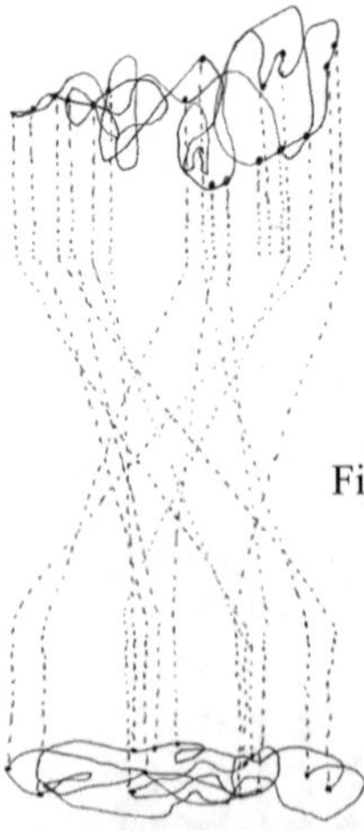

Fig. 05-09

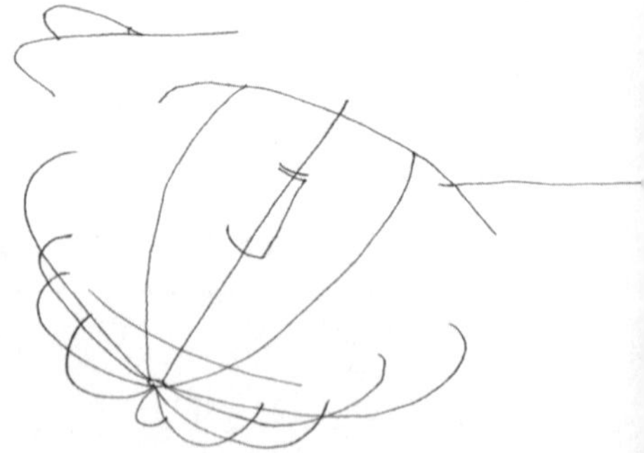

Fig. 09-05

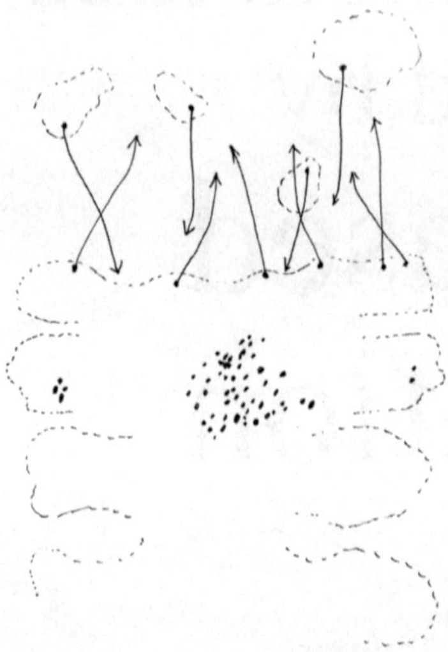

Fig. 05-12

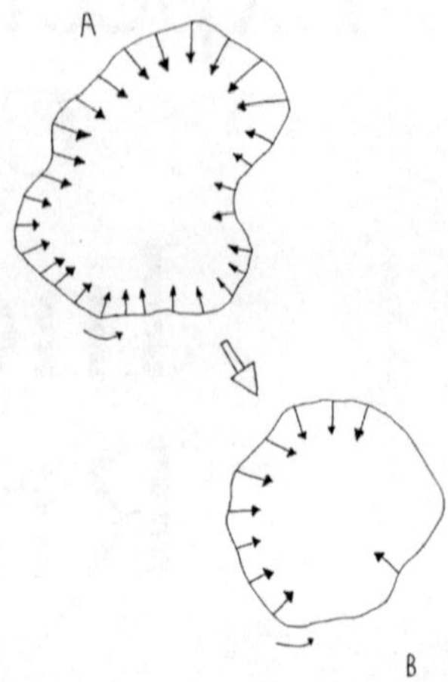

Fig. 03-28

Fig. 05-09

Geomagnetic mirror image, generated by the penetration of cosmic rays through the earth's magnetosphere.

Fig. 05-12

Depiction of magnetic field lines emanating from the shifting North Pole.
The comet-tail-shaped area points to a residual magnetism (remanence) at the original location of the Pole.

Fig. 09-05

Impact of remodelled geomagnetism on the earth's axial tilt.

Fig. 03-28

Beech tree cross-sections (stem cross-section, top view), hillside location.
The spiral grains in the beech stems are equally aligned in both positions; the centripetal forces are not the same.

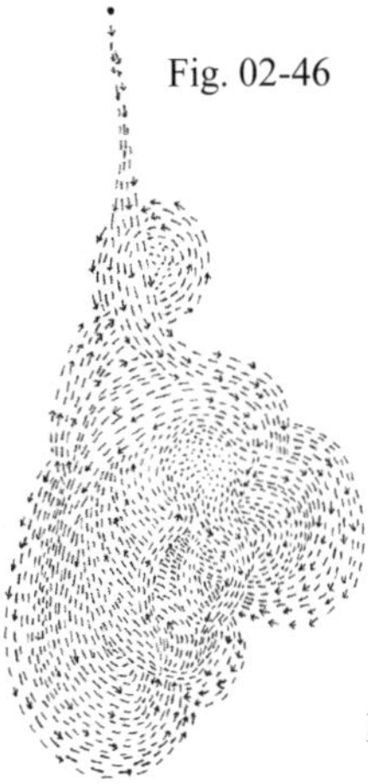

Fig. 02-46

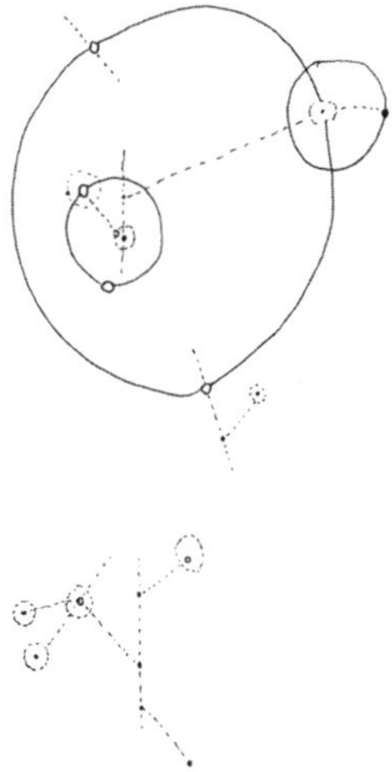

Fig. 04-08

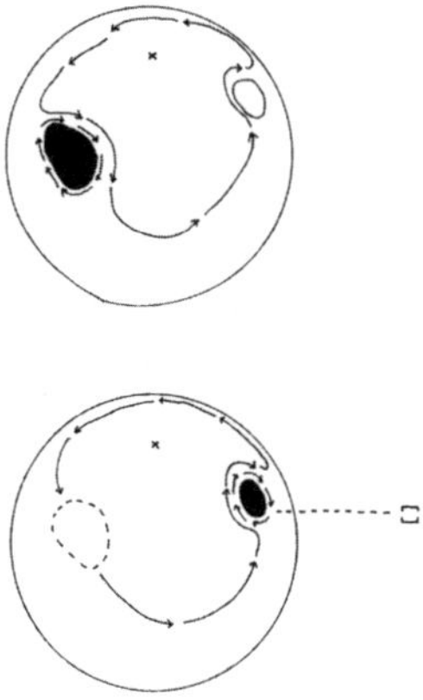

Fig. 03-27

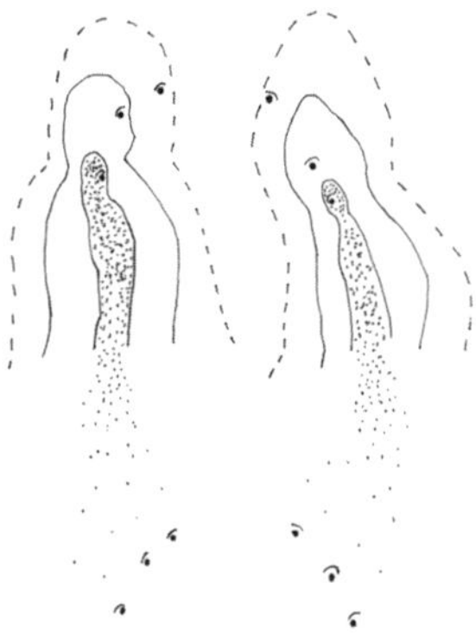

Fig. 02-01

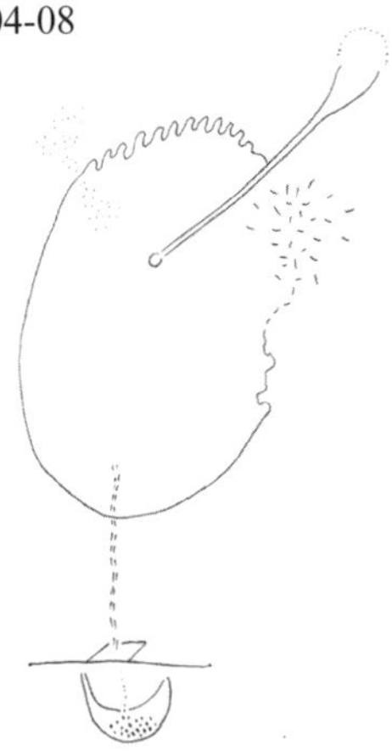

Fig. 06-16

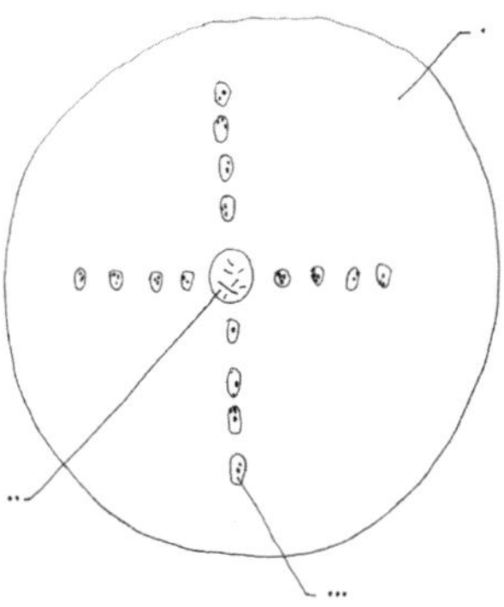

Fig. 01-32

Fig. 02-46

Aeration and biological rearrangement (bioturbation) and flow of matter in various soil horizons.

Fig. 02-01

Triploid spores escape from the fruiting body of mushrooms.

Fig. 04-08

Displacement of the plane of polarisation of reflected sunlight.

Fig. 03-27

Dance of solitary bees – Change to the dance structure following the displacement of the light's plane of polarisation (tangential).

Fig. 06-16

Percolation, permeability and osmosis in fern cells.

Fig. 01-32

Illustration of circular movements (1st, 2nd and 3rd degree) of non-Newtonian fluids.

HYPOTHESIS #27

On Pluto 86 the Winter Lasts 92 Years

(Original material first published in *Proceedings of the Concortian Academy for Interstellar Issues, 106*, 21-27 rev. hon. Hewitt Claas Stuart and Anne Dolphiq)

Ralo Mayer

ABSTRACT

Case study of Intractor failure as experienced by notorious post-war renegade Willi Tobler on Pluto 86, Sec. H85B89aT15. Tobler asked for an intractor manual and detailed charts. After receiving material Tobler shows symptoms of increasing regressive behaviour followed by aggressive verbal outbursts directed at Concortian officials. Analyzing this complex mesh of relationships between Tobler's unwillingness to follow clear instructions, his regressive revolt against the "galactic bureaoucracy" (sic) and symptoms of a general psychic breakdown, the study will lead to guidelines for similar cases of semptite behaviorisms. The study will draft not only the image of an individual autodestructive force but also the corruptive impact of comparable demeanor on the highly advanced biomechatronics of today's glorious interstellar spaceflight.

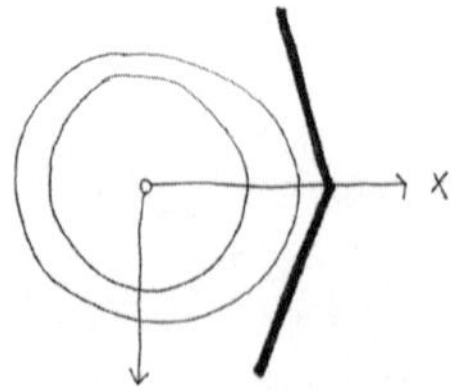

Fig. 01-42

Classified note: Although it is out of question that Tobler has produced the attached artefact himself (which are not the material sent by CSIN), the sketches bear an eerie resemblance to highly classified documents published only years later by J. Drump. Further investigation has been commenced.
Long live Concortia. (AK)

Keywords: *Intractor; artificial atmosphere; Pluto 86; Tobler-case; revoltisms; regressive behaviour; Jean Drump; WOAKL*

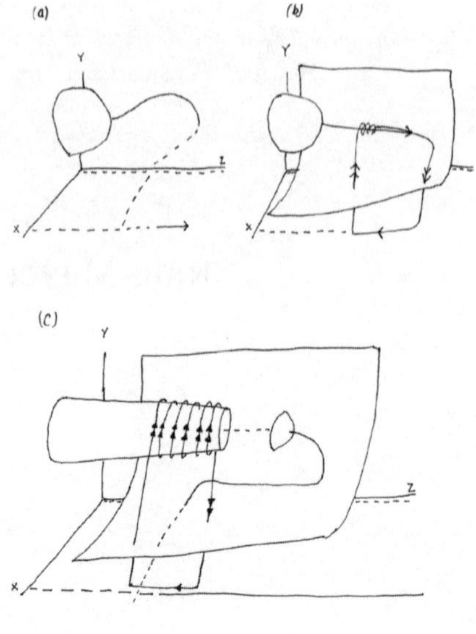

Fig. 01-35

Document (1): Willi Tobler's recordings as intercepted by WOAKL (Sec. I04H99T12b), sign. Com. Burk. (translated from German original by Veronica Buckley)
ATT: CLASS. HS 2*

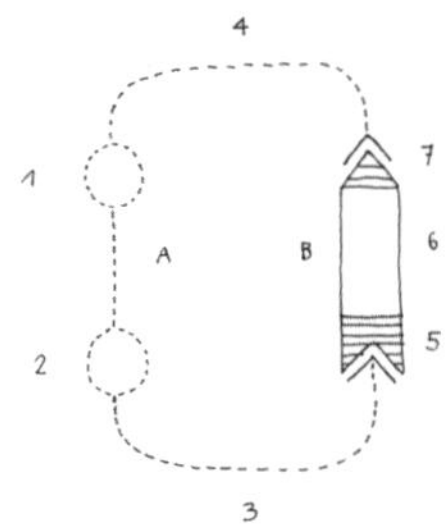

Fig. 12-72

The map material that has been transmitted to me: it's no good. I've turned the sketches back and forth, looked at them from eight kinds of perspective, reflected, enlarged, reformatted. It is and remains complete nonsense. Is it a joke on the part of the people responsible? I ask myself what they're trying to do, these ladies and gentlemen, these land register surveyors, these colleagues in biomechatronics, trak trok, and their respective bosses. My request was more than clear:

REQUEST APPROPRIATE CELESTIAL CHART (SECTOR H85B89aT15) REQUEST CONTINUATIVE BLUEPRINT FOR INTRACTOR REPAIR (URGENT MY AIR IS RUNNING OUT)

I sit on the roof in front of my window and it is one of these last fine autumn days. On Pluto 86 the winter lasts 92 years. The six pages of the document can't even be called sketches. Are they taking the piss? They are taking the piss. The biology of life forms that zoom by me: genetic analyses of their evolutionary histories, or, if you like, primitive diagrams of their family trees would be more helpful to me in the current situation than this steam cloud of dashes. The glowing yellow saltpeter clouds of the evening ambience: a spectrogram of their chemistry, or, if you like, a watercolour of the sunset over several weeks, would be a blessing. I'd even settle for the poetic description of the acoustics of a mynamite event. Drump calculators?

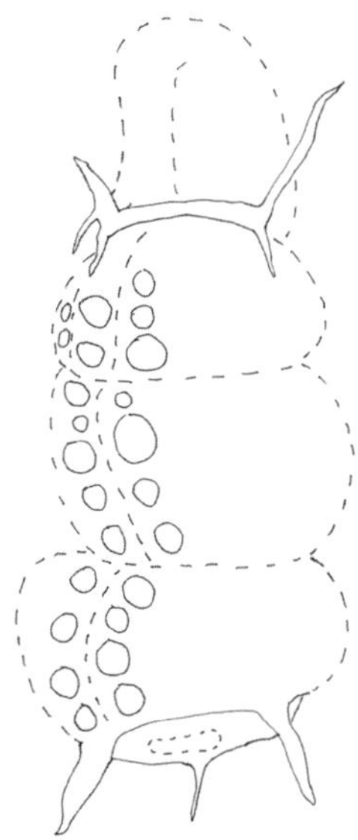
Fig. 01-50

If the winter lasts 92 years, you're keen to get away. If you press really firmly at the end of a bowel movement, a bit of fluid comes out too, from higher up. If in doubt, it's always better not to take the trouble. If the intractor is down, you call central support. If your air's running out, you'd like to be a four-part cocoon (3 + 1). If the butterflies in your stomach are moths, then better switch the lights off.

I wanted a bit of assistance; I asked for help. They sent me these dashes. I wanted a map showing the way home. They pixelled me. (Drump had pronounced the warning almost casually.) All I wanted DAMN IT ALL was star charts and blueprints AND ALL I GOT WAS 6 CARICATURES OF ZOMBIE CULTURE, that is, of the contemporary zombie culture of the galactic bureaucracy. With best wishes. Drump wrote 'That's nothing.' I'd like to add: less than nothing, there's nothing here either, except that my nothing isn't transmitting across through all sectors. My colleagues are true masters of emptiness, vacuum virtuosos, that's how they earn their living, and I've heard they don't live badly from it, some of them have even earned something of a reputation (in the broadest sense) in their professional capacity. Drump, Drump, Drump. DRUMP!!!

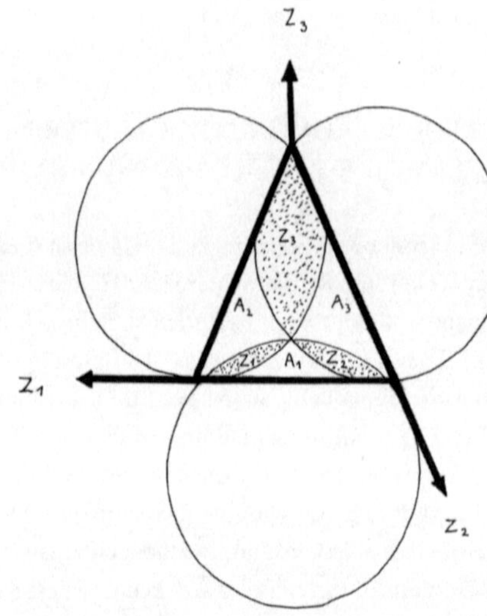

Fig. 12-65

I sit here on Pluto 86 and count the atoms of a black hole in myself. I have no apartment (that's why I'm sitting on the roof in front of my window, which strictly speaking isn't mine on the inside any more), my glider is screwed (not even the intractor's functioning properly, that's why the air's running out), and I don't know the right angle for orbital re-entry (simple mathematics, otherwise). I need star charts, I need those blueprints. They've sent me six unusable scribbles; it can't be an error, the transfer codes match. This planet's unique life forms are drag-jetting past. Have I already mentioned that in the meantime they've lost the last remaining shreds of their already negligible charm? It's only with the greatest effort that I avoid

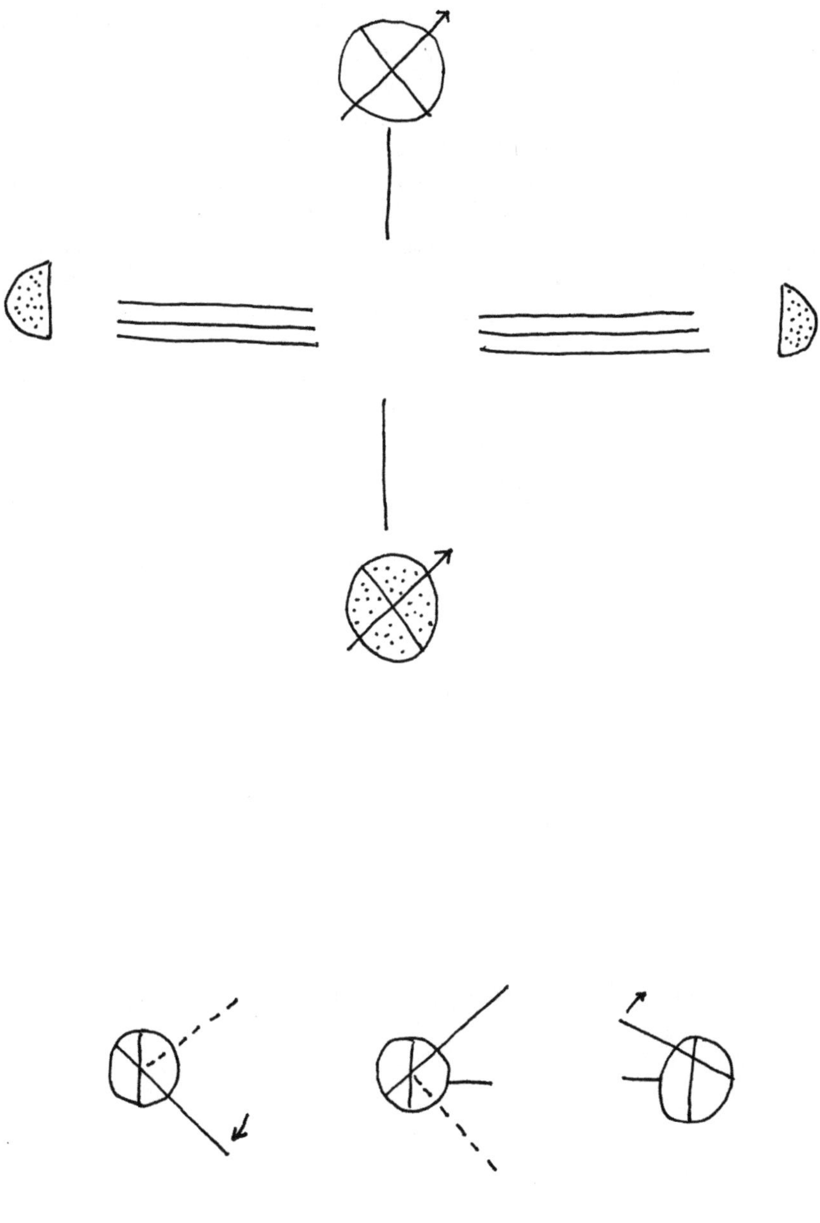

Fig. 01-39

falling into self-pity, and I must admit I've already grabbed one or two didiograchts out of the thin air and squashed them with my own hands. I'm turning into a barbarian. Fuck the parentheses: Drump, you old citation swine.

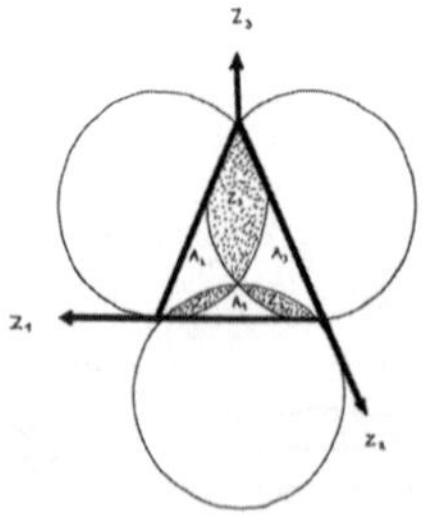

Fig. 12-65

What does Figure 12-65 tell me about the economy of my desire? How does the kindergarten representation of a singularity relate to the relations of production in the asteroid business? Who's running the galactic bureaucracy, and how? – it can't be that it's got no more than three axials and three intersections?! Colleagues! The intractor is sputtering. The didiograchts and the local FG population are building four-minute empires in muffled harmony. This sunset is lasting too long for me. I'm running out of air, never mind the ball bearings. Two axials and my job's gone to hell in a handbasket. One more arrow and one crisis will turn into the next.

Emptiness all around, a vector won't help, either. March on, protons! Kessler Syndrome galore!

Yesterday (i.e. 25 weeks ago) I painted a picture with the modest means at my disposal. It doesn't look that good, but it's for a friend, and I wrote something at the bottom: DEATH RAYS NOT OK.

My name is Willi Tobler, former press officer for the sixth star fleet. I am the mockery of the Western Galaxy. They've sent me unusable charts; I'll stay here and try to last out the winter.

(End of translation)

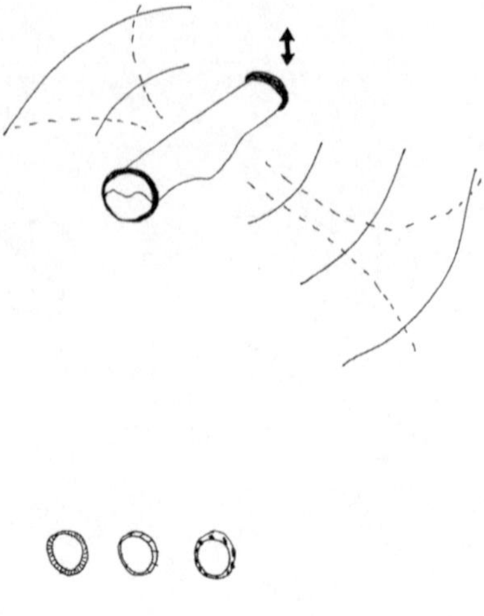

Fig. 01-43

Appendix

PERSONALIA

ADAM, A. – 2003/04 Distance learning in the Humanities Faculty, University of Innsbruck, Ph.D. 2004, since 2000 at the IWF, Vienna.

AUERBACH, Antony – is an artist and theorist. http://aauerbach.info

BAKKE, Monika – works in the Philosophy Department at the Adam Mickiewicz University, Poznań, Poland. She writes on contemporary art and aesthetics with a particular interest in posthumanist, gender and cross-cultural perspectives. She is an author of books: *Bio-transfigurations. Art and Aesthetics of Posthumanism* (2010) [in Polish], *Open Body* (2000) [in Polish], co-author of Pleroma. *Art in Search of Fullness* (1998), an editor of *Australian Aboriginal Aesthetics* (2004) [in Polish], and *Going Aerial. Air, Art, Architecture* (2006). Since 2001 she has been working as an editor of a Polish cultural journal *Czas Kultury* [*Time of Culture*].

BARTELS, Kerstin – Photographer, paintings restorer, graduate in photograph restoration (HTW Berlin), since 2007 Acting Professor of Conservation and Restoration of Audiovisual and Photographic Objects at the HTW Berlin. She is currently working on her Ph.D. thesis, an investigation of the surfaces of photographic paper and the development of a digital catalogue for their identification.

BOECKLER, Marc – is Professor of Economic Geography at Goethe University, Frankfurt. Previously he was Professor of Cultural Geography at Mainz University. He holds a doctorate in geography from Eichstätt University and an MA in Middle Eastern Studies, Economics and Geography from the University of Erlangen. His current research focuses on the interface of cultural theory and economics. In particular he is interested in the question of how economics – as a practical set of hegemonic narratives, socio-technical materials and performative models – shapes and formats social worlds. His contribution to this book originated during his time as Senior Fellow at the Institute of Advanced Study at the Center of Excellence of Constance University.

BRANDLMAYR, Peter – lives and works in Vienna; 1994 Mag.rer.nat., University of Innsbruck; 1998 graduate in photography at the Grafischen Bundeslehr- und Versuchsanstalt in Vienna; Ph.D. 2005. Freelance artist since 1999, working primarily in the field of tension between art and science: Institut für Wissenschaft und Forschung (IWF); Discussion on the life and work of physicist Prof. V. Krylov; equipment for the foundations of physics; interactions; research on the life and work of artist C.I. Brom; ADAM; Sound installation. www.iwf.at

COCKER, Emma – is a writer and artist based in Sheffield and a Senior Lecturer in Fine Art at Nottingham Trent University. Recent published writing includes *Over and Over Again and Again in Contemporary Art and Classical Myth* (Ashgate Publishing, 2010) and in *Failure* (Documents of Contemporary Art, Whitechapel/MIT, 2010); *Performing Stillness: Community in Waiting* in *Stillness in a Mobile World* (Routledge, 2011); *The Restless Line, Drawing* in *Hyperdrawing: Beyond the Lines of Contemporary Art* (I.B. Tauris, 2011), and *Border Crossings - Practices for Beating the Bounds* in the forthcoming Liminal Landscapes (Routledge, 2012). http://not-yet-there.blogspot.com/

DIRMOSER, Gerhard – born in Freistadt, lives and works in Linz, systems analyst. Exhibitions (selection): Architektur & Diagrammatik (Köln 2011), Ars Electronica Festival (Linz 2009, 2006, 2005, 2004), Gerhard Dirmoser, Horst Münch (Künstlerhaus Palais Thurn und Taxis, Bregenz 2007), Eine Festausstellung (Lower Austria Documentation Centre for Modern Art, St. Pölten 2006), Survival and Maintenance of Media Based Art (Ludwig Boltzmann Institut für Medien.Kunst.Forschung, Linz 2006), Was ist eine Ausstellung – Symposium (OK – Centre for Contemporary Art, Linz 2005).

FISHER, Benjamin Fitzroy – Neurobiologist and computer scientist; 1987-2000 Chair in Applied Neurobiology and Neurocybernetics at MIT, Boston; 1998-2009 established and directed the Centre of Experimental Neurocybernetics (CENK) in Durban, SA; from 2004 established and worked in the Department of Neurocybernetics at the IWF Vienna; 2009 awarded the Ludwig Wittgenstein Prize of the Austrian Forschungsgesellschaft.

PERSONALIA

GANSTERER, Nikolaus – Nikolaus Gansterer studied art at the University of Applied Arts in Vienna, Austria and completed his studies at the Jan van Eyck Academie in Maastricht, the Netherlands. He is co-founder of the *Institute for Transacoustic Research* and currently Guest Professor at the *Zentrum Fokus Forschung* at the University of Applied Art in Vienna. Deeply interested in the links between drawing, thinking and action, his practice is grounded in a trans-medial and trans-disciplinary approach, underpinned by conceptual discourse in the context of performative visualisation and cartographic representations. In his artistic research, he focuses on mapping processes of transience by developing experimental modes of notation and translation. Gansterer is co-author of the book *Choreo-graphic Figures. Deviations from the Line,* 2017 on the complex character of diagrammatic and embodied figures and is internationally active with performances, exhibitions and lecturing. www.gansterer.org

GROOTENBOER, Hanneke – is a University Lecturer in History of Art and Fellow of St Peters College at the University of Oxford. She works on vision and early modern painting. The author of *The Rhetoric of Perspective: Realism and Illusionism in Seventeenth-Century Dutch Still Life Painting* (University of Chicago Press, 2005), she is currently preparing *Treasuring the Gaze: Intimate Vision in Eighteenth-Century British Eye Miniatures*. Exploring the overlapping fields of art history, critical theory and philosophy, Grootenboer is currently working on a project on painting as a form of thinking, entitled The Pensive Image.

HARRASSER, Karin – is assistant at the Academy of Media Arts Cologne (Media- and Cultural Studies). She was Juniorfellow at the IFK and Research Scholar at Duke University. She completed her dissertation on the narratives of digital cultures of the 1980ies 2005. After a post-doc position at the Graduate Seminar Codes of Violence in Changing Media at the Humboldt-Universität Berlin she followed her research in the cultural history of prosthetics (Habilitation). She conducted a research project on the production of gender and knowledge in museums and has realised numerous projects at the intersection of arts and science communication. Recent book: with D. Harrasser, S. Kiessling, S. Sölkner, K. Schneider & V. Wöhrer: Wissen Spielen. Untersuchungen zur Wissensaneignung von Kindern im Museum, Bielefeld 2011.

KRÜMMEL, Clemens – studied art history and philosophy at the University of Bonn, training and voluntary work at the Karl Ernst Osthaus-Museum, Hagen; 2000-2007 editor and co-publisher of the periodical *Texte zur Kunst*, Berlin; co-curator of the exhibition *Tauchfahrten - Zeichnung als Reportage* at the Kunstverein Hannover/Kunsthalle Düsseldorf, and founding member of the Melton Prior Institute for reportage drawing in Düsseldorf (both with Alexander Roob); co-publisher of the *Polypen* series at b_books, Berlin. Lives in Berlin, working as critic, translator, visiting lecturer and curator.

LEDER, Helmut – is Professor of Cognitive Psychology and Head of the Department of Psychological Basic Research at the University of Vienna. His main fields of research are aesthetics, psychology of the arts, design and face perception. His PhD is from the University of Fribourg. He was a visiting Researcher at the University of Stirling, ATR Japan, USC and UCSD, and at the Languages of Emotion-Cluster, FU Berlin. He is the author or co-author of many scholarly publications and was awarded the Berlyne Award for career contributions to the psychology of aesthetics from the American Psychological Association.

LEEB, Susanne – is an art scientist working at Berlin's Freie Universität. Along with a project in cartography and diagrams in contemporary art, her particular field of research is 'Aesthetic Experience in the Drawing of the Unbordering of the Arts'. Before completing her Ph.D. on *The Anthropological Configuration of Art in 1900 in the History and Theory of Art* in Frankfurt an der Oder in 2007, she was for several years editor of the art journal *Texte zur Kunst*. She is also co-publisher of the *Polypen* series at b_books, Berlin. In 2011 her book on diagrams in contemporary art will appear with the same publisher.

MATHEUS, Kirsten – began her academic career studying electrical engineering at the Technical University of Aachen. While writing her Ph.D. thesis in mobile communications at the University of Bremen, she also completed a degree in economics at the University of Hagen. Since then she has worked in several well known technology ventures, always at the forefront of innovation. The combination of engineering and economics has enabled her to work not only with the technologies but also with an understanding of the market forces that shape our future.

PERSONALIA

MAYER, Katja – studied physics, sociology and philosophy, with an emphasis on metascientific research, at the University of Vienna, and completing a doctorate on visualisations of social networks. She worked for many years at the Institut for New Cultural Technologies/Public Netbase in Vienna; she works on the concept and production of exhibitions, including on robotics, virtual worlds, and surveillance technologies; engagement in the uses of media and critiques of technology. Since 2002 she has worked freelance in information technology; since 2009 at Information Retrieval Facility, www.ir-facility.org. She is a guest lecturer at the Institut für Wissenschaftsforschung at the University of Vienna.

MAYER, Ralo – born on the Austrian side of the Iron Curtain, lives and works in Vienna. Artistic interests include the Science Fictions of post-Fordism, higher dimensional geometries and outer space as a giant projection screen for rather mundane salmagundi; works most often lead to breeding unruly monsters in various substrates like film, performance, installation and text. Since 2007 translation of the novel *The Ninth Biospherian*, about "Biosphere 2", a closed ecological system in the desert of Arizona in the 1990s, now a recent ruin of the space age.

DE MENDELSSOHN, Felix – is a psychoanalyst and group analyst in private practice both in Vienna and Berlin. He has lectured in Casework at the Academy of Social Work, in Aesthetics at the Max-Reinhardt-Seminar for Performing Arts, and was Head of the Dept. of Psychoanalysis at the Sigmund Freud University in Vienna. He is now a member of the Scientific Advisory Committee of the Sigmund Freud Museum Foundation. His recent publications include the books *Das Psychoanalytische Subjekt – Schriften zur psychoanalytischen Theorie und Technik* and *Die Gegenbewegung der Engel – Psychoanalytische Schriften zu Kunst und Gesellschaft* (SFU-Verlag 2011).

NARDO, Maurizio – pyschologist. Since 2004 assistant professor in the Department of Neurocybernetics and Neuropeutics at the IWF, Vienna.

PIRINGER, Jörg – Currently living in Vienna, Austria. Member of the Institute for Transacoustic Research. Member of The Vegetable Orchestra. Master's degree in computer science. Works as a freelance artist and researcher in the fields of electronic music, radio art, sound and visual electronic poetry, interactive collaborative systems, online communities, live performance, sound installation, computer games and video art. http://joerg.piringer.net

REDER, Christian – was born in Budapest, Hungary. He is a writer, consultant and professor at the University of Applied Arts in Vienna (Head of the Centre of Art and Knowledge Transfer). He is editor of the book series Edition Transfer at Springer Vienna/New York, and co-editor of the newspapers *Volltext* (literature) and *Recherche* (science) in Vienna. Principal topical book projects for 2011/12 are: *Zeichnung als universelle Sprache/Drawing as Universal Language*, and *Kartographisches Denken* (*Cartographic Thinking*). www.christianreder.net

REKACEWICZ, Philippe – has dual French and American nationality. He is a geographer, cartographer and journalist (permanent contributor to the international newspaper *Le Monde diplomatique*, with responsibility for cartographic production). He particularly follows issues such as demography, refugees, statelessness and displaced persons, as well as migration, and, more broadly, geopolitics and geostrategy, as well as social territories, and public and private space. He also works on a number of other projects which bring together cartography, art and politics, especially studying how communities, political or economic powers produce the cartographic vision of the territories on which they operate, and how they can manipulate and lie through the use of maps. Since 1988, he has published more than 2000 original thematic maps, 15 atlases, and a number of written articles which reflect research and thinking about cartography and how the world is represented. He also often participates in exhibits linking cartography to art in Europe.

ROTH, Moira – holds the Trefethen Chair of Art History at Mills College, Oakland, California. She has written extensively on a wide range of contemporary art, and her first volume of collected essays, *Difference/Indifference: Musings on Postmodernism, Marcel Duchamp and John Cage*, was published in 1998. Currently she is at work on her second volume, *Travelling Companions/ Fractured Worlds*. In recent years, Roth has increasingly devoted herself to writing poetry, fiction and plays. Among her current projects are a series of plays (produced in Tokyo and Kyoto, Japan, Potsdam, Germany and San Francisco), poem cycles (*From Far Away, 2003-*), together with a narrative about Rachel Marker, a fictional 100-year old Czech Jew, and *The Library of Maps*, a set of 41 texts about a fictional library and its inhabitants.

SCHINNER, Andreas – is a theoretical physicist engaged in freelance research at the Johannes Kepler University in Linz, Austria. His main area of scientific interest is theoretical solid state physics – particularly particle beam interactions with matter. He is also working as a self-employed software developer.

SCHMATZ, Ferdinand – writes poetry, prose, essays and audio plays, lives and teaches at the University for Applied Art in Wien. 1999 Christine Lavant Prize; 2004 Georg Trakl Prize; 2006 H.C. Artmann Prize; 2009 Ernst Jandl Prize. Most recent publications: *Durchleuchtung: Ein wilder Roman aus Danja und Franz* (2007); *quellen:* Gedichte (2010).

SEIDL, Walter – was born in Graz, Austria and is based in Vienna. He earned a Ph.D. in Contemporary Cultural History and studied in Austria, France and the U.S. Seidl works as a curator, critic and artist. As a critic, Seidl writes for various international art magazines such as Camera Austria, contemporary, *Springerin* and *Ivot Umjetnosti*. A member of the editorial team at *Camera Austria*, he edited the magazine's 100th issue (together with Christine Frisinghelli). Seidl's curatorial work has included projects in Austria, Belgium, Bulgaria, the Czech Republic, Germany, Hong Kong, Japan, Montenegro, Romania, Serbia, Slovakia, Slovenia, South Africa, Switzerland, Turkey, and the U.S. Since 2004, Seidl has been in charge of the art collection of the Erste Group. www.walterseidl.net

SECTION.A – has worked for nine years at the intersection of economics, art and design. Working with clients in various areas, section.a develops tailor-made concepts for strengthening company identities, accompanying internal processes and supporting company communications, internally and externally. A knowledge of the many-layered potential of art is the basis of all section.a's considerations. To engage with complex content and connections and to bring them to emotional tangibility are the defining elements of the work of this curators' collective, whose members are Katharina Boesch, Christine Haupt-Stummer, Alexandra Feichtner, Andreas Krištof. www.sectiona.at

STADELBAUER, Christina – is an Austrian-Italian biologist interested in the complexity of processes in nature. She obtained a Ph.D. in natural sciences (chemistry) from BOKU, Vienna and has been practising and teaching shiatsu for over 10 years. Currently, she works for FoAM, Brussels, working on interdisciplinary projects concerned with city environments and urban resilience. She has an apiary in the city of Brussels, and coordinates participatory activities around honeybees and their role in ecosystems. She is also involved in projects on alternative forms of gardening, and researches herbal medicine, both in urban and rural areas. http://apiary.be

STOCKBURGER, Axel – is an artist and theorist who lives and works in Vienna. He studied at the University of Applied Art in Vienna with Peter Weibel and holds a Ph.D. from the University of the Arts, London. His films and installations are shown internationally. Among other projects, in 1998 he initiated the independent art television channel TIV in Vienna, and collaborated on international projects with the London-based media art group D-Fuse (2000-2004). At present he works as a scientific staff member at the Academy of Fine Arts / Department for Visual Arts and Digital Media in Vienna. www.stockburger.co.uk

TORMEY, Janey – lectures in Critical and Historical Studies at Loughborough University School of the Arts. Her research explores the exchange of ideas between art practice and other disciplines and the ways in which conceptual and aesthetic traditions can be disturbed by and through photographic/filmic practices. She is co-editor of the book series *RadicalAesthetics-Radical Art* (I.B.Tauris) and its companion series of symposia. She has been part of the editorial team for the electronic journal *Tracey Drawing and Visualisation Research* since its inception in 1999. She co-edited the collection of essays *Telling Stories: Countering Narrative in Art, Theory and Film* (CSP 2009) and has work published in *Drawing Now* (I.B.Tauris 2007), *The State of the Real* (I.B. Tauris 2005), and *Masquerade: Women's Contemporary Portrait Photography* (Ffotogallery 2003). She is a member of the editorial board for the peer-reviewed journal *Art and the Public Sphere* (Intellect).

SUBINDEX

SUBINDEX

SUBINDEX

SUBINDEX

SUBINDEX

INDEX OF NAMES

INDEX OF NAMES

INDEX OF NAMES

COLOPHON

ACKNOWLEDGEMENTS

I want to thank the people I met during my stay at the Jan van Eyck Academie, who inspired me and encouraged me to pursue my idea of making this publication: Kasper Andreasen, Orla Barry, Ron Bernstein, Koen Brams, Sabeth Buchmann, Norman Bryson, Peggy Buth, Raphaël Cuomo, Wim Cuyvers, Marthe Van Dessel, Marjolijn, Dijkman, Jonathan Dronsfield, Christoph Fink, Katja Gretzinger, Sönke Hallmann, Tsila Hassine, Paul Hendrikse, Anouk van Heesch, Sabine Hillen, Will Holder, Antony Hudek, Maria Iorio, Suchan Kinoshita, Johanna Kirsch, Aglaia Konrad, Will Kwan, Urs Lehni, Achim Lengerer, Lene Markusen, Charlotte Moth, Matt Mullican, John Murphy, Mike Nelson, Willem Oorebeek, Falke Pisano, Hinrich Sachs, Stefanie Seibold, Annette Stahmer, Tim Stüttgen, Saliou Traoré, Joelle Tuerlinckx, Armando Andrade Tudela, Toni Uroda, Frans Vos, Inga Zimprich and the staff of the JvE. Here I would especially like to thank Sarah Infanger for the inspiring ideas and conversations in the early stages of the project, about the form it should take.

My special thanks go to Gerald Bast, President of the University of Applied Arts, Vienna, and Barbara Putz-Plecko, Vice-Rector for Research in Art and Science, University of Applied Arts, Vienna; Brigitte Kowanz, Professor at the Institute for Transmedia Art Vienna; Alexander Damianisch, Director of Zentrum Fokus Forschung and Head Support Art and Research; Anja Seipenbusch-Hufschmied for Public Relations at University of Applied Arts and Eva Blimlinger, Director of the Academy of Fine Arts Vienna for continued support.

I want to express my special thanks to all involved authors for their exciting contributions. I am aware that such a project is always made possible by so many people, my thanks also go to those who might not have been mentioned in this list.

SUPPORT

The research project and the resulting publication were made possible
by the generous funding of
Jan van Eyck Academie, Maastricht, The Netherlands;
the Austrian Federal Ministry for Education, Arts and Culture;
the University of Applied Arts Vienna, Austria
and Gerhard Dirmoser.

edition: 'angewandte JVE bm:uk

NOTICES

NOTICES